THE EVER-PRESENT PAST

THE EVER-PRESENT PAST

The Memoirs of Tatiana Kardinalowska

---

transcribed by Assya Humesky

translated by Vera Kaczmarska

edited by Uliana Pasicznyk

Canadian Institute of Ukrainian Studies Press

Edmonton 2004 Toronto

Canadian Institute of Ukrainian Studies Press
University of Alberta
Edmonton, Alberta
Canada T6G 2E8
University of Toronto
Toronto, Ontario
Canada M5S 2J5

ISBN 1–895571–48-0

Canadian Cataloguing in Publication Data

Kardialowska, T.

The ever-present past: the memoirs of Tatiana Kardinalowska / recorded and transcribed by Assya Humesky; translated by Vera Kaczmarska.

First published Kyiv: Dnipro, 1992 in Ukrainian under title: Nevidstupne mynule.
Includes index.
ISBN 1–895571–48-0

1. Kardinalowska, T. 2. Authors' spouses—Ukraine—Biography. 3. Ukraine—Intellectual life—20th century. 4. Communism and intellectuals—Ukraine—History—20th century. 5. Authors, Ukrainian—20th century—Biography. 6. Political purges—Ukraine—History—20th century.
I. Humesky, Assya, 1925– II. Kaczmarska, Vera III. Title

DK508.83.K365A3 2004 947.7'0841'092 C2003–904970–1

This book was published with generous support from the Michael Kowalsky and Daria Mucak-Kowalsky Endowment Fund at the Canadian Institute of Ukrainian Studies.

Printed in Canada

CONTENTS

ILLUSTRATIONS

PREFACE

My mother died in 1993 at the age of ninety–four. Her memoirs end in the year 1934, leaving the last sixty years of her remarkable life unrecorded. It is my intention—indeed, my duty—to pick up the thread of her narration and bring it to its true conclusion. Of course, that story will be as much mine as hers, for it will be told from my own perspective and in my own way—Mother's style is inimitable, in any case.

The present memoirs were a collaborative effort. Mother would relate an episode or two as I typed. Later, when I read the typed text to her, she would make changes or additions. The work proceeded at a snail's pace, taking ten years to complete. At last, in 1992, the memoirs were published in Ukrainian in Kyiv, under the title *Nevidstupne mynule.*

For this English edition, I have supplied some notes to her story, primarily to bring it up to date. Some material in the original Ukrainian version (mainly quotes from other memoirists) has been omitted.

The fact that the family photographs included in this book survived is a small miracle. In 1943 I was being deported from Ukraine by the Nazis for forced labor in Germany. Not wanting us to be separated, my mother decided to join me and brought along my little sister, Mirtala, as well. All Mother took with her were a few items of clothing and our family photos, which she packed in Mirtala's schoolbag. During the many Allied air raids we lived through while in a German forced-labor camp, Mother always made sure she grabbed that schoolbag when we and the other prisoners ran for shelter. We also took the photos with us when we escaped from the camp and walked over three hundred kilometers across the Tirolean Alps. After many more adventures, they were still with us when we finally made our way safely to the United States a few years later.

I sincerely thank Vera Kaczmarska for translating my mother's memoirs and Uliana Pasicznyk for her skillful editing of the translation. I am grateful to the late Professor George S. N. Luckyj and to Dr. Frank E. Sysyn for the insightful foreword and personal remembrance. I also express my gratitude to the Canadian Institute of Ukrainian Studies and to Roman Senkus and Dr. Marko R. Stech of CIUS Press for supporting and preparing this book's publication.

ASSYA HUMESKY
ANN ARBOR, DECEMBER 2002

FOREWORD

During the 1930s, Ukrainian literature was subjected to a devastation of staggering dimensions and consequences. In the course of that decade, hundreds of Ukrainian writers, critics, and scholars were arrested, incarcerated, and shot or otherwise killed. This incredible bloodbath, carried out on Stalin's orders, went unnoticed in other parts of Europe and in the Western world as a whole. In the decades that followed, émigré Ukrainian scholars tried to draw attention to that devastation and to the man-made famine in Ukraine that claimed millions of peasant lives. But not until 1988, during Gorbachev's era of glasnost, did the world community hear and begin to comprehend accounts of the Soviet regime's genocidal practices. The Russian researcher Eduard Beltov was one of the first to present clear evidence that the "literary purges" were much more devastating in Ukraine than they were in Russia: more than five hundred lives were lost. Today, researchers in Ukraine have finally gained access to the archives of that era, so long buried in secrecy, and accounts revealing and detailing the dimensions of the tragedy will undoubtedly be written. But today relatively few witnesses remain to tell us the human story behind these horrible crimes.

The memoirs presented here are truly exceptional testimony about those times. They are the personal, very readable, and yet highly informative recollections of Tatiana Kardinalowska (Tetiana Kardynalovska), widow of the Ukrainian writer Serhii Pylypenko. During the period of Ukrainization, her husband was the leader of the large association of peasant writers called Pluh (The Plow). Like many other writers' groups, this organization played an important part in Ukrainian literary life. In the 1920s, when Pluh was organized and flourished, the Communist Party tolerated the free development of Ukrainian language and literature. But with Stalin's rise to power in 1930, official Soviet policy changed. In 1932 all literary organizations were dissolved by Party decree, and a Soviet writers' union controlled by Moscow was created. Ukrainian writers soon lost their autonomy and, all too often, also their lives as Stalin's great purge of intellectuals began.

Tatiana Kardinalowska was a remarkable woman in her own right, and her description of events is both authentic and moving. She was born to a Russified Ukrainian family, the daughter of a tsarist general. During the Revolution of 1917, she married Vsevolod

Holubovych, one of the leaders of the Ukrainian Central Rada, the first Ukrainian government, which lasted only a year. It was during that time that Tatiana recovered her Ukrainian identity and refined her knowledge of the language. Her colorful account of those stormy days vividly conveys the fragility of the leadership of the Ukrainian People's Republic as well as the romantic aura of life under it. The story is presented through the eyes of a young woman in love not only with her husband, but with her newly discovered country. When independent Ukraine collapsed in 1919, she chose not to emigrate. It was through her second marriage, to Serhii Pylypenko, that she came to know the members of the Ukrainian intellectual elite of the 1920s who are described here in some detail.

Tatiana's chief personal qualities were honesty and humaneness, and these permeate the memoirs. Through her we become acquainted with prominent writers as individuals, rather than as cultural activists or literary figures. In these pages, Mykola Khvylovy, Volodymyr Sosiura, Valeriian Polishchuk, Ostap Vyshnia, Yurii Smolych, and others come alive, with faults and virtues in full view. Equally true to life are the officials of the Soviet secret service and the prison authorities to whom Tatiana went to try to save those she loved. Her personal charm and beauty were important in these and all her adventures. Reading her words affords us the pleasure of sharing her company and observing her solicitude for her children and friends. The grim reality of the 1930s that she depicts is relieved somehow by the evidence of her courage and good will that we find here. The public and personal horrors and ordeals of that decade broke or destroyed many people. Tatiana was among the few who not only survived but remained unbroken and true to herself.

The Polish writer Witold Gombrowicz once wrote: "In the great pressure of the life of the collective on the individual, resistance is possible only by delving into one's innermost self and reposing there." That is what Tatiana Kardinalowska succeeded in doing. She refused to be either a victim or a mere survivor. She fought back and lived to tell her story. Now it is here before us—to read, to ponder, and to share.

George S. N. Luckyj
Toronto, May 2001

TATIANA KARDINALOWSKA: A PERSONAL REMEMBRANCE

I first met Tatiana Kardinalowska in the 1970s in Cambridge, Massachusetts, when I was a graduate student at Harvard University. At that time the Ukrainian community had just endowed Harvard's first chair in Ukrainian studies, also the first at any North American university, and was responding to the inspired challenge of Professor Omeljan Pritsak to endow two more chairs and a research institute there. In those heady days, academics, students, and Ukrainian intellectuals, eager to formulate great plans and initiate or revive important projects, gravitated toward the Ukrainian program's first small office on Cambridge Street and then, after 1973, to the institute's commodious if somewhat rickety house on Massachusetts Avenue. The presence and participation of Tatiana Kardinalowska, who was then living in Cambridge and teaching at Boston University, helped us all to connect the study of Ukrainian culture and the Ukrainian past with the period of Ukraine's independence in 1917–19 and the Ukrainian cultural revival of the 1920s.

During the summer, when her daughter, Professor Assya Humesky, came to Cambridge to teach Ukrainian courses at the Harvard Summer School, Tatiana Kardinalowska would meet with students and staff to share her reminiscences. These were always memorable occasions. In her unpretentious and direct way, she would speak of the extraordinary events and people she had known and make them come alive, repeatedly conveying important insights in seemingly random comments. My understanding of the 1920s was shaped by one such comment. Many of us who hoped for a Ukrainian cultural revival or political presence within the Soviet Union looked to the period of Ukrainization and Ukrainian National Communism as a model. After returning from a trip to Ukraine in 1973, Tatiana Kardinalowska described to us her very personal journey there. She mentioned that in meeting with Ukrainian cultural leaders, she was struck by how little fear they seemed to have, in contrast to what she knew had been felt by the Ukrainian intelligentsia of the 1920s. History's record of literary achievements, publication statistics, and political debates had given me one vision of Ukraine in that decade. That evening, through one insightful comment, followed by others, Mrs. Kardinalowska helped me to comprehend reality as it was actually lived at that time. That was an insight hardly to be found anywhere else, following the obliteration of a cultural generation and its personal effects.

In a number of cases, a speaker's talks before Harvard summer-school students led to the taping of the material presented. These projects preserved, for instance, the recollections of Lusia Demydenko, granddaughter of Mykhailo Drahomanov. The stimulus for Mrs. Kardinalowska's writing of her memoirs came in part from the taping of summer-school presentations. Also, during a meeting in Ukraine in 1973, the writer Yurii Smolych insistently told Mrs. Kardinalowska that it was her duty to record and publish her story. At that time, despite the thaw and rehabilitations of the 1960s, uncensored memoirs could not be published in Ukraine. Then, just two years later, there began a new repression and silencing of the Ukrainian intelligentsia, which extended to the end of the 1980s. In 1992, shortly after the Soviet regime collapsed and Ukraine regained its independence, the Ukrainian-language original of Mrs. Kardinalowska's memoirs was published in Kyiv. With the publication of the present volume, the English-language reader, too, gains access to the story of her remarkable past.

Tatiana Kardinalowska tells us at the outset that she is not a historian and that she will relate only what she herself saw or heard from those close to her. In reading the work of a memoirist, particularly one who continued to read about and discuss the period he had lived through, it must be kept in mind that the writer has been informed by subsequent opinions and analyses. At the very least, this might be expected to influence the selection of content. Mrs. Kardinalowska's account, however, is pervaded by a sense of fresh reaction, as if the perceptions and views of so many years ago were being relived and captured. For instance, in her presentation she has eschewed a recitation of the "who," "what," and "when" of everything she relates. Such information would have made her account easier to follow for those not well versed in the events and personages of independent Ukraine and Ukrainian literature during the 1920s. But it would also have dulled the immediacy of her account, and altered perspectives and evaluations. For example, her reader is left without a definitive statement about Holubovych's fate and without a genealogy of the Kysilevsky family. Nor did she herself add an explanation of the use of the term *zhyd* that so offended her when she was a primarily Russian-speaking young woman, still unaware that in the language of Western Ukraine, unlike in Russian, the term is not derogatory, but a neutral word for Jew (as it is in Polish). By limiting introduction of subsequent knowledge and understanding, Mrs. Kardinalowska preserved the authenticity and immediacy of her account.

In tracing a life that began as the privileged child of a tsarist army officer and became that of an impoverished woman in exile with two young daughters, Mrs. Kardinalowska was spurred by a desire to share her recollections of major historical and cultural figures. She moved in those circles primarily because of her marriages, first to Vsevolod Holubovych, prime minister under the Ukrainian Central Rada, and then to Serhii Pylypenko, head of Pluh Association of Peasant Writers. Because of her tendency to understate her own accomplishments and influence, Edward Kasinec, librarian at the Ukrainian Research Institute at Harvard, was first to note at one of her presentations that Mrs. Kardinalowska was the translator of over thirty books and that her debates on collectivization and literary politics with Pylypenko were incisive and well informed. Nor did she dwell on her personal appearance, which clearly had a considerable influence on her circumstances and position. Very telling in this connection, however, is her account of how the religious activist Volodymyr Chekhivsky tried convincing her to accompany him on a proselytizing mission as a symbol of the Madonna.

The *Ever-Present Past* documents one of the most important shifts in the political and cultural map of Eastern Europe. What appeared at the beginning of the twentieth century to be a small band of Ukrainian cultural and political activists in the Russian Empire had, by 1917, succeeded in enlisting tens of thousands of intelligentsia to the nation-building cause. With the rapid spread of modern Ukrainian identity among the masses, the Ukrainian movement even survived the failure of statehood, emerging as a force strong enough to oblige the Bolsheviks to seek accommodation with it. That process of Ukrainization formed a new Soviet Ukrainian intelligentsia, one which had a strong pre-1920 component. The remarkable cultural flourishing of the 1920s was achieved by dynamic forces that matured and bloomed between 1905 and 1930.

In outlining her own development, Mrs. Kardinalowska speaks to the issue of Ukrainophile sentiments by depicting the devotion of her father, Mykhailo Hryhorovych Kardynalovsky, to Ukraine's greatest poet, Taras Shevchenko. In conjuring up the archaic and colorful world of her youth in tsarist times, she illustrates how the seeds of Ukrainian identity were present in the educated upper classes in Ukraine, seeds that could, in changed circumstances, take root and grow. Tatiana

Kardinalowska's father, despite his relatively progressive views, could not imagine the existence of an independent Ukraine, but her first husband was part of the small cadre of prerevolutionary Ukrainian political activists. Although she does not dwell on Vsevolod Holubovych's influence on her own personal development, it is clear that his views and career ushered the young girl toward a full, modern Ukrainian identity.

As for so many members of the young Ukrainian intelligentsia of central and eastern Ukraine of that time, Russian literature was Tatiana's spiritual and cultural reference point, in a way that now, at the beginning of the twenty-first century, is difficult to imagine. Eventually she would find herself among writers who sought to create a Ukrainian literature that could compete with Russian literature, and she would even move toward Khvylovy's slogan, "Away from Moscow." But, of course, all these writers were themselves formed by Russian literature. And before a viable Ukrainian culture could be fully established, the experiment itself would be stamped out by Stalin and a new era of Russification would reestablish the primacy of Russian literature. For Tatiana Kardinalowska, the link between the Russian and Ukrainian cultures lasted a lifetime, as is reflected by her choice of a poem by Ilia Ehrenburg to begin her story.

Although the wish to depict the prominent individuals she had known prompted Mrs. Kardinalowska to record her memoirs, it is her characterizations of less notable people that are some of the book's most revealing. The significance of Ukrainian independence becomes clear to us through such figures as the Kuban Cossack who decided his national identity on the basis of Semen Petliura's speeches, the clerk who was honored to provide a picture frame gratis for Holubovych's portrait, and the youth in Poltava who was committed to continuing the struggle for Ukrainian identity and independence. The nature of Stalinism can be perceived, if not comprehended, in Mrs. Kardinalowska's account of the woman who desperately sought, as she herself did, to see Andrei Vyshinsky, the chief Soviet prosecutor, in an effort to save her husband's life.

Students of Ukraine's revolutionary times will turn to these memoirs to gain insight into the characters of the major cultural leaders of the age. They will find valuable material on, among others, the writers Ostap Vyshnia, Vasyl Ellan-Blakytny, and Mykola Khvylovy. Above all, the figure of Serhii Pylypenko emerges clearly from these pages. Tatiana Kardinalowska's love for her second husband hardly qualified her as an objective observer, but it meant she knew him as no one else did. Here she shares much of that knowledge with us.

When Mrs. Kardinalowska shared her experiences with students and others at the Harvard Summer School, the famine in Ukraine of 1932–33 was continually a focal point. At that time, Soviet authorities were asserting that no famine had occurred, many Western specialists did not perceive the Soviet regime as culpable, and the general public had virtually no knowledge of what had taken place. Today, when that man-made famine has been acknowledged and has become the subject of historical study in Ukraine and the West, her recollections still give us some of the most poignant information we have about its horrible toll.

Tatiana Kardinalowska lived with her remarkable past ever present. She lived to see her daughters—Assya Humesky, professor of Slavic languages and literatures at the University of Michigan, and Mirtala Bentov, noted sculptor and poet—become established in the new world the three of them had entered together. She also lived to see many of the writers she had known, once branded non-persons by the Soviet regime, returned to the canon of Ukrainian literature and culture. She even lived to witness the rebirth of an independent Ukraine. Today, her memoirs will find resonance in the ever-growing community in the West that endeavors to understand reemergent Ukraine.

FRANK E. SYSYN
TORONTO, MAY 2001

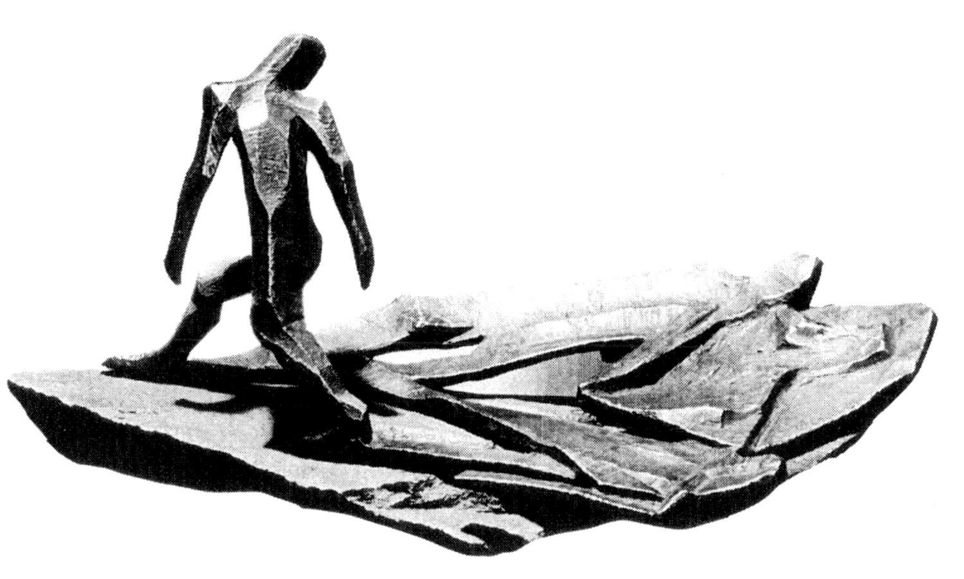

The Ever-Present Past

INTRODUCTION

When the sun inclines toward the earth—
shadows grow longer;
When life's lines approach their end—
thoughts get clearer[1]

As I embarked on my memoirs I kept thinking: "What was interesting in my life?" I lived through four wars during those long years—Russia's war with Japan, the war with Germany, the civil war in Ukraine, and World War II. I was imprisoned and witnessed famine and the whole range of human suffering. Fate blessed me with the opportunity to associate closely with many of the distinguished figures of the age—talented artists and writers, individuals who were creating Ukrainian literature and history. I was more than a passive observer. Life threw me into the vortex of unfolding events, demanding immediate and often risky decisions. It taught me to evaluate people, to trust my own judgment and intuition, to fear nothing and no one. I approached life thoughtfully; my memoirs reflect my thinking and observations. Actual dates and historical events appear in my story only when "history" intruded on my personal life. I am not a historian; therefore, I speak only about those things that I saw with my own eyes or heard from people who were close to me.

Once, during the civil war in Ukraine, I heard the poet Ilia Ehrenburg recite his then unpublished poem, "Our Grandchildren." It became etched in my memory as the truest expression of the spirit of those days.

Our grandchildren will puzzle and wonder
As they leaf through the history books—
1914 … 1917 … 1919….
How did they live, all those poor wretched souls?
Children of the new age will read of the battles,
Will learn the names of the leaders and orators,
The number of the dead
And the dates,

---

[1] From my daughter Mirtala Bentov's collection *Thought Forms: Sculptures, Poems* (Boston, 1975). A sculpture by Mirtala, also called *The Ever-Present Past,* is reproduced as the frontispiece to these memoirs.

They will not learn how sweet on the field of battle
Was the scent of roses,
How clearly amidst the din of cannon the chirping
Of swifts was heard,
How beautiful it was then to be
Alive.
Never, oh never, was the sun's laughter so joyously spent
As over a city's destruction,
When the people crawling out of their dark basements
Marveled: the sun is still there!...
Mutinous speeches rang out,
Enraged armies perished,
But the soldiers discovered what fragrance snowdrops can impart
Before an attack starts.
Escorting at dawn, executing in firing squads,
They alone discovered the meaning of an April morn.
In the slanting rays the cupolas blazed,
Yet the wind implored: Oh please wait! One minute, just one
more minute!...
Embracing, they could not tear themselves from those sad lips,
Nor release the grip of firmly clasped hands,
They loved—I will die, will die:
They loved—burn on, little flame, in the wind:
They loved—oh where are you, where?
They loved, as they can love only here, on this mutinous and
tender star.
In those years there were no gardens with golden fruit,
Only a brief flowering, one doomed month of May.
In those years there was no "goodbye,"
Only a short, resounding "farewell."
Read about us and marvel.
You didn't live with us—mourn your loss:
Guests on the earth, we came for only one evening.
We loved and destroyed, we lived at the hour of our death,
But above us stood stars eternal,
And under them you were conceived.
In your eyes our anguish still burns.
In your words our mutiny still echoes.
We spilled far into the night and unto ages and ages to come
Our extinguished lives.

CHAPTER 1

I was born in Kyiv in 1899 into the family of a career officer of the Russian imperial army. My childhood was spent in an environment typical of military circles in those days, although our family itself was far from typical. Readers today can gain a general idea of that milieu from the works of Anton Chekhov, Aleksandr Kuprin, and Mikhail Bulgakov. My "eyewitness" accounts may provide a somewhat different perspective.

My father, Mykhailo Hryhorovych (Russian: Mikhail Grigorovich), was of noble ancestry, though his family was impoverished. Our surname, Kardynalovsky (Russian: Kardinalovsky),[2] often elicited interest and wonder, for it derives from *kardynal* 'cardinal' and there were no cardinals in the Russian Empire. One distant relative became sufficiently intrigued by the name to investigate its origin. He discovered a Kardynalovsky who had come to Ukraine from Hungary some two hundred years before: our ancestor was apparently of Polish origin, for his family coat of arms depicted a white ram with a bloodied side (red and white are the Polish national colors) against a green meadow. But with that the relative's search came to an end: he discovered nothing more about our ancestor or surname.

My paternal grandfather was also an officer. Although then no longer a young man, he took part in the Turkish campaign. Returning home with his unit, he was riding through a small village near Kyiv, not far from Fastiv, when he saw an extraordinarily beautiful young peasant woman standing by a well. The events that followed could have been taken straight out of a romance by Yevhen Hrebinka, who wrote "Dark Eyes" ("Ochi chernye"):

> I remember, I was a mere sixteen, no more.
> Our army was dispatched to fight a war.
> Dusk was falling as I stood beneath a tree
> Watching soldiers ride their horses down the street.

---

[2] The spelling of my surname, Kardinalowska, reflects both German orthography and my gender. This was how my name was written by the authorities during the German occupation of Ukraine in the Second World War, and I retained the spelling after emigrating to the West.

A young nobleman rode up to me and prayed,
"May I ask you for some water, pretty maid?"
As he drank, he leaned down and looked into my face,
Firmly pressed my hand, and gave me an embrace.

As in the song, the girl gave my grandfather water to drink and captured his heart. He ordered his soldiers to set up camp in the village and spent three days there. He met the young woman's parents, proposed, and married her.

I remember my paternal grandmother as being tall and svelte and as having very black hair that did not go gray even in old age. We children dubbed her "Black Grandmother" because of her hair, thus drawing a distinction between her and our other, "White," grandmother, whose hair did turn gray. Because she was not of noble birth, our "Black Grandmother" felt slighted by the label, and Mother strictly forbade us from calling her by that name.

"Black Grandmother," whose name was Oleksandra Dominikiivna, was of Polish peasant ancestry, but she spoke only Ukrainian—I don't recall if she knew any Polish at all. Her manner was rather severe, and she always had her own opinions. For example, she never wanted to master any grammar, because she felt that, as a peasant, she was unworthy of the undertaking, and neither Father nor the rest of us could convince her otherwise. Such views also manifested themselves later, when she would not permit her adopted daughter, Raia, to attend secondary school. She felt that as a poor orphan Raia should "know her place." Nevertheless, Grandmother had a very deeply ingrained sense of her own dignity. She loved her only son devotedly, but his high position interested her very little and she was certainly unimpressed by it. When he was promoted to the rank of general and several military orderlies were assigned to our family, Grandmother never regarded these men as somehow inferior or subordinate. On the contrary, she treated them with kindness and concern and without any trace of superiority. As children we observed this, and her behavior undoubtedly made a strong impression on us.

"Black Grandmother" was not known for her religiosity. I don't recall ever seeing her pray, and she never went to church—a fact that set her completely apart from "White Grandmother," who was forever visiting monasteries, attending church devotedly, and observing every church ritual and tradition. "White Grandmother" did all this despite the fact that she could not tolerate the local village priest, who fleeced the peasants mercilessly for every baptismal, nuptial, or funeral rite he performed. Sometimes this priest would refuse to bury some poor soul for days on end until he received prepayment for his services. Grandmother never kissed his hand in church, nor did she ever invite him to her home. In an effort to instill some piety in me, she took me along on her visits to the monasteries, but the sight of the well-fed monks elicited neither my regard nor respect, while the Church Slavonic language they used simply did not enter my consciousness.

My maternal "White Grandmother" was of noble birth, but her family, too, was impoverished. Her maiden name was Makhno—something I learned only during the revolution, when Nestor Makhno, the famous partisan anarchist, made his appearance in Ukraine. Grandmother feared that he might be a relative, especially because they both came from the same town, Huliai-Pole, and was relieved to be assured that Nestor Makhno was not from a noble family. (In fact, the surname was very common in that part of the country; there was even a village called Makhnivka whose residents were almost all named Makhno.)

There were ten children in the family of "White Grandmother": nine sisters and a brother. Their parents died when the children were young, and they were parceled out among relatives. My grandmother was taken by a family of wealthy landowners and received an education commensurate with people of that class. In my childhood I read a lot of Nikolai Gogol's work, and for me "White Grandmother" was the very incarnation of an Old World landowner. She was always enthusiastically cooking some kind of "confitures," as she called them, and readying endless jars of the sweet concoctions to dispatch to us in town. These were prepared in huge copper kettles following all the principles of Old World culinary art. There were jams made of boysenberries, raspberries, wild strawberries, rose petals, apples, pears, and sour cherries. In the sour cherry confitures, the pits were replaced with walnuts—imagine how time-consuming that whole process was! Though Grandmother always got the credit for making the confitures, she in fact had a whole staff of helpers. Grandmother herself admitted that the whole jam-making procedure was a throwback to the time of serfdom. In addition to the confitures, Grandmother also knew how to make all sorts of fruit liqueurs. Once she was preparing *vyshniak*, a liqueur made of sour cherries. After letting the sour cherries ferment, she had them pitted and ordered that the pits be thrown away. Without giving the matter any thought, one of the servants dumped them in a corner of the yard, where our geese sampled some and found them quite tasty. Eating the pits to the very last one, they dropped down in a stupor. Soon a frightened servant ran in shouting "Mistress! All our geese have died! They're lying motionless in the yard!" Grandmother, distraught at the news, ordered the servants to pluck the feathers off the geese, so at least these would be of some use. When the servants started the plucking, the geese suddenly regained consciousness and created a tremendous racket! This incident was long a topic of conversation in our family, and it always elicited gales of laughter.

I don't remember "White Grandmother" as an avid reader, but I do recall one book she regarded very highly as a guide on how to live well. It was a kind of housekeeping manual, written by Elena Molokhovets, that was popular among ladies of the time. It contained exhaustive advice on how to cook, how to conduct oneself with servants, how to dress, how to rear children, and so on. I saw this same thick, heavy hardcover volume in many households even after the revolution.

My "White" grandmother liked tending to her health, so she was always interested in anything new in the medical field. Somewhere she heard about homeopathy as a new branch of medicine. She was told that homeopaths used herbs in their work, sometimes even poisonous ones in microscopic amounts, and that intrigued her. When she learned that a homeopathic doctor had set up a practice in their area, she went to visit him. He prescribed some medicine, and she brought home several bottles of multicolored pills. Leaving these bottles on the table, she went out of the room for several minutes. In the meantime, my mother, who was then three years old, came into the room, saw the beautiful "candies," and began sampling them. When my grandmother returned, her small daughter was just finishing the last pill. The whole family fell into a panic and braced for something terrible to happen—but nothing did: Mother had not so much as a bout of diarrhea. The experience made Grandmother lose all faith in this branch of medicine, however, and she swore never to visit a homeopath again.

"White Grandmother" had an enormous repertoire of romantic stories she liked to tell. Our favorite was about the beautiful Halshka, princess of Ostroh. Memory of her was still very much alive in the area where Grandmother had spent her childhood and youth. Grandmother even visited the church where Halshka's body was kept in a glass coffin. But by that time not a trace of the princess's legendary beauty remained, and the whole episode gave Grandmother quite a fright. Halshka's story was immortalized by the Russian writer Vsevolod Solovev in his historical novella "Kniazhna Ostrogskaia" (The Princess of Ostroh, 1876). He was obviously intrigued by her incredible adventures, and indeed her life story was excellent material for an adventure novel. Few would have believed it, had it not been for some contemporaries of hers who corroborated the details. I told Halshka's story to my own daughters, and they were just as fascinated by her as I myself had been as a child. It's strange how memory is passed down from generation to generation.

Grandmother also liked to tell a true story about the eighteenth-century Cossack rebel and brigand Semen Harkusha—a tale with an extraordinary semblance to Pushkin's novella about Dubrovsky. Harkusha was a handsome young man with impeccable manners. He would appear unexpectedly at some grand estate as a ball or family celebration was in progress, pretending that his carriage had just broken down. Harkusha would enter the salon and manage to spirit away the possessions of the host and his distinguished guests. He would then immediately give all this wealth away to impoverished villagers. Our grandmother never had the opportunity to meet this Ukrainian Robin Hood, but she was acquainted with several landowners who had had the dubious pleasure of experiencing his visits firsthand. Apart from these romantic personas, Grandmother's imagination was also fired by the famous Polish hero Tadeusz Kościuszko, whose escapades she described with great gusto.

Now, looking back over time, I see how such stories influenced my character and even my worldview. I was fascinated, too, by stories of Joan of Arc and Kaspar Hauser, as extraordinary people who were forced by circumstances to act against society and history itself and yet never faltered in pursuing what they set out to do.

I know little about my maternal grandfather—only what my mother and grandmother told me. He traced his lineage back to a Zaporozhian Cossack named Kysil, who began calling himself Kysilevsky after being elevated to the nobility. Grandfather lived on his estate and took an interest in public affairs. Local landowners named him to the post of community arbitrator, a position created after the abolition of serfdom to facilitate implementation of reforms. It was a government position, and each person's candidacy had to be approved by the governors and ratified by the Russian State Duma. Naturally, the community arbitrators usually favored the noblemen. But there were exceptions. Sometimes a humane arbitrator would attempt to redress a peasant's grievances. Perhaps my grandfather was one of these exceptional arbitrators, for he was known as a very amiable and well-intentioned person. Years later, his son Aliosha found this part of his father's biography potentially incriminating and sought to hide it from the Soviet authorities, for whom humanitarianism, in any case, had little meaning.

Grandfather played the cello well, and my mother accompanied him on the piano. He also loved to listen to songbirds. Peasants who knew this often brought him birds that had fallen out of their nests or injured their wings. Once they brought him a songster with a broken leg. He bandaged the leg and fashioned tiny crutches for the bird. To everybody's surprise, the bird quickly learned how to hop along on these and would wander throughout the house, whistling the Ukrainian folk song "Oi, ne khody Hrytsiu ..." (Don't Go to Evening Parties, Hryts), which my grandfather taught it. Grandfather turned the veranda into a bird sanctuary, and the birds in it became totally domesticated. Grandfather would go about whistling arias from operas, romantic ballads, or Ukrainian folk songs with a bird perched on his shoulder. The birds quickly learned an entire repertoire of songs and performed for Grandfather's guests.

Like most landowners of his time, Grandfather was an avid hunter. He had a pack of hunting dogs, one of whom he called Herr Miller in honor of the German who had given him the dog as a gift. The peasants, not understanding these words, simply called the dog Harmyder (which means "disorder" in Ukrainian), a name that suited the boisterous dog perfectly. Harmyder had a voracious appetite and made a habit of entering the kitchen just when meat patties were being fried. Despite the cook's best efforts, he always managed to snatch one right out of the frying pan and dash out a door or window, savoring his catch.

Mother also told stories about another dog, a huge Newfoundland named Fingal. This dog was the embodiment of benevolent patience. As children, my mother Olha and her brother Oleksii, who had the nickname Aliosha, would tug at his tail and ears or mount him like a horse. Fingal bore it all with total composure. When Mother was a toddler, she was let out on the veranda that stretched around the house. Since there was no railing, Fingal was delegated to protect her. He was a wonderful nanny: whenever Mother approached the edge of the porch, he blocked her way, and no amount of pushing and shoving would make him budge.

True to his breed, Fingal felt a responsibility to save people by dragging them out of the water. When guests came to the estate to swim in the river, he had to be locked up in the house. Otherwise he would throw himself into the water and start "saving" everyone. One day, Mother, then a small child, was let out into the garden for a walk, and, as usual, Fingal accompanied her. Suddenly screams, barking, and the stomping of feet resounded on the street adjoining the garden. Mother, curious, stepped out into it. A dog came running sideways towards her, foam dripping from its mouth. A crowd of peasants was giving chase and screaming, "Rabid! A rabid dog! Save yourself!" Oblivious to the danger, and accustomed to considering animals her friends, Mother approached the "little doggie." And then something incredible happened. Instead of running from the mad dog as instinct would dictate, Fingal attacked him and managed to kill him—but not before the mad animal had bitten his flesh. When the peasants ran up to him, Fingal was still breathing but lay motionless. They carried him to an old beekeeper in the neighborhood who was renowned for his use of herbs to cure rabies. The old man made every effort to save the faithful animal. After lying sick for three weeks, Fingal recovered somewhat. But he never regained his health fully. Becoming sickly again, he soon died, surrounded by our family's affection and gratitude.

CHAPTER 2

That was how my grandparents lived. I'd like to say more now about my father, Mykhailo Hryhorovych Kardynalovsky. When he was just seven years old, Father was sent to the Kyiv Cadet Corps. He never spoke to us about his childhood or about the years he spent in the corps, but once, in 1915, when he returned from the front, he wanted to visit the corps and invited me to come along. As we walked through the park encircling the school. Father found the bench on which he had carved his initials. When we entered the building, Father immediately became excited: "The smell! That familiar smell!" he exclaimed. There was indeed a distinctive odor, which obviously had lingered all those years. The vestibule walls were covered with marble plaques with the names of graduates who had achieved the rank of general engraved in gold. Father found his own name among them. This was the only time I remember seeing my father deeply moved by memories of the past.

Father was a very good student, and he excelled in mathematics in particular. As he himself used to say, he had inherited this aptitude from his famous ancestor, the mathematician Mykhailo Ostrohradsky (Russian: Mikhail Ostrogradsky), whose life story he had heard from his own father. He often recounted this story with pleasure, though in general he did not like to speak about his family. As is often the case with narratives transmitted orally from generation to generation, the "family" version differs somewhat from the official biography, and I would like to share it.

In his youth, Ostrohradsky was such a poor student that he was nearly expelled from school. His family lost hope that anything would come of him, and his father was ready to apprentice him to someone who could teach him a trade. He wrote to his brother, a mathematics professor at St. Petersburg University, complaining that his son was not interested in anything and that he only wandered about taking measurements and jotting them down. His brother was intrigued by this description of his nephew's actions and requested to see the boy's notes. To his astonishment, it turned out that his nephew's jottings were complicated mathematical calculations. The uncle suggested that Mykhailo be sent to him so he could prepare him for university. And that was how Ostrohradsky got on the path that led to his becoming a scientist.[3]

[3] In reality, Ostrohradsky's uncle was not a professor at St. Petersburg University; but he did persuade Mykhailo's father to send the boy to Kharkiv University. This is mentioned in Andrii Konforovych and Mykola Soroka's biographical novel *Ostrohradsky* (Kyiv, 1980).

My brother and I shared our own father's interest in math, and I, too, liked to take all kinds of measurements. Much later, when I finished my secondary education and enrolled in the Department of Road Construction at the Kyiv Polytechnical Institute, I had the opportunity to take that interest in a professional direction.

After his graduation from the Kyiv Cadet Corps, Father's love of math led him to enroll as a student in the Mikhailov Artillery Academy, where Ostrohradsky had taught until 1841. Half a century later my father taught higher mathematics there too. (How fitting that the academy was named Mikhailov![4]) Father's education and natural aptitude enabled him to make extraordinarily rapid strides in his military career: he never remained at any rank for more than two or three years. By the time he was thirty-two, he was already a major general. Soon he became a lieutenant general and, subsequently, a "general of the artillery," that is, a full general: military newspapers of the time reported that my father was the youngest general of this rank in the empire. As was customary for all officers at the time, Father received a medal of distinction or an order with each promotion. He also won innumerable medals for bravery. The last military distinction he received was the Order of the White Eagle—the highest honor in the tsarist army. On learning of the award, Father joked, "This is my last award, for there are no more to be had." The joke became a sad reality, for he died at the front soon after and this last honor was awarded posthumously. His military decorations were put to good use later, when my family was in very difficult financial straits after the revolution: Mother sold them to help us survive.

Besides the orders, Father received the Golden Sword of St. George, awarded for his service in the war with Japan. The words "For Bravery" were engraved on it. This weapon would later have a tragicomic role. When my husband Serhii Pylypenko was arrested in 1933, the sword was "discovered" during a search of our apartment—it hung in the pantry—and documented as proof of a military plot. Such incidents would be quite common then. For instance, in searching one writer's apartment, the secret police found a cannonball on his writing desk. The writer had kept it as a reminder of the day during World War I when it had fallen at his feet but failed to explode. The police documented this too as evidence of an insurrection in the making.

---

[4] That is, a name based on the the possessive form of "Mikhail."—*Eds.*

As mentioned, Father fought in the war with Japan. I remember some of the episodes he related about this war. One time, at a bazaar in Manchuria, he witnessed the following scene. Crowds of people were pushing and shoving. In the center of all the commotion was a man who had fallen to his knees. His hands were tied behind his back and his neck was enclosed in a wooden brace. Suddenly there was the swing of a sword and the man's head rolled to the ground. Father, an amateur photographer who always carried a camera with him, captured this moment on film. As children we gazed at this picture with terrible awe as we listened to Father's account of what had happened.

Father spoke about how people became fatalists in wartime. For example, the orderly assigned to him was told by a gypsy fortune-teller that he would not be killed or wounded in the war. This man believed in his "lucky star" to such an extent that he fearlessly brought Father his meals at the front even during the fiercest battles. And he did indeed survive the war unscathed. The same gypsy told one of the officers that he should have no fear of bullets, for he would die of a lightning bolt. After hearing this, the officer stopped paying bullets any mind, but he became terrified of storms. Whenever there was any lightning, the officer would try to find a crowd and make his way into the center of it. Amazingly enough, during one storm a lightning bolt found the unfortunate man and struck him dead. Whenever Father told us this story, we could tell that he himself saw a connection between the fortune-teller's predictions and the men's fates.

In Father's own life there were many incidents that seemed to point to the existence of some higher power that held sway over people's lives. The following was among them. Father was an excellent horseman. Despite his rather stout figure, he could jump up on a horse like a young man, as a soldier simply stood by to steady the stirrups. Father had a half-thoroughbred pony named Femida that saved him from harm many a time. During one battle, Father was galloping out in front of the soldiers, as was his custom, and accidentally tugged at the bridle in such a way that the horse reared up, throwing back his head. At that very moment, a bullet aimed at Father whistled through the air, passing right through the horse's gaping mouth and just grazing his lip. Father's sudden tug saved both their lives.

In January 1917, however, my father's luck finally ran out. During the war Father was an artillery inspector in the army. Given his high position, he should have been at military headquarters rather than out at the front. But Father always preferred to be out with the troops. He wanted to set an example of courage, like the commander about whom the Kuban Cossacks sang:

> Our commander is no coward,
> Riding always up ahead.
> He was very badly wounded
> In the chest by Polish lead.

Father was like that—he repeatedly risked his own life to be with his men. As he was riding at the front on that January day in 1917, he was shot by a German sniper, his stately figure on easy target. Father was evacuated to a medical unit, but his wound proved fatal. Mother was sent a telegram summoning us to his deathbed. Before we could gather our things for the journey, there came a second telegram, informing us of his death. Mother was asked where she would like him to be buried, and she chose the old cemetery at Lukianivka, not far from our home. The funeral was extraordinarily solemn. Many staff officers accompanied the coffin to its final resting place. Father's orders were carried on a pillow, and his Golden Sword was carried separately. Many years later I returned to Kyiv and found my father's grave, which had had a stone cross at its head.[5]

Father was a reticent person by nature. He did not have many friends. Nor did he associate much with the other officers, for he had nothing in common with them, neither shared interests nor common political views. He acquired his only true friend toward the end of his life. General Klembovsky was a renowned military man whom father met during the war. Klembovsky did not emigrate after the revolution, nor did he join the Red Army. He taught at the Military Academy. The men were drawn to each other not only by a personal affinity, but also by shared political views. Father was not a supporter of absolutism; he favored the constitutional monarchy espoused by the Kadets,[6] and his ideal of a statesman was Pavel Miliukov. No portrait of the tsar hung in our house, something that always surprised military officers who came

---

[5] Over time, the cross disappeared and the grave could no longer be found. Now, thanks to L. A. Protsenko, a historian and archivist who spent nearly twenty-five years establishing the identities of those buried at the Lukianivka cemetery, my father's grave has been found once again. My niece, Roksolana Kardynalovska, had another iron cross placed over it, with an inscription written in Ukrainian.

[6] That is, members of the Constitutional Democratic Party.— *Eds.*

to visit. Father loved Ukraine and considered himself a Ukrainian. He often hummed and sang Ukrainian songs at home, and a copy of Taras Shevchenko's *Kobzar* lay open on his writing table. We children did not understand Shevchenko's poetry very well at the time, for we spoke Russian at home, but Father would translate and explain it to us. Yet Father's Ukrainophilism did not extend so far as to dream of Ukraine's independence. He was convinced that Russia would never allow that to happen. Today, in retrospect, I see how extraordinary it was that my father, though raised from early childhood in an atmosphere that propagated ultra-monarchism, maintained his independent views and love for his own people throughout his life.

Father was tall and weighed well over two hundred pounds. In the military, a man of his rank was entitled to two or three orderlies. One of them served as a messenger and personal servant, helping him dress and put on his boots (Father's size and gout prevented him from managing that on his own). An amusing story is connected to Father's gout. Someone told Father about an alcohol-and-ant mixture that was heralded as a tried-and-true folk medicine for treating the condition. It called for burying a half-empty bottle of vodka in an anthill, with the neck of the bottle barely sticking out. Ants were supposed to flock to the bottle and fall in; their bodies would then ooze out acidity into the vodka, creating the healing concoction that was then to be rubbed into the legs and feet. Father found the remedy intriguing and decided to try it. He told his orderly to take a bottle of vodka and bury it in an anthill. A few days later, he sent him to retrieve the bottle. The orderly came back empty-handed, saying the bottle had disappeared. In consternation, Father gave him another bottle and the same instructions. The results were the same. Deciding that the orderly had shared the potential remedy with his friends, Father finally abandoned the experiment. In the end, the orderly's temptation certainly proved greater than Father's dedication to treating his gout.

Father's spirit of democracy was remarkable. It was evident in his relationships with orderlies, soldiers, and common people. I do not remember a single incident when Father was rude to a soldier or shouted at one, though that was customary among the officers. I do, however, recall incidents of brutal behavior toward orderlies by other officers and their wives.

One incident made a particularly strong impression on all of us. It happened in Kyiv in the family of the officer who lived above us. He was away fighting at the front, and his wife, who had four small children, was assigned an orderly. She overworked him, shrieked at him, and often slapped him across the face. The soldier tolerated her cruel treatment for almost a year. Finally, he could stand it no longer and decided to kill his tormentor. He took a revolver and went to her room, but seeing that she was sitting on a sofa and reading to her children, he took pity on her. Instead he ran out of the room and fired a bullet into his own chest. My brother, who happened to be in the garden, heard the shot. He ran to the soldier, finding him blood-soaked but still breathing. My brother summoned the police, and the soldier was taken to a military hospital. As he lay dying, the soldier revealed the particulars of how he had been treated. But the officer's wife was not brought to trial, and she was soon assigned another orderly.

Tatiana's father, Mykhailo Kardynalovsky (1916 or 1917)

Of course, that was an exceptional case, but such behavior was not uncommon in the military. In contrast, the orderlies assigned to our family were treated so well that when their three-year tour of duty was over, they often begged Father to extend it. When they first arrived, they did not know how to cook, so Mother patiently taught them. Some of them became quite expert at it and even later found jobs as chefs. The culinary arts did not interest me, however, and I grew up not knowing how to cook at all. Later, during the revolution, when I had to live alone, I taught myself to cook hot cereal and boil an egg, but that was about the extent of my repertoire. Once a commissar who had moved into our apartment wanted some *halushky* (dumplings). He ordered me to prepare them and left, leaving me completely at a loss. I had never made *halushky*. When the commissar returned and discovered that I hadn't made any because I didn't know how, at first he was stunned. Then he became furious, calling me a good-for-nothing princess with two left hands who didn't know how to make *halushky* and yet had the nerve to call herself a Ukrainian. That was during the first days of the revolution. Later life obliged me to learn to do everything—cook, sew, wash laundry, and chop wood.

Instead of addressing our mother by the usual "*barynia*" (noble lady), our servants called Mother by her name and patronymic in Russian, Olga Nikolaevna. The servants were good friends to us children, and they called us simply Tania, Liza, and Seriozha. When we came to the kitchen, they would tell us about their war experiences, play cards with us, and sing us soldiers' songs. Our favorite was the song about the sinking of the Russian warship called the *Varangian*. We also liked a song about the Boer War that went "Transvaal, Transvaal, My Country—You're All Aflame," as well as one about Suvorov[7]:

> First one, then another, felled by a stray bullet,
> Will tumble into a bottomless chasm.
> Falling from the heights, against rocks and brush
> Their state-owned bodies will be torn asunder.

We also heard the story of Arkhyp Osypiv, both from our orderlies and from Father. In the orderlies' version, Osypiv gained legendary stature and the tale was embellished with many details, so that even the location of events was changed. That popular version went as follows.

During the time of the Crimean War, a Russian fortress was surrounded by the Turks. The situation of the Russian garrison was hopeless, for their ammunition and food had run out. They decided to abandon the fortress and dig a passageway under the fortress wall. When everything was ready, Arkhyp Osypiv, an artillery man, volunteered to stay behind to blow up the fortress. The Russian soldiers fled during the night, and early in the morning the Turks broke in. Suddenly there was a great explosion, and the fortress blew up with the Turks in it—Osypiv had denoted the explosives and died there together with the enemy. Afterwards his regiment started a new custom: each morning at roll-call, an officer would call out "Arkhyp Osypiv!" and one of the soldiers would reply, "Died a hero's death!" That tradition continued up until the First World War.[8]

---

[7] A song about the difficult crossing of the Alps from northern Italy by Generalissimo Aleksandr Suvorov's Russian army to fight the French in Switzerland in 1799.—*Eds*.

[8] Osypiv was born in the village of Kaminka in Lypovets county, Kyiv gubernia. He served in the Tenginsk Infantry Division and distinguished himself during the Russo-Persian and Russo-Turkish wars, for which he was decorated for bravery. In 1837 his battalion was

We were friends with not only the orderlies, but also the cooks. Sometimes this "fraternizing with the common people" had unexpected consequences. One evening some ladies came to visit Mother. Usually she did not allow us in the living room during such visits, but this time one guest persistently asked to be "shown the children," so Mother summoned me to the room. I was very shy and embarrassed in the presence of the elegant ladies, but when one of them asked me to recite a poem, I mustered my courage and recited a gem I had recently learned:

Tatiana's mother, Olha Kardynalovska (née Kysilevska, 1907)

My beautiful spouse
In the street lies soused,
The coachmen cuss
'Cause the horses fuss.

One can imagine the consternation my performance caused in this genteel company—and my mother's embarrassment! To make matters worse, when asked where I had learned the poem I innocently responded, "In the kitchen," eliciting a roar of laughter from the guests and more embarrassment for Mother.

My childhood memories are tied much more closely to my mother than with my father. Though Father was kind to us girls, he concentrated most of his attention and energy on our brother Serhii, whom everyone called Seriozha, and pinned great hopes on his future.

---

stationed at Fort Mikhailovsky on the shores of the Black Sea. In 1840, when the Adygei people of the Caucasus rebelled, the insurgents managed to take command of two other forts and were advancing on Fort Mikhailovsky. The Russians, fearing that they could not hold out, prepared to blow up the fort. On 22 April 1840, as the Adygei were forcing their way in, Osypiv blew up the ammunition dump, and with it all of the defenders and attackers. His name was then permanently kept on the roster of the regiment's first company. See "Osipov, Arkhip," in *Entsiklopedicheskii slovar*, vol. 2 (Moscow, 1953), 568.

He dreamed that his son would grow up to be a great man, a person like Miliukov, whom Father respected greatly. He left the upbringing of Liza and me largely to Mother.

My mother was a woman of medium height with dark blue eyes and fine features. She had extraordinarily beautiful hair—black, lustrous, and so long that her braid fell well below her knees. Mother was well proportioned, an avid sportswoman, and loved riding horses and swimming. I remember one family trip to Simeiz in the Crimea, just after the war with Japan, where Mother's swimming created quite a sensation. She would swim far out to sea, to a rock where none of the other vacationers, least of all the other women, dared swim. Sometimes dolphins accompanied her on these swims and frolicked alongside her.

Mother had many other talents as well. At the age of thirteen, she accompanied her father at musical performances before the Society Club. She wrote poems and had a thorough knowledge and refined appreciation of art. In general her interests lay in the spiritual and artistic realms rather than in practical matters.

Though we had a good number of nannies and governesses, it was Mother who supervised our education. She awakened our love for literature very early and directed our reading. But it was her piano playing that influenced us the most. We would listen to her play for hours. There were times when she would play through the night while we sat in some corner of the living room, enthralled by her music until, finally, we simply fell asleep.

Mother had a difficult youth. At the age of seventeen she married my father's cousin, Mykola Kardynalovsky. Soon she discovered what this young military officer had hidden from her—he had tuberculosis, which was then incurable. Overcome by a fear of death, he tried desperately to convince Mother and himself that his illness was not as dire as everyone thought. He forced Mother to drink from his glass and tried in every way to infect her with the disease. He did not succeed, however: he died within a year of their marriage, without passing the illness on to her.

At his funeral Mother met his cousin Mykhailo Kardynalovsky, and they soon fell in love. But they could not marry, because the church forbade marriages between a close relative of a deceased man and his widow. Their love was so strong that, disregarding law and public opinion, they began living together, which in those times required extraordinary courage. When their son, my brother Serhii, was born a year later, my father adopted him immediately. Shortly afterwards my parents were permitted to marry legally.

Mother's life was filled by music and her children. Like my father, she had little affinity for the military milieu. Officers' wives visited us very infrequently and only when such visits were absolutely obligatory. Mother's true friends were artistic people and her brother's university friends, with whom she kept up a lively correspondence. All of these people lived in Kyiv, whereas our family was obliged to move from place to place every two or three years, for with each of Father's promotions to a higher rank came transfer to a new location.

CHAPTER 3

My father's first transfer was to Omsk. It came on the eve of the war with Japan, and I remember it well. The journey by train took nearly three weeks. But the trip itself was of little interest to us children. The only exciting parts were the stops at small Siberian stations along the way. The approaching train would attract the local inhabitants, who would rush to the station to sell the passengers all kinds of produce—bread, eggs, milk, and the like. During one stop, Mother asked our German nanny to purchase some eggs. She came back empty-handed, telling Mother in a frightened voice that "those women sell only crow's eggs." At first Mother didn't understand what she was talking about, but then she realized what the nanny meant. The Russian word for "boiled" (*varënyi*) sounds very similar to the Ukrainian word for "crow's" (*voronyi*), and the nanny thought that crow's eggs were being sold. At another station, a group of Ukrainian peasants, dressed in embroidered shirts and speaking Ukrainian, met the train—on camels! They brought watermelons, muskmelons, and vegetables. What a strange sight that was—Ukrainian peasants on camels!

It was late autumn when we finally arrived in Omsk, and the weather was murky and uninviting. That evening we were all sitting on unpacked suitcases in our new home, located at the intersection of "Impassable" and "Old Grave" streets. The cold room was semidark. As Mother read some heartrending story, tears rolled down my cheeks and my heart was heavy, as if filled with foreboding about the joyless life that awaited us in Siberia.

In those days Omsk was a small city with unpaved streets. Instead of sidewalks, people had to walk on narrow wooden planks supported on high wooden poles. This was essential because a great deal of snow fell during the winter, and when it melted in the spring, the streets became absolutely impassable to pedestrians or any other kind of traffic. Scenes like the following one were common. A small pony pulling a very heavily loaded cart would be beaten mercilessly by the driver until the poor beast collapsed into the mixture of snow and mud and was half-immersed in the slush. The driver continued to beat the horse as he tried to pull him out, but to no avail. The horse floundered and sank deeper and deeper into the mud. A crowd gathered; someone brought the long planks designed specifically for such occasions. The planks were shoved under the horse, and a man grasped each end.

They rocked the planks up and down until the horse slid to a dry place and could stand.

We lived in Omsk twice—once before the war with Japan and then again after it ended and Father came home from the front. Both times left me with unpleasant memories of cold so brutal that birds, frozen in flight, fell out of the sky and people walked about with their breath frozen on their collars. We children had our faces smeared with lard to protect us against frostbite. Our warm parkas were made of deerskin and lined with fur. They had to be pulled down over our heads and tied at the neck. They kept us warm, but they were so heavy that when we fell, we couldn't get up without help. As a child I tended to fall a lot, which caused our Siberian nanny to exclaim, "What a child—now up, now down!" My clumsiness may have been the result of the rickets I had suffered as a child, which left me with bowed legs. I had been treated with "sand baths"—that is, my legs were buried in hot sand on the banks of the Dnipro River. Afterwards the rickets disappeared, but I was unsteady on my feet for some time.

The local people would prepare *pelmeni* (meat dumplings) for the winter, piling them into huge outdoor barrels. The *pelmeni* would freeze immediately, and then they would be cut out of the pile with an axe as needed. Milk was also sold at the bazaar, in frozen chunks. In the summer, however, everything bloomed, and in August, when the harvest was ripe, one could walk along a path in the fields and watch a rider on horseback disappear into the tall fields of wheat—Siberian horses are so short that the feet of their riders seem to touch the ground.

There were many Kirghiz people among the local inhabitants. Once we were walking with our nanny along the wooden sidewalk when we suddenly heard screams and spotted two Kirghiz men. One had a bloody knife in his hand and was chasing the other. Nanny scooped us under the arms and flew like a bullet onto our porch. We all rushed inside and our nanny bolted the door. Almost immediately there was a tremendous banging on the door, and we heard one of the men pleading to be let in. We were frozen with fear. Nanny made no move toward the door, and soon the porch was quiet. After some time, we peeked out the window. There was the body of the murdered Kirghiz, lying on the porch in a big pool of blood.

I also remember the big Siberian watchdogs. Many of them were a crossbreed with wolves, which often wandered in from the taiga to the city, especially during the spring, and frolicked with the dogs. In

Tania (right) and her sister Liza (Omsk, Siberia, 1905 or 1906)

fact, dog owners there never knew for certain whether the animal in their kennel was a dog or a wolf. Our landlord had a huge watchdog named Osman. When he broke off his leash and dashed down the street, all the neighbors would scatter, screaming "Osman's loose!" I don't know how Osman got his reputation, but we children didn't let it deter us at all. We crawled into his doghouse and played with him, and the dog never hurt us. Mother knew about our friendship with Osman but did not forbid it, to the astonishment of our neighbors.

As for the wolves, I remember hearing about something that happened one winter. The frost that year was particularly brutal, and the forest animals suffered greatly. An officer had to go to a neighboring village with his family. They set out on the journey in two sleds—the officer and his wife in the first, followed by the second with a driver, a nanny, and their infant. The road wound through a thick forest. When they had traveled about half the distance, they heard the howling of wolves. The horses sped up, but the wolves' cries got closer and closer. The first sled was quicker, leaving the second somewhat behind. The driver beat the horses to make them speed up, but the hungry wolves, jumping out onto the road, started to gain on it. The driver, turning his head, saw that the infant had fallen out of the sled. He pulled on the reins, but it was impossible to stop the terrified horses. As the sled sped away, the wolves attacked the child and tore it to pieces. Later, under questioning, the nanny swore that a wolf had leaped into the sled and had torn the baby from her arms. The driver, however, declared that she had thrown the child from the sled to the wolves. The judges apparently found the nanny's testimony more believable, for they exonerated her.

CHAPTER 4

At the end of the Russo-Japanese War, Father was transferred to Pavlovskaia Sloboda, a former Arakcheev settlement near Moscow.[9] The settlement buildings were arranged in a square: the center was an area for drills, and around it stood the soldiers' barracks, officers' quarters, stables, and other buildings. Located at one end was the sports equipment: vaulting horses, ropes, rope ladders, and the like. My sister Liza, who was then five, climbed the ropes like a monkey. Her skill was greatly admired by the soldiers and the training officer, who often asked her to demonstrate it.

The soldiers were taught to ride, and Father enrolled us too in a series of riding lessons. Because we were small and could not sit in saddles, we were seated directly on the horses' backs, with saddle blankets as our only cushions. The horses knew instinctively what kind of riders we were, and they soon resorted to antics—they would stop suddenly and lower their heads, causing us to slide down their necks to the ground together with the saddle blankets.

Another episode involving horses and Pavlovskaia Sloboda took place one winter's day. My parents had been in Moscow and they had returned by train. The station they arrived at was thirty kilometers from Pavlovskaia Sloboda. A driver had been dispatched with a carriage and a pair of horses to meet them. The train was late, so the horses had been confined in a stable for a long while and were restive. Anyone who has worked with horses knows that when they are uneasy, horses can suddenly bolt and tear off, oblivious to any efforts to restrain them. And that is precisely what happened. My parents had hardly settled themselves in the sled when the horses took off. The driver pulled on the reins with all his might, but in vain. The reins tore into the horses' mouths, but they kept on galloping wildly. Luckily, the carriage robes were fastened tightly around my parents; otherwise they would have fallen out when the carriage careened around the curves. The driver finally stopped trying to guide the horses; instead he prayed they would get to their destination safely and that the Sloboda's gate would

---

[9] The first Arakcheev settlement was created in 1810 by Aleksei Arakcheev, the head of military affairs in the Russian Empire. The peasant inhabitants of the settlements were forced to perform lifelong military duties besides corvée, and to live under strict army conditions, including limitations on marriage. The settlements were abolished in 1857.—*Eds.*

be open. And that happened. The horses galloped the entire thirty kilometers, dashed through the Sloboda's narrow opened gate, made a sharp turn at the square to the stables, and came to a dead halt.

One day a young officer named Boris Nikanorovich Sitniakovsky was transferred to Pavlovskaia Sloboda. When he caught sight of Liza, he was struck by her resemblance to his young sister, whom he had loved dearly and who had died a short time before. Liza promptly became a favorite of his. He would seat her on a pillow before him on horseback, and they would ride about the Sloboda grounds together. One day Boris Nikanorovich received a letter that his mother was coming to visit. He became anxious, for he didn't know how he would introduce Liza to his mother. But his worry proved needless. When his mother first heard of his attachment to a girl who resembled her deceased daughter, she was distraught, but when she met Liza her agitation eased and she soon became fond of her. Several years later, during the war with Germany, Boris Nikanorovich visited us in Kyiv. He was married by then, but the marriage was not a happy one. By this time Liza had become a tall and beautiful young woman. Boris Nikanorovich's warm feelings towards her were rekindled and now developed into romantic ones. But Liza continued to relate to him as she had in childhood, with warm girlish friendship and trust, and there was no chance of a romance developing between them.

From early childhood we had live-in tutors whose task it was to prepare us for secondary school, that is, entrance into a gymnasium. They lived with us for years, and several—for instance, our teacher of German, Fräulein Liebe—became like members of the family. I also well remember our teacher of botany. My sister and I were not in the least bit interested in botany, but we adored butterflies. Our brother Seriozha had a butterfly collection, and Liza and I loved to capture new butterflies to add to it, always asking the botany teacher, "And what is this butterfly's name, according to your botany?" Above all, we loved animals, as did our whole family, especially Mother. She taught us to treat them well. We never hurt any animals who happened to come into our lives; on the contrary, we always took care of them as best we could. Knowing this, the soldiers would sometimes bring us squirrels, hedgehogs, or other animals. Once they brought us a small polecat. When I trustingly put out my hand to him, the frightened animal seized my finger with its teeth and bit it right down to the bone. A polecat usually sinks its teeth into its victim in a death grip. Once this one got hold of my finger, it held fast for about ten minutes, until someone managed to pull it off. I endured the incredible pain stoically and did not cry—it was typical for me not to cry from pain. For instance, when I was twelve I ran down the stairs holding on to the rail, not noticing the nail that was sticking up from it. The nail slashed my arm open almost to the elbow, so severely that the sinews were exposed. When I was taken to the doctor, he took one look and ordered everybody out of the room—he was certain I would scream horribly when he cleaned and stitched the wound. To his surprise, I uttered not a sound.

We children dreamed of having a dog. One day we found out that a dog had wandered into the house of our neighbor and that she wanted to get rid of it. We immediately ran to her house and met the small dog—a black, short-haired Manchester terrier, whom the neighbor had already named Ralf. We all liked Ralf very much and he seemed to be taken with us, for he immediately began playing and chasing after us. When we found out that the dog was a female, she became Ralfochka. She lived with us for ten years and became part of the family. Ralfochka knew each of us by name, and when we sat down to dinner, she would come up to the table expecting to play her favorite game. We would send her from one of us to the other, calling "Ralfochka, go to Tania!" "Go to Seriozha!" and so on, as the dog happily ran from one of us to the other.

All of us liked to read, but Seriozha read with special interest and fascination. He was never without a book, and every family photograph showed Seriozha with a book in his hand, a finger holding his place. The themes of our games always seemed to derive from whatever book Seriozha was reading, in particular the novels of Alexandre Dumas, James Fenimore Cooper, and Thomas Mayne Reid. He would assign us names to match. I was "White-Haired Eagle," Liza was "Quick-Footed Doe," and Seriozha himself was "Creeping Snake." The village boys took part in our games with immense enthusiasm. Officers' wives usually forbade their children to play with peasant children, but our mother readily let us play in the village. We swam in the river with our friends and went mushroom and berry picking with them, often disappearing for the entire day. For our outings Mother sewed special bags on which she embroidered our names. We would fill them with food and set out on our journeys feeling like real adventurers.

Once we went to the river by ourselves and found a small raft tied up at the shore. At Seriozha's proposal, we got on and set sail. First we sailed along the shore, but soon the current carried us out to the middle of the river. Seriozha, keeping his wits about him, ordered us to lie down on our stomachs and use our arms as oars. The raft was very narrow—it could barely hold the three of us. We all began flailing away but produced little momentum—after all, we were only small children. Finally, our raft started to drift back to shore. When I recall those times now, I wonder that Mother did not worry about our being out alone like that. Yet I also marvel at her wisdom in allowing us to try out our own strength and become independent and courageous, qualities that would help us greatly later in life.

When it came time for us to enroll in secondary school, there of course arose the question of what gymnasium to choose. Father decided that my brother should attend the Rostovtsev Gymnasium in Moscow, then considered one of the best. He thought that the best choice for my sister and me was the Smolny Institute in St. Petersburg, but Mother was resolutely opposed. So Father selected instead the Alelekova Gymnasium for Girls in Moscow, which he had heard was an exceptionally good school. Consequently we children and Mother moved to Moscow itself, while Father remained at the Sloboda settlement.

In Moscow we settled in the part of town called the Arbat. At that time the Arbat was a peaceful neighborhood, with brick pavements and small buildings set in the midst of greenery. We loved to walk along its quiet streets with our mother. Leo Tolstoy came to Moscow at that time and settled in the same area. It was said that on his walks along the streets he enjoyed meeting and chatting with children. One morning we spotted Tolstoy walking along, dressed in a Russian peasant shirt: he looked just like the photographs of him we had seen in books, so we recognized him immediately. Speaking quietly, Mother urged us to go and greet him. But we were overcome by frightened shyness and hesitated: "What if he asks us which of his books we've read—or talks about one that we don't know?" Mother tried convincing us that Tolstoy would not ask such questions, but we refused to budge. While we sparred back and forth, Tolstoy passed by and the opportunity vanished. We never came across him again. Later, as an adult, I greatly regretted that I had let the chance to meet him slip by.

In the fall of 1910, Sergei Utochkin, one of the first Russian aviators, came to Moscow. Leaflets announcing he would fly an airplane were posted all over Moscow, and the public was invited to gather at a military firing range just outside the city to witness the event. While out on a walk with a friend, my mother spotted a leaflet and decided to go, for she was very curious to see how a human being could fly. She and her friend set off together for the field. When they got close, it turned out that the field was encircled by a tall barricade, and one had to have a ticket to get in. When Mother asked where she could get one, she was told that they were all sold. Mother, genuinely disappointed, decided to do something she had never done before, that is, make use of her "high position." She declared that she was a general's wife and showed her passport as proof. When it became clear that she was telling the truth, she and her friend were seated in the very first row, with a good view of Utochkin's takeoff. Those sitting in the back could hardly see it at all, for his plane flew very low to the ground. But the best view was from the other side of the fence, from the tops of a row of tall trees that some enterprising young boys had climbed.

Fall came and school began. I clearly remember our first day. The other girls surrounded us and showered us with questions: "Who is your father?" "What estates does your family own?" Our reply that Father was a general seemed to satisfy them, but the fact that we did not own any estates aroused the girls' consternation. And when they heard that we had arrived at the gymnasium by streetcar instead of private carriage, they lost all interest in us. Many of these young girls came from titled families, and the parents of many were millionaires. All the girls were fluent in French, whereas the only foreign language we knew was German. Then, too, we weren't accomplished at "dancing the mazurka." All in all, we felt totally alien in this milieu. To our great joy, in the spring of 1910 Father was transferred to the Caucasus, and we left both that school and Moscow. Our destination was Temir Khan Shura, then the capital of Dagestan.

CHAPTER 5

The town of Temir Khan Shura was very small—its population was about three thousand, as I recall. It was located some forty-five kilometers from the seaport of Petrovsk, the train's final stop. From Petrovsk one had to travel to Temir Khan Shura by carriage across the mountain range described in the stories of Aleksandr Bestuzhev-Marlinsky. The governor's residence was in the town, and it was here that the Fifty-second Artillery Brigade was stationed. My father was assigned to be its commander. Although the brigade was considered to be a part of the Russian army, local mountaineers comprised over a third of it. They wore wine-colored, gold-trimmed Circassian coats with red-lined brown hoods. In these uniforms they cut very handsome figures, for they were slender and had amazingly small waists. They were also excellent horsemen. On tsarist and religious holidays there would be military parades in the city square, after which there were performances of trick riding. This truly beautiful spectacle attracted all the city's inhabitants, as well as people from outlying villages. The riders performed unbelievable tricks. For example, galloping at full speed on horseback, they would bury a dagger into the ground up to its very handle. Riding off a ways, they would then wheel their horses around and, galloping at the same dizzying speed, bend low from their saddles and pluck the dagger up from the ground with their teeth. In the evening there were performances of dances called the *lezginka*. Girls in beautiful national costumes danced as if they were floating over the ground. Chadors of light fabric pinned to their hair covered their faces. As they turned away from their partners, they would unveil their faces, and each girl's partner danced around her as if in pursuit. The passionate and surging vitality of the men, contrasted with the shyness and grace of the girls, made the dance very expressive and beautiful. Afterwards the men would dance separately. Their dances were also extraordinary and lovely to watch, but I always trembled with fear when the dancers held the tips of the daggers close to their eyes and started to spin and leap at incredible speed.

There were two schools in Temir Khan Shura—a boys' secondary school that focused on scientific subjects, and a gymnasium for girls. There were seven grades in the boys' school. The mountain boys who attended had a very poor knowledge of Russian; they were indifferent students and were expected to complete only four of the school's seven grades. They would then go on to the Elizavetgrad Cavalry School, entrance to which required only four years of schooling. As a rule, it took the mountain boys twelve years to complete these four years of school! Each grade could be repeated three times, and most of the boys took full advantage of that. By the time they graduated at the age of twenty, all of them were married and had children.

At the girls' gymnasium that my sister and I attended, the local girl students also commonly repeated a grade several times. Most of them married very young, and few completed the full eight grades. Their parents demanded that they bring their chadors to school in case the teacher happened to be a man. The route to school took me and my sister through the square where the boys' school stood. Invariably, the windows would be flung open and the boys would throw us kisses, calling out, "Hello there, sweetie!" Father, who was familiar with local customs, made sure that his orderly always walked us to and from school. Though we were only ten and eleven, there was reason for concern, especially after the following incident. A fruit dealer from the mountains visited our home. Seeing me, he told my father he would like to buy me to be his wife. When Father refused, the man, thinking that the offer must be too low, raised it several times. This continued until my father lost patience and ordered him to leave. The man left in anger, and when Father's friends heard of this, they warned him that the man might try to kidnap me. After that Father ordered us never to leave the premises unaccompanied by one of our orderlies.

My sister and I were always close, and probably that was why we felt little need to make friends among our peers. I became friends with only one of my classmates—a Tatar girl named Khabira Tabasaranskaia (Russians living in the Caucasus called all the mountain people Tatars). Khabira came from a wealthy and distinguished family that regularly hosted formal galas in their home, which we girls from the gymnasium were invited to attend. The galas were held in a huge hall with large windows and narrow floor-to-ceiling mirrors. The spacious toilet in the house also attested to the wealth of Khabira's parents. Instead of toilet paper, guests were provided with silver jugs filled with water (my first encounter with the custom).

Apart from Khabira, I remember a Georgian girl who attended one of the upper classes. She was strikingly beautiful—tall and slender, with long black hair. She was very popular at school dances, where the boys swarmed around her. I did not know her well, but enjoyed watching her from a distance. Once she invited me and several other classmates to her home. In her room we saw a large photo of her eleven brothers. All of them were cavalry officers, and we were told that they all were very fond of their sister. Sometime later, terrible news swept the gymnasium: the Georgian girl had committed suicide. It was said that she had become pregnant and could not bear the shame she had brought on herself and her family. I was totally stunned by this news. I could not understand how eleven brothers could fail to protect their beloved sister, or why pregnancy should bring shame upon a woman in the first place. Also, at the age of eleven, I couldn't understand how she could be pregnant without being married.

Our brother Seriozha also had few friends. Indeed, he had only one friend, a Georgian named Vania Alkhazov. Vania was the son of a piano tuner and had a passionate love of music. Everyone in his family was musically gifted—Vania and his brother inherited perfect pitch from their father. During his frequent visits Vania used to sit in the corner of the living room, near the piano, and listen to our mother play. Sometimes he would sit down at the piano and play from memory his favorite works by Mozart and Beethoven he had heard Mother play. He would recreate them with unbelievable subtlety and accuracy, conveying all the nuances beautifully. Once Mother took him with us to Tiflis (now Tbilisi) to attend a performance of *Carmen*. The opera had a great impact on him—he sat motionless and totally absorbed throughout the performance. The following day he came to our house and, as usual, sat down at the piano. Once again we heard the overture to *Carmen*, followed by all the rest of its music: the extraordinary boy had memorized the whole opera!

I suspect Vania was somewhat taken with me, though he never spoke of it. He only told my brother that he dreamed about having his picture taken with me. I knew this, and one day as we were passing a photographer's studio I suggested that we go in and have our picture taken together. Vania beamed with happiness, and as a result I have a picture of myself with Vania.[10] We stayed in touch with him long after our family left Temir Khan Shura—he even visited us in Kyiv several times during the First World War. To our sorrow, he was later killed at the front.

The families of Russian officers living in Temir Khan Shura did not dare go to the mountains and rarely ventured outside the town—and then only for organized group picnics. As usual, our family was different.

---

[10] Unfortunately, this photo could not be found.—*Eds.*

Mother often took us to the mountains. The orderlies accompanied us, and for long trips there were also hired guides. Sometimes we spent the night in a *saklia* (a Caucasian type of stone house) belonging to friends of the guides. The mountain people were famed for their hospitality, and to us, as friends of friends, they were particularly kind. We were always asked to share a meal with them. At first we did not have the courage to eat their food, because they added *cheremsha* (a garlicky and sharp-smelling spice) to practically every dish. Its odor permeated their clothes and living quarters. Finally, though, after much coaxing by our hosts, we tried some—and promptly forgot all about its odor. After that we gamely ate anything that was offered to us. These mountain hikes remain among my most pleasant memories from those years. We would wander in the mountains for hours on end, beautiful new vistas opening before us at every turn.

One time I climbed up a cliff and sat on its very edge, drinking in the lovely view. I had been sitting there for quite some time when I suddenly realized that an eagle was soaring above me. It was circling slowly and dropping altitude with every turn—my presence on the cliff had obviously captured its interest. I became uneasy. The bird was enormous, and I recalled how the guides had told us that eagles sometimes descended to snatch up goats and sheep. In no time at all I was scrambling back down the cliff.

Another day we were out in the mountains with our orderlies, this time without any guides. First we rode on horseback, and then we traveled on by foot. It was a beautiful day, and we wandered about the mountains, discovering fresh beauty everywhere. When evening came, we started looking for a place to spend the night. Mother noticed a quiet little hollow under a cliff and we decided to camp there. We had started to take out our tent and sleeping bags when suddenly we heard someone say, "What are you doing here?!" The speaker, a highland hunter, was approaching us. He had spotted us quite by accident at a distance and had come to warn us that, the day before, he had seen a bear and her cubs sleeping in this very spot—no doubt they would return. We quickly packed up our things and left for a safer location.

Tatiana (in Temir-Khan-Shura, former capital of Dagestan, Caucasia, 1912)

CHAPTER 6

Relations between the Russians and the local inhabitants were more or less civil, but hostility could surface at the slightest provocation. For instance, Russian soldiers would often entertain themselves by calling over a mountain boy, giving him a piece of meat to eat, and then telling him, "That was pork!" When the boy fell to the ground in anguish, screaming that he had committed a sin, the soldiers roared with laughter. Naturally enough, the family of the boy would gather, pull out their daggers, and a fight would ensue.

Deaths were known to occur. If a local student received a poor grade in school, his teacher's life might be at stake. At that time Dagestan was only partly "subdued." The mountaineers were a freedom-loving, bellicose people, and periodically a confrontation of some sort would develop between them and a Russian detachment in one of their villages, each of which was called an *aul*. In 1910 real warfare broke out over Zelim Khan, whom the Russians saw as a bandit but the mountaineers viewed as a patriot and hero.

Zelim Khan, the leader of a small but daring band on horseback, sought revenge against the Russians, who had conquered his fatherland. Attacking swiftly, he would rob and kill any Russians he could and then distribute all his gains among the inhabitants of the nearest *aul*. A special cavalry division was organized to deal with this Caucasian Robin Hood. It included not only Russians, but also a good number of mountaineers who had personal vendettas against Zelim and his associates. They soon realized it was impossible to catch him. One time our father, with evident delight, told us the tale of how Zelim Khan, threatened with imminent capture, had ridden into an *aul*. Telling his people to scatter, Zelim continued riding his horse in full view of the Russians. Then, suddenly, he vanished, as if the earth had swallowed him up. It was certainly true that Zelim had sympathizers in every *aul* who were ready to spirit him away and shelter him.

Another episode demonstrated the extent of Zelim Khan's prodigious courage, adroitness, and wit. He was riding a horse alongside a ravine, on a path so narrow that it was impossible for two travelers to pass each other: it was said that whenever a mountaineer rode onto this path, he would fire a shot to warn anyone who might be at the other end to wait until he had passed through. In any case, two Russian detachments had cornered Zelim there and now stood guard at either end, waiting for him to appear. The officer in command, certain that he was about to capture his quarry at last, sent a messenger to Zelim with a note that read, "Give yourself up, Zelim Khan! I have you in my pocket!" But Zelim did not surrender. As night approached, the Russian detachments pitched camp for the night, knowing that Zelim had no way to escape. Toward dawn, they heard a loud noise—could it be that Zelim Khan was so foolhardy as to bolt on horseback down into the ravine? The Russians were stunned—they didn't expect such a tactic even from someone as brave and reckless as Zelim. Both detachments hurriedly left their camps and cautiously made their way down into the ravine to capture the rebel. Meanwhile Zelim calmly proceeded along the now unguarded path, went up into the mountains, and disappeared. The sound the Russians had heard was Zelim pushing his beloved horse over the edge of the cliff and into the ravine: by sacrificing the animal, he saved his own life. The following day the Russian officer received a note from Zelim: "Prince, there's a hole in your pocket!"

By a strange coincidence, many years later, when my daughters and I were already in America, my elder daughter Assya found out from her publisher, Israel Rausen, that he had taken part in the pursuit of Zelim Khan. Rausen was astonished that Assya knew the story. In all his years of living abroad, he had never before met anyone who knew anything about Zelim. Rausen spoke excitedly about the mountain rebel and his adventures, mentioning the incident when the commanding officer found he had "a hole in his pocket." He said Zelim's death was finally brought about by a jealous woman who betrayed his hiding place to the Russians (no wonder the French always warn, "Cherchez la femme"!). Acting on her information, the Russians encircled the house where Zelim was hiding. He returned fire for a long time, and then there was silence. The soldiers waited until finally the door slowly opened and Zelim appeared on the doorstep. Not knowing whether he had run out of ammunition or had decided to give himself up, and fearing a trick of some sort, the soldiers dared not move. Zelim Khan fired a few more shots at his enemies and then fell dead to the ground. Only then did they approach him, and froze in amazement: his whole body was riddled with bullets.

The fighting spirit of the mountain people played a tragic role in our family. One spring, after school was out, an overnight trip to the mountains was arranged for the honor students at the boys' school. My brother Seriozha, who was then twelve, was among those invited to go. The teachers were to accompany the students, but Mother still worried that something might go wrong. She feared that the students, disregarding the rules, would bring along alcoholic beverages and get drunk. Our dog, Ralfochka, also sensed danger. The moment Seriozha left, she came to his room and started whining. She was sent outdoors, where she settled herself down under his window and howled continuously until dawn. The next morning, two teachers arrived at our door. One of them addressed Father: "Your son has sustained a slight wound." Father went pale and asked, "Where?" The teacher silently pointed to his temple. It turned out that what Mother feared had indeed happened. A drunk student had played a stupid joke and had taken aim at my brother with a rusty old pistol. My brother had tried to persuade him to desist from the drunken and dangerous folly, but the other boy continued aiming the pistol at Seriozha and said boastingly, "If you were a robber, I would shoot you like this—" and then pulled the trigger. A shot rang out and a bullet hit my brother in the left temple. Seriozha fell, unconscious. He was taken to the military hospital in Vladikavkaz, where he remained in a coma and hovered between life and death for several months. The student who had shot Seriozha was so guilt-ridden that he tried committing suicide. He was to be brought to trial, but Father refused to press charges, saying that that would not put anything to rights and that the boy was already being punished by his own remorse. The school administration wanted to expel the boy, but Father rejected that too, saying sadly, "That won't make me feel any better."

The doctors in Vladikavkaz felt it was beyond their competence to operate on my brother and advised my father to contact a specialist—a surgeon in St. Petersburg. The specialist named an exorbitant sum of several thousand rubles for his services, to which Father agreed. When the specialist arrived, he examined my brother and angrily exclaimed, "Why did you bring me out here to tend to someone who is dying?" Taking his payment, he left without even trying to help Seriozha. The local doctors then undertook the operation themselves. The trepanation of the skull they performed did not locate the bullet: it was deeply imbedded in a bone at the back of the head. The doctors did not dare to do anything more. My parents took my brother to St. Petersburg, to the famed Bekhterev Hospital, while my sister and I stayed behind in the Caucasus with our grandmother. After a time, Father was obliged to return to his brigade in Temir Khan Shura, but Mother remained in St. Petersburg to be near Seriozha.

Father suffered immensely throughout this ordeal. He became self-absorbed and nearly forgot about my sister and me. Later, however, he sought my company. He taught me to play chess and we played for hours—apparently that soothed him. He obtained postcards on which the words and music of some old Cossack *dumy* were printed, including his favorite, "The *Duma* about the Cossack Morozenko."[11] He asked me to learn to play this song on the piano, and I had to play it for him every evening. I can hear its sad melody in my mind even now:

O Moroz, Morozenko,
You Cossack of great deeds!
It is for you, Morozenko,
That all Ukraine weeps.

Ukraine weeps, but your dear
Mother she cries even more.
Morozykha[12] burst into tears
Standing by the door.

"Don't cry, don't cry, Morozykha,
To grieve there's no need.
Come join us Cossacks now,
Have a drink of mead!"

"Mead, my dear Cossacks,
Has lost its taste for me,
For my son, my Morozenko,
Is fighting the enemy...."

Seriozha was given a private room in the hospital, and another bed was placed there for Mother. Seriozha was two and half years older than I was, and though we were very close, I had not realized how

[11] The *dumy* were Cossack epic songs and originated in the 16th century. They were performed throughout Right-Bank and Left-Bank Ukraine by itinerant minstrels to the accompaniment of a kobza or bandura as late as the 1920s. See *Ukrainian Dumy: Editio minor,* trans. George Tarnawsky and Patricia Kilina, intro. by Natalie K. Moyle (Toronto and Cambridge, Mass., 1979); and Petro Odarchenko, "Duma," in *Encyclopedia of Ukraine*, vol. 1, ed. Volodymyr Kubijovyč (Toronto, 1984), 769–70.—*Eds.*

[12] Morozenko's mother.—*Eds.*

much he cared for me. Mother later told that he called out my name the whole time he lay unconscious. All the hospital personnel who tended him knew he had a sister named Tania.

Dr. Botkin, the personal physician of the tsar and his family, made frequent visits to the hospital, and he would often stop by to see Mother. A friendship developed between them, and Botkin spoke to her at length about the tsar's family and about Rasputin. He said that Aleksei Nikolaievich, the heir to the throne, was very attached to Rasputin. At times Rasputin treated the boy rudely, but Aleksei never complained. Botkin confirmed the rumors that Rasputin had the power to stop a hemorrhage and that the man was a clairvoyant. He related one strange incident that he himself had taken part in. One evening Rasputin and the doctor were out walking together and they passed a drunken woman fast asleep on the steps of a building. They kept walking on, until suddenly Rasputin stopped, turned back, and went up to the woman. He shook her out of her sleep and told her, "Go home immediately! Something terrible has happened there." The woman roused herself and made her way unsteadily down the street. The doctor decided to follow her. It was a long way—the woman lived on the other side of town. When she finally turned into her own street, Dr. Botkin saw a crowd gathered outside one of the buildings. He soon learned the reason: a young girl had died suddenly—and she was the woman's daughter. The doctor knew scores of such incidents involving Rasputin.

Seriozha spent nearly a year in the hospital. His life was saved, but he was never the same, never a whole person again. Before his second operation, he began having epileptic seizures, which were to plague him to the end of his life. Also, the whole right side of his body was paralyzed, and his arm bent in at the elbow. At first, he could not move his right leg at all, but with therapy Seriozha learned to walk again, without even use of a cane. But the fact that he had suffered brain damage was the saddest part of all. For the rest of his life Seriozha remained a pleasant and kind person, but his mind was that of an adolescent. Although he did not become antisocial, he felt best when he was outdoors and alone—he would often wander off in the woods, gathering mushrooms. Animals had no fear of him at all—squirrels would come right up to him and sit on his shoulder while he fed them. Seriozha lived with us and at times with our uncle, and he always tried to be helpful and no burden to anyone. He was very gentle and considerate, and he was capable of very deep feelings. Once he fell in love with an acquaintance of ours and, wanting to give her something nice, gathered flowers in the woods for her. It was painful for our family to observe all this and know that there was nothing we could do to help him.

One day, several years after he left the hospital, Seriozha was sitting in the kitchen with our orderly, watching him clean his rifle. The man accidently pulled the trigger and a bullet flew just millimeters from Seriozha's head. Smiling sadly, Seriozha said, "It would be better if that bullet killed me." What irony! Seriozha's joyless life came to an end in Kyiv during the German occupation, when he found himself alone without any means to provide for himself. By the time I reached him, it was too late—Seriozha had died of starvation. Rest in peace, dear brother!

CHAPTER 7

About a year after the accident, my sister and I moved to Kyiv with our "Black Grandmother." Mother and Seriozha were already there. Father remained in the Caucasus until war broke out in 1914, and then he went directly to the front. We settled in Lukianivka, a suburb of Kyiv, on tree-lined and peaceful Velyka Dorohozhytska Street, where most of the residents were pensioners. A streetcar ran along the street to the center of town. Our house—number 44—stood on a hill. It was owned by the brother of the renowned art historian Ihor Hrabar. The house had a large garden in the back that extended down to a deep ravine, beyond which lay a workers' settlement. It was in a house at the bottom of the ravine, right behind our garden, that the body of a boy surnamed Yushchinsky was found: some newspapers were carrying reports that he had been killed in a ritual murder by a Jewish man called Mendel Beilis. It was said that blood from a live Christian was needed to make matzos and that that explained the numerous knife wounds on the little boy's body. In time the case against Beilis was brought to trial. Our family discussed the proceedings at length. None of us doubted that all of the "evidence" against Beilis was fabricated. The charge of inflicting wounds on a living person could have been verified by an autopsy, but the court would not allow one to be performed: it overruled the defense on the matter time and again. The whole city hummed with talk that if Beilis were found guilty, a pogrom would be inevitable. I was distraught over newspaper accounts detailing the horrible murder and maintaining that it had been committed for ritual purposes.

Any mention of a pogrom brought back one of my childhood memories. Mother and I were riding in a carriage when suddenly, somewhere in front of us, we heard muffled sounds—a combination of screams, singing, and the stomp of many feet. From around the corner a crowd appeared, led by a priest carrying an icon. As these people marched and sang liturgical songs, Jews were running out in panic from the side streets. Our driver turned to us and said anxiously, "It's a pogrom! But don't worry—I'll turn into the first alley!" And so he did, driving the horses at breakneck speed.

The day Beilis was to be sentenced, a crowd of people gathered and filled the enormous square in front of the government offices where the trial was held. We went there too. The atmosphere was extremely tense as everyone waited for the verdict. Finally an official appeared on the balcony and announced that the court had found Beilis not guilty.

What took place in the square then is impossible to describe. The crowd, which must have numbered over a thousand, let out a roar. People clasped and embraced one other, exuberantly shouting "Hurrah!" If there were dissenting voices, they were drowned out in the thunder of jubilation. Soon afterwards, Beilis appeared at a door, accompanied by several people. They all got into a car and drove off immediately through the crowd. Their destination was the railroad station, where a special train was waiting to take Beilis out of the country.

Our apartment on Velyka Dorohozhytska Street had eight spacious rooms. It accommodated my immediate family as well as Mother's brother Aliosha, his wife Zhenia, and their small daughter Oksana. Aliosha was then a student at the Kyiv Polytechnical Institute, while Zhenia was seeking admission to the Kyiv Medical Institute. At that time, it was very difficult for women to gain entry to medical school. Zhenia took the entrance exams several years in a row. She failed time after time, yet stubbornly kept preparing and reapplying. She finally managed to gain entrance to the School of Medicine in Zurich and then went on to complete her diploma there. Subsequently she was admitted to the Kyiv Medical Institute and became a physician. A woman with democratic convictions, Zhenia became a country doctor. She encountered many difficult and curious cases in her practice. Her first encounter with peasant women was a case in point. Several of them arrived at her clinic together and silently sat down. Zhenia waited a few minutes for one of them to speak, but they did not say a word. Finally she asked, "What health problems are you having? What ails you?" The women looked at one other and replied with evident scorn, "If you don't know, what kind of a doctor are you?"

One incident could have cost Zhenia her life. A woman who had contracted smallpox came to her for help and Zhenia prescribed treatment. The woman asked if she could keep breast-feeding her child despite the illness, and Zhenia assured her that she could continue without doing the infant any harm. The woman's husband, suspicious about the diagnosis, consulted another doctor, who said that continuing to breast-feed was out of the question, for the child might become infected and die. The husband tore into Zhenia's office in a rage and threatened her with a pistol, shouting, "If my child dies, I'll kill you!" Luckily, the child did not become ill and the case ended without incident.

Zhenia worked selflessly all her life. Many years later I learned that she was mobilized during the Second World War and worked as an army doctor, earning a medal for her services. After the war Zhenia continued practicing medicine. One day, while returning home from the clinic where she worked, she suffered a heart attack and died.

Aunt Zhenia was not a particularly important figure in my life, but her husband, my uncle Oleksii Kysilevsky, whom we all called Aliosha, was. A vibrant person with a great sense of humor, he loved poetry and was also a talented painter. After completing a degree in chemistry at the polytechnical institute, he got a job as an engineer at a sugar refinery. But soon the primitive and unhygienic production methods used there made him realize that the work was not for him, and he decided to change his profession. He returned to the polytechnical institute and enrolled in its Department of Road Construction. After several years of study, he became a highway engineer. He became well known and was well regarded throughout his long career. He also studied at the Kyiv Art School, where he worked in watercolors and became an accomplished landscape artist. His love of painting fitted in well with his new profession. Wherever his jobs took him—to the Altai, Mongolia, the Pechora River—he returned with beautiful watercolors he had painted. His friends tried convincing him to exhibit his work, but he refused, preferring to give his paintings away or stash them in a trunk. He was wary of attracting any attention from the authorities, fearing that they might discover his father's role as a community arbitrator and that might harm his career. For the same reason, Aliosha never published his travel notes, which were full of fascinating stories. One of them was about Mongolia and its fearsome blizzards. On one of Aliosha's expeditions through the steppe, dark thunder clouds suddenly appeared on the horizon. The members of the expedition, knowing from experience how rapidly such blizzards could descend in that region, began putting up shelters. The tent of a Mongolian nomad stood nearby: its owner was sitting at the entrance, calmly smoking a pipe and watching his cow graze nearby. Aliosha, puzzled by his calmness, asked the Mongol why he was not driving his cow to the corral. The Mongol screwed up his eyes, took the pipe out of his mouth, and said, "Why should I? Am I here to serve the cow, or is the cow here to serve me?" And troubling himself no further, the man continued sitting as impassively as before.

Another time Aliosha observed how the Mongols in one small settlement buried their dead. The deceased was wrapped in linen and placed on a low hearse that sloped to the ground. The driver whipped the horse, and the wagon bumped along the road until the corpse fell off. According to local belief, wherever it fell was the place designated by the gods or fate for the repose of the deceased, and no one was permitted to move the body from that spot. The corpse was simply left for dogs to devour—great packs of them wandered the streets. Aliosha mentioned that the stench from such "funerals" was incredibly strong and could be smelled miles away.

Aliosha told another anecdote having to do with odors, this one not about the Mongols, but about the inhabitants of the Pechora region far to the north. As Aliosha's party approached one settlement, they were struck by the stench of decaying fish. Coming closer, they saw huge pits half-filled with such fish. It turned out that this was the way the local inhabitants stored food for the winter. Throughout the brief summer and fall, until the first frosts, they caught fish and threw them into these pits. The fish started decaying, of course, but the fishermen continued eating them throughout the winter. Why these people were not poisoned as a result is baffling. Perhaps they developed some kind of special immunity to what they were eating.

Aliosha gathered hundreds of such observations, and he related them with colorful descriptions and dry humor. Once, while traveling on the Trans-Siberian Railroad, he struck up a conversation with a fellow passenger in his compartment. The passenger listened to Aliosha's stories with great interest and declared that he must write them down, promising that they would be published. It turned out that the man was one of the editors of the Russian journal *Novyi mir* (New World). Disconcerted by his attention and praise, Aliosha assured the editor that he would write down and submit his stories. To my knowledge, however, he never did.

During the time we were living on Velyka Dorohozhytska Street and Aliosha was studying at the polytechnical institute, Liza and I were still gymnasium students. There was a twenty-year age difference between Aliosha and the two of us, his nieces, but that did not stop our threesome from enthusiastically undertaking joint literary projects. One of them was collaborating on parodies of the work of Aleksei Tolstoy, Aliosha's favorite poet. We would write everything down in a special "journal," which we titled the "Dorohozhytska News." Aliosha was, of course, the main contributor, but Liza kept pace with him. I, however, lagged somewhat behind. Aliosha would also make comic drawings to complement our poetic output. Here is one of our poems, a parody of Tolstoy's ballad "Sadko":

Poor Liza is sad, at school she pines,
While outside a glorious morning
Announces spring—as it sparkles and shines,
It fills her with wondrous yearning.

The streetcar below rolls aloud with a noise,
The cars run along with a sputter,
The freedom out there every creature enjoys
As happy birds twitter and flutter.

And here the school mistress, still barely awake,
Is gazing at her without emotion,
And noisy schoolmates throughout recess
Annoy her with all their commotion.

A German translation in front of her lies,
But lost in her thoughts she is dreaming.
To the Prince of Albania her fancy now flies,
And beautiful visions are streaming.
She sees the Albanian mountains so steep,
Caressed by the azure-blue waters.
The sea is so calm and mysteriously deep,
And is dotted with sailing boaters.

And here comes the Prince, and he says with a smile,
"Elizabeth, dear—my sweetheart!
Oh, why is your countenance sad all the while?
Your secret to me do impart.

Perhaps the sweet sherbet we ate, my dear Beth,
Did not meet with your approbation?
Or maybe our etiquette bores you to death,
As well as our whole population?

Reveal all your thoughts and emotions, I pray,
To share them with you is my pleasure.
An Albanian sailboat on this sunny day
We will take to the sea without measure.

The sea gulls so swift and the fish we will feed
With French bread so good and nutritious,
And thus chase away with lightning speed
Your thoughts and bad mood so pernicious."

And presently Beth and the Prince go aboard
Their yacht, with the retinue trailing.
They carry the train of her dress in accord
With rules they obey without failing.

All at once something struck like a thunderbolt
And everything instantly vanished.
Liza found herself under sudden assault
Back at school, where she had been banished.

The girls left and right, as if in a game,
All shove her and shake her, relating
That the German instructor has called out her name
Three times in a row and is waiting.

Poor Liza jumped up, grabbed the book in her hands,
But the lines of the German translation
All blurred, and she could not at all comprehend
Their sense, to her great consternation.

The furious German pulled out the grade sheet
And entered without hesitation
The fateful grade "F," which no one can delete,
Leaving Liza without consolation.

Another of our joint creative efforts was a takeoff on Pushkin's "The Upas Tree," which describes a scene at a pawnshop. Our version included the following lines:

No beast nor fowl would be inclined
To go near such forbidding places,
Yet folk with bundles wait in line,
With resignation on their faces.

A man was sent to this abode
By someone's look of plaintive pleading,
He took his threadbare overcoat
And pawned it there, his heart bleeding.

Aliosha was a frequenter of pawnshops, so the topic was a familiar one to him. His financial situation was precarious throughout the time he was a student at the institute. His wardrobe consisted of a single suit, which he periodically took to the tailor to be turned, just like the hero in Gogol's "Overcoat." The tailor was a very colorful person, a character straight out of the stories of Sholom Aleichem. His name was Meislik. As a child, I thought his name was a diminutive and meant that everyone liked him. Indeed, Meislik was a good-hearted man. He sewed for our whole family. I can see him now, sitting on a table drawn up to a window in his basement flat. Able to see only the legs of passersby, he sat Turkish-style, plying a needle back and forth while his children played around him. He had many children and was forgetful of their names. When his children became very boisterous, Meislik, wanting to scold them but not remembering who was who, would shout out, "Hey, Boria, Misha—you, whoever you are! Stop it!" Meislik was poor, but he strove to teach his children to amount to something. Apparently he succeeded: most of them became professional people, and some graduated from university.[13]

In addition to being writers of poetry, Liza and I were avid readers. One bookstore in Kyiv, Idzikovsky's, also housed a very good library. We borrowed many books from it, primarily works of contemporary Russian literature. Our home constantly reverberated with conversations about literature, music, and art, and we children participated in these. We matured under the influence of the adults in our family, who were people of culture, well educated, and talented. We often went together to concerts, the opera, and art exhibits. We loved frequenting the Solovtsov Theater,[14] which staged superb productions of Chekhov's, Ibsen's, and Leonid Andreev's plays. The Moscow Art Theater troupe would often appear there while on tour.

---

[13] Many years later, in Ann Arbor, Michigan, I met Dr. Jerry Meislik, an ophthalmologist whose family came from Kyiv. He believed that the tailor Meislik must have been one of his relatives, since they shared a very uncommon surname.

[14] A Russian theater in Kyiv founded in 1891 by the actor and director Nikolai N. Solovtsov (1857–1902). It was nationalized in 1919 and renamed the Second State Theater of the Ukrainian SSR.—*Eds.*

Tatiana as a gymnasium student (Kyiv, 1915)

My sister and I went to see that troupe's performance of Gogol's "Inspector General." The famous actor Stepan L. Kuznetsov played the role of Khlestakov. He looked extraordinarily handsome and acted beautifully. Liza and I were captivated by him, and we went to every one of his performances. Finally we mustered up the courage to try to see our idol close up. We successfully made our way backstage and, with our hearts in our throats, knocked on the door of his dressing room. The actor opened the door in a gentlemanly way and ... horror of horrors! Before us stood an aging man, his face covered by a thick layer of greasepaint. The look of disenchantment on our faces must have spoken volumes. The actor laughed and said, "Young ladies, never seek to examine close up what looks beautiful from a distance." I have always remembered this wise piece of advice.

Kyiv also had a Ukrainian theater in those days. The plays performed there were attended largely by people from the working class. Liza and I sometimes went there with our mother, but more often we went with our orderlies or cooks. Hryhorii Kvitka-Osnovianenko's *Svatannia na Honcharivtsi* (Matchmaking at Honcharivka) and *Oi, ne khody Hrytsiu ta i na vechornytsi* (Don't Go to Evening Parties, Hryts) were the kind of plays staged there, because the tsarist censors permitted nothing more serious. In contrast, all of Kyiv would come out to listen to performances of the famous Ukrainian choir led by Oleksander Koshyts, so that getting tickets to them required both effort and luck. Our family never missed an opportunity to attend. The choir was made up mostly of students, so its members were constantly changing. Yet Koshyts was able to meld them into an excellent group of singers, and listening to them was a real pleasure.

We also enjoyed visits to the circus, particularly the acrobats' floor performances. Their aerial tricks frightened us, though, because accidents sometimes happened. Liza and I liked one of the acrobats so much that we decided to present him with an album of reproductions of ancient Roman and Greek sculptures. After long deliberation, we came up with an inscription for the luxurious and quite expensive edition: "Here, for you, the living embodiment of the creative genius of the great masters, are the lifeless monuments of their achievements." Naturally enough, the acrobat was extremely pleased and flattered by our gift.

Following Aliosha's advice, we enrolled in courses at the Kyiv Art School and attended it for the next two or three years. There we learned to draw from real life, to paint with watercolors, and to sculpt. Later my creativity expressed itself in the little animals I made from play dough for my children and in drawings and paper cutouts. My classmates at the gymnasium were enthusiastic about embroidering, but I had absolutely no interest in it. We were all instructed in sewing and embroidering, but after it took me an entire year to cross-stitch one handkerchief, my teacher lost all hope of teaching me anything more. However, a love for embroidering must have lain dormant in my Ukrainian blood, for many years later, in England, I took to embroidering pillows in traditional Ukrainian patterns. British ladies then bought them eagerly—and for a song.

CHAPTER 8

What I have described were the circumstances in my life during my formative years, when my likes, dislikes, and understanding of the world were developing. What kind of a person was I at the age of sixteen? Liza and I were often compared to Pushkin's Olga and Tatiana. Liza was active and agile, loved gymnastics, and rode horseback beautifully, whereas I was clumsy and thought of myself as uninteresting, plain, and unlike any of my friends. I had no romances or even lighthearted flirtations. Men paid court to me, and my appearance sometimes caught the attention of passersby—"Look at those eyes!" they would say—but that made no impression on me. I remained convinced I was not at all attractive. In character I took after my father—from childhood I was not very sociable, and after Seriozha's accident I became even more introverted. Reading became my one true pleasure, and it substituted for real life. I read serious literature not meant for a girl my age and yet had a deep understanding of it. By the age of thirteen or fourteen I had already read Dostoyevsky's *Karamazov Brothers* and *Crime and Punishment*, which had a profound, if depressing, impact on me, and Tolstoy's *Anna Karenina* and *War and Peace*, which I found more enjoyable.

I was thrilled by Tolstoy's philosophical and religious works, especially his treatise *The Basis of My Faith*. At that time I was very concerned with issues related to the meaning of life. Among other Russian classics, I was deeply moved by Ivan Goncharov's novel *The Precipice*. For some time his heroine, Vera, was my ideal, and the figure of Mark Volokhov, the strong-willed nihilist with a Romantic type of courage, stirred my imagination. From childhood I myself was courageous and decisive. Of the three of us children, I was the only one not afraid to enter a dark room. This characteristic was later captured with humor in our "Dorohozhytska News" in a poem based on Vasilii Zhukovsky's ballad "The Glove":

> "Liza and Tania, which one of you
> Will go down to the dairy?
> I would send Peter, but today
> I let him go out to town."
> And with these words our mother took
> Her purse and the search began.

Liza and Tatiana with their mother, Olha (Kyiv, ca. 1916)

Three nickels was all that she could find,
And she looked at us again.
"For being so brave I will let you use
A nickel to buy any sweets you choose."
At first she received no response, but then
Tania got up from her seat
And marched resolutely out the door
Into the darkness and sleet.
And everyone thought in fear and anguish,
"Oh, Tania! In getting some yogurt
You'll perish!"

I was compassionate toward people and animals who were hurt, helpless, or weak, and I was always ready to help them. Perhaps that is why I developed a wish to become a doctor. I remember that as I was returning home from school one day, a young man approached me and asked for help, saying he was hungry and had no money. "I was drawn by your face," he said. "You look like a kind person to me, and that is why I dared to approach you. Please don't be afraid of me—I'm not a beggar. I'm simply an unfortunate person." The man looked truly pitiable. But although he was dressed in ragged clothes, his face had a look of refinement. Without hesitation, I gave him the two rubles I had in my pocket and then suggested that he come with me to our apartment. When I brought him home, I told Mother that he was an unfortunate, hungry person who needed help. Without asking any questions, she led him to the kitchen and gave him some food. He was deeply moved by our kindness to him and soon told us his sad story. He was a musician, a violinist who had completed the music conservatory. But he had started drinking, and when he could not stop, he lost his job. Now he found himself out on the street, without shelter, friends, or any hope. He told his story with sincerity, and it was evident how embarrassed he was by what he was sharing. He thanked us and left, but later he made several more visits to our home. He seemed changed, and he told us he had stopped drinking and had a job. I don't know if the change lasted, but he did tell us that our family's compassion had saved his life.

Episodes like this one recurred in my life, as if someone knew I had a compassionate nature and sent all sorts of hapless and helpless beings, both people and animals, my way. I have lost count of the number of dogs and cats I saved—those I found on the street and those that found their own way to me. Whenever I failed to be of help to any of them, I suffered terribly. One autumn in Kyiv, storm windows were being installed in our apartment. The workers did not notice that a big green fly had flown in between the two sets of panes. The insect buzzed about frantically, beating against the pane, finding escape from its prison impossible. The spectacle made me cry, and I begged that the poor thing be freed somehow. But my pity for an insect seemed silly to everyone else. I recall to this day how that fly suffered for several weeks before it finally died.

Like everyone in my family, I loved poetry. Though later I would be enthralled by Vladimir Mayakovsky, Sergei Yesenin, and Aleksandr Blok, when I was in high school I liked Nikolai Nekrasov, primarily because of his democratic spirit and compassion for the common man. I also liked Semen Nadson, the general favorite of young people at the turn of the twentieth century. But my favorite poet was, and still is, Mikhail Lermontov. In those years the intelligentsia took a lively interest in questions of civic morality, and our family was no exception in that regard. Nikolai Chernyshevsky's ideas were looked upon favorably in our milieu, and his book *What Is to Be Done?* was a real revelation to me. I was particularly taken by ideas on women's liberation. I read with avid interest a book called *The Biological Tragedy of Women*. I cannot remember the name of the doctor who was the author,[15] but I do recall that he

[15] The author's name is Anton V. Nemilov. The English translation of his work was published in New York in 1932.—*Eds.*

wrote compassionately about the fate of women as essentially enslaved by their families and limited to bearing and raising children. Later I read with similar interest a book by Victor Margueritte entitled *La Garçonne* and attended a performance of Henrik Ibsen's *Doll's House*. Most influential in developing my worldview, however, was the philosophy of Max Stirner as espoused in his treatise *The Ego and His Own*. In it he confirmed the intrinsic value of the human individual and his or her life experience ("The world exists to the extent that I exist in it"). Stirner also expressed the idea that even when love is selfless and self-sacrificing, a person always loves out of egotism, that is, because he or she needs to love and this brings personal satisfaction. I was absolutely stunned by this idea, because it went so against the grain of the principles of morality and behavior generally held at the time. I accepted it, however, and added my own interpretation: that love was a gift I gave people freely and that therefore it obligated no one to me. I passed this idea on to my daughters, teaching them that they did not have to love me simply because I was their mother and took care of them. I did not need their love "out of duty" or as a reward. The girls understood, and our relations were based on mutual love and respect, to the surprise and delight of everyone who knew us.

When I was fourteen, my uncle Aliosha got me a subscription to the journal *Byloe* (The Past), which was devoted to the history of the revolutionary movement in the Russian Empire. (Today it seems amazing that the authorities allowed such publications to appear in those times.) The journal provided detailed information about the fate of people who had fought against autocracy at various times in history. In it I read, for example, about Mikhail Gots, the famous socialist about whom even Leo Tolstoy, who disliked revolutionaries, spoke with respect. Gots was an idealist, the "soul" of the Russian Party of Socialist Revolutionaries, and completely committed to the socialist idea. He spent many years in prison, where he contracted tuberculosis. *Byloe* also mentioned that, as a result of "intense interrogations," Gots was paralyzed—he had lost control of his legs. When he was finally released from prison, his party immediately sent him abroad, from where he supervised revolutionary activity.[16] It was also in *Byloe* that I read about imprisoned revolutionaries who had gone on hunger

[16] In Ann Arbor I also met Gots's relative, Dr. Alexander Gots. He revered Mikhail and collected all the material about him that was available abroad. He was pleasantly surprised that I knew about Mikhail, for he had not long met anyone who had heard of him.

strikes to protest against tsarist prison authorities. Knowing about this method of protest became important later, when I myself was placed under arrest.

I read other books on political issues, borrowing them from Idzikovsky's library, and found nothing paradoxical about the fact that I, the daughter of a tsarist general, should be reading such "anti-government" literature. Yet it never occurred to me to become active in any political party. Even later, when I was pulled into the very nucleus of the political struggle during the civil war in Ukraine, I remained on the sidelines of any real political involvement.

My first contact with revolutionary circles was through my friend Galia Melnikova, my classmate at the gymnasium. Galia's father, Yuvenalii Melnikov, was one of the founders of the Russian Party of Socialist Revolutionaries in Ukraine; he had died by the time I met her. I often visited Galia's family and became well acquainted with her mother and her brother, who was also named Yuvenalii, or Yuva, after his father. Galia, her brother, and I were close friends and often went sailing together on the Dnipro. Once Yuva's friend, Petia, joined us and the four of us went for a sail. We were out all day and came back home exhilarated. Yuva and his friend went home, while Galia remained at our house with me. We had sat down to have some tea when suddenly someone banged on the window (the room we were in was in the basement and the window was at ground level). It was Yuva's friend Petia bearing tragic news: "Yuva has shot himself!" We were stunned. We had just parted company, and Yuva had been so happy! Nobody—neither his friends nor his mother—ever found out why he committed suicide. For me this was another distressing experience. Fate seemed to be preparing me from an early age for the traumas that would befall me in the future.

Galia often spoke about her father, though she had seen him only a few times in her life, between his arrests. In all the photos of him she showed me, he was dressed in prison garb. Though Galia's life was sad, it was better than that of those children left without any home at all after their parents were imprisoned for political reasons. Yet even in those "accursed tsarist times" there were government agencies that supervised the care of such children. Through such agencies, these children were sent to peasant families who provided them with foster care at government expense. The funds received must have been adequate, for the peasants gladly took such children into their homes. Galia's mother worked for many years in one such agency, checking to see whether the peasants made proper use of the money they received; she found that the majority of them did. In some cases the peasants would compete for a child: one little boy was so sweet and lovable that peasants literally stole him from each other!

I don't recall whether Galia's mother was a party member. Shortly after the Revolution of 1917, the Bolsheviks started seeking out old revolutionaries. One newspaper published an article that referred to Yuvenalii Melnikov as a Bolshevik. As a result, Galia's mother received a letter inviting her to join the organization of old revolutionaries. She wrote back with indignation that neither she nor Melnikov had ever been Bolsheviks and categorically refused to join the organization. Her letter was published. I don't know what happened to the family subsequently.[17]

[17] In the 1920s Velyka Dorohozhytska Street was renamed Melnikov Street, in honor of Yuvenalii Dmitrovich Melnikov.

CHAPTER 9

My carefree years at the gymnasium were drawing to a close, and fateful historical events were brewing. The war with Germany, which had lasted several years, was still going on. Father was fighting at the front and rarely came home. During one of his furloughs he was visited by an officer, a distant relative whom he had never met before. The officer was also serving at the front. Upon arriving in Kyiv he had looked us up through the address bureau (people named Kardynalovsky were all interrelated). Father did not maintain ties with his family, and I knew little about them. There was a Kardynalovsky in Odesa who held some high post—possibly that of the town's chief administrator (*gradonachalnik*)—and had the reputation of being a rabid reactionary. Another Kardynalovsky had lived in St. Petersburg at the end of the last century. He must have been a good person, for he was spoken of with affection by people I met in the 1930s in Kalinin (before 1931 the city was called Tver[18]).

The officer Kardynalovsky who visited us in Kyiv was from the Far East. He turned out to be extremely rich and also extremely unlikable. He tired Father with talk about the benefits of military service in that area, praising the higher salary paid there and various other opportunities for accumulating wealth (that is, by collecting bribes). He advised Father, as a fellow Kardynalovsky, to follow his example and seek a transfer to Siberia. Father listened to this advice with undisguised displeasure and parted from him coldly. The officer left, obviously offended. But he came back and visited us several more times, for Kyiv was the nearest large city where he and other officers could come and spend their accumulated cash. Every time he came to Kyiv, he would order huge boxes of chocolates for Liza and me, and once he asked Mother's permission to take us to a jewelry store and buy us small presents there. Mother reluctantly let us go, advising us to choose something very inexpensive. He took us to Marshak's, a very chic jeweller, where Liza and I spent a long time looking at the rings and bracelets on display, not knowing what to choose. Finally, we saw some very simple gray rings with blue stones, which appeared to us to be very inexpensive. When Mother saw what we had chosen she was horrified—it turned out that our "gray rings" were sapphires set in platinum.

---

[18] The original name of this Russian provincial capital, located between Moscow and St. Petersburg, was restored after the collapse of the USSR.—*Eds.*

After our brother was wounded, at first guests rarely came to our home. But with time that changed and many new friends came by to see us. Our most frequent visitors were Aliosha's friends from the institute, Ivan Pylypovych Nemolovsky, whom we all called Vania, and Vsevolod Oleksandrovych Holubovych. Both of them later became members of the first Ukrainian government—the Ukrainian Central Rada—and also members of our family.

Vania Nemolovsky's family was prominent in the upper circles of the Ukrainian intelligentsia, and everyone in it was active in Ukrainian civic life and culture. On his mother's side, Vania was related to the Kosach family (his mother was a cousin of Lesia Ukrainka), and he used "Kosach" with some pride as his pen name.[19] Vania's father, Pylyp Ireneievych Nemolovsky, was a doctor with lofty humanitarian ideals. He worked in a zemstvo hospital, where he tried to gain the trust of his peasant patients and to understand their psychology. For example, in giving a prescription to a peasant woman, he would tell her that the medicine had to be taken before sunrise and with the "first" water from the well. His sympathetic manner and understanding of people's psychology made him an extremely popular physician and gained him the reputation of being someone who "understood sickness" and knew how to "drive it out."

Vania had been Aliosha's friend during the years they were both gymnasium students. When Vania graduated from gymnasium (in Hrodna, I believe) he went to Gent in Belgium to study at the polytechnical institute there. He studied there for almost two years, gaining training in the technical sciences and simultaneously attending art school. When he returned to Ukraine, he enrolled at the Kyiv Polytechnical Institute and graduated from it with a degree in engineering. Vania was an excellent student, talented and educated in many fields. He also graduated from the Kyiv Art School and was an accomplished artist—indeed, art was his true vocation. He would probably have become a famous painter if war had not broken out. In 1914 Vania was mobilized, and almost immediately he sustained an

---

[19] The Kosaches were a family of prominent Ukrainophile cultural figures in prerevolutionary Ukraine. The most famous member of that family is the poet and playwright Larysa Kosach-Kvitka (pen name Lesia Ukrainka; 1871–1913). Her mother, Olha Kosach (pen name Olena Pchilka; 1849–1930), the sister of the famous Ukrainian socialist and federalist Mykhailo Drahomanov (1841–95), was well known in her time as an ethnographer, feminist, writer, publisher, and translator. Lesia Ukrainka's nephew, Yurii Kosach (1909–90), debuted as a writer in interwar Galicia and continued his craft as a postwar émigré in Germany and the United States.—*Eds.*

injury to his right hand. He was brought back to Kyiv for treatment, but he never regained full control of that hand. As a result Vania was forced to give up the artistic pursuits he loved.

Vania was a socialist from the time he was an upperclassman in the gymnasium, when he joined the ranks of the Party of Socialist Revolutionaries. When the 1917 Revolution began, Vania took active part in organizing the Ukrainian Central Rada, which was dominated by the Ukrainian Socialist Revolutionaries. For a very short time, he was the general secretary of military affairs. Vania met our family when he was still a gymnasium student and would come to visit Aliosha. Although my mother was thirteen years his senior, in the course of his visits Vania came to love her. This platonic love endured for years. On Mother's side there was initially only a feeling of friendship, but in time that too developed into strong affection. Neither Mother nor Vania concealed how they felt. My father knew about their platonic feelings for one another and did not interfere.

I should mention that in the last years of their married life, relations between my father and mother were somewhat cool, at least outwardly. To me, as a teenager, this seemed fitting, for I believed there was no such thing as marital love—a conviction that stemmed from my reading of romantic literature. I was a poor psychologist at that age and failed to recognize that Father's restraint was part of his personality. There was something else in their relationship, however, that puzzled me: what I had heard of Father's unwillingness to seek medical help when Mother was about to give birth. Each of her pregnancies was very difficult, with labor lasting for days. There was always fear that she would not survive. Yet Father refused to summon a physician, on the grounds that bearing children was a woman's natural function. As testimony to that he would cite examples of pregnant peasant women who worked in the field right up to the last minutes before childbirth: how the woman would then give birth to her baby, rest a short while, and walk home carrying the newborn in her arms. I assume he inherited such views from his peasant mother. To me, Father's attitude was proof of his callousness, or even cruelty, towards Mother. In any event, by this time their passion for each other had cooled and Mother had truly fallen in love with Vania.

In Vania's relationship to our family there developed a situation of which Mother was totally unaware: Vania also became smitten with Liza. Vania's feeling was strong and deep, and it caused him much

Front row: Olha Nemolovska (Tatiana's mother), Serhii, and Liza; back row: Ivan Nemolovsky and Tatiana (Kyiv, 1917 or 1918)

anguish. Yet he could do nothing about it. Liza tried to avoid him as much as she could, and the two of us did our best to prevent Mother from suspecting anything. One time Vania became very ill and was taken to the hospital. In his delirium he kept calling for Liza. We decided that I should go in her stead. I spent several nights at Vania's bedside. We told Mother that I did it at his request, and so the secret was kept.

When Father died at the front in January 1917, Mother married Vania. She lived with him through the brief years of Ukrainian independence and civil war. After Soviet rule was consolidated in Ukraine, Vania worked in the Ministry of Education for some time. At the end of the 1920s he was arrested as a "bourgeois nationalist" and exiled to Karaganda in Kazakhstan. Like other members of the Kosach and Nemolovsky family, Vania suffered from tuberculosis. Under the conditions of exile, the disease began progressing rapidly. He also contracted dysentery. Mother received a letter from him describing his wretched condition and the total absence of medical care: in the

Vsevolod Holubovych (Kyiv, ca. 1916)

letter Vania begged Mother to intercede on his behalf, for otherwise he would not survive. Mother went to see an NKVD[20] prosecutor. She showed him the letter and begged him to do something to save Vania's life. After glancing at the letter, the prosecutor snapped, "Well, if he's sick, he will either recuperate or die. There is nothing I can do." A short time later Mother received word that Vania had died.

Our second frequent visitor, Vsevolod Holubovych, was the son of Oleksander Holubovych, a priest who had a parish in Tulchyn in Podillia gubernia. When Vsevolod and his sister were teenagers, their father suddenly lost his sight. Instead of giving up his parish and requesting a pension, he continued serving as a priest. His wife would walk him to church and aid him during the liturgy, going as far as the iconostasis (women cannot go behind it), at which point a male would step in to help. One day members of the church hierarchy arrived in Tulchyn: they had heard rumors that a blind priest was pastor of the parish, which contravened church law. Father Oleksander was faced

[20] The acronym for Narodnyi komissariat vnutrennikh del (the People's Commissariat of Internal Affairs), then the name of the Soviet secret police.—*Eds.*

with losing his beloved work, for which he had a true calling. At this critical moment, all the parishioners voiced support for their priest. They convinced the authorities that he was fully capable of fulfilling all his obligations and vowed that they didn't need or want another priest. The authorities acquiesced, and Father Oleksander continued ministering to his parish with the help of his devoted wife until he died. Vsevolod's parents had an idyllic relationship. When they married, they made a vow to each other that when one of them died, the other would not go on living (how they understood this in practice is a mystery—I don't think they had suicide in mind). In any case, Father Oleksander's wife outlived him by several years.

As a priest's son, Vsevolod could study at the seminary free of charge. That was important to the family, for they were in dire financial straits. Vsevolod enrolled in the seminary even though he did not intend to become a priest, and he completed his studies there with honors. His real interest was in becoming an engineer, but that meant completing two more years of study and obtaining a "certificate of maturation" (issued by all secondary schools in the Russian Empire except seminaries). When he was at last admitted to the Kyiv Polytechnical Institute, Vsevolod enrolled in its Department of Road Construction. Aliosha also transferred there at this time. Vsevolod was a very good student, and as soon as he completed his studies he was offered a post as engineer with the Odesa Railroad Administration. Unlike other engineers, Vsevolod became involved in all aspects of the job—he would travel all the routes by handcar and check all work in progress personally. It came as no surprise to anyone that his was a splendid career. In three years he became one of the best railroad engineers in the Southwestern Land, which was what Ukraine was then called.[21]

---

[21] Several years ago, I read an obviously monarchist and anti-Ukrainian article in the Russian émigré newspaper *Novoe russkoe slovo*, in which the author scornfully referred to Vsevolod as a "half-educated seminarian" and an inept engineer, and then vilified him because he had been a member of the Central Rada delegation that had negotiated a separate peace between Ukraine and Germany in Brest-Litovsk in 1918. A few days later, as I was composing a response to this scurrilous article, I was surprised to learn that a Russian engineer who had worked with Vsevolod in Odesa had already written a rebuttal, in which he described Vsevolod with respect as exceptionally talented and well-educated.

CHAPTER 10

In 1916, around Christmas time, my father arrived home from the front for his last leave. Vsevolod happened to be in Kyiv at the time. He dropped by, and he and Father spent the whole night talking about impending events. They both agreed that a revolution had begun, but Vsevolod believed that it was connected to events in Russia proper, whereas Father thought that it had started right at the front. Vsevolod said that anti-war propaganda was being spread throughout the entire army by young ensigns sent to the front by their political parties. "The soldiers are becoming disobedient," he said. "The antagonism between them and the officer ranks is growing." Father was a witness to the brutal treatment of soldiers at the hands of officers, many of whom would later be found with bullets in their backs or to their heads. Both Father and Vsevolod were convinced that a revolution in Ukraine was inevitable, and that the struggle would be protracted and bloody. But while Vsevolod had a burning desire to become involved in the struggle for Ukraine's independence, Father, though he sympathized with the idea, believed independence was unattainable because it conflicted with Russia's imperial interests.

In March 1917, as news came that the monarchy had fallen, a national government was created in Ukraine. Vsevolod immediately joined the leading circles of the Ukrainian national renaissance and took part in the formation of the Central Rada. Nearly a year later he was offered the post of prime minister.[22] He had been a member of the Ukrainian Party of Socialist Revolutionaries (UPSR) since his days in the seminary, and by 1917 he was a member of the party's Central Committee. Before the revolution the UPSR was the largest party in Ukraine. It defended the interests of the peasants, whereas the Ukrainian Social Democrats oriented themselves on the workers, whom they considered the vanguard "people's class." In Ukraine the majority of people were peasants, and that is why the UPSR was popular among the Ukrainian intelligentsia. It was small wonder, then, that members of the UPSR dominated in the Central Rada and that a person like Vsevolod—talented, energetic,

[22] Holubovych was prime minister of Ukraine from 31 January to 24 March 1918.—*Eds.*

with strong national and socialist convictions—rose to prominence in the government. Holubovych's later fate was closely tied to the fate of the Ukrainian Revolution, the Central Rada, and the events that followed the Rada's departure from the political arena. And my personal life became intimately tied with him and those political events as well.

I was a sixteen-year-old gymnasium student when I first met Vsevolod. He was thirteen years older. He fell in love with me with all the force of his passionate nature, whereas I, being rather naive in romantic matters, became interested in him as a hero of the revolution and the great political activist being written about constantly in the papers. I was flattered by the attention a person of his stature was paying me. I liked his intelligence and his sense of humor, his daring romantic nature, his inclination to take risks, his strong will, and his ability to inspire people and make them follow him. One could sense his tremendous dynamism and ability to accomplish great things. At the same time, Vsevolod had a great measure of spirituality—not the spirituality of structured religion (the years he spent at the seminary dispelled any illusions he might have had in this regard), but a kind of spiritual idealism gleaned from the writings of the ancient sages, which he knew well and loved to quote. Vsevolod loved literature. His favorite writer was Jack London, whom I also liked. Among poets he was fond of Igor Severianin, a poet popular at the time, whom I also liked but did not take very seriously. Just as Severianin bestowed imaginary riches on his queens and princes, Vsevolod loved valuables and frequently gave me rings with costly stones as gifts. I was totally indifferent to jewelry and so just put these away in a box. Whenever he came to visit, Vsevolod would speak more with my mother than with me: their talk was primarily about politics, which Mother understood very well. Though I was intrigued by this talk, I did not understand a great deal, so usually I just listened. In our romance the initiative was entirely Vsevolod's. When Vsevolod declared his love for me, I was taken aback—I had not thought of getting married. Nonetheless I gladly accepted his proposal.

We were married in the church of the Kyiv Cadet Corps from which my father had graduated. The site was Father's idea, but I supported it enthusiastically. Our wedding "banquet" was held at our home on Velyka Dorohozhytska Street. Only a few guests were invited. Mykhailo Hrushevsky, who was the president of the Central

Rada, and some other members of the government attended. Semen Petliura sat on my right and spoke to me very courteously.[23] The food was served by our orderlies. They were excited by the opportunity to see Petliura, whom they adored and all of whose public appearances they attended. One of our orderlies, a Cossack from the Kuban named Petro, especially idolized Petliura. If once he had been unsure of his national identity, now, under the influence of Petliura's fiery speeches, he became a true Ukrainian, ready to die for Petliura and for Ukraine. I also went to such meetings and listened to Petliura's speeches eagerly, but I did that only occasionally, for huge crowds assembled wherever Petliura appeared and it was nearly impossible to make one's way through them.

A humorous incident occurred as a result of one meeting I attended. The speaker was speaking in Ukrainian, which at the time I did not understand very well. Suddenly someone in the crowd shouted, "Hang the *prapor*!" In Russian this word is the colloquial short form for *praporshchik* (ensign), so I believed some officer was about to be hanged. Terribly shaken, I rushed out as fast as I could. When I got home and told my family that an ensign was going to be hanged in the square, everybody started laughing and then explained that in Ukrainian *prapor* means "flag." The incident was long the subject of mirth in my family, but it also had a positive result. I started studying Ukrainian seriously. In time I mastered it to such a degree that I could work as a copy editor and translator in Ukrainian publishing houses.[24]

The Central Rada's Ukrainianization policies aroused a good deal of dissatisfaction in Kyiv. Some people protested because of their disdain for all things Ukrainian; others objected to the way it was being imposed as the official language. The newspaper *Russkaia mysl*

---

[23] Petliura (1879–1926), a prominent Ukrainian journalist and social democrat, was the general secretary of military affairs and commander in chief of the armed forces of the Ukrainian People's Republic from June 1917, and president of the republic (and later its government in exile) from February 1919 until his assassination in Paris.—*Eds.*

[24] I had to overcome several obstacles in my quest to learn Ukrainian. During the early Soviet years of the Ukrainization policy, every time I sought work at some institution, I was asked to demonstrate my knowledge of Ukrainian by translating a text from Russian. In one text, the word *protsent* (percent) appeared several times. I got confused about how to say the word in Ukrainian, so I wrote "*protsent*" instead of the more Ukrainian *vidsotok*, and did not get the job. The incident reminded me of one of Ostap Vyshnia's feuilletons, in which two Russian-speaking officials boast about how easily they passed the test in that "primitive" language and got a job; meanwhile, a Ukrainian peasant woman laments that because she did not know what "genitive case" means, she failed the test and did not get a job cleaning.

(Russian Thought) published long lists of signatures under the heading "I protest against the forceful Ukrainianization of the Southwestern Land." Most of the signatories' names were Russian, but there were also Ukrainian ones.

Aliosha joined the ranks of these protestors. He had a strong aversion against force being applied for any purpose. He knew Ukrainian, considered himself a Ukrainian, loved his nation, its songs and its soul, and wished to live in Ukraine. It was he who later prevailed on us to move back to Ukraine from "Katsapiia."[25] But he also felt that Ukrainianization was a manifestation of intolerance and nationalism. Later, when the Ukrainian intelligentsia was being destroyed en masse under Stalin, Aliosha remembered his protest with shame and bitter regret.

My relationship with Vsevolod Holubovych also played a large role in my own "Ukrainianization." Thanks to him, I began to feel more Ukrainian, and Ukrainians accepted me as one of their own. People would often recognize me on the street, for photographs of Vsevolod with me appeared regularly in the newspapers. People came up to greet me and sometimes even applauded, saying to one another, "Look—it's Holubovych's wife!"

---

[25] A derogatory term for Russia.—*Eds.*

CHAPTER 11

Early in 1918 Vsevolod and I moved to the former palace of the tsarist governor-general—the residence assigned to Vsevolod as prime minister of the Central Rada. This palace was enormous. A wide flight of stairs led upstairs to a great hall, where the floor was covered by a fluffy gray-and-pink carpet and gilded white chairs stood against the walls. It was in this room that official receptions were held.

Vsevolod and I occupied several rooms on the third floor, in what had been the private apartment of the governor-general and his family. I was struck by the curtains in the bedroom—layers of cream and rose-colored drapes over transparent curtains, flanked by heavy, burgundy velvet panels that were tied shut at night. I examined all of this luxury with interest and amazement—it spoke volumes about the life of the former tsarist viceroy. The governor-general's butler, a holdover from those times, came up and introduced himself to us. He had lived in the palace for many years and continued to have the utmost respect for his former masters. The revolution had destroyed his entire way of life, and he suffered everything that was happening deeply, viewing it all as a national and a personal tragedy.

After the governor-general and his wife had departed, leaving the old butler and the rest of the servants to fend for themselves, the palace had been occupied by every new regime that ruled Kyiv, each of which plundered the premises of everything it could. The butler spoke with great anguish about how much one female warlord distinguished by her brutality had plundered the palace's furnishings. He even mentioned Volodymyr Vynnychenko, who was not above taking some paintings and kilims when he left.[26] I listened to these stories with embarrassment, for I knew that in the butler's eyes I was part of yet another set of these "unlawful" rulers. But when the old man asked me who my father was and I told him he had been a tsarist general, I saw that he was greatly impressed. He became excited, because I represented a world that was familiar and dear to him. After this, he treated me with utmost regard and courtesy. For instance, he served me every morning from a special service whose tray, cup, sugar

[26] Vynnychenko (1880–1951), the most popular Ukrainian prose writer and playwright before the revolution, and a prominent Ukrainian social democrat, was chairman of the General Secretariat of the Central Rada from 28 June 1917 to 31 January 1918.—*Eds.*

bowl, creamer, and coffeepot were all made of gold. The old butler said the service had been a gift from the governor-general to his wife, and he urged me to take it all: "Please take it, dear lady—otherwise it will disappear or fall into unworthy hands!" When I categorically refused to take part in any further plundering," he became very depressed. To cheer him up, I said it would be dangerous for me to take the service and that I would take a light-brown ceramic ashtray instead. This item had no monetary or artistic value—there were many like it in every room in the palace. This "historical" ashtray survived among my possessions for many years.

My "expropriation" of that ashtray brings to mind the episode in Bulgakov's play, *The Days of the Turbins,* in which Shervinsky takes a gold cigar case—accidentally left behind in the same palace by Hetman Pavlo Skoropadsky—for himself as a memento. Indeed, while reading Lidiia Yanovskaia's biography of Bulgakov,[27] I was struck by the extraordinary similarity between the milieus to which my family and Bulgakov belonged—the same cultural level and spiritual needs, and an interest in music, theater, opera, literature, and art. Also striking, however, was a most fundamental difference: the contrast between Bulgakov's Russian chauvinism, monarchism, snobbism, and hostility and disdain for everything Ukrainian, and my family's democratic convictions and sympathy for the Ukrainian cause.

Vsevolod and I occasionally went out to restaurants. Once we went to a garden restaurant where tables were set out under trees and flowers bloomed all around. We ordered, and were served food that we found to be especially appetizing. Our waiter, however, was young and obviously inexperienced: he dropped first a fork and then a napkin, and he spilled tea on the table. Vsevolod, annoyed by the waiter's ineptitude, muttered something under his breath, and instantly my lyrical mood disappeared. When it came time to pay the check, Vsevolod suddenly took out five *karbovantsi*—a large sum at the time—and gave it to the waiter, saying sarcastically, "This is for the brainless service you gave us." The poor fellow blushed violently and stood before us, dumbfounded. I felt sorry for him, and I was embarrassed by Vsevolod's behavior. When I told Vsevolod how I felt, he recognized that his behavior had been unkind. For some reason, memory of this incident stayed with both of us.

---

[27] *Tvorcheskii put Mikhaila Bulgakova* (Moscow, 1983).—*Eds.*

From the time I was a student, I liked going for walks in the cemetery. These walks would evoke gloomy thoughts and a quiet mood, and during them I would often read the inscriptions on tombstones. Some of the inscriptions were touching, and others were quite dramatic. I remember one in particular that sent Liza and me into gales of laughter: "On this spot, with thunder and lightning, the maiden So-and-so quietly departed this life." Vsevolod also enjoyed such walks. Once we went to the cemetery together and wandered along its paths to the far end, where everything was in disarray. A large stone cross barred the path in front of me. I walked around it and went on. Vsevolod, who was walking a little behind me, took note of my doing this and for some reason was very moved by it. After all, as a nonreligious person, I could have easily stepped on and over the cross, yet I did not do so. In this he saw my respect for things others held sacred.

At that time in my life I was learning to drive a car. I had been provided with a German automobile—a Benz, I believe—and a chauffeur. He was a jovial fellow, thrilled by the car, by his job, and by the chance to serve me. He drove me around the Tsar's Gardens with immense enthusiasm, and under his tutelage I began driving the car myself. I had a great deal of time on my hands then. I hardly saw Vsevolod—he would immerse himself in work for days on end, sometimes not even coming home to sleep. From time to time he would bring me some money—his salary—which I stored in the drawer of a night table. Friends advised me to deposit these Ukrainian *hryvni* in the bank, but I had absolutely no idea how to do that and thought it unnecessary. I didn't need to buy anything because everything was provided. But the main thing was that I didn't feel I had the right to use this money. For instance, at one point I needed a new coat and so asked my mother, "What do you think—is it all right for me buy myself a coat?" Mother laughed and said, "Of course it is." Nevertheless, I didn't work up the courage to buy one. When I became the prime minister's wife, I was suddenly obliged to act like an adult. But that meant I was being expected to act in accord with the experience that life gives, experience I did not yet have.

This fairy-tale life soon came to an end. It was dangerous to continue living in the palace, because the civil war was raging all around us and power was changing from hand to hand. Control of Kyiv changed some seventeen times in that short period, and every time someone seized power, he occupied the palace as a matter of course. Vsevolod's friends advised us to move into a private apartment, and we did.

Here I must interject something that happened decades later, during my trip to Ukraine in the 1970s. While in Kyiv, I visited the building of the Writers' Union with Yurii Smolych.[28] As we were ascending the stairs, it struck me that this stairway was familiar, as were the remnants of an old carpet on the stairs and, indeed, the building itself. "I think I remember this building," I said, turning to Smolych, "as if I lived in it once. When could that have been?" Smolych, who knew something of my personal history, smiled and said, "Perhaps in 1918? During the time of the Central Rada?" It turned out that the Writers' Union was now located in the building that had once been the governor-general's palace.

The new apartment to which Vsevolod and I moved was in the famous residential building designed and built in Kyiv by the architect Vladyslav Horodetsky. It was wonderfully asymmetrical, and various animal skulls hung on the interior walls. An avid hunter, Horodetsky had brought back various trophies from his travels in Africa—the skulls of antelopes, rhinoceroses, and other animals, which I found frightening. His wife lived in the building too. She was not very friendly towards us, fearing, understandably enough, that Vsevolod's presence did not bode well for peace and quiet. Her fears were not groundless. During the civil war, armed people seeking Vsevolod would knock on the doors of our apartment on Velyka Dorohozhytska Street. Some brought news, while others came to arrest him. I remember one such incident. We were fast asleep and suddenly someone started banging on the front door and yelling "Open up!" Mother was frightened and didn't know what to do. The person continued hammering on the door, practically breaking it down, until Mother finally opened it. A man ran into the room, bedecked from head to toe in firearms and rounds of ammunition. "I'm the Odesa satrap," he shouted, "I'm being pursued! Please, give me shelter—I must spend the night here." Without a word, Mother pointed to the couch. The "satrap" spent the night and disappeared the following morning. Vsevolod later explained that he knew the man, who indeed had the code-name "Odesa satrap" and was connected in some way to the Central Rada.

One night I went out to search for Vsevolod. As I have mentioned, he often worked late at the building of the Central Rada and did not spend the night at home. This time, though, he had been absent for several days and I had begun to worry. By then

---

[28] Smolych (1900–1976) was a prominent Soviet Ukrainian writer.—*Eds.*

we had moved from the Horodetsky building to an apartment in a building in Chekhov Lane owned by some doctors. Though I didn't know it yet, I was pregnant at the time. I set out for the building that was formerly the Pedagogical Museum and was now where the Central Rada held its sessions, determined to find Vsevolod. As I approached, I saw that the building was surrounded by military men. I was taken aback—why were there so many guards? But in those days there were so many men in uniform everywhere that I didn't attach any particular significance to them. I headed for the door. One of the soldiers turned to me and asked what I wanted. "I'm looking for Holubovych," I answered. At that, the soldiers all burst out laughing, "We're looking for him ourselves," they declared. It turned out that in the past few days Hetman Skoropadsky had led a coup against the Central Rada and the Rada's members had been forced to go into hiding. The young Hetmanite soldiers were apparently so amused by my ignorance of political developments that they didn't bother detaining me.

CHAPTER 12

I hurried to Velyka Dorohozhytska Street to find Mother and Vania. There I found a family conference in progress—what should we do now? No one knew. It was hopeless to search for Vsevolod, and staying in the apartment was dangerous. Suddenly Vania had an ingenious idea: we should all depart for Moscow. That was the only safe place for us to go, for no one would search for members of the Central Rada there. No sooner was the idea voiced than we took action. Grabbing together a few things, we headed for the railroad station. There was no train schedule, so we had to be very careful in determining where each train was headed. We were lucky, for we immediately came upon a cargo train bound for Moscow. We found a boxcar with empty space, climbed in, and sat down. The train began moving. A young officer sat next to me. He had a very friendly face and somehow inspired my trust, for I believed that his situation was similar to ours. Dispensing with any shred of caution, I told him everything—who we were, where we were going, and why. The soldier listened with great interest and, it seemed to me, compassion. At the train's first stop he got out, saying that he would be right back. But when the train started again, he had still not returned. My heart froze—what had I done? I didn't know him at all: he would report us, and we would all be arrested! I rode the entire distance to Moscow expecting disaster to strike at any moment. But none did. I'll never know whether the soldier reported us and then came back too late to find us, or whether, on learning who we were, he became fearful of traveling in the same wagon and decided to go elsewhere. I told no one of my impetuous trust and imprudence, but I never forgot this incident. Later it served me well when I was in a situation where I could have said too much and hurt others: then I passed the test honorably, without compromising anyone.

We were going to Moscow without any idea of what we would do there or where we would live. We had no friends or acquaintances in the city. On arrival, we decided that Mother would remain at the station with Liza and Seriozha while Vania and I went in search of an apartment. The whole city was buzzing like a beehive. Those were the days when the capital was being transferred from St. Petersburg to Moscow. We walked the streets, peering into windows and looking for signs advertising apartments or rooms for rent. We kept walking on and on, not daring to enter any of the apartments posted as being available, for we did not know what kind of people we might encounter. Finally we found ourselves on a very quiet street. A sign on a two-story building said that there was a furnished three-room apartment for rent on the first floor. We knocked, but no one answered. We tried the door: it was open, and we entered. All the furniture was in disarray—some five or six beds, and some tables and chairs. Evidently the occupants had left in a hurry. Vania went up the stairs to the second floor and found the landlord. We soon came to terms, and with that our strange life in Moscow began. We lived in this apartment for several months. At first, we relied on the provisions we had brought with us, and when these began running out Mother began bartering Father's military decorations—his gold crosses and medals—for food. Thus those decorations helped us survive.

One day, while walking down the street, Vania noticed a broadside pasted to a fence. In those days newspapers were always posted this way, but this one was different—it was in Ukrainian! Vania's curiosity was piqued—what sort of Ukrainian newspaper was being published in Moscow? He started reading and was thunderstruck. The last page carried the following notice: "I have the honor to request the distinguished editors to publish an appeal to the persons I am seeking—Tatiana Holubovych and Ivan Kosach—to come forward." The address of the editorial offices to which one should apply appeared just below. The announcement had undoubtedly been written by a Galician from Western Ukraine. I was struck by its unique manner of expression and have remembered the text word for word.

Vania and I hurried to the address given. There we were told that the man who had placed the announcement had been looking for us for several days. We immediately made contact with him. He turned out to be a messenger from Vsevolod who had brought forged documents for us. Having lost hope of finding us, he had been getting ready to return to Ukraine. He gave us the documents, and very soon we were on a train bound for Kyiv. The man told us that Skoropadsky was no longer in power and that a new coup had taken place: the Central Rada had been restored to power as the Directory of the Ukrainian People's Republic (UNR). In areas removed from the capital, the Directory's authority was so unstable that its opponents used to say derisively, "Here's the Directory, and beneath it [i.e., the train in which they were travelling] lies its territory."

The Galicians I first met during the civil war seemed to be people from another nation altogether and not like us at all. They looked different and behaved differently somehow. What made the biggest impression on

Ivan and Olha Nemolovsky (Merefa, ca. 1926)

me was their language. At times it was even difficult for me to understand them. But to be honest, the Sich Riflemen[29] did bring with them two songs I especially liked and related to—"Chuiesh brate mii" (My Brother, Do You Hear?) and "Yikhav strilets na viinonku" (A Rifleman Was Leaving for the War). They enjoyed instant popularity, and soon all of Ukraine was singing them. There were, however, other Western Ukrainian songs that seemed strange and comical to me, with verses like "Yest u mene topir, topir, / Shche i kovana fliashka" (I have a hatchet, a hatchet, / as well as a forged canteen) or "Hop, chuk-chenchyk, / Chenchyk ladnyi, / Na chenchyku / Pas iedvabnyi" (Hey, little friar, /Charming little friar, / The little friar's wearing / A satin sash).

---

[29] Former soldiers of the Austro-Hungarian Army from Western Ukraine who had escaped from Russian POW camps and come to Kyiv to help build an independent Ukrainian state. Constituted as a battalion in November 1917, the Sich Riflemen later became a division of the Army of the Ukrainian People's Republic (UNR). They helped to overthrow Skoropadsky, and until December 1919 they fought against Bolshevik insurgents and the Red Army during the Ukrainian-Russian War.—*Eds.*

I disliked the way Western Ukrainians spoke to Jews: "Hey, *zhyd*! Bring us this or give us that." They used the word *zhyd* without anger or a desire to be offensive, but as a normal form of address. Of course, they were totally unaware of how degrading this word was.[30]

Later, in the 1920s, I became acquainted with Ukrainians from Western Ukraine of a very different kind, including the famous theater director Les Kurbas, the actor Yosyp Hirniak, and other cultured, intelligent individuals who had made valuable contributions to Ukrainian culture. Thenceforth I saw these Ukrainians in a completely different light.

---

[30] In Russian-ruled Ukraine this age-old Ukrainian word for "Jew" had acquired a pejorative meaning because the Russian word *zhid* was a term of abuse and derision. But in Western Ukraine, which did not experience Russian rule until the First World War, and then not again until the Second World War, *zhyd* was used in its original, standard and neutral sense.—*Eds.*

CHAPTER 13

We were on our way back to Ukraine. At first our train journey went well, and the miles passed by uneventfully. By our calculations we were not far from Kyiv when suddenly the train stopped in the midst of the steppe. What could be the matter? Anxious passengers peered out the windows and asked each other what was going on. Soon we had our answer, as shots rang out all around. We were in the middle of a combat zone. Hurriedly we jumped down from the train and ran for the whistle-stop nearby. We hid ourselves there, but Vania kept peeking out the window. He caught sight of a peasant who was unhurriedly making his way towards his wagon. It was unclear whether this man had a typically phlegmatic Ukrainian nature ("Things will turn out all right somehow") or whether he was so accustomed to gunfire that he paid it no mind. But he clearly intended to go somewhere in his wagon. It suddenly occurred to Vania that he might take us along. He called out, "Can we get a ride with you?" The old man readily agreed to take us as far as his village.

At first we rode alongside the railroad tracks, and then we made a turn and set off through the steppe. Suddenly a group of riders on horseback appeared. They were heading straight in our direction. There was no place to hide, so our elderly driver continued urging his horses on. A minute later the riders caught up to us. The one in front—apparently the leader—pointed his rifle at us and barked, "Stop! Who are you? Show your documents!" We took out our meager papers, which stated we were innocent teachers on our way to take up posts at a village school and that we had no connection to politics whatsoever, as in a popular Russian song:

> The little fried chick,
> The little steamed chick,
> Went on Nevsky Boulevard for a stroll.
> But they nabbed it,
> They arrested it,
> Demanded its I.D. and all.
> "I'm not a Soviet,
> I'm not a Kadet,
> You could crush me with ease.
> Please do not shoot me,

Don't execute me—
Chicks too want to breathe."

We were caught in one of those decisive moments that happened all the time during the civil war. Not knowing who might stop them at any given moment, people carried several different sets of documents in separate pockets. If one was lucky and happened to show the "right" document at the right time, one lived to go on. If not, one bade the world farewell. And so it was with us.

The rider, who was armed to the teeth, examined our documents, clearly skeptical of every word. He scrutinized our party again—it included three women, one of them pregnant. Our appearance must have convinced him that we weren't worth bothering about. He handed us our documents. Then, wheeling around to his men, he called, "Forward, lads!" Turning back to us for a moment, he added, "Why are you heading straight toward the conflagration?! Imbeciles!" And off he and his companions rode, kicking up a cloud of dust. We breathed a sigh of relief and continued on our way. When we reached the village, we learned that the Directory of the UNR was no longer in power. All the members of its government had left for Kamianets-Podilskyi, and Kyiv was now occupied by the Bolsheviks. What were we to do now? It was decided that Mother and Vania would go on to Proskuriv (present-day Khmelnytskyi, near Kamianets-Podilskyi), where they had friends. Liza and Seriozha would accompany them. But I was expecting the birth of my child any day now and could not risk such a long journey. It was agreed that I would go to the apartment building on Chekhov Lane in Kyiv where Vsevolod and I had lived, and that Mother would join me there as soon as she could.

So I ended up alone in Bolshevik-occupied Kyiv. The building on Chekhov Lane had been built by a group of six doctors to house their families. All of these physicians had been mobilized and were serving on the front, but their families were still there. Vsevolod and I had rented a room in the apartment of a Dr. Smirnov. But when I showed up at the building, his wife told me that all the obstetric clinics in Kyiv were closed and there were no physicians to be found: in other words, I couldn't count on any medical help. A few days later, when she saw that I was about to go into labor, Mrs. Smirnov left, saying that she did not want to hear my screams. I was left completely alone. Luckily a neighbor's kindhearted servant came to visit and offered to help me give birth. The labor went quite smoothly, and I gave birth to a daughter. I gave her the name Lesia.

I had never had any experience with infants and knew nothing about feeding, changing, or caring for them. Moreover, I had very little breast milk, for I was undernourished. Three weeks later, when Mother finally managed to join me in Kyiv, she was appalled at my desperate condition. She prevailed on me to move to the village of Prokhorivka near Kaniv, where Zhenia and Aliosha were living at the time. Zhenia was working there as a zemstvo doctor, and Aliosha was overseeing some building construction. I was preparing to leave when suddenly a messenger from Vsevolod arrived. He took out a letter—it was actually a note—written on very thin paper that had been sewn into the stiff collar of his military shirt. It was from Vsevolod and read: "If you have given birth to a son, name him Viacheslav, and if to a daughter, name her as you wish." That message angered me to the depths of my being. I was insulted for myself and for my daughter—for our common female sex. I had been treated like a slave—expected to bring male children into the world for her master and told how to name them. In typically Asian fashion, my baby daughter was considered unimportant, so I was allowed to give her any name at all, as if she were a kitten. On top of that, to my mind my husband was showing a total lack of consideration for my psychological and physical state—for everything I had suffered and endured. I could not forgive Vsevolod what I saw as his harshness and male condescension. At that moment I could not think calmly. I sat down and immediately wrote him a reply: "I have given birth to a daughter, and neither she nor I need you any more." I sewed my note into the messenger's collar and he left, bearing it away.

CHAPTER 14

I managed to get to Prokhorivka with the baby, and Zhenia met me there. She had found a place for me in the home of a peasant woman called Haida, whose husband worked in Aliosha's construction detail. Zhenia had also found me a job in her clinic, and therefore I could earn some money for food. By this time, however, my breast milk had totally disappeared. My infant daughter became ill and grew weaker day by day. Within two months she died. By that time I had fallen into a state of stupor and apathy and nothing could affect me. I accepted my child's death without emotion. Little Lesia was buried in the village cemetery.

A small wooden church stood next to the cemetery. It was kept locked except for funeral services, which were infrequent because by then hardly anyone was being buried in that cemetery. A local legend had it that this was the same church Gogol had described in his horror story "Vii." That legend had aroused my curiosity earlier. But the first time I was able to step inside the church was for my daughter's funeral service. What I saw there surpassed anything I might have expected. In the semidarkness, to the right of the entrance, I saw a huge depiction of the face of Christ that covered the entire wall. In keeping with the traditions of Byzantine iconography, Christ's penetrating eyes seemed to be looking straight at me regardless of where I stood. The distinct impression created was that the eyes moved as I did. On the opposite wall was a floor-to-ceiling depiction of sinners being thrown into the fires of hell. These murals elicited a kind of mystical horror in me, and I began believing the story about Gogol and his "Vii." Later Aliosha sketched a watercolor of the church's exterior, but it was lost. The church itself was destroyed during the Second World War.

The peasants of Prokhorivka told other fantastic tales, especially about the Maksymovych family's estate that lay beyond the village, on the high bank of the Dnipro. They claimed the ghosts of Mykhailo Maksymovych, the renowned ethnographer and professor who was the first rector of Kyiv University, and of his son and grandson wandered about the estate. Their graves, like those of all the Maksymovyches, were not in the cemetery, but on the grounds of the estate. The villagers believed those ghosts existed so completely that they categorically refused to enter the estate's grounds even during the day. Still, they were very proud that the famous professor had lived so near their village. They were convinced that the popular song "Stoit hora vysokaia" (A Tall Mountain Stands) was composed by a group of poets who had been invited to the estate and that the song celebrated the colorful landscapes around Prokhorivka. In fact, the song's lyrics were by Leonid Hlibov,[31] but they could easily have been about that countryside:

> A tall mountain stands serene,
> And at its foot there lies
> A little glen, lush and green
> Like paradise.
> Nearby a winding river flows,
> It sparkles so like glass.
> Its path along the valley goes,
> Who knows where it will pass.
> And at the shore, where boats are tied
> In a secluded spot,
> Three willows bend, as if immersed
> In mournful thought.

This song was very popular in Prokhorivka when I was there, and hardly a day went by without someone singing it. In my memory it is connected with the story of a hapless young couple in love. The girl was from a wealthy peasant family, and her parents refused to allow her to marry her beloved because he was poor. The whole village knew about this unhappy affair and sympathized with the two lovers. In the evenings the young man would come out to the bank of the Dnipro and start singing this song, calling for his beloved. She would come out to join him, the two of them would sit by the bank and sing together, and their wonderful harmonies would echo above the river all the way back to the village.

The peasants of Prokhorivka would often mention Taras Shevchenko's visits to Maksymovych's estate and point to the old oak tree under which the poet liked to sit.[32] Some of Shevchenko's paintings

---

[31] Hlibov (1827–93) wrote poetry in Russian and Ukrainian, feuilletons, and some plays. He is best known for the over one hundred Ukrainian fables he wrote.—*Eds.*

[32] While visiting Maksymovych at his estate, Mykhailova Hora near Prokhorivka (seven km. south of Kaniv), Shevchenko painted portraits of Maksymovych and his wife and wrote his poem "Mariia." In July 1859, he was arrested there. In 1964 a memorial museum was opened in Maksymovych's house.—*Eds.*

hung on the walls of the Maksymovych family's house. I hope that both that building and Shevchenko's paintings have been preserved.[33]

In the nearby village of Sushky lived an old gentrywoman who knew the famous Taras. In 1918, when I made her acquaintance, she was 104 years old. She talked about the Ukrainian writers and poets who used to gather at Maksymovych's estate and the soirees she attended there as a young girl. The one thing she related about Shevchenko was that he enjoyed a drink and that she had often admonished him not to drink so much.

Chernecha Hora (Monk's Mountain), the hill where Shevchenko is buried, is not far from Prokhorivka—two hours upriver by rowboat against the Dnipro's current. Before the Great War began, our family became acquainted with the very colorful old man, called Grandfather Ivan, who had tended the poet's grave for many years. He lived in a rickety shanty at the foot of the hill and had been carrying out his labor of love since 1861, when Shevchenko's remains had been brought from St. Petersburg for burial in Ukraine. Ivan, then a teenager, had attended the bard's funeral, and it was then that he volunteered to tend Shevchenko's grave. In time a small cottage was built for Ivan so he could live near the grave. Half a century after Shevchenko's death, on the eve of the war in 1914, that cottage was falling apart, but its elderly occupant had no money to repair it. Our family—especially Vania Nemolovsky—was very fond of Grandfather Ivan, and we decided to help him. Each of us donated whatever money we could; in the end we collected a hundred rubles, a considerable sum at the

---

[33] One of our own family's stories pertains to both Shevchenko and Maksymovych, one of the earliest collectors and publishers of Ukrainian folk songs. A copy of the first edition of Maksymovych's *Malorossiiskiia pesni* (Little Russian Songs, 1827) found its way to Harvard University's Widener Library, and my daughter Assya came across it there as a student at Harvard in the 1950s. Impressed by the poetic beauty of the songs' lyrics, she began copying them and their musical notations. While doing so, she found that someone had underlined and marked the text and written comments in the margins in pale ink. On one page, next to an annotation by Maksymovych, she found a sardonic remark, and under it the words "Shevchenko's words" and the signature of one of Shevchenko's friends, the prominent writer, ethnographer, and historian Panteleimon Kulish (1819–97). Kulish's note indicates that the book had been in Shevchenko's possession and that the poet had marked images and motifs in it also found in Shevchenko's own poems. Assya told her professor, Dmytro Chyzhevsky, who was then teaching Russian and Ukrainian literature at Harvard, about her discovery, and he published a brief note about it in the *Harvard Library Bulletin*. Today this copy of Maksymovych's book is kept in the rare-book collection of Harvard's Houghton Library. In the 1960s the Soviet embassy in Washington tried to obtain it, but Harvard refused to part with it.

time. The old man was moved to tears by our gift: at last he could pay someone to build a new cottage for him, which he did without delay.

I now realize what a tremendous role Shevchenko played in the life of our family. After reading the great Taras's *Kobzar,* my father became fully aware of being Ukrainian. Shevchenko's writings were an important presence in my own childhood, and as a young woman I visited his grave in Kaniv and was reminded of him when I stayed in Prokhorivka. Years later my second husband, Serhii Pylypenko, would travel throughout Ukraine and even beyond the Aral Sea to gather information about the poet; Serhii also became the director of the first Shevchenko memorial museum in Ukraine.[34] Many years after that, our daughter Assya, while a university student in America, would find her "roots" after discovering the *Kobzar* for herself, and would write several articles about the bard's works. Later still, our second daughter, Mirtala, used a recording of Shevchenko's ballad "Dumy moi" (My Thoughts), performed by the Ukrainian Bandurist Chorus,[35] in a video film about her sculptures.

---

[34] The museum was founded in 1932 at the Taras Shevchenko Scientific Research Institute. In 1933 the museum's holdings were transferred to the new Shevchenko Picture Gallery in Kharkiv. In 1948 and 1949 all of Shevchenko's art works at the gallery were transferred to the new Shevchenko State Museum in Kyiv.—*Eds.*

[35] A famous male chorus formed in Detroit in 1949 by bandura players and singers who were postwar refugees from Soviet rule. Over the years the chorus has toured extensively, produced many recordings of Cossack *dumy* and other Ukrainian songs, and attracted new, mostly American-born, members. For many years its musical director was Hryhorii Kytasty.—*Eds.*

CHAPTER 15

After my Lesia died, I went to live with another peasant couple in Prokhorivka, who had two daughters and two sons. The father was at the front, and the elder son had joined the partisans and was rarely at home. At first this son was wary of me and remained silent in my presence. But when he learned that I was Vsevolod Holubovych's wife, his attitude changed completely. Subsequently he went out of his way to show me the utmost respect and, no longer reticent, told me a great deal about his partisan activities. The whole family was staunchly Ukrainian and wholeheartedly supported the national-liberation movement. They were peasants of average means, with two horses, two cows, and a bit of land that they worked with great vitality and devotion. Never in my life, either before or since, have I met people who were so hardworking. They put all of their energy, thought, and desires into their work. For them work was not merely a means of existence or even a means of acquiring wealth—it was what gave their life meaning.

They toiled from morning until late at night, the mother working alongside her children and energetically keeping pace with them. In the evenings she would cook borscht, adding to it not one of the usual sorts of meat, but pigeon. The family raised pigeons, and every evening the younger son would climb up the ladder to the top of the threshing barn, catch a few, twist their heads off, and bring them to his mother. The borscht she cooked would be left in the oven overnight, and it would still be hot when the family arose at 4:00 a.m. Breakfast always consisted of this borscht, hot cereal, buns, and other baked goods. The sons and daughters would then go out into the fields, taking food with them for the whole day. They would usually return at sunset, but if there was an unusual amount of work to be done that day, they would simply sleep out in the field. In the evening they would work in the house, stable, or vegetable garden without any respite, day after day.

The family was also very close-knit and, as was typical of Ukrainian peasant families, extremely respectful of the mother. During the winter the girls would embroider or spin cloth, and the blouses they finished embroidering were put into a chest that was nearly as tall as a full-grown adult. This was also where they stored clothes handed down from previous generations, all of them made of homespun linen and with beautiful embroidered designs. In the summer, when they worked in the fields, the sisters and brothers would change shirts once a week, throwing the dirty ones into a separate chest. At summer's end, after their work in the fields was done, the women would start the task of laundering, which lasted two weeks. They would carry the dirty clothes to the river, wash them by beating them against the rocks, and then lay them out on the grass to be bleached by the sun. The clothes became white as snow. To me this family epitomized the industriousness and high moral standards of the Ukrainian peasantry.

I also observed how the peasants of Prokhorivka harvested buckwheat. I learned that the entire crop must be gathered in a single day, when it is fully ripe but has not yet begun loosening on its own and falling. Determining the precise, optimal moment for the harvesting was no mean feat: knowledge of special signs was required. One old man in the village had inherited this knowledge from his parents: it had been passed down in his family from generation to generation. Everyone in the village waited for this old man to say when the harvest should begin. When he finally announced, "Tonight, it will be ripe," everyone, young and old, went out to the field before dawn, and by noon all the buckwheat was harvested. I wonder how the harvesting is done today, given our "advanced technology." I suspect much of the crop falls to the ground, where it is harvested by gophers and birds.

Life in Prokhorivka brought me closer to the common people. By that time I was completely fluent in Ukrainian, and I felt very much at home with the peasants. They treated me with warmth and friendship. The girls and women would often come to admire the bouquets of field flowers I gathered and arranged, and they would beg me to teach them how to make such arrangements. The men and boys greeted me kindly; they always asked if I needed a lift anywhere and offered to take me there if I did.

During that time, the civil war was raging all around us. Time and time again it burst in on the life of the village. Once I was walking down a street when a cavalry division suddenly appeared—partisans of some kind were entering the village. Crying "Here's a Jewess!" they surrounded me and dragged me to their leader. Luckily, several peasants saw what had happened and ran up to the partisans, assuring them that they knew me well: I wasn't Jewish at all, they declared, but the niece of the widely respected local doctor. The partisans listened to them skeptically and then took me to the clinic to find out whether their story was true. Zhenia confirmed that we were related, of course, and the partisans let me go. Before they left, they apologized to me, saying that it was my attractive appearance that had led them to take me for a Jewess. This was one of the many times in my life when I was taken to be Jewish.

Another time, at Easter, some partisans again rushed into the village, and rumors spread that a pogrom of Jews was about to begin. When Zhenia heard word of this, she quickly put together an Easter meal, laid it out on the table, and asked all the local Jews to come. Someone told the partisans that all the Jews were hiding in the infirmary, and the partisans rushed there. When they burst through the door, they saw the table with its lighted candles, the Easter meal, and some guests sitting peacefully and eating. When they asked if any Jews were present, Zhenia gazed at them wide-eyed, burst into laughter, and said, "Christ be with you! What kind of Jews could there be here?" With that, the embarrassed partisans departed.

Living and working in the town of Zolotonosha, not far from Prokhorivka, was Zhenia's good friend and colleague Petr Nikolaevich Zhebenev. He often visited Prokhorivka, and that is where I met him. An extraordinary person who dispensed help freely, Dr. Zhebenev was very popular among his patients. Legends circulated that his very touch would help a sick person get well. When a typhoid epidemic broke out, his infirmary was quickly flooded with patients. In those days treatment of typhoid was quite primitive, and during the revolution and subsequent years of civil war no medicine was available. Petr Nikolaevich spent entire days in his infirmary, providing whatever help he could and comforting his patients in his quiet, compassionate way. And these people, responding to his tender touch and gentle voice, did indeed get better. Soon sick people from outlying areas were brought to his infirmary. Not only was it filled to capacity, but the ill who could not be brought inside lay in carts and wagons outside its doors. So, after spending a whole day in the infirmary, Petr Nikolaevich would come out and tend to the sick and dying there. Through the night and into the morning, he would go from one cart to the next, placing his hand on each patient's forehead, speaking softly, and doing what he could. Whether because of their deep faith in the doctor's touch or his real medical skill, many of the sick did recover.

Zhenia admired Dr. Zhebenev greatly, and I also liked and respected him. But a problem developed: Petr Nikolaevich developed a strong romantic attachment to me. I knew about it, but what could I do? I had no such feelings for him. Zhenia, who knew the state of my relations with my husband, tried to persuade me to divorce Vsevolod and marry Dr. Zhebenev. She could not accept my total disinterest: she thought I was simply being capricious, and took umbrage at what she thought was my "heartlessness." Later Petr Nikolaevich married a woman who, it was said, reminded him of me. But the marriage was not a happy one.

When Dr. Zhebenev noticed I was steadily losing weight, he urged me to move from Prokhorivka to Zolotonosha and even went to the trouble of finding me an office job there. Allowing myself to be persuaded, I moved to Zolotonosha and settled there in a small house with a garden in the back.

CHAPTER 16

One day I returned from work to find an unexpected guest—my husband, Vsevolod, in ragged clothes, dirty, and unshaven. He had received my note and had risked his life to reach me, crossing a number of front lines on his way from Kamianets-Podilskyi. Along the way, somewhere near Proskuriv, he had fallen into the hands of the Reds. They took him to the train station and locked him in what had once been a storage room. It was already filled with people the Reds had arrested during that day's roundup. In his ragged clothing, Vsevolod looked suspiciously like a deserter, and he was noticed at once. Three people conducted the interrogations, which were brief: "Who are you?" "Where are you going?" "Where are your documents?" Those who had documents stating where they were going were let go. Most of those who had no documents were shot; a few were pressed into the Red Army. Vsevolod had a fake document that was very similar to the ones we had once carried—it stated he was a teacher on his way to a post at a village school. That was so at odds with his appearance that Vsevolod was certain it would be disbelieved and that he would be summarily executed. So when he was called in for questioning, he did not even show this "document."

The prisoners were taken out in groups to endure their fate. The turn of Vsevolod's group came, and they were taken out into the courtyard. Here Vsevolod had a severe attack of diarrhea, a result of his nervousness about what was to come. He begged the guard to take him to the outhouse. At first the guard refused, but finally he relented and took him to a small wooden building not far from the railroad tracks. Vsevolod stepped inside, while the guard stood outside and leaned against the door. Vsevolod looked up. The roof was pitched—like a house made of playing cards. Below the roof there was an opening just big enough for a person to slip through. He quickly stood on the seat, jumped up, and, grasping the edge of the opening, raised himself up to it. He wiggled through and tumbled down to the ground. Luckily, some twigs were stacked below, and these cushioned his fall. Behind the building there was open land and a forest in the distance. Vsevolod headed for the forest, forcing himself to move as silently as possible, which meant not running. But once he got to the woods, he ran as fast as he could, until he fell to the ground from exhaustion. He lay there for a long time, expecting to be seized at any moment. But no one pursued him—he had escaped.

"And now I'm with you once again," he said, finishing his story. Then he added, "And I'm not going anywhere without you." I didn't know what to say. I felt sorry for him—after all, he had risked his life on my account. But my feelings toward him were not the ones I once had, and I did not want to live with him any longer. I simply could not do that now, and I told him that openly. We also had another problem to deal with: Denikin's troops were in Zolotonosha, and it was dangerous for Vsevolod to remain here. What, then, should we do? I resolved I would return with him to Kamianets-Podilskyi, where the Central Rada was based, but that we would live separately, to which Vsevolod agreed.

The following day I went to work as usual. Vsevolod went out into the garden and lay down under a tree to rest. My neighbor across the fence was an officer in Denikin's army. His orderly stepped out into the yard and saw Vsevolod. Noticing the intensity of his gaze, Vsevolod knew that he had to leave immediately. That evening, when I returned from work together with Dr. Zhebenev, Vsevolod told us what had happened. Petr Nikolaevich said that he could get us the necessary documents and a different set of clothes for Vsevolod. We got our things together for the journey. Within an hour, everything was ready, and we left that same night. Later we learned that Denikin's security agents had come to the house the very next day.

We arrived at the train station and got a place in an army transport filled with Denikin's soldiers. In order not to call attention to ourselves, I sat in one car and Vsevolod sat in another. I found myself among officers traveling together with some women. The officers were enjoying themselves, and laughter and shouts rang out continually. One officer sat down next to me, ready to have some fun. Suddenly I felt his hand on my leg, moving upward. I cried out and shoved his hand aside, but he did not stop. Then, with all my might, I kicked him. That, at last, had the desired effect—the officer understood that I was not the kind of woman he thought. This was the only time during the civil war, or my life, for that matter, that anyone approached me in that way.

Finally we reached Kamianets-Podilskyi. Vsevolod found a room for me there and then immersed himself in work. At that time he was editing a Socialist Revolutionary newspaper called *Chervonyi shliakh* (The Red Path), and work was also found there for me.[36] Pavlo Mykhailovych Hubenko—who later became famous as a writer and humorist under the pen name Ostap Vyshnia—was also working at that newspaper then. I became friends with Pavlo Mykhailovych, and that friendship continued for many years. Another friend I made there was Valeriian Polishchuk, then a student at the new Ukrainian university in Kamianets-Podilskyi and later a well-known poet.

Valeriian was very handsome and always in love with someone. He became enamored at first with me and then with my sister Liza, who had then come to Kamianets-Podilskyi. Liza was living with me and was also working at the newspaper. Valeriian and Liza, whom he called "Miss Li," began a correspondence in verse—a poetic dialogue, so to speak. For instance, Valeriian spontaneously wrote her the following poem in Ukrainian:

> On the grass beneath the tree
> I was sitting with Miss Li.
> Evening fell so softly
> On the cherry blossoms,
> And itty-bitty bats flew
> Overhead.

To this Liza replied in Russian:

> Don't offer me orchids, my friend,
> I'm not fond of their fanciful shape,
> I prefer the friends of the fields—
> Cornflowers of a deep blue shade.

Later Valeriian and I became such good friends that I addressed him by the familiar form "*ty*" (thou), which was unusual for me.

Among the people I knew in Kamianets-Podilskyi, I also well remember Volodymyr Chekhivsky, who became prime minister in the

---

[36] It appears that Mrs. Kardinalowska inadvertently misnamed the newspaper. At that time the central organ of the UPSR, *Trudova Ukraina* (Laboring Ukraine), was being published under Holubovych's editorship in Kamianets-Podilskyi, and Ostap Vyshnia debuted there as a humorist. Also published in that city was *Trudovyi shliakh* (The Labor Path), and this is probably the paper Mrs. Kardinalowska had in mind. Its first issue appeared on 26 June 1919. See Arkadii Zhyvotko, *Istoriia ukrainskoi presy* (Kyiv, 1999).—*Eds.*

[37] Chekhivsky (1876–1937) served very briefly as prime minister and foreign minister (26 December 1918–11 February 1919). A member of the Russian State Duma in 1906 and a

UNR government under the Directory.[37] Chekhivsky was a close friend of Vsevolod's. Their acquaintance dated from the time they were both at the Kamianets-Podilskyi Theological Seminary—Chekhivsky as a teacher and Vsevolod as a student. Chekhivsky was a very religious person and an impassioned preacher. Every Sunday, after the liturgy, he would preach with great fervor, gathering crowds of listeners. He traveled around to villages and towns, always preaching his sermons to great effect. At our first meeting, Chekhivsky was struck by my appearance—he said I embodied his idea of the Madonna. He also tried to persuade me to travel with him to the villages and help in his proselytizing. When I asked him in surprise how I could help, he replied, "Just stand next to me when I speak. Let people gaze at your face." This was not the first time someone saw a Madonnalike quality in me. In my adolescence, when my brother Seriozha was in the hospital in Moscow, another patient there who was an artist begged Mother to be allowed to paint me as a Madonna: Mother held firm and refused.[38] Although I liked Chekhivsky very much, I declined his proposals, explaining that I had no connection with the church.

I would see Chekhivsky in Kharkiv years later, in 1930, when he was a defendant in the show trial of the Union for the Liberation of Ukraine. I remember entering the courtroom and sitting down in one of the front rows. When Chekhivsky noticed me, he smiled and waved to me in greeting, to the surprise of the others present. After that day I never saw him again.[39]

---

prominent Ukrainian Social Democrat, from 1919 he was a leading figure in the Ukrainian Autocephalous Orthodox Church. A defendant along with forty-four other prominent Ukrainian intellectuals in the 1930 Stalinist show trial of the so-called Union for the Liberation of Ukraine (Spilka vyzvolennia Ukrainy), he was executed by the NKVD on 3 November 1937 while serving a ten-year term in the infamous prison complex on the Solovets Islands in the White Sea.—*Eds.*

[38] In 1945, after the Second World War ended, an Italian artist I met asked me whether I would pose for a painting he was calling "Lazarus Resurrected": he thought my countenance illustrated well the look Lazarus had when he came back from the dead.

[39] The defendants in the show trial were sentenced on the basis of fabricated charges, and almost all of them perished in the 1930s in Soviet prisons or concentration camps. See James Mace, "Union for the Liberation of Ukraine," *Encyclopedia of Ukraine*, vol. 5 (1993), ed. Danylo H. Struk, 491–2; and Oleksandr Sydorenko, "Sud nad perekonanniamy," in *Represovane "vidrodzhennia,"* ed. O. I. Sydorenko and D. V. Tabachnyk (Kyiv, 1993), 63–153.—*Eds.*

CHAPTER 17

In Kamianets-Podilskyi I became acquainted with a former landowner who owned a large library. His fascination with the occult had led him to amass many books on spiritualism and parapsychology, the majority of which were translations from English. During the revolution his collection was confiscated and became part of the city library. However, for some reason it was designated a classified collection and access to it was restricted. The collector was unhappy that his books were not freely available to potential readers. This piqued my curiosity, so I went to the library. There, saying that I was a journalist, I requested books on the occult. Once I received permission to use the collection, I became engrossed in reading the volumes. They opened up an extraordinarily interesting world of mysterious and supernatural phenomena. I should note that the occult was not foreign to me. Everyone in my family, with the exception of my father, had an avid interest in spiritualism, and we often held seances. My mother and her brother were acquainted with Madame Blavatsky and belonged to a student spiritualists' club. My father poked fun at them for this, but one day something happened to make him reconsider his view and take a somewhat different stance.

That day we were sitting in the dining room, summoning "spirits" and holding hands over a saucer. The general consensus was that our mother was the best medium among us, for in her presence the saucer would move with particular intensity. In this instance, it began moving almost immediately, and we asked, "Spirit, who are you?" The saucer started to point to the letters of a name—a Russian surname none of us knew—followed by the words, "Ask your father, he knows me." Amazed, we called Father, who was sitting in his study. Upon our mentioning the surname, Father jumped up and dashed to the table, where he began firing questions in rapid succession: "Tell me, were you guilty? How did it all happen?" We didn't understand what was happening, but Father's excitement was contagious: we were caught up in it too and followed the "conversation" with intense interest. Later, after he found out what he wanted to know and the seance ended, Father told us the following story:

"During the Russo-Japanese War there was a soldier by that surname in my brigade. He was accused of plunder and murder and was brought to trial before a military court. My high rank demanded that I participate in the review of his case. The evidence was convincing, but for some reason I had doubts about the case. The judges were divided in their opinion, and I found myself on the side of the dissenting minority. The soldier was sentenced to be shot by firing squad. The memory of this incident hung over me all these years, because I could not shake the feeling that an innocent soldier had been executed."

Father had never told us about this incident until now, when the "spirit" of the executed soldier appeared to tell him the truth. It named the actual culprit and gave a full picture of what had happened, down to the last detail. Now, at last, Father understood what had happened and was fully convinced of the soldier's complete innocence. I'm not sure whether this incident changed Father's attitude toward the occult altogether, but certainly he, like all of us, was very moved by it.

As a young girl, I knew of encounters with the "netherworld" that were related to our "Black" grandmother. For instance, in 1919, during the height of the civil war, Grandmother was living with her ward, Raia, in Shuliavka, a suburb of Kyiv. The small old house in which they lived had windows facing a long winding street, which dipped steeply downward. The windows had wooden shutters that were locked by latches. One winter's day, a deep snow blanketed everything except for a narrow path that had been cleared from the doorway. Grandmother, who was nearly ninety years old at the time, suddenly got the urge to visit her native village—to bid farewell before dying, she said. In those years, the only trains in operation were military ones, and people who needed to go somewhere asked soldiers to let them ride along in the cars of these trains. When we learned of Grandmother's intentions, we all tried to dissuade her from embarking on such a dangerous journey, but, in a manner consistent with her temperament, she refused to listen and set out. Remaining in the small house were only Raia and a friend she had invited to stay with her during Grandmother's absence.

About five days later, Raia was awakened in the middle of the night by the rattling of the shutters. Thinking that Grandmother had returned, she ran to the window and shouted through the closed shutters that she was coming to the door immediately. But when she got to the door and opened it, no one was there. She opened the window and the shutters, but saw no one. Surprised, Raia shut the windows and exchanged looks with her friend, who had also been wakened by the noise. They went outside and walked around the house, but they saw no one. And there were no footprints in the snow other than the ones they themselves had just made.

It was a moonlit night, and the empty street was brightly illuminated. Standing near the gate, the girls asked each other how they could possibly have heard what they did. Just then, Raia spotted my grandmother far off at the bottom of the hill, making the ascent with her basket. Both girls ran to meet her, calling, "Where have you been you? Where are you coming from?" "Why, from the train station, of course," Grandmother replied in surprise. "But you were just knocking at our window," the girls said, and then told her the story. "That was Death coming after me," said Grandmother with finality, "I'll die soon." The next day she did not get up from her bed. Grandmother had contracted typhus on her journey, and she died a few days later.

A second strange incident occurred shortly after Grandmother's death. Mother and I were then living in Kyiv, in a large building, on the third floor. That day I was out and Mother was at work. When she returned home, the landlady asked, "Did you see your friend?" "What friend?" asked Mother in surprise. "The one who was just here a short while ago. She just left. You couldn't have missed her," replied the landlady, puzzled in turn. "She did not introduce herself, but waited for you for almost an hour, asking a lot of questions about you and particularly about your daughter, Tania. She said that Tania's fate worried her greatly. Is it possible that you did not see her?" Mother, bewildered, asked the landlady to describe the guest. "She looked rather strange," began the landlady. "She was dressed in an old-fashioned coat, in a style that nobody has worn for a long time; and she was wearing rubber boots, though it's not raining or snowing outside. She had on a fur hat, with a black kerchief tied over it. But it was her discolored teeth that made the greatest impression on me. They were totally black, as if they had been painted." Mother went completely pale and said: "You've given an exact description of my mother-in-law, who died a short while ago." Now it was the landlady who went pale. Mother told her that our "Black" grandmother refused to accept anything modern and always dressed in the same old-fashioned way, just as the landlady had described her. As for the black teeth, in her youth Grandmother had suffered toothaches and was told to rub nicotine into her gums. The nicotine acted as a narcotic and eliminated the pain. Grandmother became used to it, and after many years of nicotine being rubbed into her gums, her teeth had turned completely black.

These are only a few of the many puzzling and incomprehensible incidents I experienced or heard about from someone who was close to me. In the course of my story, I shall share more of them.

CHAPTER 18

A few months after our arrival in Kamianets-Podilskyi, members of the Central Rada who had been in the Ukrainian government began fleeing abroad. Once again Vsevolod declared that he would not go anywhere without me: "If you don't come with me, I'll stay behind too." I faced a choice that would determine the course of the rest of my life—whether or not to emigrate. Those who were part of the Central Rada—and, especially, their wives—insisted that I leave and appealed to my sense of duty and patriotism. But it was precisely patriotism that was holding me back—I was very committed to Ukraine and did not want to leave it. The arguments these individuals advanced did not convince me, for they did not have the same meaning for me as they did for people who were politicians. Furthermore, there was another factor, which these people were unaware of but for me was decisive—my feelings toward Vsevolod. Leaving with a person whom I no longer loved seemed totally absurd to me.

Just before their departure, the members of the Central Rada made a last attempt at convincing me to go. They sent a government car for me, but I refused to get in it. Then Vsevolod declared he would remain in Kamianets-Podilskyi as well. That decision had grave consequences for him—shortly thereafter he was arrested, and later he was sent to a concentration camp. I've carried a sense of guilt about this all my life. Yet in an objective sense I was not guilty, for I acted in accord with my heart and my conscience. Later, during the Second World War, when the Germans seized my daughter Assya and sent her to a forced-labor camp in Austria, I made the decision to go with her instantaneously. Then I had no doubt whatsoever about what to do, for I knew that if we became separated I would never see her again, and I followed the dictates of my heart. I was the only mother who went voluntarily with her child to the camp, to which the four hundred young people seized at that time were sent.

Fate conspired in such a way that I again met the people who had tried convincing me to emigrate. It was after the Second World War in Graz, Austria, where the wives of former members of the Central Rada was then displaced persons. Once again I had to listen to many bitter reprimands and accusations of being selfish and lacking patriotism. None of these women seemed to want to understand the emotional state of a very young woman who was being exhorted to abandon her country and family and go abroad with someone she no longer loved for the sake of political ideals. Though I knew I had made the right decision, I could not free myself of the guilt I felt, which probably stemmed from an inherent mind-set of self-sacrifice that I and many women of that time had.

After the exodus of the Ukrainian government, I resolved to return to Proskuriv, where Mother and Vania were still living. The suitcase I packed with my belongings was so heavy that I could barely lift it with both hands. The station was overcrowded with refugees waiting to board any train going west. I managed to drag my suitcase to the platform and looked around for a conductor. A soldier was standing, waving to someone and calling out, "Semen! Come this way! The train to Proskuriv is over here." I was overjoyed to hear this much-needed information. Semen made his way over to his comrade. They both sat down on some crates and lit up cigarettes.

"Could you possibly tell me when the train will depart?" I asked Semen's comrade.

"Not very soon. There's probably at least an hour's wait," he answered. "So sit down, Miss, and have a rest."

I took his advice and made myself comfortable on my valise. A group of soldiers gathered around us. One of them had an accordion and began playing the song "Yablochko" (Little Apple), a lively ditty popular at the time. Everyone joined in the singing. A young sailor stepped forward; saying "Move aside, guys," he began tap-dancing. He was a wonderful dancer—he tapped very rapidly, grinning the whole time. All the spectators cheered and beamed with pleasure at the entertainment. After a while the accordionist began playing the Ukrainian dance called the "Kozachok" (Little Cossack) and a young fellow dressed in a Ukrainian embroidered shirt jumped into the center of the ring and began dancing. He made incredible turns, unlike any I had seen before. Only a professional dancer could have danced with such dexterity. His performance was both audacious and humorous, in the true spirit of the Ukrainian Cossacks. I was so mesmerized by his dancing that I was oblivious to what Semen was saying to me as he and his friend got up. It was only after hearing voices in the crowd shouting, "Look, the train for Proskuriv is leaving!" that I remembered where I was and jumped to my feet. Freight cars filled with soldiers were slowly moving past me. I stood stock-still, not knowing what to do. The train was gathering speed and its last cars were approaching. Suddenly I heard a voice from one of the cars, "Miss, get in here! Give me your valise!" It was my new acquaintance, Semen. Stretching out his hand to me, he cried, "Hurry! Hurry up!" Then something incredible happened: I picked up the huge valise and, lifting it up above my head, handed it to the soldier. He grabbed it and then pulled me inside the car. Only after my breath came easily again did I realize what had happened. It was physically impossible for me to pick that valise up with one hand, let alone lift it above my head. Yet I had done just that. The act made me recall something someone had once told me about an incident in the Caucasus he had heard about. A mountaineer was fleeing from some men who were pursuing him. In the chase he came to a wide mountain stream that completely blocked his escape. Having no alternative, he mustered his will and strength and in a superhuman effort jumped to the other side. His pursuers were so stunned that they abandoned their pursuit. Later I learned that such feats of "supernatural strength" in moments of extreme duress are not as rare as one might think.

Thankfully, the rest of the train trip was uneventful, and I reached Proskuriv and found Mother and Vania without difficulty. The following day, Mother and I were walking down the street when we suddenly overheard part of a conversation: "Did you hear the news?" one person asked another. "They've arrested Holubovych in Kamianets-Podilskyi." I felt as if I had been struck by lightning. In an instant, all my resentment toward Vsevolod vanished: I declared to Mother that I was going to Kamianets. I didn't consider what I would do there—all I knew was that I had to go there and do whatever I could to save Vsevolod. Mother understood and made no attempt to dissuade me. Soon I was boarding yet another train, headed back to Kamianets.

When I reached my destination, I went directly to the local headquarters of the Cheka, the Soviet secret police. I was told that Vsevolod was no longer there: he had been transferred to Vinnytsia. I took the train to Vinnytsia, and there again I went to see the head of the local Cheka. In difficult or dangerous situations, I always went to the person in charge. In Vinnytsia that turned out to be a young man. He told me that Vsevolod and other arrestees were in the ice cellar beside the Cheka building. "They've all been sentenced to execution by firing squad," he said. Then suddenly, to my great relief, he promised to try to persuade the other members of the Cheka tribunal not to shoot Vsevolod, but to transfer him to Kharkiv instead. He told me to come back every day to check on developments and said he would let me know how things were going.

It dawned on me that the Chekist had taken a liking to me and had decided to help me for that reason. The next morning and every one thereafter, as I left the house where I was staying, I found a bouquet of roses on the porch—a gift from the enamored young Chekist. During my daily visits he told me he was having difficulty convincing the other members of the Cheka to spare Vsevolod, for they feared an attack by anti-Bolshevik partisans, who were extremely active in the area and would surely try to free Vsevolod if they found out he was being held there.

Finally, when he encountered me in the street one day, the Chekist told me that he no longer had the power to save Vsevolod. The only recourse remaining was to get an order for Vsevolod's transfer from Kamianets-Podilskyi to Kharkiv from Volodymyr Zatonsky, the head of the Galician Revolutionary Committee,[40] who was then in Przemyśl. I immediately decided to go to see Zatonsky. As Vsevolod once told me, Zatonsky had been the rector of the Kyiv Polytechnical Institute and knew Vsevolod well when he was an exemplary student there. I therefore had some hope Zatonsky would be sympathetic and would help Vsevolod.

On the eve of my departure a young man came to visit me. He said he was a student working for the Cheka on secret orders of the Central Rada: he had learned that I was planning to visit Zatonsky and wanted to help me. He handed me an official-looking packet addressed to Zatonsky. "This is a letter to Zatonsky from the Central Committee of the Communist Party in Moscow," he said. "Taking such a long journey without documents is dangerous. This letter will help you." I thanked him, and to add to the packet's importance I wrote "VERY URGENT" on it.

At the train station I found a military train heading west. I showed the "document" I had received and immediately discovered its magical powers: I was taken to the engineer, who seated me right beside him! There were several changes of train along the way, and the packet was of help at every one. In those days the trip from Vinnytsia to Przemyśl usually took several days, but I made it in twenty-four hours. The train station in Przemyśl had been bombed, so the train stopped several kilometers from the city. I got off the train and stood there, not knowing

[40]This was the name of the Soviet provisional government during the Red Army's occupation of eastern Galicia in the summer of 1920. Zatonsky (1888–1938) served in various senior Soviet Ukrainian government and Party posts until he was arrested by the NKVD in 1937. He was later executed.—*Eds.*

how to get to the city. Suddenly two young men approached me and asked where I wanted to go. Hearing the name Zatonsky and seeing the package, they gallantly offered me a ride in their car. Of course, I accepted the fantastic offer, and the three of us settled into the front seat, with me in the middle.

During the ride the fellows entertained me with humorous stories, paid me compliments, and overall behaved in a most gentlemanly manner—I wasn't sure whether that was because of me or the packet with the magical powers. When we arrived at the building that housed the Communist government's headquarters, the two young men offered to wait for me in the car and then take me back to the train.

I entered the building, showed the packet, and was taken to Zatonsky immediately. When he saw what I carried, Zatonsky presumed that I was a messenger from the Central Committee in Moscow and greeted me very graciously. But as soon as I mentioned Vsevolod's name and stated the purpose of my visit, Zatonsky's manner changed abruptly and his face became severe. Nonetheless, he listened to what I had to say. When I finished speaking, he promised to order Vsevolod's release. Writing something on a piece of paper, he stuffed it into an envelope, sealed it, and handed it to me. I thanked him and left.

The young men were waiting for me. I got into their car and we drove off. One of them took out a small book. Writing an inscription inside, he gave it to me, saying "This is for you to remember me by. It's a collection of poems I wrote in English when I lived in Canada." I didn't know any English, but I took the book and thanked the poet. Years later, a friend noticed the book in my library and opened it: he asked if I knew what was written in the dedication on the first page. When I shook my head, my friend laughed, read the inscription, "I love you," out loud, and then translated it for me. Later still, when I was working as an editor, I crossed paths again with the poet who had lived in Canada: his name was Ivan Kulyk, and he reminded me of our first meeting.[41]

[41] Kulyk (1897–1937) was a socialist activist in North America from 1914 until he returned to Ukraine in 1917 and became a member of the first Soviet government there. He was a member of the Galician Revolutionary Committee (1920) and the Hart proletarian writers' group; the Soviet consul in Montreal (1924–27); a founding member (1927) of the All-Ukrainian Association of Proletarian Writers; chair of the organizing committee (1932) and head (1934–37) of the Writers' Union of Ukraine; and a member of the Central Committee of the Communist Party (Bolshevik) of Ukraine (1937). He wrote many newspaper articles, eight poetry collections, and several collections of prose, and translated an anthology of American poetry into Ukrainian before he was arrested by the NKVD. He perished during the Yezhov Terror.—*Eds.*

The young fellows drove me back to the station and bade me farewell. I decided to go to the ladies room and check what Zatonsky had written. I was overcome by doubt that he had kept his promise. My intuition was right: the note read, "I consider Holubovych to be dangerous and recommend that he be executed immediately." I tore the note to shreds and flushed it down the toilet. The train arrived, and soon, filled with desultory thoughts about the failure of my rescue mission, I was sitting in one of its heated cars.

The train was slowly moving eastward when it suddenly stopped. Two military men jumped up into our car. They quickly looked everyone over and then one of them pointed to me and shouted, "Here she is!" The two of them grabbed me, picked me up, and dragged me off the train and into the station. There they questioned me. "Where are the papers you took from Zatonsky's office?" I was totally confused: "What papers? I neither saw nor took any papers." "Really? Then what are these?" they said triumphantly, pulling a whole sheaf of papers out of my handbag. The head of the station started checking the documents and comparing them to the list he held. Convinced that they were all there, he smiled and said, "You're lucky that nothing is missing. You say you don't know what's in them? It's Vynnychenko's correspondence with our government."[42] When he said this I was overcome by fright, for I expected to be arrested and perhaps even summarily shot. To my amazement, they let me go.

This unbelievable episode continues to be a mystery to me. Were the papers hidden in my bag so they could be recovered later, or were they planted as a provocation against me? Should I suspect that the two young men who drove me to the station had a concealed purpose? To this day, I cannot say.

Once back in Vinnytsia, I immediately went to the Cheka headquarters there. To my surprise, I discovered that the Chekist who had befriended me had somehow succeeded in persuading the tribunal to transfer Vsevolod to Kharkiv and that he had already been taken there. I breathed a sigh of relief and soon left for Kharkiv.

---

[42] Vynnychenko resigned as president of the Directory of the UNR in February 1919 and moved to Vienna, where he headed the Foreign Group of the non-Bolshevik Ukrainian Communist Party, which promoted the creation of a completely independent Ukrainian socialist republic. In 1920 he visited Moscow and Kharkiv for high-level discussions with Lenin and other Bolshevik leaders. Disillusioned by their positions and policies, he rejected the invitation to become deputy chairman of Soviet Ukraine's Council of People's Commissars and people's commissar of foreign affairs. In Vienna, and later in France, he remained a vocal left-wing critic of the Soviet regime.—*Eds.*

I recently read a book of memoirs about the Ukrainian anarchist leader Nestor Makhno. According to them, the young Chekist in Vinnytsia who had been so friendly toward me, and seemed to be so humane and even a good person, was an infamous sadist who was captured and hanged by partisans.

CHAPTER 19

As soon as I arrived in Kharkiv, I went to the prison and said that I wanted to speak to the warden. When I asked him whether Vsevolod was there—and acknowledged that I was his wife—that official confirmed that Vsevolod was an inmate. I thanked him for the information and left, surprised not to have been detained. I was only a few streets away when a man caught up with me. "Are you Holubovych's wife?" he asked. When I replied I was, he asked me to return to the prison to answer a few questions. I went back with him, and this time I did not emerge—I was placed under arrest and spent the next nine months in prison.

At first I was put in a huge preliminary detention room with hundreds of other people. The room was so packed that it was impossible to turn around. Some people were standing, others sitting. There were men and women, military people and civilians. We were brought food once a day—a pot filled with some mush that passed for soup. Everybody pounced on this pot and tried to get at the food with any utensil they had. I had no implement with me, and in any case the beastly battle around the pot filled me with disgust. I didn't eat for two days. On the third day my neighbor, who appeared to be an officer in Denikin's army, turned to me. Extending his cup toward me, he said, "Take it. I won't be needing it anymore—I'll be shot today. Take it!" I looked at him in terror, not wanting to take a gift from a person about to die. But he insisted, and I did take the cup from him. That same day the officer was taken out of the room, and he did not return.

After a time I was transferred to another prison, on Hubernatorska Street. In the early 1920s, the Kharkiv offices of the Cheka were housed in several buildings on that street, which had once been where the town's affluent people lived. It was here, in their mansions, that the Cheka set up its administration. Prisoners were kept in the mansions' cellars, and many were shot there.

I was brought to a large room that had obviously once been a parlor but was now filled with bunks. Some fifty or more women were sitting on the bunks or on the floor. The room's windows faced out onto the street, and across from them was the Cheka's information bureau. The mothers, sisters, and wives of those arrested would make daily trips there to learn the fate of their loved ones. They stood in long lines, making their way one by one to the information window. Time and again we would hear an agonized cry as yet another woman was told of the execution of her husband, brother, or son. After all these years, those cries still echo in my ears, and I remember how I shuddered at every one.

There were women from all walks of life in our cell—prostitutes and thieves, as well as political prisoners. Each one found a spot for herself as best she could on a bunk bed or on the floor, putting something under her head and throwing a coat over herself. I had nothing with me—it was summer when I was arrested, and all I had was the summer dress I was wearing at the time. I slept on the bare boards. When my neighbor received two pillows from home, she gave me one. One night, as I was settling down to sleep, I saw the pillow move. I picked it up—and saw that a mouse had given birth to several babies under it! What a commotion the women made then!

They fed us so miserably that we suffered constantly from hunger. Consequently all the women talked about was food. They took turns describing how to cook one dish or another, savoring every detail. Food and culinary affairs had never interested me, so I did not participate in these discussions. That immediately set me apart and alienated me from the other women. In addition, the prison administration assigned me to clean the halls, a job that entitled me to an extra portion of food. This set the women against me even more, and they displayed their hostility and jealousy at every turn, making my imprisonment doubly hard to bear.

One day a group of young schoolgirls was brought to the prison. No more than thirteen or fourteen years old, they had been arrested in Poltava together with the schoolboys of the same age who were their friends. These youngsters had a patriotic and national frame of mind: they were convinced that the cause of the Ukrainian revolution was not yet lost and that they could be of service to it. They had formed an "organization" they believed was secret but was, in fact, well known to the Cheka. The girls had stayed in Poltava, while the boys traveled around "to set up contacts." They carried on a lively correspondence in which they shared their plans and hopes for the future. The letters were delivered on time, even too punctually, but the young people never suspected that these were being monitored by the Cheka. One day they were all arrested. The evidence against them was iron-clad, and it was certain that they would be executed. Their desperate parents went to see the writer Vladimir Korolenko, whom some of them knew, and implored him to intercede on their children's behalf. Korolenko immediately wrote to Moscow and then traveled there himself. He begged the Party to spare the children, arguing that their actions were all child's play and adolescent enthusiasm, that their "organization" had no political clout at all and posed no threat to Soviet rule. Korolenko even came to Kharkiv and visited our prison to see these young people. But all his efforts were in vain—the children were condemned as "enemies" and sentenced to be shot. The sentence was carried out. I remember that as the boys were being led past our cell on the way to their execution, one of them shouted out "Farewell, Halia!" to the girl he loved. The prosecutor later told us with what courage the boys had faced their execution and spoke about their heroic deaths with genuine admiration.

Oddly enough, this prosecutor quite often came to our cell to talk to us. We were given considerable freedom of movement in prison—the doors to the cells leading into the long hall were open at all times, and we prisoners could wander through from cell to cell. I recall a woman inmate who walked into our cell one time: she came up to me and started telling me about all the thefts in which she had taken part. Another time, the sister of one of our prison mates ran into our cell. Her husband was an officer in Denikin's army who had been wounded and remained behind when Denikin's forces were retreating from the city; he had been caught and arrested together with his wife, and both were sentenced to death. As this woman ran in, someone in the hallway was calling out in a loud voice the names of people who were to be led away to be shot. On hearing her own name, the woman caught hold of her sister's hands and cried, "I beg you, swear to me that you will not abandon my children!" Her sister, our prison mate, swore that she would take the children into her home and care for them. At that moment, the officers on duty came in and led the woman away. For a long while afterwards her distraught sister could neither eat nor drink and just kept repeating her vow that she would take care of the poor orphans: she was released from prison a short time later, I believe. There were many such episodes in prison: the toll of human suffering I saw around me was too great for me to remember it all.

Five months later, I was transferred to the old prison on Kholodna Hora (Cold Mountain) in Kharkiv. Kharkiv was then the capital of Ukraine, and this prison was probably the principal one in the country. It was here that Vsevolod was incarcerated together with his colleagues, as was my stepfather Vania, that is, Ivan Nemolovsky. The news that Holubovych's wife was also now an inmate spread through the prison like wildfire. The other Ukrainian prisoners started sending me food and sharing their packages from home with me. Among the prisoners who cleaned the halls and brought the meals were supporters of the Central Rada, and they all tried to be of help to me. Through them I promptly established contact with Vsevolod, and that continued throughout my imprisonment.

Once a gift from Vsevolod was passed along to me—his portrait drawn on a piece of gray paper that had been a book cover. It was done in pencil and had undoubtedly been drawn by an incarcerated artist, for it was a very good likeness. The portraitist had captured Vsevolod's facial features very well, and it was clear that he was a true artist. Beneath the portrait Vsevolod had written "My last prayer is your name, my love." I kept this portrait for years. I remember the day, months later, when I went to Dietrich's, a German store selling art supplies on Prorizna Street in Kyiv, to buy a frame for it. The clerk, seeing the portrait, immediately recognized Vsevolod and excitedly exclaimed, "Ah, isn't this Holubovych?!" She had obviously seen his photograph in the newspapers during the time of the Central Rada and remembered it. Her every gesture made it clear that she had great admiration for him. She diligently searched for the frame that would best suit the drawing and then refused to take any payment for it. In 1933 this beautiful, even historic portrait was confiscated by the secret police who had come to arrest my second husband, Serhii Pylypenko, and search our apartment. Perhaps it still exists, filed somewhere in their archives.

After a short while I was transferred to the main prison building, and there I was at last interrogated. The questioning lasted almost a full twenty-four hours. The interrogators took turns in shifts, while I continued to sit in the same position the whole day. They asked me about the members of the Central Rada and their activities. They also asked questions related to party matters—something I knew nothing about. For example, in my attempt to say positive things about Vsevolod and convince my interrogators how revolutionary an individual he was, I recalled the slogan "Long live the International!" which I remembered reading in the Socialist Revolutionary paper Vsevolod had been editing. To my surprise, my interrogators broke out in peals of laughter and asked: "Now, do you know what International they were referring to?" It was only then that I learned there were several internationals: the second one was supported by the Socialist Revolutionaries and the third—completely different—by the

Bolsheviks, and that was the major principle on which they had parted ways. When Vsevolod and his friends heard about my "testimony," they laughed harder than the interrogators had. For a long time after that my ignorance and naïveté sparked great mirth among them. Nonetheless, it was these qualities that actually saved me and the members of the Central Rada who had been arrested: not knowing any of their secrets, and guided by my intuition, I answered cautiously but truthfully and managed not to betray anyone. I didn't know that at the time, however, and after the interrogation I greatly feared that I might have said something that would harm these people. Once I was returned to my cell, I wrote down all the answers I could remember giving and passed them on in a note to Vsevolod. He responded quickly, reassuring me that I had answered superbly and that he and his friends were very grateful to me. Several other inmates who were friends of Vsevolod's also sent me notes of gratitude.

Several months went by, and I was not recalled for questioning. Somehow the idea occurred to me that I should go on a hunger strike to protest being held behind bars without cause—after all, I remembered reading the stories in *Byloe* of hunger strikes by revolutionaries imprisoned by the tsarist authorities. I asked that the prosecutor be informed of my intention to refuse food. He promptly appeared in my cell and tried to convince me that hunger strikes were valid only in tsarist times and that now, under Soviet rule, they were totally uncalled for. Furthermore, he said, "This is the first time since the revolution that anyone in this prison has mentioned a hunger strike. Drop this silly notion of yours." I firmly refused. The prosecutor, apparently at a loss for words, turned on his heel and left. I put my plan into action even though I was convinced that nothing would come of my "silly notion." On the third day of my hunger strike I received an official letter: it informed me that my case had been suspended and that I was free to go. I couldn't believe my eyes! That very same day the prison door opened and I walked out, a free person once more.

CHAPTER 20

Upon leaving prison, I was at a total loss as to what to do. I had no family or friends in Kharkiv. Where should I go? Where should I spend the night? I decided to go to the train station, where at least there would be people milling about and waiting for trains.

It was summer again, as it had been the day I was arrested. I was wearing the same thin dress I had on then, except now I was barefoot—I had thrown away my dilapidated shoes. Walking along the street, I noticed that I was not the only person without shoes. Many people were walking on wood soles tied to the bottoms of their feet with straps of leather or rope. Times were hard, and shoes were not easy to find. I went barefoot for months after leaving prison, and during that time my feet were often bloody.

I spent that night dozing fitfully at the train station. The following morning I resolved to find a job. While walking down a street, I caught sight of the building of the Council of People's Commissars. "Why not try my luck there?" I thought, and went directly to the building. A man came up to the building alongside me and politely held the door as I stepped into the lobby. Turning to me, the man asked, "Are you looking for anyone in particular?" Without hesitation, I said, "Yes, I'm looking for the chairman of the commissariat." To my surprise, the man smiled and said, "I am the chairman. What can I do for you?" I told him everything frankly—who I was and where I had been. The chairman—it was Rakovsky himself[43]—heard me out and then, without asking anything more, offered me a job as registrar. I had no idea what the job involved: the one connection that kept spinning in my head was Gogol's character Akakii Akakievich, who had a similar position and spent day after day copying official papers. I confessed to Rakovsky that I had never worked in an office, but he assured me I would soon learn whatever I needed to know. True enough, the job turned out to be very straightforward. And that is how I became a Soviet civil servant. Such miracles could

---

[43] Khristian Rakovsky (1873–1941), who was of Romanian origin, was a Bolshevik functionary from 1918. He headed the Soviet Ukrainian government (January 1919–July 1923) and served as the Soviet ambassador to Britain (1923–25) and France (1925–27). He was expelled from the Party in 1927 for belonging to the Left Opposition and exiled to Astrakhan (1928–34). He was rearrested in 1937, tried as a spy, and shot in an NKVD prison.—*Eds.*

happen only then, when Soviet institutions lacked educated or even literate people.

I worked at that institution for almost two months, and then someone advised me to look for a job in a publishing house. I learned that Vasyl Ellan-Blakytny, who had been a member of the UPSR and then became a Borotbist, was now editing the daily newspaper *Visty VUTsVK* (The All-Ukrainian Central Executive Committee News).[44] I knew that at one time he had been close to Holubovych and Nemolovsky, and I hoped he would help me.

Ellan-Blakytny greeted me in a very friendly manner. He listened sympathetically to the story of my imprisonment and that of Vsevolod, who was still behind bars. But when I asked about a job, he said with regret that there were no positions available at his newspaper. However, he offered to introduce me to Serhii Pylypenko, the chief editor of *Selianska pravda* (Peasant Truth), where, he said, there were some openings.[45] We walked down the corridor to the offices of that newspaper, which were located on the same floor, and there Ellan-Blakytny introduced me to Pylypenko. Serhii listened to my story quietly, just as Ellan-Blakytny had. When I finished, he offered me a job as copy editor and translator. He explained that his newspaper received all its material from Moscow in Russian, which then had to be translated into Ukrainian. By this time I was fluent in Ukrainian, so I was confident I had the skills necessary for the job.

My first translations were of news reports about the 1921–22 peasant famine in the Volga region and Ukraine. These reports, which came to our editorial offices daily, gave detailed accounts of all the famine's horrors, including cannibalism. In practically every case the latter involved hunger-crazed mothers killing their infants and

---

[44] Ellan-Blakytny (1894–1925) was a prominent early Soviet Ukrainian poet, journalist, critic, and satirist. He was also one of the leaders of the Borotbists, the large left faction of the UPSR that formed the pro-Ukrainian-independence UPSR (Communists) in March 1919 and merged with the pro-independence left faction of the Ukrainian Social Democratic Workers' Party to form the Ukrainian Communist Party (of Borotbists) in August 1919. The latter party, with some 15,000 members, voluntarily merged with the Bolshevik Party in March 1920. Many former Borotbists played important roles in Soviet Ukraine in the 1920s and were repressed and killed during the Stalinist terror.—*Eds.*

[45] *Selianska pravda*—originally called *Selianska bidnota* (The Peasant Poor)—was the organ of the central committees of the Bolshevik Party and the Committee of Poor Peasants in Ukraine, published daily in July 1921 and then three times per week until December 1925. Members of Pluh, which Pylypenko headed, were frequent contributors, and the paper did much to popularize Ukrainian literature among the peasantry. Pylypenko left *Selianska pravda* after it was merged with *Radianske selo* (The Soviet Village).—*Eds.*

feeding their flesh to their older children. Such horrors would be repeated during the great famine of 1932–33, which, unlike the famine of 1921–22 in the aftermath of the civil war, was not the result of a poor harvest, but an artificial one created by the Party to smash all opposition to its policies.

The poor harvest of 1921 did not affect all of Soviet Ukraine, and consequently many peasants came there from the Volga region in search of salvation. Help and food for the starving came from abroad, including from the American people via the American Relief Administration. But the millions who perished during the famine of 1932–33 received no help from anyone. The Soviet government regarded them as "enemies of the people" and strictly forbade anyone to assist them.

At the newspaper I met people who soon became my friends. The staff consisted of three people—the editor, Serhii Pylypenko; Ostap Vyshnia, my old friend from Kamianets-Podilskyi; and Ivan Kyrylenko. Ostap Vyshnia was the newspaper's secretary, and his desk was next to mine. He had no enthusiasm for his job and often did not show up at work.

One day Ellan-Blakytny paid a visit to our office—he liked dropping by to see Pylypenko, with whom he was on very friendly terms. Ellan-Blakytny was a cultured and well-educated man with a gentle nature. However, he deliberately adopted coarse mannerisms and peppered his conversation with obscenities in an effort to show he was "close to the common people." The men who printed our newspaper sometimes complained to me about their superior's behavior, protesting that they themselves did not use such language, especially in front of women. They considered his manner personally demeaning—something I'm sure the "proletarian writer" Ellan-Blakytny never suspected.

One particular morning Ellan-Blakytny entered the editorial office and, seeing that Ostap Vyshnia was not at his desk, muttered to no one in particular, "You mean that dirty rascal hasn't shown up yet?" These words irritated me immensely. With unaccustomed sarcasm, I retorted, "I've been here since early morning, and before you arrived there was no dirty rascal here." For a moment Ellan-Blakytny was stunned, but then he began roaring with laughter. "That's really well put!" he commented, and with that he turned on his heel and left. My coworkers burst out laughing and congratulated me on my wit. My retort was quoted in our offices for months afterwards.

Ostap Vyshnia (1928)

Vasyl Ellan-Blakytny (early 1920s)

There was another incident involving Ellan-Blakytny and me. One day he suddenly took note of my wedding band, which was wide, heavy, and made of dull gold, as was the fashion in those days. "What do you have there?" he said, "Let me see that." Surprised, I extended my hand. He grasped it, slid the ring off my finger, and threw it out the window, muttering, "Oh, these bourgeois superstitions!" Later I went out into the courtyard and tried to find the ring, but it was hopeless—the area was totally covered with trash.

One day, however, fate itself played a joke on Ellan-Blakytny. He had fallen gravely ill and had gone to a sanatorium to recuperate. During his absence word spread that he had died. On their own initiative the workers at the print shop composed an obituary of him and printed it in his own newspaper. Shortly afterward Ellan-Blakytny returned from the sanatorium. Everyone was embarrassed, but he turned the whole matter into a joke, saying: "Not everybody is lucky enough to read his own obituary." The joke soon became a sad one, however, for he died a short while later.

In 1926 a monument to Ellan-Blakytny—a bronze bust on a marble pedestal—was erected at the intersection of two paths in the Myronosytskyi Public Garden. It stood there a short while, only a few months, and then it disappeared one night without a trace. Even the cobblestones were reset so that there was no way of finding where the monument had been. Ukrainian Communists were perplexed, for there had been no official notice or explanation for its disappearance. Everyone perceived the act as the authorities' desire to erase public memory of a Ukrainian patriot and former member of the UPSR and, simultaneously, to issue a grave warning to others involved in the Ukrainian national rebirth. Soon every Ukrainian with even a bit of national consciousness—every "bourgeois nationalist," in Soviet jargon—would be in danger.

CHAPTER 21

I liked my work at the newspaper. The atmosphere there was friendly and cheerful, owing largely to the inexhaustible humor of Ostap Vyshnia, whom his coworkers addressed by his real name and patronymic, Pavlo Mykhailovych. He had an amazing talent for punning—and he did so nearly effortlessly. At times, as we were all working, one of us would say something quite prosaic and Pavlo Mykhailovych would pick it up and give it such a twist that we would all burst out laughing. Pavlo Mykhailovych introduced me to his brother and sister, both of whom turned out to be as witty as he was. He assured me that, in fact, his sister had a much better sense of humor than he had and that the wittiest person in their family was their father.

Pavlo Mykhailovych loved Ukrainian folk songs: he liked to hum them and listen to bandurysts sing them.[46] He had many friends in the State Banduryst Kapelle, and he often invited them to his house. He also befriended an old and blind banduryst who used to come to the Myronosytskyi Garden with a boy guide. This banduryst knew a great number of old songs and *dumy* and performed them masterfully. Every day, when he and his guide arrived in the garden, people who had come especially to write down his songs would already be waiting for him. That banduryst was admired by many Ukrainian writers, who loved to come to hear him sing. His songs always reminded me of my childhood trips with my "White" grandmother on holy days to the

---

[46] Bandurysts (*bandurysty*) or kobzars (*kobzari*) were originally itinerant, often blind, minstrels who preserved and sang Cossack *dumy* and historical and other folk songs while playing the bandura or kobza, both of which are many-stringed musical instruments. Known since the sixteenth century, these musicians travelled about the countryside and performed for alms. Bandurysts were persecuted by the tsarist regime during the nineteenth century, particularly in the cities. They survived, however, and banduryst ensembles were organized in Ukraine after the revolution of 1917. The traditional itinerant bandurysts were persecuted by the Soviet regime as carriers of Ukrainian national consciousness, and many of them perished in Soviet prisons and concentration camps in the 1930s. Nonetheless, bandura playing became a popular musical form that has survived in Ukraine to this day. See M. Hnatiukivsky [Mykola Mushynka], "Kobzars," in *Encyclopedia of Ukraine*, vol. 2 (1988), ed. V. Kubijovyč, 575–6; and Natalie Kononenko, *Ukrainian Minstrels: And the Blind Shall Sing* (Armonk, N.Y., and London: M. E. Sharpe, 1998).—*Eds.*

monastery in Mezhyhiria, where blind bandurysts, surrounded by rapt listeners, would sit and sing under the monastery's walls.[47]

Of other people who joined our editorial staff, I particularly remember an agronomist named Pushkarov, whose articles had appeared in journals and newspapers even before the revolution. He told us about his work among the peasants and attempts at changing the agricultural practices they had inherited from their forebears. For example, he tried convincing them hawks were a positive presence on a farm because they fed on field mice. But the peasants continued chasing away and shooting the hawks because "they stole the chicks." Pushkarov would say, "But each one of those birds eats a hundred field mice a day! The loss of a few chicks is worth that benefit!" His arguments fell on deaf ears. One of his colleagues had a similar experience while trying to reeducate the peasants. She created a model garden in her yard, and soon peasants from the surrounding villages were coming to see the beautiful vegetables she had grown. Shaking their heads in amazement, they would say, "Oh yes, the vegetables here are beautiful, but in our fields they won't grow like that." In protest, the woman would assure them they would and offer to teach them the cultivation principles she applied. They would smile politely and leave, convinced that for them that kind of achievement was impossible. The woman's work was not totally futile, however, for some of the more literate peasants would borrow Pushkarov's articles from her to read, thus opening their minds to new possibilities. Pushkarov became a good friend of mine and, being older, served as my protector. Indeed, everyone at the editorial office treated me very well.

I was asked to translate various Russian literary texts into Ukrainian. Many of these texts were already translations from Czech, Polish, German, English, and other languages. So, for example, I translated Mayne Reid's *Osceola the Seminole*, a novel that presented the life of the Seminole Indians respectfully and portrayed Osceola as a very admirable character.[48] I also translated a good number of books

---

[47] The Transfiguration Monastery was established no later than the sixteenth century in Mezhyhiria (now Novi Petrivtsi), some twenty kilometres north of Kyiv. It long benefitted from support by the Orthodox nobles and metropolitans, Cossack hetmans, and Zaporozhian Cossacks. The monastery was closed down by the tsarist authorities in 1786, and its main edifices were destroyed in a fire in 1787. It was allowed to reopen in 1886. The Soviet authorities closed down the monastery and confiscated its valuables in the early 1920s and had it demolished in the 1930s.—*Eds.*

[48] Many years later, I visited an Indian reservation in Florida named after Osceola. The Seminoles did indeed appear to be a very dignified people. Proud and independent, they

on politics, including works by Lenin. I did scientific translations as well, even helping to compile the first Russian-Ukrainian dictionary of chemistry. In all, I translated over thirty titles.[49]

Naturally enough, Serhii Volodymyrovych Pylypenko was the major figure in our office. He was not only an editor, but also an inspiration to his coworkers and everyone who came into contact with him. The *Pluzhany*—members of Pluh, the large Soviet Ukrainian peasant writers' association that Pylypenko had organized—adored him and affectionately called him "*Papasha*" (Papa). Many retained a deep gratitude to him throughout their lives. Typical were the sentiments about Serhii that Dokiia Humenna,[50] a former member of Pluh, expressed: "The number of encounters I had with Pylypenko can be counted on the fingers of my hands. But they are etched in my memory as the brightest moments in my literary life. All of my tentative steps in literature are connected in some way or another to this noble, kind, and fatherly person. I can name three specific times when I was on the edge of despair. Each of these times a miracle happened: Pylypenko would stretch out his hand and pull me out of the abyss."[51]

Mariia Romanivska, another member of Pluh, wrote the following about Pylypenko: "I see a tall, broad-shouldered figure wearing a lambskin hat, a long sheepskin coat trimmed with gray fur, and high boots. A manly face with a proud, chiseled nose, black moustache, and a sharp, cleft chin looks out from under his hat. The eyes behind his glasses look out at you benevolently. But his entire countenance seems stern and his voice is low, as wise *Papasha*'s should be...." For her, this nickname expressed everything—warmth, fatherly support, humaneness, and friendliness. In a word, his was the strong shoulder of a father one could lean on and fear nothing."[52] In her article Romanivska relates

---

treated tourists with a reserve bordering on hostility, which is understandable, given their history and struggle for freedom and independence. The Seminoles are the only Indian nation that has not signed a peace treaty with the American government. Thus, they are theoretically still at war with it.

[49] Edward Kasinec, then the librarian at Harvard University's Ukrainian Research Institute, told me he had identified thirty-four titles I had translated.

[50] Humenna (1904–96) survived the Stalinist terror and lived as a postwar refugee in the United States, where she published over fifteen books of prose.—*Eds.*

[51] Cited from my article "Mii borh Serhiievi Pylypenkovi," *Ukrainski visti* (Detroit), 20 February 1979.

[52] "Pluhatar Ukrainy," *Vitchyzna* (Kyiv), 1968, no. 1, 197. I must say that Serhii's seemingly severe countenance was a disguise. He had a gentle nature and, as he admitted to me more than once, grew a moustache to hide the soft contours of his mouth.

how *Papasha* Serhii did all he could to get a winter coat for the writer Oleksander Kopylenko; how, when she herself fell ill with tuberculosis, Pylypenko used his own money to buy a permit for her to convalesce in the Crimea; and how he sat up all night correcting his colleagues' reports and stories, texts for which they had already been paid.

The list of Serhii's good works goes on and on. For example, at the Taras Shevchenko Scientific Research Institute, where Serhii served as director, there was a nearly destitute cleaning woman who worried about how she would be able to buy a winter coat for her son.[53] Serhii gave her his permit card for the purchase, saying he didn't need a new coat (even though his was a decade old). Another time, in the early 1920s, Serhii was riding in a train. It was cold outside, the train was packed, and all the windowpanes were broken. Serhii was sitting in a window seat. The woman sitting next to him had an infant in her arms. The baby was shivering, coughing, and crying. To protect the infant, Serhii stood in front of the window, his broad shoulders cutting off the chilly wind. He had on his famous sheepskin coat—the one he is wearing in Oleksander Dovzhenko's drawing of him. Serhii spent the entire four-hour trip at that window. As a result, he contracted a nearly fatal bout of double pneumonia.

I have never encountered anyone who knew Serhii and didn't speak of him as an extraordinarily noble and sensitive human being. He seemed to have a unique ability to sense people's needs. With his innate democratic convictions, he treated everyone with equal respect, regardless of what position a person held. His idea of creating Pluh grew out of his admiration for the Ukrainian peasantry and their many talents. He believed there could be many talented writers among them and all they needed was direction and a better education. From dawn to dusk he was involved in this cultural mission—teaching, patiently explaining, and helping by both word and deed. Contemporary critics accused Pylypenko of "massism," saying he allowed everybody who showed the slightest interest in literature to join the organization, thereby giving rise to many mediocre scribblers. Serhii always rebuffed

[53] Pylypenko was the managing director of the Taras Shevchenko Scientific Research Institute. Established in Kharkiv by the People's Commissariat of Education in 1926, it was the primary research institution in Soviet Ukraine devoted to the study of Shevchenko in particular and Ukrainian literature in general. It ceased functioning after most of its scholarly associates were repressed during the years 1930–33, and its archives and library were transferred to what is now the Institute of Literature of the National Academy of Sciences of Ukraine in Kyiv. See Roman Senkus, "Taras Shevchenko Scientific Research Institute," in *Encyclopedia of Ukraine*, 5: 162–63.—*Eds.*

Pylypenko (second row, fifth from the left) and other Pluh members (Kharkiv, 1923)

his critics, saying that increasing the involvement of the common people in literature was a positive step and time would show how many good writers would emerge from the ranks of Pluh.

Indeed, if one were to name all the writers whose literary careers began in Pluh, the list would be quite long.[54] Some of these writers eventually left Pluh to join other organizations, and some even preferred to forget their humble beginnings in Pluh and omitted references to it in their official biographies. But the facts speak for themselves. Thanks to Pylypenko's selfless work with novice writers and his extraordinary organizational talents, a new Ukrainian literature developed in the 1920s. This fact has been discussed widely in modern-day Ukraine. In an article in the Kyiv magazine *Ukraina* in 1971, Vitalii Oleksiuk wrote: "Young beginners oriented their voices ... on this active, wise person.... The Pluh Association of Peasant Writers with Serhii Pylypenko at its head ... gave wings to an entire generation of creators of literature."

In 1981 the Kyiv literary journal *Dnipro* published an article commemorating the ninetieth anniversary of Serhii's birth. Its author, Volodymyr Basiuk, emphasized Serhii's role as "the organizer of literary forces in Ukraine" and cited Petro Panch: "Pluh ... was the

[54] It would include Volodymyr Sosiura, Petro Panch, Ivan Senchenko, Andrii Holovko, Vasyl Mynko, Leonid Pervomaisky, Oleksander Kopylenko, Natalia Zabila, Sava Bozhko, Vasyl Chaplenko, Volodymyr Gzhytsky, Kost Hordiienko, Oles Donchenko, Hryhorii Epik, Vasyl Mysyk, Dokiia Humenna, Mariia Romanivska, and Yurii Lavrinenko.

Soviet writers' first cradle ... this cradle nurtured writers who laid the foundation of Soviet literature and enhanced it."[55] This point was stated even more succinctly by the postwar émigré critic Yurii Lavrinenko in a letter he wrote to my daughter Assya: "... as an organizer and leader of Ukrainian publishing, *Papasha*, as everyone called him, was, in a real sense of the word, the father of the Ukrainian literary renaissance of the 1920s. For this he paid with his life.... [He played] a historic, unique, and incomparable role as the organizer of an independent publishing base, without which there would have been no ... literary renaissance."

Lavrinenko was referring to Serhii's role as the chief editor of the State Publishing House of Ukraine, which published works by Ukrainian writers with diverse literary styles and profiles. Serhii also played numerous other roles: he was secretary of the Federation of Soviet Writers of Ukraine; chairman of the editorial board of the scholarly journal *Literaturnyi arkhiv* (Literary Archive); managing editor of a number of scholarly editions of the Ukrainian classics; compiler and translator of an anthology of Belarusian poetry in Ukrainian translation and of an anthology of Ukrainian poetry in Russian translation; and the Ukrainian representative at the First All-Slavic Congress of Philologists, which was held in Czechoslovakia in 1929.

Serhii's contribution to Ukrainian scholarship deserves particular mention. Hryhorii Kostiuk assessed that contribution in these words:

> Pylypenko was not a degree-holding scholar, but as the director of a scholarly institution[56] he accomplished everything that was possible under the circumstances. He personally selected students for postgraduate work. He kept a close eye on every talented student enrolled in the Department of Literature of the [Kharkiv] Institute of People's Education,[57] sought out those who displayed an aptitude for scholarly work, and made sure they enrolled in postgraduate studies. It was thanks to his efforts ... that an important scholarly library was created and valuable archival material was collected. Under his editorship, the [Shevchenko] institute published irregular but solid *Arkhiv* collections containing many materials and documents that

[55] "Talanovytyi orhanizator i pysmennyk" (A Talented Organizer and Writer), Dnipro, July 1981, 130–1.

[56] That is, managing director of the Taras Shevchenko Scientific Research Institute.—Eds.

[57] In the 1920s the Soviet government transformed every university in Ukraine into an Institute of People's Education (Instytut narodnoï osvity). See I. Bakalo, "Education and Schools: 6. The Ukrainian SSR," in *Ukraine: A Concise Encyclopaedia*, vol. 2, ed. Volodymyr Kubijovyč (Toronto, 1971), 347–8; and "Institutes of people's education," in *Encyclopedia of Ukraine*, 2: 335.

> are still valuable today. Thanks to his initiative and direct involvement, an art gallery containing many valuable works of art was established at the institute. Owing to his initiative the famous exhibition "Fifteen Years of Belles Lettres in the Ukrainian SSR" was held in 1932. On display were many extremely rare publications that were thought to be lost. This exhibition was also remarkable in that it was illustrated by numerous portraits of Ukrainian authors and cultural figures. It was a unique presentation of objectively selected works that were excluded forever from future [Soviet] exhibitions.[58]

Serhii's capacity for work was nothing short of phenomenal. He often worked through the night while chain-smoking several packets of cigarettes—a habit that resulted in grave damage to his lungs. His life's motto was "To work with one's hands, / To work with one's mind, / To work without rest / Both day and night."

Little has been written about Serhii's literary legacy, for literary critics do not hold the genre of fables in high esteem. As a fabulist, Serhii himself alluded to this in his *Baikivnytsia: Chvert kopy baiok* (Collection of Fables: Fifteen Fables, 1922)[59]:

> If you should see a collection of fables,
> Hold back your scornful label,
> Let me remind you, if I may,
> Of what the old folk used to say:
> "Sing some songs!"
> —"Don't know how."
> "Tell some fables!"
> —"Don't dare now."
> What do you think, my dear,
> Whence comes this sudden fear?

At the end of the 1920s, literary critics were involved in a heated debate over this old and once venerated genre in Ukrainian literature. Then, as the literary critic Viktor Kosiachenko wrote, "a certain segment of the Proletkult critics did considerable harm to this genre."[60] Serhii's *Baikivnytsia* was the first collection of fables in

---

[58] Hryhorii Kostiuk, *Zustrichi i proshchannia: Spohady*, vol. 1 (Edmonton, 1987), 413.

[59] A *kopa* consists of sixty sheaves of grain; hence a *chvert* (quarter) is fifteen.—*Eds.*

[60] In the early 1920s, the theoreticians of the Soviet literary mass movement called Proletkult (Proletarian Culture) were opponents of Ukrainization and the Soviet Ukrainian literary

Soviet Ukrainian literature, and his neologism *baikivnytsia* became part of the Ukrainian language and literature. Although Serhii was also the author of short stories and military sketches, he considered his fables to be his true contribution to Ukrainian literature. He often said that "should my name ever be included in Ukrainian literature, it will be as a fabulist." He recalled how the poet Oleksander Oles hailed his literary debut, saying: "At last Ukrainian literature has acquired a talented new fabulist." It was Oles who published Serhii's first fable, "Voly" (Oxen) in his newspaper. Incidentally, it was this fable that later brought trouble on Serhii's head—it was seen as a manifestation of "Makhnivshchyna,"[61] this is, of anarchism, and as anti-collectivization propaganda. The fable goes:

The old master died,
  and to his son
Went all the land
  and all thereon.
A neighbor to his oxen said:
"You must be overjoyed,
The old whip you can forget,
For you are now employed
By a new master,
Luck is on your side
At last."
"Not so fast," one ox replied,
"They're all the same brand—
The young Cossack has a heavy hand.
No matter who the boss may be,
An ox will stay
A slave.
Wicked fate will flog us—you'll see."

You know, my friend, of course,
All power relies on force.
Want no ruler in the nation?

renaissance in general. See George S. N. Luckyj, *Literary Politics in the Soviet Ukraine,* rev. ed. (Durham, N.C., 1990 and Ivan Koshelivets, "Proletkult," in *Encyclopedia of Ukraine,* vol. 4 (1993), ed. Danylo H. Struk, 237.—*Eds.*

[61] The pejorative term for the anarchist insurrection and army headed by Nestor Makhno (1889–1934) against the Central Powers, the Russian Volunteer Army, the UNR, and the Bolsheviks in Left-Bank and Southern Ukraine during the years 1918–20.—*Eds.*

Join the Global Federation—
Workers only. Lords—out the door!
Oxen-slaves we'll be no more!

I found it gratifying to read not long ago that "Serhii Pylypenko is rightly considered one of the most notable initiators of the fable genre in Soviet Ukrainian literature." In his book *Ukrainska radianska baika* (The Soviet Ukrainian Fable [Kyiv, 1972]), Viktor Kosiachenko devoted much space to Serhii's works, pointing out the originality of their plots and use of literary devices, in particular Serhii's introduction of new allegorical characters, rhythms, meters, and strophic structures. Kosiachenko concluded that "Pylypenko's approach significantly broadened the formal search for new forms in Ukrainian fable writing."

As for the ideological focus of Serhii's involvement in literature and civic life, there is no question that it was governed by his deep-seated conviction that Communist ideas were just. He truly wanted, as Romanivska wrote, "his *Pluzhany* to grow up to become ... the apostles of socialism and future communism." Serhii was a convinced internationalist, but, of course, he also had profound sympathies for Ukraine. Though he subscribed to the Marxist theory of class struggle, at heart he was an idealist and a humanist of the purest kind. He dreamed of a "universal commune," of a society united by mutual love and harmony where complete freedom would reign. He dreamed of the same kind of society that Shevchenko, his favorite poet, dreamed about: "and there will be a son, and a mother, and people on the earth." Serhii honestly believed that communism was the right path to the achievement of that noble goal. He loved the Ukrainian people, and for that he was accused of being a nationalist. He aspired to complete freedom for the individual, and for that he was labeled an anarchist. He loved all human beings, and for that he was castigated as "an idealist" and "abstract humanist," that is, an anti-Communist. And in the end he paid for his convictions with his life.[62]

Serhii was born in Kyiv in 1891. His father, Volodymyr Pylypenko, was a school teacher who traced his ancestry to non-landowning Cossacks. One official version of his biography stated that Serhii's

---

[62] In his memoirs, Hryhorii Kostiuk described his last meeting with Serhii. Serhii came to him with the sad news that he had been "not only banished from the institute," but "was also ... a non-Party citizen." Kostiuk, greatly distressed, asked, "What are you saying? When did this happen?" Serhii replied, "Yes... Just now... Thrown out... For fifteen years I was ... I fought ... I risked my life ... I was ready to die ... because I believed that this was for the

father was a member of the Russian revolutionary terrorist organization Narodnaia volia (The People's Will), and that he took part in revolutionary activity. According to another version, his father merely had "a revolutionary temperament" and sympathized with Narodnaia volia's ideas. He was unable to keep a job for any length of time and switched from one civil-service post to another, until finally he was labeled politically unreliable and lost the right to work for the government. Consequently the family became impoverished, and Serhii was forced to work and support his family at a very early age. He had two brothers, Yurii and Borys, and a sister, Liudmyla. Serhii, who was the eldest sibling, inherited his father's independent spirit. At the age of thirteen he began reading the forbidden works of socialist writers, including Ivan Franko and Mykhailo Drahomanov, and became interested in the anarchist views of Peter Kropotkin, but this interest soon evaporated. He received his secondary education at the First Kyiv Gymnasium—the same school where the Russian writer Konstantin Paustovsky was a student, a year ahead of Serhii. Serhii spoke of the atmosphere that prevailed in the school and also of several of the same teachers that Paustovsky described in his memoirs.

Serhii's literary talents manifested themselves early on, and upon graduating from the gymnasium he enrolled in Kyiv University's Faculty of Philology. He was interested in Slavic folklore, and he researched and wrote about Serbian epic poetry. This may have stemmed from his interest in his mother's ancestors, Serbs who had migrated to Russia during the time of Catherine the Great.

At the university Serhii became a member of a student group of Socialist Revolutionaries and was given the task of disseminating banned literature. When the police uncovered this group during his third year at the university, he was expelled and banished from Kyiv. In the nearby town of Boryspil he found a job as a teacher of history, literature, psychology, and logic and took part in the activities

---

people's good, for the future happiness of my nation, for Ukraine... And it turns out ... I'm a *kontra* [counterrevolutionary]. They threw me out... They probably want to throw me out of existence as well... But ... they won't throw me out of literature... Never!" (*Zustrichi i proshchannia*, 1: 414). In trying to understand why the Party destroyed people like Serhii, Kostiuk writes: "Pylypenko, Richytsky, and people of their ilk, though organized members of the Party, were nonetheless organic sons of their nation—they were Ukrainians. Everything having to do with the fate of the Ukrainian people and its culture was dear to them. And this, obviously, is what made them dangerous to the Party" (ibid., 403). In other words, the destruction of people like Serhii was dictated by the deliberately anti-Ukrainian policies of the Party in those years.

Serhii Pylypenko at the front during World War I

of the local Socialist Revolutionary organization. When the Great War broke out in 1914, Serhii volunteered for duty at the front, on the party's orders—his job was to disseminate propaganda among the soldiers. He served at the front near Riga until it collapsed. He returned to Kyiv in 1918 on the eve of Hetman Skoropadsky's coup. He fought alongside other Socialist Revolutionaries in the popular uprising against the hetman, was taken prisoner, and was incarcerated for three months. When the Directory of the UNR regained power, Serhii was a member of the Central Committee of the UPSR. While still at the front near Riga he had edited a socialist newspaper called *Ukrainskyi holos* (The Ukrainian Voice), and now he became an editor of *Narodnia volia* (The People's Will).[63]

As we know all too well, Ukraine's independence did not last long. The Bolsheviks moved a huge military force into Ukraine and occupied the country. Kyiv fell to the Red Army. Like Holubovych before him, Serhii had to make fundamental decisions—how to live and whom to support. Like many other members of the left faction of the UPSR, he joined the Bolshevik Party, in March 1919. He also continued his journalistic career, as a technical editor of the newspaper *Bilshovyk* (The Bolshevik); in time he became a member of its editorial board. Once again, however, the vortex of the civil war drew him in and forced him to take up arms, and he took part in battles against Denikin's Russian Volunteer Army and against the Poles.[64]

---

[63] This daily newspaper was published in Kyiv from May 1917 to February 1919 by the Ukrainian Central Co-operative Committee. The organ of the Ukrainian Peasant Association (Ukrainska selianska spilka), a fraternal civic organization of the UPSR, it was the most widely read Ukrainian newspaper of its time. Pylypenko edited the paper until the end of 1918, the year he was a member of the Central Committee of the UPSR, and published his fables in it.—*Eds.*

[64] Serhii organized a partisan detachment and later commanded a brigade of the Thirteenth Red Army.—*Eds.*

When hostilities finally ended, Serhii resumed his editorial career. He worked as an editor for the newspapers *Visty VUTsVK* and *Komunist* (The Communist), the publishing co-operative Knyhospilka (Book Association), the press of the literary journal *Chervonyi shliakh* (Red Pathway), and the State Publishing House of Ukraine (DVU). Serhii led the initiative group for the creation of Pluh in 1922, and he served as that association's one and only head until its liquidation in 1932. Concurrently he was the editor of *Selianska pravda,* in whose offices we first met.

CHAPTER 22

I liked Serhii from the moment I saw him, and I soon learned he liked me as well. But neither of us did anything to initiate any intimacy. In those years people began and ended affairs easily, but that did not appeal to Serhii. For my part, I had been so traumatized by my relationship with Vsevolod that I had no interest in a romantic attachment. By that time my husband Vsevolod had been released from prison and our relationship had ended, though we did meet from time to time, usually in a park. I recall one such occasion. While we were sitting on a park bench, Vsevolod told me how sorry he was that our baby Lesia had died and how he would never stop loving me. His words moved me, but I knew in my heart that our relationship had ended and could not be revived.

One day my friend Valeriian Polishchuk asked me how it could be that I was working with such an interesting person as Serhii and we were not spending any time together. "You've never gone out with him? Not once, not to the theater or even for a walk?" he asked incredulously. His words struck me and started me thinking in a new direction. The following day I suggested to Serhii that we go to the movies. He was not at all surprised and promptly accepted the invitation. Later he admitted to me that Valeriian had also expressed his surprise to him about the formal relationship Serhii and I maintained. We went to the movies, and a few days later Serhii asked me to dinner and to a concert. That is how our closer relationship began, and it soon deepened into strong mutual feelings.

Overall our friends and families were very happy at this turn of events. But a few of his friends expressed dismay that he, a Communist, had fallen in love with a tsarist general's daughter. Serhii turned this into a joke, saying that they should view the development as yet another Communist victory. As for Vsevolod, soon after he learned about Serhii and me, he remarried. His wife was Jewish, and I subsequently heard that when guests came to visit, Vsevolod warned them against telling any anti-Semitic jokes. I do not know what later happened to Vsevolod or his wife. After I emigrated to the United States, I found a reference to him in an encyclopedic dictionary at Widener Library. It stated that he had been rearrested and sent to Siberia, but was later released. There was no mention of his death. Later Dmytro Kyslytsia, editor of the monthly magazine *Novi dni* (New Days), published in

Yivha Mykolaivna Pylypenko

Toronto, told me that Vsevolod's wife was said to be living in Argentina. But Adam Antonovych, editor of *Ekran* (Screen), had other information—Vsevolod and his family had lived in Berlin, and when Vsevolod died his wife and their son moved to the United States and lived in Chicago. I had neither the desire nor opportunity to verify this information.[65]

My relationship with Serhii was welcomed especially by his sister Liudmyla, a tall, beautiful woman with curly brown hair. The fact that her brother was still unmarried and paid no attention to women had begun worrying her, and she fully approved of me as his choice. But as Serhii began spending more time with me, Liudmyla became jealous, and in the end we did not become friends. I did become very close to Serhii's mother, Yivha Mykolaivna Pylypenko. She was a charming, sensitive woman, and Serhii loved her dearly; indeed, all her children and grandchildren adored her. When Yivha Mykolaivna decided to give up her job as linen-keeper at the Selianskyi dim (Peasant Residence) apartment building, where she lived, and to move in with one of her children, they vied with each other for the opportunity to take her in. We were fortunate to have her live with us for some time. Our friends, many of whom were writers, respected her intelligence and taste. They would often drop by to read their works to her, and they usually heeded her comments. Yivha

[65] In fact, Holubovych died on 16 May 1939 in an isolation cell in the Yaroslavl prison. A defendant in the show trial of seven UPSR members held in Kyiv in May 1921, he was released from prison in October 1921 but kept under police surveillance and not allowed to work for some time. He later found employment in Kharkiv at the Supreme Council of the National Economy. In 1931 he was again prosecuted during the show trial of the fictitious "Ukrainian National Center" and then imprisoned for the remainder of his life. See Anatolii Bolabolchenko, *Vsevolod Holubovych i "sprava UPS-R"* (Kyiv, 1993), published in the year that Tatiana Kardinalowska died.—*Eds.*

Mykolaivna was an incredibly beautiful woman: statuesque, with curly hair, a high forehead, and classic features, she attracted attention wherever she went.

Serhii physically resembled her in many ways. He was also tall, and extremely well built. During his student days he had often worked as an artist's model. He engaged in athletics and was an excellent swimmer—on several occasions, he saved people from drowning. In fact, he received twelve medals for his heroism. Whenever we went to the river for a swim, it seemed that someone was drowning and Serhii would have to drag the poor soul out of the water. One of Serhii's youthful romances began with his rescue of a peasant girl from drowning during a summer vacation. Subsequently she fell hopelessly in love with him. When he went back to the city at the end of that summer, the girl kept hoping he would return to her. Serhii later learned she had never married, and that information distressed him.

Serhii loved marathon running. As a student, he and a friend would often race each other, keeping pace with the fastest horses pulling carriages through the streets of Kyiv. He laughed as he told a story of how he was once running down the street and overtook a carriage rolling along at high speed. An old woman passing by was so startled that she began to crossing herself at the sight. Serhii and his friends continued jogging during the winter months—as much to keep warm as for the exercise, since they could not afford winter coats.

Although Serhii had very little money during his student years, unlike other students he did not go in for gambling. Once, however, his friends coaxed him into going to the racetrack and betting on a horse. They teased him, saying, "Perhaps you'll get lucky and win a thousand rubles." Serhii acquiesced and bet a ruble on the horse least likely to win. To everyone's surprise, the horse led the race right to the finish line, crossed it first, and then dropped dead. Serhii's one-ruble bet won him a great deal of money, since he was the only one who put money on this horse. I don't remember how much money he got, but I do know that he spent it all on renting a yacht for a sail down the Dnipro and a dinner party on board—complete with orchestra—for his friends.

Among other sports that Serhii practiced was Greco-Roman wrestling. This physical conditioning proved life-saving during the First World War I, when he was wounded in four places by a single bullet that went through his arm into his chest, passed through his lungs, and exited through his back. Blood spurted from all four wounds, and his trench coat was drenched in blood. Serhii had no idea how long he lay on the ground unconscious. Finally he heard the voices of medics searching for casualties who were still alive. They saw Serhii, but, thinking he was dead, started to pass by. Mustering his last bit of strength, Serhii pressed the trigger of the revolver he was still holding. The shot rang out, summoning the medics back to him. They quickly moved him to the field hospital, where he was operated on immediately. The medical staff could not believe that his body was able to withstand such a severe loss of blood—he had lost almost two-thirds of it.

Serhii had another experience in which his physical conditioning and stamina saved his life. He had fallen asleep on wet ground and caught double pneumonia. The doctors told his mother that the crisis would come during the night ahead and solemnly expressed doubts he would survive. When the doctors left, Yivha Mykolaivna sat by his bedside, refusing to let her son die: summoning all the force of her love, throughout the night she kept repeating to him that he would live. The doctors thought it miraculous that Serhii weathered the crisis.

Serhii spoke very little about his wartime experiences. The only information he volunteered was that he never deliberately sought out and aimed at the enemy. Once, however, he came face to face with a German soldier, who had emerged from nowhere. Serhii's only choices were taking the German's life or relinquishing his own. They started shooting at each other, darting around trees, until Serhii's shot finally felled the German. His war experiences were reflected in his story collection *Tysiachi v odynytsiakh* (Thousands One by One, 1928) and in his military diary.[66]

When Serhii and I first married, we lived separately. I had a tiny room in an apartment owned by a poet and translator, which had been assigned to me through my job. Serhii continued living with his mother and brother in the building called Selianskyi dim. Later, when I was expecting a baby, we were assigned a room in a three-story building. The room was very large, and we put up dividers in it to create a five-room "apartment" of sorts. One of the "rooms" was set up as a nursery. Having five "rooms" was considered a great luxury, but this apartment of ours was actually part of a communal one, with a shared kitchen and lavatory. Three families lived in it: Serhii and I, a lawyer and his wife,

---

[66] In 1963, after Serhii was posthumously rehabilitated, a small collection of his works was published under the title *Baiky ta opovidannia* (Fables and Stories). Unfortunately this collection does not include the stories Serhii considered his best.

and an old Communist and retired miner named Dubovy and his wife. The Dubovys were a pleasant couple. She was a typical peasant, illiterate but blessed with innate intelligence and a good heart. I taught her to read, and it was a pleasure to see her joy at being able to understand once-mysterious street signs. During her long life she had given birth to many children—at least twelve—all of whom had died as infants except for one: a son named Ivan, of whom the Dubovys were both very proud. Her account of his whereabouts was confusing, but I gathered that he had a high-level position in the Red Army.

One day, when the Dubovys were out, a military man knocked on our door and inquired whether they lived there. Thinking that he was their son Ivan, I asked him in. Soon I learned that the fellow was a messenger sent to find Commander Dubovy's parents. Shortly afterwards Ivan himself arrived. A very handsome man, he was a much-decorated hero of the civil war who did indeed hold a very important position. Later, in 1937, during the Yezhov Terror,[67] Ivan Dubovy and another prominent military leader, Yona Yakir, were arrested. They were both shot as "enemies of the people."

---

[67] Nikolai Yezhov (1895–1940) was appointed the USSR commissar of state security in January 1937 by Stalin himself. Yezhov initiated the largest of the Stalinist purges, targeting Party members and military officers as well as ordinary citizens. Lasting until late 1938, It has been popularly known as the "Yezhovshchina"—*Eds.*

CHAPTER 23

We lived in that apartment for several years. Our daughter arrived during the first year. At first we called her Esta, a combination of the first letters of our names—"S" and "T." But later, when other children began teasing her about her unusual name and she insisted, we changed it to *Asia*, now spelled "Assya" in English. There was no comparison between my first pregnancy and this second one, which brought me great joy. The time before Assya's birth was filled with happy expectation at creating new life. I listened with interest to what doctors said about the various stages of fetal development and tried to follow all of their recommendations. To me it was vital to influence the intellectual and spiritual development of this new human being as positively as possible. I attended concerts, went to art exhibits, and tried to remain calm, knowing that all these things had an effect on the child. The birth of our baby was a wondrous event for everyone in our family.

When Assya was born, it was rumored in the maternity ward that babies were sometimes sent home with the wrong parents, so new mothers like me feared they might be sent home with someone else's infant. Resolving to take precautions, I had my last name written on our newborn's back with an indelible pencil. "Kardynalovska" is a very long name and barely fit across such a small back! Once the baby and I were home, the letters did not wash out for a long time, much to the amusement of our family, who loved teasing me about it.

I was very involved in my work as a translator, so we hired a nanny and I continued working at *Selianska pravda*. Later, when our second daughter was born, we hired a second nanny and a cook. Such "upper-class" ways were commonplace then. Peasant girls were eager to work as housemaids, for they welcomed the opportunity to come to the city and earn some money, while urban women preferred continuing their education or working professionally to staying at home caring for children and keeping house.

We found a very sweet peasant girl named Kylia to take care of Assya. She had previously worked for the family of man named Kharytonenko, who had owned a renowned sugar factory in Kharkiv.[68]

---

[68] Probably Ivan Kharytonenko (1820–91), who was one of the wealthiest industrialists in prerevolutionary Ukraine and a well-known philanthropist, or one of his sons.—*Eds.*

Serhii Pylypenko and his daughter Assya (Merefa, 1926)

Kylia always spoke highly of the Kharytonenko family, saying that they were good-natured, kind to their servants, and well liked by everyone, including the people who worked in their factory. Kylia had taken care of the family's small son and had become very attached to him. At the age of five the child contracted scarlet fever and died. This was a great tragedy for the family, especially for the grandmother, who loved her grandchild dearly. The funeral was solemn and grand, and the child's coffin was a lavish one made of silver, or perhaps even gold. Many people followed the pallbearers as they carried it down the road from the church to the cemetery, along a path that had been covered by Persian rugs.

I, too, would know overwhelming grief at the death of a beloved child. Two years after Assya was born, I gave birth to a son, whom we named Rostyslav. He was a beautiful boy, with green eyes like mine and a bewitching smile. We adored him and enjoyed spending as much time with him as we could. When he was three months old, Assya and I took a trip to our dacha at Merefa, near Kharkiv. When we returned, Serhii told me that our little boy had contracted grippe. I wasn't overly worried; this is a very common illness, especially in children. But the following day I heard an awful scream. Our infant son was writhing in his crib, his tiny body racked with pain. I ran to him, called the doctor, and later listened to his diagnosis: the grippe had brought on complications, and our son now had meningitis. We were stunned—in those days there was no cure for meningitis. Serhii and I lived through three days of hearing our baby scream constantly in pain, each scream tearing at our hearts. He died on the third day. My grief knew no bounds—it was feared I might lose my mind. I looked so grief-stricken that friends would cross the street to avoid seeing me. For months I visited his grave daily and spent hours in total forgetfulness there. Finally life reclaimed me and forced me to come back to my senses. But the wound did not heal for years—I could not stop remembering the baby son who had left us so young and so tragically.

Two years after he died, I gave birth to another daughter, whose arrival was quite extraordinary. When my labor pains began, I went to the hospital, where the cramps continued coming with increasing frequency. I did not scream, but other women did, and I recall that these sounds brought to my mind some lines from a poem by Aleksei Tolstoy: "Even psychopathic women do not scream the way / Those seized by pain did as they in labor lay."

Suddenly I noticed one pregnant woman walking around the room without any indication that she was in pain. Soon the nurses were persuading her to lie down, for she was about to give birth. And, indeed, no sooner did she lie down than her child was born. This made a tremendous impact on me. "Obviously," I thought to myself, "being in pain is not obligatory." I began to wonder whether what was crucial in labor was the woman's thoughts and will power. If this woman was able to dismiss pain, why shouldn't I try to be devoid of it as well? Lost in thought, I didn't realize that my own pain had lessened and then totally disappeared. When I did realize this, I thought something was amiss and called a nurse to examine me. She assured me that everything was proceeding normally, that the contractions were coming at increasingly brief intervals, and that the child would be born soon. And, indeed, our daughter soon arrived without my experiencing any pain at all! Later, when I told doctors about this, they said that instances of painless childbirth were not all that rare, and that in my case auto-suggestion might have played a role.

We named our second daughter Mirtala, after the heroine in a historical novel by the Polish writer Eliza Orzeszkowa, which I had read in Russian translation. Based on historical fact, the work portrayed the life of a beautiful courtesan of ancient Rome who knew many senators and was influential in politics, but died a tragic death. But to me this story was essentially insignificant—I named our daughter Mirtala simply because I loved the name.

On the topic of names, I should note that when I married, I retained my maiden name, which was quite common in those days and is not infrequent today. An amusing incident occurred in connection with this. At the end of the 1920s Serhii and I traveled to Moscow with a group of Ukrainian writers to attend a conference. Our delegation was staying in a hotel, and that is where Serhii and I took a room. Tired after the day's travels, we went to bed early. In the middle of the night we were awakened by a loud knock on our door. A rough voice called out, "Get rid of the woman!" When Serhii voiced bewilderment at what was going on, the hotel official stated succinctly that his establishment operated on strict moral principles and that only married couples were permitted to stay in the same room. Since Serhii and I had different surnames, to him we were obviously not married and therefore I had to vacate the room. The official would not entertain any explanation: I had to go to another room. Serhii was more amused than angry, and the next day he told the members of our group about our adventure. One of them related the incident to the editor of *Literaturnaia gazeta* (The Literary Gazette), who made it into a story called "Likvidiruite zhenshchinu" (Get Rid of the Woman), published in the 15 July 1927 issue.

Our family now included two small children. In time Liza's daughter Roksolana—whom we called Roksanochka and Roksia—joined our ranks. Liza's life had become very difficult after the revolution. For a while she lacked any professional training and had difficulty finding a job. Later she found work as a translator and illustrator and also studied part-time at the Department of Architecture of the Kharkiv Art Institute, where in 1930 she received a degree in art and architecture. Her interest in literature did not abate, however, and she continued translating from Russian and Belarusian. She also wrote poems, children's stories, and novelettes. Together we wrote a fantasy we called "We Want Sun!" Liza's stories for children always had interesting plots and revealed deep insight into child psychology. Children were especially fond of the ones titled "The Wolf and Ralf," "The Benz," "The Train," and "Hanusia and the Pests." Liza had a gift for language: during the revolution she had mastered Ukrainian and become enchanted by it. She adored the poetry of Pavlo Tychyna and memorized all of the poems in his first collection, *Soniashni klarnety* (Sunny Clarinets, 1918).[69] Her artistic talent was also noteworthy: later, during the Second World War, she supported herself by selling her watercolors.

Liza was somewhat shy and unsure of herself, and her personal life was not as adventurous as mine. But she too experienced pain and distress in a personal relationship. At the end of the 1920s she

[69] Tychyna (1891–1967) was one of the greatest Ukrainian modernist and Soviet Ukrainian poets.—*Eds.*

met a chemical engineer named Ivan Kostiuk. He became the father of her daughter Roksolana, but they separated when the baby was just a year old. Liza and her daughter came to live with us in the Slovo (Word) apartment building, a residence for writers and their families in Kharkiv. Though she was not a member of the Writers' Union, her literary accomplishments were sufficient for Serhii to get her a small room of her own in the building. She lived with little Roksolana and worked day and night on her translations. Whenever Roksolana woke up crying during the night, Liza would pick her up and hold her in one arm while continuing to type with her free hand, until the monotonous clatter of the keys being struck lulled the baby back to sleep.

When Roksolana was a little older, Liza would leave her with us during the day. In time Roksolana's bed was moved to our apartment, and thereafter the three girls grew up together like three sisters. Roksolana's family now consisted of her two "sisters," her uncle Serhii, who loved her dearly, and two "mothers"—"Mama Liza" and "Mama Tania."

All too soon the terrible year of 1933—the year Serhii would be arrested—would be upon us. That year Liza would lose her job, and the doors of every publishing house would close to her. When that happened, she returned to work as an architect. She also worked as an illustrator, making just enough to support herself and her child. Later, when my children and I were exiled from Ukraine, Liza felt alone and abandoned. She needed attention and support, and Kostiuk extended a helping hand. They got together again. Roksolana was five years old when she saw her father for the first time since she had been a baby. Their family life was quiet and peaceful, but it did not last long. In 1937 Kostiuk's former wife, driven by jealousy, denounced him, and he was arrested. The woman was a witness at the trial, which for some reason was an open one. During the proceedings she withdrew her charge, admitting that it was a complete fabrication. But the court refused to dismiss the case. The judge insisted that Kostiuk had admitted to his "crimes" and that the charges against him could not be dropped. As an "enemy of the people," Kostiuk was sentenced to four years of hard labor at Kolyma. When his term ended, he was given to understand that if he returned to Ukraine, he would be imprisoned again, and so he remained in Siberia for many years, working at a factory. Only after the Second World War, when he was already in his seventies, was Kostiuk able to return to Ukraine and live out his life with his family. With the earnings he had saved during his long years of exile, he and

Tatiana's sister, Liza (Kharkiv, 1926)

Assya, Mirtala, and Roksolana (1932)

Liza bought a home in Kyiv. That is where their daughter Roksolana and her husband live today.[70]

---

[70] Roksolana's husband, Marian Malovsky, a talented artist, died in 1993.—*Eds.*

CHAPTER 24

The year Mirtala was born, Serhii traveled to Czechoslovakia to attend the First All-Slavic Congress of Philologists. There he and Professor Kostiantyn Nimchynov represented Ukraine.[71] Czechoslovakia made a great impression on them. They loved its beautiful, well-ordered cities and the level of civilization and culture they saw. Serhii spoke with great enthusiasm about how the Czech farmers tended their land. All of them had collected small, personal libraries of publications having to do with farming, and those who grew special crops or raised animals subscribed to journals devoted to these topics. Serhii was equally impressed by the farmers' industriousness. On one occasion he noticed a farmer working his field at night—to make that possible, he had strung up electric lights the length of the plot.

Serhii brought gifts from Czechoslovakia for me and the children: a wind-up phonograph for the girls and a portable, German-made typewriter with a Russian keyboard for me. At the border he had a great deal of trouble with these gifts, and in the end the customs agents refused to allow them through. Serhii later had to write to several different ministries for permission to bring in these "scarce" and "bourgeois" items, especially the typewriter (Soviet law prohibited anyone from owning a personal typewriter, because it was assumed that it would be used to produce anti-Soviet propaganda). Eventually Serhii succeeded in convincing the Soviet bureaucrats I needed the typewriter for translations I produced at home. Later this wonderful typewriter literally saved our lives: when Serhii was arrested and I was sent from Ukraine to live in Kalinin, I used it to subsidize the meager salary I earned at the pedagogical institute by typing students' dissertations and professors' papers at home. It was a miracle no one denounced me than as the owner of a forbidden item.

In addition to his work as an editor, Serhii headed the State Publishing House of Ukraine. He was paid a mere two hundred rubles per month, the so-called *partmaksymum* (the maximum salary allowed a Party member regardless of his position). Serhii's salary was less than

---

[71] Nimchynov (1899–?) was a professor of Ukrainian linguistics and a lexicographer in Kharkiv during the 1920s and 1930s. He was arrested in 1937 and was most likely killed by the NKVD in a prison or concentration camp.—*Eds.*

what an accountant earned, but he considered that to be completely fair. Moreover, as a committed Communist, he wanted to be closer to the people and so worked the night shift at a factory as an ordinary worker. But even with his prodigious strength and good health, he would probably not have been able to endure such a schedule for long. As things happened, an accident intervened—a heavy metal tool fell on Serhii's foot, and the injury made it impossible for him to continue working at the factory.

In regard to Serhii's health, there was one incident that gave some basis to a rumor that he suffered from a nervous condition. A fellow writer got the idea of visiting the Kharkiv Psychiatric Hospital and talking with the patients there. About ten other writers, including Serhii and Mykola Khvylovy, became intrigued with the idea, and the visit was arranged. On the appointed day they went to the hospital, where the doctors briefed them on the medical histories of the patients they would be seeing. When they actually met the patients, however, the writers were at a loss and asked things like "Where did you study?" and "Where did you spend your childhood?" The doctors, taken aback by the writers' simplistic questions, protested that even if the patients gave answers, they would shed no light on their mental problems.

One young doctor was particularly annoyed by the writers' visit and decided to turn the tables on them: he offered to make a psychiatric diagnosis of the writers themselves. The writers agreed, became animated, and started cracking jokes. The doctor spoke with the writers one by one, interviewing each for about five minutes. Then he made a solemn declaration: "I must say that not a single one of you can be said to enjoy full mental health." The writers became very uneasy, for the doctor seemed to be absolutely serious. Then one of them said: "Well, perhaps the nerves of the rest of us are not completely in order, but surely you cannot say that about Serhii Pylypenko. After all, he's a most calm and well-composed person." The doctor laughed sarcastically and said, "You are mistaken. He suffers from hysteria, and his condition is actually quite acute. He only gives the appearance of being calm." The writers were shocked: not one of them had suspected that the doctor was giving them a comeuppance. Gratified by the effect he was having, the doctor lectured the writers further: "You see, the concept of 'being normal' is very relative. All of you have lived through the civil war. We doctors see the effect this has had on your nerves. On top of that, writers are creative and very sensitive people—which my observations today confirm." Later, when Serhii told me about all this,

Serhii Pylypenko (center of the middle row) among Ukrainian writers, painters, and composers (Kharkiv, 1923). Front row from left: Maksym Rylsky, Yurii Mezhenko, Mykola Khvylovy, Maik Yohansen, Yukhym Mykhailiv, Mykhailo Verykivsky, Pylyp Kozytsky; middle row: Natalia Romanovych-Tkachenko, Mykhailo Mohyliansky, Vasyl Ellan-Blakytny, Serhii Pylypenko, Pavlo Tychyna, Pavlo Fylypovych, Savelii Khutoriansky; back row: Dmytro Zahul, Mykola Zerov, Mykhailo Drai-Khmara, Hryhorii Kosynka, Volodymyr Sosiura, Todos Osmachka, Volodymyr Koriak, Mykhailo Ivchenko, Borys Yakubsky

I saw that he gave credence to the diagnosis of his "latent hysteria." I gave it some credence too, even though it contradicted common sense, for in the ten years of our married life together I had never once seen Serhii lose control or yell hysterically.[72]

Khvylovy must also have believed Serhii's "diagnosis," for the protagonist of his short novel "Sanatoriina zona" (The Sanatorium Zone, 1924), a hysteric named Anarkh, bears a physical and psychological similarity to Serhii; indeed, Khvylovy dedicated the work to Serhii. Also, Khvylovy's description of Anarkh's emotional state closely parallels the doctor's "diagnosis": "It was hysteria, and it could not have been otherwise—after the long years of the civil war in which he took active part, Anarkh could expect to fall prey to this illness. And with it came emotional imbalance—heightened sensitivity,

[72] Only when I began composing these memoirs did it occur to me to check this "diagnosis of hysteria" with an American psychiatrist who is a friend. When he heard that the diagnosis was based on a five-minute interview, he laughed. From the medical point of view, it is impossible to determine "latent hysteria" on that basis.

eccentricity, attacks of depression and fear." In fact the character Khvylovy created resembles Serhii only slightly. Anarkh is more a reflection of the author's thoughts about himself, his generation, the individual's role in a Communist society, and particularly the role of the writer compelled by the Party to sing of the "heroism of everyday life." To quote Khvylovy's novel, "heroic day-to-day life is more difficult to depict than a heroic holiday.... I accept day-to-day life with both my heart and my mind. Still, there is anguish."

The quarrel between Khvylovy and Serhii on matters of principle is well known. It was evident in the public polemics they carried on with each other, which were not always couched in politeness. Khvylovy tried directing the development of Ukrainian literature along Western lines, while Serhii felt that it should follow its own path, which he believed would be closer to Russian literature. In this debate I sided with Khvylovy. This was one of the rare instances in which my view on aesthetic matters differed from Serhii's.[73]

Serhii and Khvylovy had a common goal: creating a Ukrainian culture with its own national profile. But their goal turned out to be threatening to the Soviet authorities. For that reason it was condemned as "nationalist," in other words, counterrevolutionary. As for their personal relationship, I recall that it was not inimical, but, on the contrary, quite cordial. The émigré critic Yurii Lavrinenko wrote that Khvylovy highly valued Pylypenko as a civic activist and a person. The truth of his statement is evident in Khvylovy's "Sanatoriina zona" and in his story "Redaktor Kark" (Editor Kark), whose protagonist has some similarity to both Serhii and Ellan-Blakytny.

---

[73] Soviet critics later declared that the differences between Khvylovy and Pylypenko were insignificant, because both of them were Ukrainian nationalists who opposed Russian culture. For example, in an article about Pluh published in the Soviet Russian-language *Literaturnaia entsiklopediia* (Literary Encyclopedia), vol. 8 (Moscow, 1934), 733–4, Dmytro Kosaryk wrote that "in conducting his polemics with Khvylovy on narrow organizational issues, he [Pylypenko] nonetheless was in agreement with him and his nationalist program of severing Ukrainian culture from Russian socialist culture." This official explanation does not reflect the true picture. Hryhorii Kostiuk has a much deeper understanding of both Pylypenko's and Khvylovy's positions, an understanding based not only on their polemics, but also on their actions. Noting that he personally supported Khvylovy's stance, Kostiuk states: "In my consciousness I have come to understand that these were people of one generation and one era who had a common goal, but that they had different intellectual and emotional temperaments and were talented in different ways. What Pylypenko did for the establishment of Ukrainian culture could not have been done by Khvylovy. And vice versa. They followed different paths and the steps they took were different, yet the goal they were pursuing was the same" (*Zustrichi i proshchannia,* 1: 413).

That story contains a detail that probably has little relevance for the general reader but was meaningful to us: namely, mention of the bust of a Roman that stood in an editor's office. A bronze bust of this kind did indeed belong to the editor of a local newspaper. Larger than life and very realistic, it stood on a pedestal inscribed with the words "Civis Romanus sum." After the revolution that newspaper's editorial office on Sumska Street became the headquarters of the Communist newspaper *Visty VUTsVK*, and its editor in chief was, alternately, Serhii or Ellan-Blakytny. At first Ellan-Blakytny paid the bust no mind, but after a time its presence began annoying him and he decided to get rid of it. When Serhii learned of this, he declared that he liked the sculpture and wanted to take it home. And so the Roman was brought to our apartment and put on the buffet in our dining room, where we thought it would be safely out of everyone's way. But we forgot about our children's favorite game, which was running around the dining-room table, with "briefcases" under arm. They would race about, pretending to be dashing off to their "offices" as they chanted this verse from a favorite children's book:

> Chief bookkeeper's running fast,
> Tries to catch his breath at last,
> Can't be late to work, no way—
> Lots for him to do today.
> "I'll be done perhaps by noon
> And will enjoy my kasha soon."

Naturally enough, the stomping of small feet would make the bust shake, and we constantly feared that it might come crashing down on the children's heads. Soon the Roman found himself relegated to another room.

CHAPTER 25

We were staying at our dacha outside Kharkiv when Serhii returned from the city one day looking distraught. Holding a newspaper in his hands, he said: "Listen to what it says here! Andrii Holovko shot his wife and little daughter![74] He's been arrested and is awaiting trial in Poltava. I know him—he's a member of Pluh. Something's not right about this—I must look into it."

The following day Serhii placed a call to Poltava. He was told that Holovko had probably committed the crimes while temporarily insane and that he had been placed in a psychiatric ward for medical observation. Because he knew Holovko well, Serhii was asked to come to Poltava and see him. Serhii and I made the journey there together. Upon arriving we were received by the hospital's chief psychiatrist. He told us that we would probably detect nothing odd when we spoke with Holovko, for he was speaking logically. Serhii asked whether it would be too stressful for Holovko to talk about what had happened. The doctor assured him that, quite to the contrary, Holovko spoke about it willingly. Then the psychiatrist asked that the patient be brought in. Holovko looked dreadful. He was wearing a pair of long underwear; one leg was ripped off at the knee and the other was ragged. His shirt was torn to shreds, and his body was bruised and blood-stained.

Taking no note of us, Holovko threw himself at the doctor. "What are you doing to me?" he asked angrily. "Why did you put me in a room with raving lunatics? They beat me unmercifully! Look at what they have done to me!" The doctor was horrified: "I didn't give any order to put you in a room with lunatics! There has been some mistake." He immediately summoned an orderly and told him to transfer Holovko to another ward. At this point Holovko noticed us. His face brightened and he shook Serhii's hand, thanking him for coming. "I want to tell you everything that happened. Everything," he said. And then he poured out his story.

He and his wife were both teachers, but their jobs made it necessary for them to live apart. Holovko's wife lived with their daughter in a small village near Poltava, and they would come to visit Holovko in

---

[74] Holovko (1897–1972) was a member of Pluh and a well-known Soviet Ukrainian novelist. He survived the Stalinist terror and remained a writer, receiving the Shevchenko State Prize in 1969 for the first two volumes of his trilogy, *Artem Harmash*.—*Eds.*

another village where he was teaching. The visits were rare, and he suffered greatly from the separation. He loved his wife passionately, indeed, practically deified her—she was the only woman he had ever loved. The feelings did not mellow with time—on the contrary, they intensified to the point of obsession. He was tormented by the fact that they were poor and had to live apart. But what upset Holovko even more was the fact that his constant thinking about his wife was preventing him from doing any writing. Gradually he became convinced that his love for his wife and child was the source of his misery and that he had to rid himself of them. He decided that the only solution was to kill them both. He became more and more convinced of this as time went on, and he began writing down these thoughts in his journal.

During their winter vacation, Holovko's wife and child came to visit him. He was away when they arrived. His journal lay open on the table, and his wife began reading it. When Holovko returned, he found her in tears. She cried out that she never wanted to interfere with his writing and declared that she would leave immediately with their child and he would never see them again. Holovko tried to calm her, saying that he no longer felt that way and that all would be well. They talked until dawn, and his wife was somewhat consoled. They agreed that it would be better for them to separate for a while. After his wife and child returned home and some time passed, Holovko wrote asking that they both come for a farewell visit before they parted ways.

By that time it was late spring or early summer. The weather was warm and sunny. Holovko suggested they ride out into the woods for an outing, and his wife agreed. The three of them boarded a train, rode a few stops, and got out. They were in an area of meadows and woods where people had summer homes. They walked through the woods the whole day. Holovko's wife wanted to stop and rest, but he kept coaxing her to walk a bit farther. Finally, completely exhausted, she lay down on the grass, saying that she could go no farther. Holovko did not insist, but said that he would go on with their daughter a bit. In a few minutes the little girl also begged to rest—after all, she was small, only three or four years old. He sat her down under a tree and told her to wait for him, that he'd be back soon. He returned to his wife, who had fallen asleep. Taking a red kerchief out of his pocket, he covered his wife's face and shot her in the head.

Then Holovko returned to take his daughter to the station. There they boarded a train and, after a few stops, got off again. When his daughter asked where her mother was, Holovko replied that she would join them shortly and led the child into the woods. Evening was approaching. The little girl was stumbling from fatigue. Holovko finally laid her down on the grass, sat down next to her, and asked what children's stories she would like to hear. He told her all her favorites until she finally fell asleep. Afterwards, he took out another red kerchief from his pocket, covered the child's face, and shot her. After that Holovko went back to the station, boarded the train, and went back to Poltava.

He rented a room in a hotel and stayed there for two days. On the third day he read in the paper that a woman who had been shot in the head had been found in the woods near Poltava and that in another area a little girl shot to death had been discovered. In both cases the faces had been covered with a red kerchief. Holovko immediately went to the hospital where his wife had been taken—she was still alive, but unconscious. Holovko told the doctor he had killed the child and had also tried to kill his wife, but the kerchief must have gotten in the way. He insisted that he be allowed to see his wife. Promising to obtain permission, the doctor left the room and called the police, who arrested Holovko. At this point Holovko ended his story. He took a deep breath and said, "Now I feel free."[75]

After he had been led away, the doctor asked Serhii whether he had noted something especially peculiar about Holovko's story. Serhii answered that one detail in particular had struck him—the red kerchief. Holovko had written a story by that title. His "Chervona

---

[75] The case has prompted interest to the present time. The summer 1990 issue of the student journal *Khoma Brut* (Zhytomyr) printed the official record of Holovko's interrogation after his arrest. Although it contained some discrepancies with the account Holovko gave Serhii—for instance, it said that his daughter was killed the day after his wife was shot—the facts and motives he gave to the police were identical to those he related to Serhii. In his brochure *Ukrainskyi renesans XX stolittia* (The Ukrainian Renaissance of the Twentieth Century [Toronto, 1953]), Prof. Hryhorii Vashchenko mentions the double murder and says that the motive was Holovko's desire to get rid of his family in order to marry another woman: "While living in Bilyky, Holovko fell in love with a beautiful young teacher at an orphanage. In order to eliminate any obstacle to his getting together with the woman, he decided to get rid of his wife and daughter in a criminal way." Vashchenko provides the following false information: that Holovko's daughter was saved by peasants, that he merely feigned insanity, and that he became a member of the Writers' Union after his release from prison. These statements make Vashchenko's testimony very suspect. In regard to Holovko's second marriage, Volodymyr Kulish writes in his memoirs, *Slovo pro budynok "Slovo"* (A Word about the Word Building [Toronto, 1966], 15), that Holovko's second wife was not a teacher at an orphanage, but a niece of the Yiddish writer Lev Kvitko.

khustyna" was set during the time of the civil war and included an episode in which a little girl covered the face of a peasant murdered by Haidamakas.[76] The story had been published the previous year. The doctor thanked Serhii for the information, saying that it shed some light on what had taken place.

After spending two months in the hospital, Holovko was discharged, having been judged to be completely sane once more. Later he remarried, and the doctors advised the couple to live with Holovko's brother. The three of them came to live in the Slovo (Word) apartment building, where we too were living then.

---

[76] Most likely a reference to members of one of two formations in the Army of the UNR: (1) the Haidamaka Battalion (*Haidamatskyi kish*) of Slobidska Ukraine, which became the Third Haidamaka Infantry Regiment of the Zaporozhian Corps in March 1918, a brigade in June 1919, and later that year mutinied against the UNR and acted independently until it was destroyed in 1920; or (2) the Haidamaka Cavalry Brigade, which also became part of the Zaporozhian Corps in March 1918.—*Eds.*

Tatiana and her brother Serhii (Kharkiv, ca. 1925)

Tatiana and her daughter Assya (ca. 1928)

Tatiana, Serhii Pylypenko, and their daughter Assya (Kharkiv, 1927)

Serhii Pylypenko and his daughters Assya and Mirtala in the country near Kharkiv (1931 or 1932)

CHAPTER 26

The Slovo building and its inhabitants deserve some discussion. The idea of establishing a building cooperative of "our own" was the brainchild of a group of writers in Kharkiv at the end of the 1920s, and Serhii was the idea's prime mover. According to the plan, each shareholder was to make annual payments for his apartment for some fifteen years, after which it would become his private property. The plan was never realized, however, because most of those who developed it were arrested and imprisoned the 1930s and their families were exiled.

Construction of the building proceeded at the usual Soviet tempo: it took three years, from 1927 to 1930. When it was finally completed, Serhii and some other members of the founding group were given the opportunity to choose their apartments, and the other shareholders were asked to draw lots. The future residents had to choose whether to heat their apartment by coal or gas; the majority chose coal because they had heard stories of people being poisoned by gas. So coal was brought to the building and left in the basement for every resident to drag up the stairs to his apartment (there was no elevator). The charred remains of spent coal were taken out and dumped in the backyard. Over time they formed hills of considerable size, on which the residents' children loved to play.

The apartments were spacious and had a great deal of light. Each had a living room, a study, a kitchen, one or two bedrooms, a pantry, a bathroom, and a small balcony. The entire building, including the balconies, was made of reinforced concrete. The balconies had high parapets, which were not attractive but made the balconies quiet and safe and thus a good place for children to play. The balconies also served as coolers—ours was where we kept our milk, eggs, meat, and produce. After a while we noticed that our food was disappearing. Other residents on the first floor and second floors began noticing that their food was disappearing too. Who was stealing it and how? We soon had an answer to the mystery: the police called to tell us that they had caught the culprits—a gang of adolescents. When the residents were told they could attend the interrogation of these juvenile delinquents, we decided to go and hear what the culprits had to say.

The teenagers, who were homeless and dressed in rags, said the main impediment to their foraging for food was the fact that writers did not go to bed at a reasonable hour but sat at their desks writing until the wee hours of the morning. This meant that the thieves had to wait late into the night until, at last, all the lights were out. As for the second-floor balconies, the young people said that they had no difficulty reaching them—the drainage pipes along the walls facilitated that. In the end, as I remember, the punishment the judges meted out to them was not very harsh. These were the years immediately after the civil war and the famine of the 1920s, when orphans numbered in the thousands. They would wander about in packs or alone, foraging for food, begging, and stealing. Sometimes they acted in gangs: some would whistle and raise a commotion so that others could snatch women's purses. I developed the habit of wrapping the strap of my handbag around my hand several times and clutching it close to me whenever I walked down the street.

While the Slovo building was being constructed, the workers often stayed there overnight and brought food with them. The food attracted mice, rats, and bedbugs, which soon multiplied so much that it was impossible to get rid of them. We tried, though: we got a cat and placed traps throughout the apartment. Our cat was rather lazy and soon figured out there was no need to expend any energy hunting mice. Instead he would simply lie in the kitchen and listen. As soon as a trap snapped, he would run to one of us, meowing to announce that his dinner had been caught.

Our battle with mice and rats made a great impression on little Mirtala, who was then nearly four years old. We discovered this the day she surprised us by writing, in block letters, "KLADOVKA. KRYSY. KLADOVKA. MYSHI" (PANTRY. RATS. PANTRY. MICE). We never suspected she had learned the alphabet and could write, let alone write words in verse with alliteration, rhythm, and a semblance of rhyme. We should have known then and there that she would grow up to be a poet.

Mice figured in several of our family's recollections and life experiences. The first such incident happened many years earlier, at the end of the nineteenth century. The Kyiv Military Commissary was then home to millions of mice. The authorities had tried everything possible to get rid of the pests—poison, traps, cats—but to no avail. Then one day, just as in the old legend about the Pied Piper of Hamelin, there appeared a man who promised to get rid of the mice. He asked a handsome price for his services, and his sole other condition was that no one interfere with what he was doing, to which the authorities agreed. That evening the man visited all the storage rooms and pantries and inspected all the mouse holes; the following day, at dawn, he began playing a reed pipe. The unbelievable happened: mice started appearing from everywhere—in the hundreds and then thousands. They squealed, dashed about back and forth, and obediently followed the man, who walked toward the Dnipro while continuing to play his pipe. When the mice came to the river, they jumped into the water, and all of them drowned! This event was reported in the daily newspaper and was remembered by Kyiv's denizens long afterwards. The story was related to me by our "White" grandmother.

Another incident happened during the civil war, when Aliosha, Mother, Seriozha, Liza, and I were living in Bessarabia (Aliosha had gotten a job there). We had settled in an abandoned country house, where the mice reigned supreme. They lived off the books in the library, where their feast of choice was the leather-bound volumes. They were so much at home that they dashed through the rooms without any concern for us at all, and when we sat down to eat they brazenly ran across the table! One night, when there was a full moon, I witnessed an amazing sight: mice standing on their hind legs in a circle and squealing as they gazed up at the moon.

CHAPTER 27

Although I was a member of the Writers' Union, I did not participate in its literary debates, for they were of little interest to me. But I gladly accompanied Serhii to Pluh meetings, where, in a very amicable atmosphere, people read and discussed the new works of Pluh writers. Serhii was very diplomatic in his comments, for he understood that many of the young writers had to learn their craft from scratch. Ostap Vyshnia wrote a humorous sketch describing how new members were admitted to Pluh:

—Is there anyone else here today who writes? Here's someone. Greetings! Who are you?

—Me? I'm Semen Liubystok!

—Are you a writer?

—No!

—Perhaps you're a writer anyway. Are you writing anything at the moment?

—Why, yes. I just wrote a letter to my father asking him to send me money for postage stamps.

—There you are! And you said you're not a writer!

I also paid visits to the Blakytny Building, which was a meeting place for the writers, artists, and composers who comprised Kharkiv's Ukrainian intelligentsia. The gatherings there were always boisterous and lively: people drank, sang, and engaged in animated conversation. There Ostap Vyshnia reigned as master jester supreme. Whenever I entered the room, I immediately knew where he was, for invariably peals of laughter were reverberating from that direction. Elsewhere in the room there might be people reading from their latest literary work, drawing pictures, reciting poetry, or acting out scenes from a play. Yosyp Hirniak, the famous actor from the Berezil Theater,[77] was often

[77] The avant-garde Berezil (March) Theater association (1922–33) was the brainchild of its famous and influential artistic director, Les Kurbas (1887–1937). Based in Kyiv from 1922 and in Kharkiv from 1926, Berezil staged modern plays by European and Soviet Ukrainian playwrights, including those by its playwright in residence, Mykola Kulish (1892–1937). Berezil was closed down in 1933 after Kurbas and his ideas were condemned by the regime and he was dismissed as artistic director. Both he and Kulish were arrested—in December 1933 and December 1934, respectively—and killed on the same day, 3 November 1937, by the NKVD after years of imprisonment in the Solovets Islands prison complex. Many of Berezil's actors were also repressed, but not all of them perished, for instance, Yosyp Hirniak (1895–1989) survived and reached the U.S. after the Second World War.—*Eds.*

there—he excelled at impersonations. Once a Georgian poet came to the club and demonstrated his skill at playing glasses. Having filled several glasses with varying levels of wine, he tapped them lightly with a fork to determine the pitch. Then he played some sad and hauntingly beautiful Georgian melodies.

Among the Blakytny club's many regulars was the talented storyteller Antin Dyky.[78] Writers would listen spellbound as he related his civil-war experiences. He gave them permission to use episodes from these stories in their own writing. Everyone, including Dyky himself, thought he had no writing ability, but this proved to be untrue: in 1925, he began, and his works were subsequently published.

One of the rooms in the Blakytny building had a billiard table, and one day a humorous incident occurred there. Vladimir Mayakovsky had arrived in Kharkiv for a poetry reading. Scheduled to appear after him was the Ukrainian poet Ivan Kulyk. Kulyk's poetry was hardly on the same level as Mayakovsky's, and it must have taken some courage for him to appear together with the renowned poet. When Kulyk began reciting his verses, Mayakovsky went to one side and stood there, rocking back and forth on his heels, keeping his hands in his pockets. He made a point of looking down from his great height at Kulyk, who was not a tall man. Mayakovsky was well aware of what a comical scene he was creating. Someone in the audience began laughing, and soon everyone had joined in the hilarity. Poor Kulyk had to stop reciting and leave the stage. Soon enough, however, the tables were turned.

After the reading Mayakovsky was invited to meet with local writers at the Blakytny club. When he arrived, he spotted the billiard table and announced that he wanted to play. Mayakovsky was known to be an excellent player, so no one was in a hurry to take up the challenge. Confident of his skill and eager for an opponent, Mayakovsky urged someone to step forward, suggesting that whoever lost the match be obliged to crawl around under the billiard table on all fours. A poet who was a member of Pluh accepted the challenge. This time it became Mayakovsky's turn to be embarrassed—he lost the game and had to crawl around under the table as a roomful of people roared with laughter.

---

[78] Dyky (1900–54) was a member of Pluh. He was repressed during the Stalinist terror, but was not killed by the NKVD.—*Eds.*

I liked Mayakovsky's early work very much, as did my mother and Liza. Serhii, however, was more impressed with the poetic gifts of such Russian poets as Fedor Tiutchev. He also loved the works of the Ukrainian poets Tychyna, his contemporary, and Shevchenko. Serhii revered the great Taras and wrote many articles about him. He also wrote a biography of Shevchenko in verse for children. It began:

> There once was a boy by the name of Taras,
> Who watched over lambs while geese fed on grass.
> His family owned a small shack by the road,
> Merchants with salt rode by with their load.
> No tooting of engines was heard in those parts,
> Oxen and horses still pulled all their carts.

Our daughter Assya first learned of Shevchenko from this poem, and it played the same role in her life as my father's reading of the *Kobzar* did in mine.

Serhii made it a goal to collect as much material about the great poet as he could find. To accomplish this he traveled to the Aral Sea coast, where Shevchenko had lived while in exile. He was lucky enough to locate the descendants of the commandant, Uskov, whose home Shevchenko had frequented; Shevchenko had also painted portraits of the commandant's wife.[79] This family revered the memory of Shevchenko and had carefully preserved letters, drawings, and small items related to their acquaintance with him. They gladly donated these memorabilia to the museum that Serhii established and directed. Today the former holdings of this museum are part of the Shevchenko State Museum in Kyiv. When I visited that museum in the early 1970s, I saw a large portrait at the entrance—it was of Ellan-Blakytny! Very much taken aback, I asked the guide why his portrait was placed there. After all, Ellan-Blakytny had nothing to do with the museum, for its creator was Serhii Pylypenko. The woman nodded her head fervently in agreement and said, "But you know, today people have forgotten—nobody remembers that." And, I thought, someone was clearly making sure that people forgot. I wonder if that portrait still hangs in the museum today.

[79] As commandant of the Novopetrovsk fortress, Major Iraklii Uskov (1810–82) allowed Shevchenko to paint while the poet was exiled there (1853–57) and often invited him to his home. Shevchenko drew a portrait of Uskov and painted three of his wife Agafiia, including one with her daughter Nataliia.—*Eds.*

Other writers I got to know well in the 1920s were Mykola Bazhan, Petro Panch, Vasyl Mynko, and Yurii Smolych. I worked with Smolych for a time. During my trip to Kyiv in 1973—when I saw my sister for the first time in thirty years—I met with Smolych and we talked about the past. I reminded him of an episode in his life that he had totally forgotten. Once Serhii, Smolych, and I, together with a number of other writers, traveled to the Caucasus, to a place not far from the Soviet-Iranian border. We had wandered in the mountains the whole day, and that evening we sought some place to get something to eat. We found a small restaurant and were led out into its garden, where the three of us—Serhii, Smolych and I—sat down at a small table. We ordered bowls of soup, and when these were brought out we started eating. Suddenly a bird landed in Smolych's bowl. The hot liquid splattered all over the table, but Smolych, dexterous and quick as usual, managed to grab hold of the bird. Our waiter came running, calling out excitedly: "It's a bird of paradise! It's very rare for them to fly here across the mountains from Iran! Please, let me have it!" And he related the local inhabitants' belief that a bird of paradise brings good fortune. Smolych hesitated over the request—the bird was so beautiful and exotic that he wanted to keep it. But how would he take it with him? Moreover, the waiter's entreaties to give him the unexpected avian visitor were so heartfelt that Smolych relented and let the waiter have it. Afterwards he told all his friends and acquaintances about how luck had fallen right into his soup bowl and he had let it go. When I reminded him about this incident so many years later, Smolych greatly regretted that he had not remembered and had not included it in *Rozpovid pro nespokii* (A Tale of Disquiet).[80]

Natalia Zabila, the well-known author of children's books, was an acquaintance of mine. She came from an old noble family and took pride in speaking of it. Like many women in those days, she had many lovers and several husbands who fathered her children. Before moving into the Slovo building she had an affair with the writer Sava Bozhko, and they had a son named Taras. This boy grew to be a holy terror, and all the children in our building feared him, except for our Assya, whom he befriended and even took under his wing.

---

[80] The title of the first volume of Smolych's memoirs about Ukrainian literary life and writers in the 1920s and 1930s, published in Kyiv in 1968.

When a kindergarten was established in our building, we enrolled Assya, and Zabila enrolled her Taras. The boy was constantly flaunting the teachers' rules. For example, during the so-called quiet hour, when the children were supposed to be resting, he took to teaching Assya how to count to a thousand. After a while the teachers despaired of turning these two into model students, and they asked that Assya be removed from the class because she was "a socially underdeveloped child." Indeed, many of the writers' children would not conform to the pedagogical norms of the time, and teachers regularly left our building's kindergarten because they couldn't control the pupils.

After Assya was expelled from the kindergarten, we put her in a private school. The teacher's forewarning that her methodology was not based on the principle of "Arise, ye branded by damnation" (the opening line of the Russian version of the "Internationale") or "Lie down, ye branded by damnation" certainly raised no objection from me. Assya continued her schooling there, and at the age of nine she entered the third grade. As for Natalia Zabila's son Taras Bozhko, in 1985 I read in *Ukraina* that he was a Second World War hero.

To complete the series of portraits of Ukrainian authors I knew well, I offer two more—of the poets Valeriian Polishchuk and Volodymyr Sosiura. Valeriian was a friend from the old days at Kamianets-Podilskyi, and he and I had many things in common. We even resembled each other—we both had large greenish eyes—so people often mistook us for brother and sister. Our relationship was always platonic. In fact, after Serhii and I became involved with each other, neither of us had any other romantic interests. That was something so rare in those years and in that milieu that we were pointed to as a model couple: it became common to define some close and happy relationship by saying, "they live like the Pylypenkos." Polishchuk, in contrast, had an amorous nature that seemed incompatible with monogamy. At the time he was living in our apartment building, he was in love with two sisters simultaneously. The sisters were terribly jealous of each other and finally gave Valeriian an ultimatum—choose one and marry her. So he had to make a choice. The sister who became Valeriian's wife gave birth to a baby boy, who was named Marko. He was an exceptionally handsome child with huge, dark-blue eyes and long lashes, and passers-by would stop in the street to admire him. Marko became Assya's second good friend. When he reached the age of nine or so, in the mid-1930s, his father presented him with a dagger and said, "If they arrest me, use this to avenge me." Valeriian was

Serhii Pylypenko at a meeting of the Pluh writers' association. Left to right: Pylypenko, Anatol Hak, Andrii Paniv, Ivan Dniprovsky, Sava Bozhko, Vasyl Mysyk, Volodymyr Sosiura (Kharkiv, mid-1920s)

Anatol Hak and Serhii Pylypenko in a train compartment (late 1920s)

Valeriian Polishchuk and his son Marko (1926)

Volodymyr Sosiura (1923)

arrested,[81] but, of course, there was no way his young son Marko could avenge his father. Years later I learned that Valeriian's son perished at the front during the Second World War.

Volodymyr Sosiura was another handsome man whose love affairs were legion. He was always coming into our office and talking about his current love, each time assuring us that he had finally met the woman he was destined to marry. I recall his first meeting with Serhii very vividly. He stood unshaven and in a torn military coat, having come directly from the battlefield. He opened a backpack he was carrying and took out some rolled-up sheets of paper. "These are my poems," he said, handing them to Serhii. Serhii was accustomed to reading awkward first attempts at writing, so he did not expect anything exceptional. But as soon as he started reading Sosiura's poems he realized that this former soldier had real talent. Serhii was overjoyed at the discovery and complimented the fledgling writer. He took Sosiura under his wing and literally taught him the fundamentals of writing. Sosiura never forgot that Serhii had "made a person out of him," and he always expressed great gratitude, love, and respect for *Papasha*. Sosiura joined Pluh and quickly became not only a prominent peasant writer, but also a prominent Ukrainian poet of the 1920s in general. He was very popular among young Ukrainians; his lyricism and youthful sincerity appealed to many older readers as well.

In the early 1930s, a wave of arrests among the Ukrainian intelligentsia began. One writer and then another and another disappeared from our building. Late one evening, Sosiura knocked on our door. When we opened it, he held out a roll of papers clutched in his hand, just as he had the first time he and Serhii met. In a trembling voice he said, "Please hide these poems in your apartment. I am certain that I will be arrested, if not today then tomorrow, but you—they will not dare touch you, Serhii Volodymyrovych." Sosiura had served in the UNR Army, and he was sure he would be arrested. By an irony of fate, Serhii, a Communist by conviction who was completely devoted to the Party, was arrested a few days later, while Sosiura remained free and later even received awards.

In the memoirs that were part of his autobiographical novel *Tretia rota* (The Third Company), Sosiura recalled Serhii with fondness: "Serhii Volodymyrovych's face reminded me of ancient Ukrainian frescoes. I

[81] Polishchuk was arrested in December 1934 and executed on 9 December 1937 in the NKVD prison complex on the Solovets Islands.—*Eds.*

loved him very much and regarded him as my [second] father.... We [young writers] all affectionately called Pylypenko *Papasha* and shamelessly abused his kindness by plundering his cigarette case.... [We] were ready to give our lives for him" (p. 225).[82]

[82] The novel was first published only twenty-three years after Sosiura's death: in 1988, during the perestroika period.—*Eds.*

CHAPTER 28

The horrors of the 1930s were coming closer and closer. Toward the beginning of 1933, rumors of famine in the villages began circulating in Kharkiv. The newspapers carried no official confirmations of these rumors, nor was there any mention of them at Party meetings. But before long, starving peasants began appearing on the streets of Kharkiv. They came not in groups or whole families, but individually. Most often they were young mothers with infants; less frequently they were adolescents. There was one scene that I saw over and over again. A mother with a baby would enter the city and search out a busy street. Spreading a kerchief on the sidewalk, she would lay her child on it and walk away, peering from around a corner to see if anyone picked up her infant. Invariably, no one did. She would return, pick up the child herself, and walk to another street, where she would do the same again, in an effort to save her child from the fate that awaited it.

For about three months there were few people on the streets who were obviously suffering from hunger. Then their numbers increased, becoming a steady stream of starving people. Children and mothers died first. Special trucks patrolled the streets daily and picked up the dead. The bodies were transported outside the city limits and buried in mass graves. Those who were still breathing were taken to barracks at so-called *spetspunkty* (special centers), where they received neither food nor medical care but were simply left to die slowly of starvation. The city dwellers knew this, but for a long time the peasants did not—they thought that the authorities were sending the trucks to help them. Mothers themselves lifted their children into them and gratefully climbed in themselves, expecting to be fed. Slowly the peasants realized the horrible truth about the *spetspunkty.* Then, when a mother could not find her child on the street, she knew a truck had taken the child. All she could do was lament in anguish and grief.

Soon the peasants who got to the city were so feeble that they were barely able to put one foot in front of the other. I remember walking along a street one day and seeing a teenager being held up on either side by adults, probably his parents, who could barely walk themselves. From a distance I thought the boy was smiling. But as I drew closer I realized that it was not a smile but a horrible grimace—starvation had drawn the skin on the youngster's face so tight and in such a way that his teeth were bared. Another time, while leaving a theater one evening, we saw a group of children no older than five. They were curled up in a niche near the theater's entrance and slowly drifting off into death. After that, every time I left home I took along bread and other food to give to the starving children I encountered on my way. Soon, however, many of them became so feeble they no longer had the strength to eat.

Gradually city people also began feeling the consequences of the famine, as food began disappearing from the stores. As a Party member and noted writer, Serhii received food stamps and special coupons entitling the bearer to eat dinner in the dining hall of the Radnarkom (Council of People's Commissars) building. This was a cafeteria for the privileged to which common people had no access. The first time we went there we were told we could either eat on the premises or take the food home. The next day we arrived with bowls and pots. Filling them with food—soup, meat, vegetables—we went out into the street and gave the food to a crowd of hungry children. Since they had neither spoons nor forks, we sat down on the street beside them and fed them one by one, straight from the pot. A number of mothers were with the children and they helped us to feed them. Some of Serhii's coworkers who frequented the Radnarkom cafeteria saw what we were doing and followed our example, but they were few. I should add that in addition to coupons, we ourselves received special rations and did not go hungry. The same was true of all high-ranking Party officials.

In the summer of 1932, the Writers' Union of Ukraine organized a summer vacation for members and their families at a Black Sea resort near Skadovsk, not far from the city of Kherson. On the way there I saw brimming granaries guarded by armed military personnel—not from thieves, of course, but from starving peasants. There was evidence of a bountiful harvest that year: cart after grain-laden cart was making its way to the granaries. Had some foreign tourists found themselves traveling along this route, they would undoubtedly have concluded that they were visiting a land of plenty.

As we approached the sea, we saw an expanse of sandy soil dotted here and there by shrubs. There were no buildings in sight, and the whole locality looked rather desolate and sad. Suddenly we saw movement in the distance, near the mouth of the Dnipro. As we approached, we saw hundreds of peasants who had fled there to escape starvation. Whole families were living in dugouts along the riverbank. Here they could at least catch fish and stay alive. Summer was ending, and the peasants living there were worried about the crops in their native villages: who would harvest them this year? They sent representatives back to their villages to find out. These people came back with the report that the crop of grain and produce was bountiful, but because there was no one in the villages who could harvest it, the authorities were sending factory workers from the city to do the job.

The same bleak picture greeted us in Kharkiv upon our return at the end of summer. By then extending aid to "enemies of the people" was strictly forbidden. It would have been impossible to help everyone who needed help, in any case.

One day Serhii was walking in a market on the outskirts of town, not far from our home, when he spotted a young peasant woman and was struck by her strange appearance—she was barefoot and wearing a long embroidered shirt. Her walk was unsteady, and her eyes had a peculiar, vacant look. Serhii walked up to her and asked who she was and where she was going. In a barely audible voice she replied that everyone in her village had died and she had nowhere to go. Her wretchedness so moved Serhii that he asked her to come with him, and she did. When our cook took her into the kitchen and offered some food, the young woman burst into tears—she hadn't eaten in four days. After she had eaten a little, we saw to it that she was bathed and gave her some clothes. She stayed with us for six months, and then Serhii found her a job at a factory.

This was not the only time that Serhii saved people who were in danger of dying from hunger. Nearly every day he saw people who had come from the villages in search of help from relatives who were Pluh members. Serhii tried helping them any way he could, usually by finding some kind of work for them in the city.

As a member of the Party, Serhii had to take part in the collectivization drive and the dekulakization campaign. He traveled to various villages, where he witnessed the horrors that were taking place by order of the Party. Although he suffered deeply over what he saw, he continued defending the collectivization policy, on the grounds that it was the only way the village could progress. I did not agree with that point of view. I took the position that the use of violence is evil and unjust, and that the brutal and inhumane methods used to promote collectivization were the epitome of such evil. This was the major political issue over which Serhii and I disagreed and had heated disputes. He shared Lenin's view of the peasantry as a backward, conservative mass of people steeped in the psychology of private ownership, which prevented them from seeing the benefits that would accrue to them from the collective ownership of land. In his writing Serhii consistently propagandized the idea of the "commune." Thus, for example, in his fable "Rivnist'" (Equality), he describes the progressive impoverishment of a family in which the father divides the land among his sons, who in turn divide it among their own children, until they all become beggars. The solution, suggested Serhii, lay in collective work:

> Equality, I can tell,
> Is the Commune's goal as well,
> But rather than dividing,
> It gives us this advice:
> Work all together, brothers,
> And earth, our dear old mother,
> Will always be providing
> A hundredfold for us.

In his novel *The First Circle*, Aleksandr Solzhenitsyn portrays an idealist and Communist named Rubin whose prototype was Lev Kopelev.[83] Rubin travels through Ukrainian villages to enforce collectivization, believing in the correctness of the Party's stand on the issue. But when he lands in prison, Rubin begins wondering if those policies were not a horrible mistake. Finally he must admit to himself that the Party had deceived him, and that he had deceived himself.

Several years ago Kopelev came to Ann Arbor, where he met my daughter Assya. She asked him whether he had heard of Serhii Pylypenko. Kopelev, visibly moved, said that he had not only heard of him, but had known him during the years of collectivization. And, like Rubin in Solzhenitsyn's novel, Kopelev uttered words of contrition, bitterly regretting that a true understanding of what was happening then had come to him so late. Perhaps after his arrest Serhii, too, had second thoughts about the collectivization policy.

---

[83] Kopelev (1912–97) was born in Kyiv. He was active in the Jewish section of the Bolshevik Party in Ukraine in the 1920s and was a Party agitator during the collectivization drive there. He worked as a journalist and literary scholar in the 1930s and wrote poetry in both Russian and Ukrainian. A prisoner of conscience from 1945 on, he was incarcerated for over ten years in the Gulag, where he met Solzhenitsyn. After his release in 1955, Kopelev was active in the Soviet dissident and human-rights movements. He emigrated to West Germany in 1980 and died in Köln. His first volume of memoirs, *The Education of a True Believer* (1980), contains much information about life and politics in Soviet Ukraine in the 1920s and 1930s.—*Eds.*

In the 1930s the majority of Communists in Ukraine shared Serhii's views on collectivization—they justified and supported it. This was particularly true of the young members of the Communist Youth League, who served the Party devotedly, body and soul. But there were also those who, in their hearts of hearts, had no hostility toward the peasants and did not agree with the methods being used to impose collectivization. For the most part, however, they remained silent out of fear of being denounced to the authorities. Those who ventured to criticize the policy did so only within the confines of a small circle of friends. There were, of course, opportunists who were indifferent to the sufferings of others and ready to do anything to promote their own careers. But there were also the few who spoke out openly against the genocidal policy and paid for it with their lives. This brave group included Mykola Skrypnyk and Mykola Khvylovy.[84]

Khvylovy was sent to the countryside at his own request—he wanted to see for himself that the kulaks were hiding grain from the state. But when he arrived and saw that whole villages had been depopulated, he immediately telegraphed the following to the Central Committee: "The countryside is dying. Immediate assistance is necessary." In response he received an order to return to Kharkiv and explain his message. When he did so, he was told that everything was proceeding according to plan and the Party's directives. People "at the top" knew everything that was happening and there had been no mistake: confiscating all the grain was the only way to break peasant resistance to progress. Shortly thereafter Khvylovy committed suicide. Everyone who knew him said that it was what he saw in the

[84] Mykola Skrypnyk (1872–1933) was one of the old Bolshevik leaders and a senior government official in Soviet Ukraine. There he served as the people's commissar of internal affairs (1921–22), justice (1922–27), and education (1927–33). In the latter post he was a leading proponent of national-communism and the Soviet policy of Ukrainization. After his policies and theories were condemned and he was removed from that post, he committed suicide in protest against the Stalinist mass repression of the nationally conscious intelligentsia and the physical destruction of the peasantry in the famine-genocide of 1932–33. Mykola Khvylovy (1893–1933) was the most famous and influential writer and cultural figure of the Ukrainization period. He also committed suicide in protest against the Stalinist terror and the famine-genocide. See Ivan Koshelivets, "Khvylovy, Mykola" and "Skrypnyk, Mykola," in *Encyclopedia of Ukraine*, 2: 500–2, 4: 737–8; idem, *Mykola Skrypnyk* (Munich, 1972); James E. Mace, *Communism and the Dilemmas of National Liberation: National Communism in Soviet Ukraine, 1918–1933* (Cambridge, Mass., 1983), 120–60, 192–231, 264–301; and Mykola Khvylovy, *The Cultural Renaissance in Ukraine: Polemical Pamphlets, 1925–1926*, trans., with an intro., by Myroslav Shkandrij (Edmonton, 1986).—*Eds.*

villages that made him take his own life. Then, nearly two months later, Skrypnyk shot himself. These two suicides depressed Serhii greatly—especially that of Skrypnyk, whom he particularly admired and esteemed.

Serhii and I had long talks about where the Party's policies in Ukraine were leading. By this time Ukrainization was no longer part of the Communist Party's program. Serhii told me with bitterness how he had been shown secret instructions to the All-Ukrainian Academy of Sciences from Moscow. They unequivocally "recommended" that academicians do everything they could to make the Ukrainian language as similar to Russian as possible. All Ukrainian writers, playwrights, and scholars—in fact, every member of the intelligentsia who considered himself to be Ukrainian—began experiencing persecution and harassment. In the press a relentless campaign began against these "bourgeois nationalists," who were accused of every crime under the sun. The press included increasingly hostile references to Serhii, which did not bode well for the future.

CHAPTER 29

Arrests were sweeping Soviet Ukraine. People began to disappear from our building, taken away in "black ravens"—the black cars driven by the NKVD—during the night, never to return. We noticed that our building was under surveillance day and night. Everyone wondered if his or her turn would be next.[85]

Just at that time I found myself pregnant again. Serhii and I thought long and hard about what we should do. The future was so totally uncertain—who knew what awaited us? If Serhii were to be arrested and I was left alone with an infant, none of us would survive, neither the little one, nor I, nor our two small daughters. In the end we decided I had to have an abortion.

I went to the hospital with a heavy heart, and the abortion was performed. They said the baby was a boy—we would have had a son! Thoughts about this forced murder under duress haunted me for years to come. I kept thinking that our son might have resembled Serhii, that he might have grown up to be as intelligent and handsome as his father. Much later I pondered what his fate might have been during the Second World War—whether he would have been drafted and gone to the front, perhaps to be killed or to come back disabled. What bitter thoughts these all were.

Finally, in the winter of 1933, Serhii's turn came. The first step was his expulsion from the Party. That was followed by dismissal from all the positions he held.[86] Then one night, as expected, the NKVD knocked on our door. As soon as they entered our apartment, they began going through the drawers in Serhii's study, confiscating all his papers. Then they searched the other rooms. The search lasted an unbearably long time, but finally they had taken everything they wanted, including my father's gold sword. I stood on our balcony and watched as Serhii was led to the car, climbed in, and was taken away. I

---

[85] According to Volodymyr Kulish, thirty-four people living in the sixty-six apartments in our building were arrested.

[86] Hryhorii Kostiuk describes his reaction to the news that Serhii had been expelled from the Party and the danger he would be "expelled from life itself": "Somewhere in the depths of my soul I felt acutely that the attack on Pylypenko was an attack on me and the many others like me. This was a tragedy of the whole generation of the 1920s, which had grown up under the authoritative influence of Serhii Volodymyrovych Pylypenko" (*Zustrichi i proshchannia*, 1: 415).

still see that scene vividly, as if it happened yesterday. I remember how my heart contracted with pain—and my strong presentiment that this separation would last forever.

Long, painful days ensued. I was completely devastated. I moved about numbly, doing and saying things mechanically, with grief my constant, weighty companion. I could think of nothing but Serhii. What was happening to him? I knew he was being held in the new prison in Kharkiv, not the one where Vsevolod and I had once been confined. Finally I gathered up enough strength to go there and investigate.

I was granted a visit. My first meeting with Serhii was excruciatingly painful, as all the subsequent ones would be. A prosecutor was present at all times. He would intrude into our conversation to ask questions and transform our meeting into an interrogation. He made every effort to catch Serhii in some incriminating remark and to prove Serhii was lying. The prosecutor asked me where Serhii had traveled and whom he had met, and he compared my answers with Serhii's own testimony. He did this coarsely and mockingly. At the first meeting he cynically declared: "You realize, of course, that he will never leave here a free man." Subsequently the prosecutor never missed an opportunity to reiterate that there was not a shred of hope Serhii would ever be released.

One day I came to a meeting with Serhii accompanied by his mother. All that had happened weighed very heavily on her. The prosecutor said to her: "You realize that this Tatiana was the reason for your son's arrest. It was she who pulled him into counterrevolutionary activity." Fortunately Yivha Mykolaivna knew me well and did not believe this ugly lie.

Serhii would ask me about the children. During one of our meetings he passed along a gift to them—a little house with a removable roof he had made out of his prison ration of black bread. He looked drawn and thin, but he did not complain; under the prosecutor's scrutiny he couldn't very well have done so even if had he wanted to. But I noticed that his hands trembled and that he was trying to keep them still.

Serhii came to one of our meetings without his glasses. It was strange to see him without them. He was very nearsighted and had worn glasses since childhood—without them he could barely see two steps ahead of him. And now suddenly he had no glasses. Alarmed, I asked him where his glasses were. Looking at me strangely, he replied: "Yes, I have no glasses now. I no longer need them." His reply frightened me so much that I did not dare ask any other question.

The last photo of Tatiana and Serhii Pylypenko (winter 1933)

Another exchange of this sort with Serhii makes me shudder even now. One day I brought him a package with some underclothes and soap. As he took it, Serhii held out a rolled-up towel and said, "Please wash this." Taking the towel, I noticed with surprise that the towel was not one of his and that a piece was missing, as if someone had ripped it out with his teeth. When I asked Serhii about it, he became morose and said, "Don't ever ask me about that." These words were so terrifying that I felt chilled to the bone. For a long time afterward I imagined horrible things of every kind. After all, I had heard about people being beaten and tortured in prison. I kept wondering what the secret was—what had happened that was so awful it could not even be asked about.

Immediately after Serhii's arrest I was fired from my job. All the books I had been translating were taken away from me, and I did not receive payment for the translations I had already completed. I tried to find another job, but as soon as people learned I was Serhii's wife, each of my applications was turned down. If they saw me approaching on the street, many of our friends would cross to the other side out of fear of being seen with me. At other times I would be walking down a street and hear someone's quick steps as he or she caught up with me from behind. "Please do not turn around," the person would say softly. "I'm so-and-so. I want to know what's happening with Serhii Volodymyrovych. I'll pass you in a second and walk ahead of you. Then please tell me." The person would pass and walk ahead of me, and in a low voice I would tell him or her whatever I knew.

CHAPTER 30

Several months passed. In May of 1934, I and the wives of other writers who had lived in the Slovo building and had been arrested received notice that we and our children were being resettled outside Soviet Ukraine, and that we had been stripped of any right to return. We were given three days to vacate our apartments. Furthermore, we were ordered to surrender our internal passports to the police immediately. This was a death sentence, for in the Soviet state it was impossible to get a job or a residence permit without a passport. We were thunderstruck, but what could we do? We took our passports to the police station and then came back to the Slovo building to decide what to do next. The first to speak up was the wife of Andrii Richytsky, a former UPSR member who had held an important position in the Communist Party—as a member of the Central Committee, I believe. He had been arrested and was sentenced to be shot, but every day Mrs. Richytska came to the prison and received a note from her husband that read, "I'm still alive." Now, as we wives contemplated what to do next, she voiced an idea: we should turn for help to the famous Russian writer Maxim Gorky. Everybody knew that Gorky had been a defender of imprisoned people, and surely the case of writers who had been arrested would be of concern to him. When all of us expressed support for the idea, Mrs. Richytska told us that she had already composed a letter to Gorky and proceeded to read it. But no one liked the letter's tone: it enumerated all the rights that had been stripped from us, but read like a stiff business letter. Then I volunteered to write a different letter, and everyone agreed to the plan. I went home and sat down to write. I wrote in a kind of frenzy, all the while raging with indignation at the unjust treatment we had received. My letter was strongly worded and very emotive in tone. When I read it aloud to the women, they all approved of it. But only five or six of them, including Mrs. Richytska, had the courage to sign it. Now we were faced with how to get the letter to Gorky—after all, we had to leave Ukraine in just three days. I volunteered to be the one to take the letter to him, and that same day I left for Moscow by train.

In Moscow I went straight from the railroad station to the two-story house where Gorky lived. I rang the doorbell; a servant opened the door and allowed me to enter. When I said I wished to see Aleksei Maksimovich, [87] I was told he wasn't seeing anyone but I could state my business to a secretary. One of Gorky's secretaries entered and I gave him the letter, explaining who I was and why I had come. He shook his head: "I don't have the right to take your letter. It has been a long time since my employer has accepted petitions involving imprisoned people. Aleksei Maksimovich has left strict instructions not to take letters with such pleas from anyone." "But this is an exception!" I said. "We're talking about the families of many writers, composers, and painters. Perhaps Aleksei Maksimovich will agree to help in some way." The secretary shrugged his shoulders and allowed me to leave the letter, saying he would show it to Gorky. I asked if I could return the next morning, for I had only two days to accomplish my mission. The secretary agreed. When I returned the next day, I was surprised at how the secretary's behavior towards me had changed—he smiled in a friendly manner and gave every sign of being sympathetic. "Fortune has smiled on you," he said. "Your letter made a great impression on Aleksei Maksimovich, and he decided to write a letter to Vyshinsky in this matter.[88] He asks only one thing: can you swear that everything you have written in your letter is absolutely true and that nothing has been added or changed?" I replied that I could, and indeed swore to it. The secretary then stamped the envelope he was holding with several seals and handed it to me, saying: "Here you are. Take this letter straight to the prosecutor's building. Comrade Vyshinsky will receive you."

I went directly to the prosecutor's building, on Pokrovka Street. It was encircled by a cast-iron fence. At the entrance were sentries sitting in booths, and guards patrolled the perimeter. As I approached the gate, a woman came up to me and said, "I see you're going to the prosecutor's office. May I go with you? I've come from Ukraine. My husband has been unjustly arrested and I've come to see Vyshinsky on my husband's behalf."

I thought that it might be a good thing if this woman accompanied me—if I were arrested, she could inform my family. I went up to

---

[87] Gorky's real name was Aleksei Maksimovich Peshkov.—*Eds.*

[88] Andrei Vyshinsky (1883–1954) was the principal prosecutor in major Soviet show trials from 1928 on. He was appointed chief prosecutor of the Russian SFSR (1931), deputy chief prosecutor (1933) and chief prosecutor (1935) of the USSR, deputy commissar and later minister (1949) and deputy minister (1953) of foreign affairs, and was also a permanent Soviet representative at the United Nations.—*Eds.*

the guard and said, "I need to see Comrade Vyshinsky." The guard retorted, "He's not in today." Then I took out my letter: "I have a letter here for Comrade Vyshinsky from Maxim Gorky." The guard took the letter, turned it over in his hands, phoned someone, and finally handed it back to me, saying, "All right, you may enter."

Both of us walked in, for the guard thought that we had come together. We were stopped four times and questioned where we were going, and each time we were told that Vyshinsky was not in. And every time Gorky's letter magically opened doors. Finally we arrived at the office of the deputy chief prosecutor of the USSR. The secretary there greeted us very coldly, but she took the letter and asked us to wait. She quickly returned and pointed to another door. "Go in there. Comrade Vyshinsky will see you immediately." We found ourselves in a huge hall. A very long table, draped in red material and covered with telephones, stood on the right. This table was obviously used for meetings: it could seat a hundred people or more.

Vyshinsky was standing in front of another long table at the back of the room. As I walked toward him across the entire length of that enormous hall, I felt his heavy gaze upon me the whole time. As I drew closer, I could see he was holding my letter to Gorky in his hands. "Was it you who wrote this letter?" he inquired sternly. "Yes," I replied. "Can you swear that everything you say in it is true? That all the names and all the events are indeed true?" And again I had to swear to the truth of the statements I had made in that letter. How odd, when I think about it now, that both these Soviet dignitaries demanded an oath from me, and that both of them accepted my "word of honor" without any further questions. Certainly Vyshinsky seemed satisfied by my "oath," for he declared, "Then return to Kharkiv. Go to the police there, and they will return all of your passports. I will call them from here. After that you must leave Ukraine. You may settle wherever you wish—except in Moscow and Leningrad, of course." He said all this in a very proper, even cordial, manner. I thanked him and turned to leave, when suddenly I heard the voice of the woman who had come with me and about whom I had completely forgotten.

"Comrade Vyshinsky," she said, "I have a private matter to discuss with you." Vyshinsky immediately scowled: "A private matter?" In the Soviet Union only public or collective matters were considered worthy of attention—private matters were of no concern to anyone, and it was obvious that this woman's declaration had irritated Vyshinsky. "What matter do you have to discuss?" he demanded.

"There is a feud of long standing between my husband"—she gave his name—"and Comrade Krainii, the prosecutor of the Ukrainian republic. Now that he holds such a high position, Comrade Krainii wants to harm my husband and has had him arrested." On hearing this, Vyshinsky turned pale with anger and, articulating every syllable as he simultaneously pounded the table with the side of his hand, he said: "I know that many lives have been ruined by my actions. But that does not give anyone the right to say that I did what I did in my own interest, and I can say the same for Prosecutor Krainii. Get out!"

As we left the hall, I was certain the woman with me had ruined everything by angering Vyshinsky. We were barely out the door when I turned and upbraided her: "How dare you say such things! Don't you realize you've ruined everything for me? You got to see Vyshinsky thanks to me, and now look what you've done! Caused total disaster!" The woman apologized, saying she did what she did because that was the only way she could explain to Vyshinsky why her husband had been arrested. But I was livid and barely listening. Suddenly from behind the door we heard Vyshinsky's booming voice. He was ordering the secretary to get Krainii on the phone. We froze and continued listening, giving no thought to the possibility that someone might catch us eavesdropping, even though that would have meant the end of us. Vyshinsky was shouting at Krainii over the phone: "What mess have you created!? Do you know that Pylypenko's wife just came to see me? She wrote to Gorky, and I received a very stern letter from him. He's demanding you reverse your orders immediately! It's illegal! Give them back their passports immediately! Do you hear?!" At that point I stopped listening and ran down the corridor, down the stairs, and out into the street. Only then did I pause to catch my breath. Then I went to the central post office on Gorky Street to call my mother. By that time my fellow supplicant had disappeared.

I entered one of the booths for out-of-town calls and dialed our number in Kharkiv. When Mother answered, I told her that I had just given Gorky's letter to Vyshinsky and that Vyshinsky had ordered Krainii to return all our passports. I asked Mother to tell the other women to go to the police for their passports at once, because tomorrow was the day we were all obliged to leave Kharkiv. I told her I was on my way to the railroad station and would be home very soon.

I hung up and left the booth. It had seemed to be soundproof, so I thought I could speak freely. But as I made my way through the post office, I suddenly heard a voice: "Citizen! Was that you who called Kharkiv just now?" When I turned around to see who was speaking, I was facing a man in civilian clothes. "Who were you talking to?" he demanded, as if he had the right to question me. Sensing who I was dealing with and struggling to maintain my composure, I replied, "I was speaking with my mother." "Then why did you mention such important people as Comrades Gorky and Vyshinsky? What was that about?" he persisted. "You obviously heard everything I said," I retorted. "I went to see Comrade Gorky, and he gave me a letter to take to Comrade Vyshinsky. That's all." To my surprise the man said, "All right, you can go." As I walked away, my heart sank deeper and deeper with every step, for I was sure I was going to be seized at any moment. As I walked through the post office, as I made my way to the railway station, and even after I boarded the train for Kharkiv, I expected to be stopped and arrested. But nothing happened, and I arrived back in Ukraine.

CHAPTER 31

As soon as I got home, Mother told me that there had been a number of calls for me from Prosecutor Krainii's office, instructing me to appear before him as soon as I arrived. But in the wake of all I had been through, I physically collapsed. My nerves were shattered, and I had developed a high fever. I was in no condition to go to the prosecutor's office even if I had wanted to. The next day a messenger came from Krainii's office. Mother told him I was ill and could not leave my bed, and he left. Mother started selling off whatever household items we still had, and I helped as much as I could. We sold everything for practically nothing—for example, a sofa that cost at least twenty-five rubles went for one ruble. There was nothing else we could do. Buyers descended on our home like vultures. An acquaintance dropped by and exclaimed, "They should be ashamed! They are giving you kopecks for these things." Then she turned to me and said, "Don't sell this sugar bowl to anyone else. Tell me the highest price you're offered and I'll meet it."

I was sick for two days. On the third day a military man came and said, "Since you are so sick that you can't walk, a car has been sent for you. You must come to see Prosecutor Krainii immediately." I had no choice but to heed the order, especially since Mother and I had already managed to sell off most of our belongings. I went to Krainii's office. It was furnished in much the same way as Vyshinsky's—a long hall, with a desk at the very end. I suppose the rooms of prosecutors were furnished that way intentionally, to force visitors to walk a long way before reaching the prosecutor, making them lose confidence with every step.

Krainii was sitting behind his desk. His pale, tubercular face was camouflaged by a sardonic smile: "Do you believe I am returning the passports because you went to see Comrades Gorky and Vyshinsky? I want you to know that had no significance at all. I am doing this of my own free will." I remained silent. After all, how could I admit I had overheard Vyshinsky yelling at him? I asked where I could get my passport, because when I had gone to the police they had refused to give it to me. "Yes, they refused, on my orders," replied Krainii. "I decided to return your passport personally," and with these words he handed me my passport. "You may go. But remember: when you find a place to live, you must write and give me your address so that

I can inform you about your husband's sentence." I took the passport and left.

We left Kharkiv the following day. Mother and the children went to Aliosha's in Kyiv, while I, on the advice of friends, went to Kalinin to look for a place for us to live. "Kalinin is a rather large industrial town," my friends had said. "The old Morozov textile factories, a train factory, and a good teacher's college—the best one in tsarist times—are located there. You'll easily find a factory job, and in time your daughters will be able to attend the college." But I had my own reasons for moving to Kalinin: the city was located between Moscow and Leningrad, and when my girls grew up they could attend the university of one city or the other. And, generally, the idea of being within easy reach of the Soviet capital was attractive.

When I arrived in Kalinin, I promptly found lodgings with a worker's family. I didn't really have a room, but a corner in one separated from the rest of the dwelling by a curtain. I went to the police to register my place of residence. A short time later I found other lodgings, this time not in the factory district but closer to the center, and again I registered with the police. Finally I moved yet again and registered a third time. These three moves took place in the course of two or three months. In April I decided not to wait until I found a permanent residence to write to Krainii, and I asked him to send me news of my husband's sentence to a post-office box. May and June went by, and finally in July I got a letter from Krainii's secretary. It informed me that I would have to report to the local prosecutor to find out what sentence Serhii had received. When I went to the Kalinin prosecutor's building, I was met by screams of "Why haven't you registered with the police?!" I became angry: "What do you mean? I moved three times, and each time I registered. You can check for yourself."

It turned out that someone in Krainii's office in Kharkiv had reprimanded the officials in Kalinin for failing to keep track of me and my place of residence and for not informing Krainii of my whereabouts. Naturally Kalinin's prosecutor and the police were angry with me for being the unwitting cause of this unpleasantness. I listened to all this without another word, and then I asked to be told my husband's sentence.

The prosecutor shuffled papers until he finally pulled out a sheet and started reading it aloud: "Sentenced to execution by firing squad. The sentence has been carried out." All I was able to say was,

"When?" He replied: "It doesn't say." Then I knew something was wrong. The authorities always gave the date when a sentence was carried out. It was clear to me that this was a lie and that it was Krainii's doing.[89] I knew of several cases where relatives had been told that their loved one who had been arrested had been executed and the sentence had been carried out, but no date was specified: later it turned out this was not true, and the person had not been executed but sent to a concentration camp.

I decided to go to Moscow to appeal for help to a committee headed by Ekaterina Peshkova, Gorky's wife, that provided aid to political prisoners. Its numerous lawyers worked on cases of people who had been arrested but about whom no other information was available. I gave the committee the information I had received from Krainii's office about Serhii's sentence, and it began investigating. After a time I was told the committee was unable to get any other information. "There's something strange in your husband's case," I was told. "When we called Kharkiv, they confirmed your husband had been shot, but still it's not entirely certain. It's not the usual state of affairs."

I returned to Kalinin. There, in the autumn when school started, I found a job as a typist at the teacher's college and my mother brought my daughters to Kalinin. Long, difficult, and joyless days went by, one bleak day after another. My heart was desolate. At times I was at the point of committing suicide, and if it hadn't been for the children, perhaps I would have. But the girls were totally dependent on me now, and I resolved to devote my life to them.

A year passed, and one day I unexpectedly received a letter from Serhii's sister Liudmyla. She wrote very excitedly that there was word Serhii had not been executed and was still alive. During a train trip from Poltava to Kyiv, one of Serhii's brothers, Yurii, had struck up a conversation with a fellow traveler when they were alone in their compartment and could speak freely. The other man turned out to be a member of the State Banduryst Kapelle. He told Yurii his ensemble was returning from an unusual tour—it had performed concerts beyond the Arctic Circle in special small camps holding twenty to thirty prisoners. The families of these prisoners had been told that they had been executed, but they were still alive and were living in

[89] Krainii (1889–1943), who had worked for the Cheka from 1917 to 1921 and been a GPU and NKVD prosecutor since 1923, later fell into disfavor. He was arrested in August 1937 and imprisoned in a concentration camp in Kazakhstan.—*Eds.*

complete isolation. Yurii asked the banduryst if he had seen the writer Serhii Pylypenko. The man became excited. "*Papasha*? Of course I saw him. I remember him well from Kharkiv. When we used to come and sing at Ostap Vyshnia's place, Serhii Volodymyrovych would join in, singing in his pleasant baritone. Yes, I saw him there."

When I read Liudmyla's letter, I was beside myself—could it be true that Serhii was still alive? Again I got the wild idea of saving him somehow. I traveled to Moscow and turned to Peshkova's committee for help once again. But what could I tell them? I dared not repeat what the banduryst had said—no one would believe me, and besides, anything I said would put him in danger. Moreover, I was not completely sure the information was true. So I only asked the committee to inquire again if there was any news about Serhii. It checked again, called Kharkiv, and received the same reply—"Executed without a trial." After that, I was convinced there was nothing else I could do. As I returned to Kalinin, the words of a Russian song I had once heard kept ringing in my head:

> It's so simple and so plain
> And it has been shown—
> You can't bring back again
> What is lost and gone.

EPILOGUE

Serhii was posthumously rehabilitated in 1957. Soviet newspaper accounts said he had died in 1941 or 1943.[90] One even said he died in 1951. Are the official communiques to be believed? Whatever the answer, the name of the "unforgettable" Serhii Pylypenko was mentioned again in Soviet Ukrainian publications from time to time, and several commemorative events were held to honor his memory. Also, as I have already mentioned, a small collection of his fables and stories was published in 1963.[91]

Our daughter Mirtala, a sculptor and a poet, created a bronze bust of Serhii. In 1970, for an evening in Serhii's honor held in Writers' Union building in Kyiv, I had the sculpture brought there. It was put in a place of honor among likenesses of his old friends. I left the bust with the Writers' Union as a gift, and it remained there for twenty years. Today it stands in the Museum of Literature[92] in Kyiv, in a room dedicated to Pluh and its members.[93]

In 1992, a year after Ukraine gained independence, a small but to me priceless book of reminiscences of Serhii by his relatives, friends, and colleagues was published in Kyiv.[94] My memoirs were published in Ukraine that same year.[95]

---

[90] Soviet encyclopedias and literary reference books published in the 1960s, 1970s, and 1980s state Pylypenko died on 3 March or 11 July 1943, but do not state where and do not mention his imprisonment.—*Eds.*

[91] We now know that after Pylypenko was arrested on 29 November 1933, Soviet state security (the OGPU) accused him of belonging to "a Ukrainian counterrevolutionary organization—the Ukrainian Military Organization national bloc, which aspired to overthrow Soviet rule in Ukraine by means of an armed uprising," and of "personally head[ing] a terrorist triumvirate that organized an attempt to assassinate the head of the Council of People's Commissars of the Ukrainian SSR, Comrade [Vlas] Chubar." On 11 December 1933, Pylypenko "admitted" his guilt to his interrogators, and on 3 March 1934 the OGPU Collegium in Ukraine ordered his execution. Nonetheless, researchers have been unable to find a document stating when Pylypenko died. See O. Mukomela and M. Savka, "Pylypenko, Serhii Volodymyrovych," in *Ukrainska zhurnalistyka v imenakh: Materialy do entsyklopedychnoho slovnyka*, vol. [*vypusk*] 4, ed. M. M. Romaniuk (Lviv, 1997), 216. It may be assumed that the OGPU murdered Pylypenko on or soon after 3 March 1934.—*Eds.*

[92] The museum opened in 1986.—*Eds.*

[93] A small memorial museum dedicated to Pylypenko was opened in 1996 at the Kharkiv State Academy of Municipal Administration. It sponsors an annual program in Serhii's honor and publishes the miscellany *Pylypenkivskyi zoshyt* (The Pylypenko Notebook).—*Eds.*

[94] *Pro Serhiia Pylypenka: Spohady suchasnykiv*, comp., with an afterword, by O. H. Mukomela, ed. O. H. Musiienko (Kyiv, 1992).

[95] *Nevidstupne mynule* (Kyiv and New York, 1992), the original, Ukrainian version of *The Ever-Present Past*.

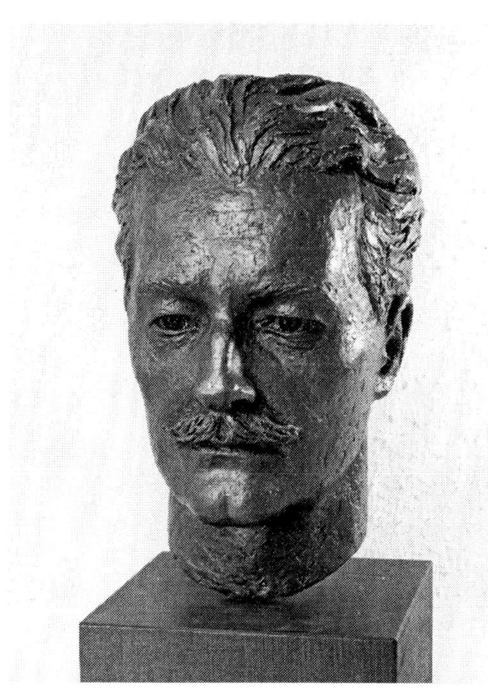

Bust of Serhii Pylypenko by his daughter Mirtala

Bust of Tatiana Kardinalowska by her daughter Mirtala

One of Mirtala's earliest Ukrainian poems was dedicated to Serhii. It also speaks for me:

For My Father

Let my voice pierce
through time, land, and sea—
I bring you my remembrance,
my love, my anguish, my sorrow.

You left
not having spoken
to the end.
You were cut off
in mid-word.
Your life
was pushed
down a steep precipice,
as though
it were not needed.

In the indifferent Siberian snow
you came to rest, by fate forgotten.
But I keep you alive
in my sorrow,
which tears have not washed away.[96]

---

[96] The Ukrainian version of this poem was published in Mirtala Kardynalovska [Bentov], *Raiduzhnyi mist* (New York, 1976), 25.

INDEX

Николай В. Кононов

Код Дурова

Издательство «Манн, Иванов и Фербер»

Николай В. Кононов

Код Дурова

Реальная история «ВКонтакте» и ее создателя

Издательство «Манн, Иванов и Фербер»
Москва, 2013

УДК 316.472.4
ББК 60.54:65.292.9
К64

Кононов, Н. В.

К64 Код Дурова. Реальная история «ВКонтакте» и ее создателя / Николай В. Кононов — М. : Манн, Иванов, Фербер, 2013. — 208 с.

ISBN 978-5-91657-546-0

Серо-голубой логотип «ВКонтакте» мелькает на всех мониторах страны. Чем так притягательна виртуальная реальность соцсети для десятков миллионов россиян от 12 и старше? Кто придумал эту игрушку и куда этот человек ведет свою необычную компанию?

Павел Дуров почти не общается с журналистами, но автору этой книги удалось проникнуть внутрь «ВКонтакте». Получилось не просто журналистское расследование, а авантюрная история, исследующая феномен сетевого предпринимателя-харизматика и его детища — а заодно и вполне материальное выражение популярности бизнеса соцсети.

УДК 316.472.4
ББК 60.54:65.292.9

ISBN 978-5-91657-546-0

Оглавление

Предисловие

С этой книжкой нам очень повезло.

Нынешняя Россия — это страна потерянных сюжетов: истории шекспировского накала и гомеровского размаха буквально-таки валяются под ногами, да некому подобрать. На наших глазах рушатся империи, люди без имени и, в общем, без судьбы становятся хозяевами вселенной, чтобы тут же быть повергнутыми в грязь, из ничего создаются многомиллиардные состояния, а иногда и целые миры — и вся эта космическая свистопляска остается совершенно не описанной, не зафиксированной, не отливается не то что в граните — а даже в книжках в мягкой обложке. На то существует множество причин: архивы засекречены, пиарщики путают следы, или же, как принято сейчас говорить, «реальность настолько неустойчива и неоформленна, что ускользает от любого описания» (что, по-моему, совсем уже гнилая отмазка). Но факт остается фактом: когда будущим ученым потребуются источники по истории России раннего постсоветского периода, им практически не из чего будет составить библиографию — придется ограничиться подшивками «Коммерсанта» и «Ведомостей» да архивами соцсетей на калифорнийских серверах.

Редкое наше везение в том, что одна из происходивших рядом с нами удивительных человеческих историй превратилась в книжку, которую вам сейчас предстоит прочитать. Притом что история эта до сих пор не была внятно отражена даже на коммерсантовских страницах. Да и сервера, которые в ней фигурируют, прописаны вовсе не в Кремниевой долине.

Мир, о котором рассказывает книга Николая Кононова, — он вроде как есть, но, с другой стороны, его как бы и нет. Если у вас есть родственники или знакомые младше двадцати, вы наверняка замечали, что в их браузере постоянно мелькает сине-голубой логотип «ВКонтакте», и то, что происходит на страницах с этим лого, почему-то кажется им более важным и осмысленным, чем так называемая реальная жизнь (если вы сами являетесь тем родственником и знакомым младше двадцати лет, то извините, что здесь приходится объяснять такие очевидные вещи, а также не очень понятно, как вы нашли в себе силы оторваться от «ВКонтакте» и взяться за книгу).

Само пространство, маркированное сине-голубым логотипом, руками не потрогать, словами не назвать — и приклеиваемые к нему ярлыки «заповедник школоты» или «клон фейсбука» никак не объясняют этого феномена, а лишь позволяют от него временно отделаться. История вопроса, масштабы происходящего и список ответственных лиц при этом остаются совершенно не ясны — а меж тем существует смутное подозрение, что этот логотип мелькает перед глазами неспроста, а мир, в котором мы живем, будет все больше переползать в сторону «ВКонтакте» просто в силу поколенческих закономерностей.

К тому же существует (и будоражит воображение) сама фигура основателя «ВКонтакте», который в двадцать с небольшим заработал миллионы долларов (которые ему, кажется, не очень нужны) и затащил в свои сети миллионы пользователей (с которыми он делает что хочет). И, как писали раньше в журнале «Афиша», — что с этим делать, решительно непонятно.

Велико искушение на основании всего вышеизложенного объявить Павла Дурова выразителем духа времени и представителем мира будущего — править которым будут полчища мини-Дуровых, зарабатывающих миллиарды, не отрываясь от экрана ноутбука. Но «цифровая элита» потому и является элитой, что попасть в нее могут единицы — для этого требуется смелость, наглость, тонкое чутье и мгновенная реакция, большинству, по определению, недоступные.

Для этого нужно мыслить глобально, действовать локально, уметь угадывать, что нужно людям, гораздо раньше, чем люди сами могут это сформулировать, не думать о миллиардах и иногда отрываться от ноутбука. Поэтому вряд ли стоит читать книгу Кононова как портрет Героя Нашего Времени или описание того, Как Все В Мире Будет Устроено, — в фигуре Дурова слишком много исключительного, не сказать, эксцентрического, чтобы делать из его истории Далекоидущие Выводы.

Возможно, правильнее было бы подойти к этому тексту как к авантюрному роману, серии удивительных приключений и сказочных перевоплощений — развязка которых, кажется, далеко не очевидна. Кажется, один из важных мотивов для Дурова — стремление сделать все назло и поперек системе, в которую его пытаются встроить, разломать рамки, в которые его стараются загнать, обмануть ожидания относительно логики собственного поведения. Это тот случай, когда ничему удивительному в его судьбе не стоит удивляться. Возможно, через несколько лет он скроется в нейтральных водах на бронированной яхте в компании какой-нибудь Леди Гаги, или купит контрольный пакет акций «Газпрома», или уединится в мансарде на Невском, чтобы рисовать собак. Герой этой книги не борется за свободу — а утверждает ее самим фактом своего существования.

В любом случае, это открывает и перед автором, и перед читателями блистательную перспективу: в том смысле, что продолжение следует.

Юрий Сапрыкин, публицист, шеф-редактор «Рамблер-Афиша»

Пролог

Поток бурлил, завивался и крутил водовороты из прохожих и зевак, глазеющих на собор и площадь перед ним. По проспекту фланировали студенты, назначившие группе встречу и теперь искавшие своих. Азиаты в водонепроницаемых пончо фотографировали особняк на углу канала.

Человеческий трафик рождал шум, который смешивался с гудками и призывами на экскурсию по городу. Течения сгущались у дома с кованым панно, называвшим первого владельца — Zinger. Медные девы-валькирии с копьями охраняли его купол, увенчанный прозрачным земным шаром.

На шестом этаже у окна в полный рост стоял человек в очках и, щурясь от света, высматривал что-то в потоке. Время от времени он приглаживал стриженые волосы и слушал голоса, звучавшие за его спиной. Шел третий час переговоров.

За столом восседал мужчина средних лет — очки, улыбка, акцент иностранца, который давно живет в России и говорит вполне бегло. Его компания слыла сильнейшим интернет-торговцем страны. Директору-экспату требовалось навязать программистам, создавшим самую крупную соцсеть в России, свои условия торговли на их территории. Захватить пространство, где ежедневно толчется 20 миллионов человек, мечтает каждый, поэтому иностранец старался нравиться.

Напротив него сидели двое. Белобрысый парень с ноутбуком и айфоном (представился главным разработчиком) и невзрачный тип в бейсболке. Каждому на взгляд — не более двадцати пяти лет. Программист отрешенно стучал по клавиатуре, а тип как в рот воды набрал, поэтому менеджер обращался к человеку у окна. Тот прославился в качестве attack dog, жесткого переговорщика, но сегодня вел себя тихо. Это немного сбивало с толку, ну что ж, бывает.

Переговорщик отвернулся от окна и спросил: «Так что, вы продолжаете настаивать, что с разных категорий товара заплатите нам разный процент?» Экспат закивал; он неоднократно обосновывал свою позицию — каждый товар имеет оборачиваемость, популярность — короче, это бизнес, ничего личного.

«Послушайте, — вздохнул переговорщик. — Мы внедряем этот сервис, „Желания", чтобы миллионы пользователей могли дарить друзьям товары. Мы выбрали вас и даем вам кнопку, которая в один клик позволяет приобрести подарок за нашу валюту. Эта кнопка приведет к вам миллионы покупателей».

Ерзая в кресле, экспат повторил свои аргументы. Он давно и железобетонно уяснил: всему есть цена, и благородные устремления существуют, чтобы набить цену. Парни просто торгуются.

«Хорошо, — произнес он. — Уважая цели вашей компании, я готов на 5 процентов по мягким игрушкам». Программист покрутил головой и продолжил стучать по клавиатуре. Переговорщик вернулся к столу, откинулся, развел руками: «Мы настаиваем — 10 процентов».

«Понимаю, — твердо сказал менеджер. — Но такая комиссия для нас неприемлема».

«Тогда 20 процентов! — неожиданно заорал тип в бейсболке. — 20 процентов! Или мы подписываем контракт немедленно, или мы не работаем с вашей компанией!» Он вскочил, сунул руки в карманы черных брюк и зашагал, чуть скособочившись и наклонившись вперед, вдоль стола. Иностранца предупреждали об эксцентричности этого деятеля, но не до такой же степени, мы здесь все приличные люди.

«Черт возьми, я думал, что мы работаем с инновационной компанией, а вы торгуетесь, как на базаре, — чеканил тип. — Мы создаем новое, совершенное средство коммуникации, а вы… что вы тут вообще устраиваете?!»

Иностранец лихорадочно соображал, как себя вести: исполнитель роли attack dog сидел совсем не там, где он предполагал, и напал неожиданно. Ему говорили, что «плохого следователя» играет стриженый очкарик, а этот, якобы гениальный программист, всегда вежлив. Хотя чего думать, надо успокаивать чертова неврастеника, пока не сбежал.

«Подождите, Павел, — экспат примиряюще развел руками. — Я прекрасно вас понимаю и ценю ваш продукт, вы работаете на переднем крае технологий…» — продолжал он, краем глаза фиксируя, что гений вернулся на стул, сбросил бейсболку, быстрым движением пригладил черные волосы и водрузил кепку обратно.

Удивительно, что за два часа у этого человека несколько раз тасовались, как карты, личности. Первая — подросток, глядящий черными глазами куда-то вбок, растерянный; подбирает слова; неестественность, выпирающие углы жестов, то плавных, то стремительных, выдают тлеющее внутри безумие. Вторая — нагловатый бизнесмен. Третья — интеллигент, с лету разбирающийся в проблеме и способах ее решения.

Об этом человеке говорили, что выше всего он ценит кодеров, а остальных людей в компании считает вторым сортом. Впрочем, много что рассказывали про его социальную сеть. Что нигде нет программистов такого класса, чтобы тридцать человек поддерживали сложную архитектуру серверов и присутствие десятков миллионов юзеров. Что «ВКонтакте» создали масоны. Или, наоборот, чекисты, а Павел Дуров — выдуманный персонаж.

Экспат взял себя в руки, отбросил иррациональную симпатию, которую вызывал нахальный противник, и аргументировал: наша компания тоже высокотехнологичная, но бизнес-резоны одинаковы для любой отрасли. Переговорщик кивал. Буря эго стихла. Можно повторить насчет 5%.

Но Дуров опять подскочил: «Вы считаете, будто мы набиваем себе цену. Вы просто тратите наше время. Два часа я слушаю вас, хотя мы могли бы договориться и запустить эксперимент. Хватит!» — и опять направился к двери.

В мозгу экспата столкнулись и заискрили несколько соображений. Эксперимент по-любому выгоден, а если безумец оборвет переговоры, то более сговорчивые конкуренты быстро заключат с ним контракт. Проклятые программисты, возомнили о себе черт знает что. А как отреагируют на объяснения о разрыве договоренности насчет сделки мои акционеры?

«Павел, подождите! — закричал экспат устремившейся к дверям фигуре в черном. — У меня есть предложение, я согласен, вы правы! Мы сейчас разгорячились, а это вредно для бизнеса. Предлагаю договориться в общих чертах, а конкретизировать условия приглашаю вас, Илью и Андрея в мое шале в Швейцарии. Встреча, отдых — все на мне. Мы спокойно посидим…»

Экспат прервался, потому что увидел, как переговорщик смеется. Программист тоже улыбался, а предводитель шайки молчал, внезапно успокоившись, будто и не бегал к двери. Наконец Дуров любопытно наклонил голову и произнес: «А вы еще и коррупционер. Интересно. Мы из вашей Швейцарии два дня назад прилетели и полетим еще, когда захотим».

Экспат вздохнул и быстро сказал: «ОК, давайте зафиксируем ваши условия».

Гостя проводили по ковровой дорожке до лифта, чья золоченая клетка наводила на мысль, что программисты сняли этаж у реликтового министерства. Затем переговорщики прошли в залу с анфиладой кабинетов. Троица так громко хохотала и обсуждала окаменевшую физиономию иностранца, что на смех начали сходиться странные люди. Они выползали из кабинетов с магнитными досками, где литерами были набраны таблички вроде: «Сквот ИЕ. Кости в танке», «Наркомпросвет», «Злые пользователи», «Музей Дурова» и т. п. Бо́льшая часть пришедших носила футболки, схваченные ремнями выше пояса, а некоторые гордо застегнули рубашки на верхнюю пуговицу.

Странные люди выглядели как кодла ботаников родом из эссе Пола Грэма Why Nerds Are Unpopular, которая сбежала с олимпиады по физике и учредила свое государство на необитаемом острове.

Собравшись в круг, нёрды вслушивались в детали переговоров. Кто-то наливал сок из автомата, выжимавшего апельсины. Кто-то, забыв, зачем пришел, обсуждал возможности языка C++.

«Классный момент был, — пересказывал главный программист. — Этот нам: „Вы хотите десять, но мы не можем дать больше пяти“. А Павел ему: „Двадцать!“» Нёрды заулыбались. Старожилы помнили, как предводитель менял себя и учился вежливо хамить.

«Так торгашей и надо троллить», — произнес кто-то. Мы занимаемся важными для будущего вещами, и зачем терять время на какие-то проценты. «Прозрачная позиция отлично работает», — добавил переговорщик. «Да, конечно, — кивнул лидер, — когда ты не врешь, тобой нельзя манипулировать».

«Павел, — спросил один из программистов, — а правда, что наш инвестор хочет слить бизнесы в один холдинг — и мы как бы войдем туда?» Пауза. «Вполне возможно, что так».

Еще пауза. Нёрды сознавали, что слияние с корпорацией может принести больше проблем, чем ярость сетевых коммерсантов. Речь шла о возможной войне за независимость, потеря которой означала бы распад их коммуны, живущей по своим законам.

Мало кто в доме Зингера догадывался, что война идет с первого года жизни «ВКонтакте» и имеет свое предназначение. Возможно, это знали медные валькирии, но никому не говорили и молчали, взирая на человеческий трафик, который тек под ними, несмотря на то что собор, мосты и весь Петербург погрузились в ночь.

***

Историю с переговорами мне рассказали ее участники со стороны «ВКонтакте», предусмотрительно записавшие беседу на диктофон (их оппонент не отреагировал на просьбу прокомментировать отношения с домом Зингера).

Я слушал и размышлял о том, что мы не заметили, как нёрды сломали картину мира. Похожие друг на друга утра: конструктор из многоэтажек; толкотня у поручня или ругань на перестраивающихся справа; метро; люди, уткнувшиеся в газеты, пусть даже в телефоны, — дело не в носителе, мало кто замечает, насколько стремительно технологии изменили сознание и психику.

Сто лет назад человек скакал на лошади к другу, позже пугался прибывающего поезда и плакал, услышав голос в трубке на расстоянии. Знание в пределах одной страны доставлялось днями, часами, наконец, минутами — теперь люди обмениваются информацией мгновенно. Человек говорит и видит абонента, следит за его жизнью в фотокартинках и видео. Люди не стали ближе, но стали откровеннее за считаные годы.

Если раньше личными переживаниями владели мы сами и отчасти наши близкие, то теперь — это любой, перед кем мы хотим обнажиться. Даже если вы не дали допуск к своим мыслям, переживаниям, фото, все равно есть люди, которые владеют выплеснутым вами содержанием жизни — то есть надеждами и страхами, горем и эйфорией, похотью и изменой, сокровенным и непростительным. Тем, в чем признаются, давясь словами, на последней исповеди, владеют люди, которых никто, по сути, близко не знает. Даже если эти люди, втащившие мир в двоичный код, держат слово, как врачи или адвокаты, все равно знание человеческой изнанки у них достовернейшего качества.

В соцсетях человечество обрело децентрализованную нервную систему — одну на многих. Кто контролирует ее нервные окончания, тот знает о людях все: профиль с интересами, биографией, фото, плейлистом сам по себе стал высказыванием и идентичностью.

Миллионы идентичностей порождают «мудрость друзей», то есть коллективное мнение многих, которое становится решающе значимым. Это вызов и раздражитель для экспертов в любых областях знания, которые оказались лишенными монополии на исчерпывающую оценку происходящего в мире.

Социальные сети — это ЦНС, регулируемая не пользователем, а хозяевами кода. Кто эти хозяева, какими качествами наделены, чего хотят, к чему стремятся?

Год назад журнал Vanity Fair выпустил номер о новом истеблишменте. Его вполне можно было бы озаглавить «Мир во власти нёрдов». Более половины списка агентов влияния на умы — программисты, воплотившие свои идеи в коде.

Услышав рассказ о переговорах «ВКонтакте», я подумал, что сценка в переговорной очень характерна и узнаваема. История отличников, которые обвели вокруг пальца мир троечников, мне была близка со школы. Как всякий чуть-чуть соображающий хорошист с трояками по нелюбимым предметам (а также отсутствием дисциплины, чтобы их выучить), я торчал между высоколобой Сциллой и быдловатой Харибдой. Одна из моих ролей заключалась в том, чтобы служить медиатором между одними и другими, проводником, который мирит, объясняет, находит точки, где одни могут быть полезны другим. Иногда процесс напоминал зажимание зубами оборванного провода связи.

Когда настала цифровая эпоха, эти два мира, две жизненные стратегии находились в точке перелома. Интернет обеспечил тех, над кем хихикали девочки и издевались гопники, шансом подчинить себе мир, облагоразумить его и упорядочить. Ботаникам в руки попало сильнейшее оружие, и им, горбатившимся на государства и мегакорпорации, открылось, что код способен изменить мир без посредников. Нажал «ввод» — и things will never be the same again.

Социальные сети — верх их реванша: весь мир создает контент, которым владеет и на котором зарабатывает сама платформа. Люди делятся фото, эмоциями, страхами, самым сокровенным — на их коммуникациях интернет-герои зарабатывают миллиарды. Сервисы вмешиваются в чужие жизни и высасывают из них самое дорогое. Хотите быстро познакомиться — Badoo, продать себя дороже — LinkedIn, составить альбом своей жизни, читая лучшее из газет и журналов и просматривая фото друзей, параллельно переписываясь с ними, — Facebook и «ВКонтакте».

Мир ловил меня, но не поймал, писал философ Григорий Сковорода. Ботаники поймали мир, и Павел Дуров казался типичным генералом этой армии ночи.

***

Год назад я колесил по Петербургу. Вокруг гремел День города, человеческие течения напоминали переплетающуюся в ручье траву. Лето еще не разбросало нужных мне людей по отпускам, поэтому мне удалось встретиться с университетскими приятелями, школьными учителями и коллегами Дурова.

Если раньше из его биографии были известны мало что раскрывающие факты («отличник с двойкой по поведению», университетский активист), то теперь кое-что прояснялось. Впрочем, сам он не откликался на письма. Лишь когда меня рекомендовали буквально со всех сторон, ответил в интернет-мессенджере, что не хочет давать интервью Forbes, так как ему плевать на деньги. Я схватился за эту соломинку и начал спорить. Выяснилось, что взгляды сторон на цель и смысл предпринимательства совпадают, и мы проболтали до четырех часов утра.

Ночной разговор послужил отправной точкой для этой книги. По мере того как я изучал путь «ВКонтакте», передо мной разворачивалась совсем другая история — более глубокая; не столько о реванше нёрдов, сколько о последствиях их революции.

Дуров оказался той же крови, что и предприниматели нового поколения, стремящиеся изобретать сервисы, которые решают глобальные проблемы (их пока меньшинство в списке Vanity Fair). Например, есть такая малоприятная штука, как непрозрачность или асимметрия информации. Facebook во главе с Марком Цукербергом толкает людей к все большей прозрачности их жизни — привыкай к тому, что твои поступки и связи видят все. Граждане переносят новые паттерны поведения, к примеру, с частной жизни на отношения с государством и бюрократией.

«Я боюсь не новых идей, а старых», — как-то написал Дуров и сформулировал ключевую ценность новых «социалистов»: движение вперед. Он, странный юноша не без снобизма и мизантропии, сначала прятался от публики, а в последнее время, напротив, чудил — разбрасывал деньги с балкона дома Зингера, придумал эротическую фотосессию моделей в своем кабинете, подписывал футболки поклонникам на Дворцовой площади. Затем вызвал лютую ярость сталинистов, написав 9 мая в личном твиттере, что нечего радоваться победе, вернувшей страну в руки палача.

Когда в декабре 2011 года поднялись протесты, он не испугался прокуратуры и не стал ограничивать количество участников группы оппозиционного политика Алексея Навального. Незадолго до этого, на свой день рождения, вывесил на личной странице коллаж из кадров разных фильмов и приписал из «Фауста»: Vi veri universum vivus vici — «[Силой] истины я, живущий, покорил вселенную». Коллаж увидели

3,6 млн подписчиков — аудитория, которой вещает Дуров, перекрывает любое печатное издание в стране.

Как ни странно, у этого пафосного человека оказалось много фанатов среди его негромких коллег — интернет-миллионеров. Мало кого принципиально смущало наличие во «ВКонтакте» порнографии и фильмов, выложенных без уведомления правообладателя.

Однажды зимой, стоя у окна цеха бывшей шоколадной фабрики, я наблюдал за рекой. Теплоходы без труда рассекали ледяную кашу по проторенному кем-то створу. В глубине зала начиналось представление, посвященное рейтингу сетевых предпринимателей Forbes. Чтобы развлечь публику, коллеги устроили голосование в нескольких номинациях.

Зная, что в одну из них — «лучший CEO» — номинирован Дуров, я устроился рядом с основателем «Яндекса» Аркадием Воложем. Нам раздали пульты с тремя кнопками — по каждой на кандидатуру. Первые две номинации Волож сидел спокойно, а когда объявили третью, занес палец над цифрой «3», полагавшейся Дурову, и держал так несколько минут, пока конферансье живописал подвиги номинантов.

Я догадывался, почему владелец компании, стоившей миллиарды и торговавшейся на бирже NASDAQ, проголосовал — как и многие другие — за сына профессора филологии. Дуров создал цифровое государство с населением сто миллионов человек — причем произвел этот финт под носом у государства, где бизнесмены переживали эпоху мелкотемья и боязни не угодить вертикали власти.

«Причина нелюбви ко „ВКонтакте“ заключается в том, что каждый считает, что во „ВКонтакте“ неправильно ведутся дела, недостаточно активно вычищается порнография и „пиратские“ фильмы, а он, дескать, знает, как правильно, — писал случайный комментатор на сайте интернет-деятелей Roem.ru. — Факт: Дуров с командой взял на себя смелость войти в тему, оседлал тренд и теперь гребет бабло, и именно потому, что выстраивает политику так, как считает нужным».

Когда я искал ответ на вопрос, что движет пользователем Twitter под ником Porn King и его командой, которые затащили в «новую нервную систему» более 100 млн человек, то не предполагал, что история стартапа превратится в триллер о сражении за свободу в двоичном коде, цифровой среде.

Исследуя путь взбесившегося и анархического государства нёрдов, каковым, безусловно, является «ВКонтакте», я спиной ощущал взгляды персонажей Бека, Вулфа, Капоте и других охотников за выдающимися историями, которые следует поймать, а не придумать.

И зачем что-то придумывать, если перед тобой люди, которые построили систему каналов, в которых бежит чужая жизнь и создаются миллионы идентичностей-гомункулов. Разговаривая с Дуровым, я чувствовал себя режиссером из первой сцены «Пиратов Кремниевой долины», которому Джобс внушает, что предстоит снять не рекламу, а блокбастер об устройстве, которое изменит мир.

Герой оказался сильнодействующим продавцом идей, и автору стоило много труда раскопать слой, лежащий в их основании. Однако я старался отсекать факты о «ВКонтакте» от интерпретаций и подвергал сомнению даже те эпизоды, которые не вызывали вопросов. Это было интересно. Как говорится, so long, and thanks for all the fish*.

* «Всего хорошего, и спасибо за рыбу!» (англ.) — юмористический научно-фантастический роман британского писателя Дугласа Адамса. Четвертая часть серии книг, известных под общим названием «Автостопом по галактике». Само название романа является прощальной фразой дельфинов человечеству из первой книги цикла, когда те покидали Землю перед ее уничтожением вогонами (чтобы освободить место для гиперпространственного экспресс-маршрута).

Глава 1
Ботанический сад

Мальчик с томом Сервантеса выходит из подъезда, огибает автомобиль, который какой-то негодяй поставил так, что пешеходы еле протискиваются мимо, и сворачивает за угол. Перед ним пустынные кварталы, поля и высоковольтные вышки, а в физиономию дует ветер — как везде в Петербурге, но в этом районе особенно. Рядом море.

Архитектор раскрасил панели домов в оранжевый и бордовый, чтобы однообразное серое не свело район с ума. Расстояния между корпусами напоминают о заполярных городах, где возводить что-либо можно лишь на сопках, а дворы имеют сторону в километр. Летом они зарастают одуванчиками, разнотравьем и камышом. Вокруг осушенные болота.

Сканируя пространство на предмет гопников, мальчик с книгой идет к трассе. Некоторые многоэтажки недостроены, а улицы недочерчены. У одного корпуса поставили стилобат, а потом, видимо, куда-то просадили деньги — осталась бетонная коробка. Внутри нее горят костры и сидят парни, курят, треплются и малюют граффити. Весной разливаются лужи, и парни сколачивают плоты, чтобы перебраться с континента «Камышовая» на континент «Ситцевая». Маячат котлованы, наполненные мутной водой. За ними чернеет лес.

Перепрыгивая через лужи, мальчик проходит недострой и выбирается к дороге, по которой век назад возили торф. Справа забор кладбища и березки у надгробий. Слева перекопанная площадь, окруженная скелетами панельных многоквартирных гигантов. Гиганты глядят свысока на рабочих в отсыревшей одежде, которые поднимаются из-под земли, где вот-вот — ожидание затянулось на годы — откроется новая станция, последняя на ветке.

Несколько лет мальчик ходил к площади по грязной тропинке, и ему казалось, что он перемещается в предместье Аида: перед ним возникал строй теней — пенсионеры и несуны с завода продавали метизы, подшипники и еще что-то из подвергшихся насилию металлов; когда метро наконец ожило, тени исчезли. Пока же метро не открылось, дорога мальчика к ближайшей станции и оттуда до школы лежит через подболоченное поле, засеянное бетонными столбами и их обломками. Наверху в проводах гудит электричество. Сереют трубы, а зиккурат фабрики, выпускающей фотоаппараты, сбегает вниз ступеньками — тупыми серыми блоками.

Оглянувшись, мальчик форсирует торфяную дорогу и упирается в поле. Перед ним заброшенный аэродром и остатки военной базы. Бомбоубежища, накрытые искусственными холмами, и закрытые на замок корпуса, бункеры. Он взбирается на холм и разглядывает дымящиеся горы мусора вдали. Когда ветер дует неудачно, сталкер ощущает присутствие ужаса квартирных маклеров — помойки. Пейзаж как бы говорит: больше трэша, больше ада.

Но в этот раз дым не долетает, пахнет морем. Мальчик, устраиваясь на крыше бункера, открывает книгу и погружается в нее. Гопники сюда не забредают, да и вообще кругом живет мало людей. Он худой, невысокий, не различает буквы на третьей строчке снизу; логопед не плакал по нему, а пожалуй, справлял тризну. И он торчит часами на крыше в одиночестве, если не считать Сервантеса.

Он мог бы пригласить с собой братьев, но старший, сводный, Михаил — взрослый, жил отдельно от матери, а средний, Николай, был настолько умен, что не интересовался аэродромом. Когда Николаю было три года, родители сажали его на свободное место в троллейбусе и выдавали книгу — например, «Популярную астрономию». Никто из попутчиков не верил, что ребенок ее читает, — рассматривает, поди, — но Николай читал. Он рано выучился арифметике, а в семь лет щелкал кубические уравнения. Однажды его даже зазвали в телевизор на шоу вундеркиндов.

Это произошло, уже когда семья перебралась с Балтики на Адриатику. Отцу, доктору филологии, предложили учить иностранцев русскому языку в Индии или Италии. Индусы манили поместьем с садом, прислугой, комфортом. Итальянцы известили, что главу Института русского языка ждут в однокомнатной квартире, но в Турине. Что выберет латинист?

В общем, «мальчика с Сервантесом» — то есть Павла — не взяли в стесненные условия и оставили бабушке, пока не наладится быт. Та жила на Невском проспекте в тридцатиметровой комнате, окруженной чистилищем коммуналки. По блокадной привычке крутила страшное количество консервов и заполоняла полки банками. Семья не сообщила Павлу, что летит в урезанном составе. Когда объявили едва ли не в последний момент, он, четырех лет от роду, не переварил это известие и начал бить банки предательства.

Бабушка паниковала и жаловалась родителям: мальчик капризный и неуправляемый. Среди ночи он щелкал кнопкой телевизора и пялился на экран. Показывали заседание во Дворце съездов, и его, как многих детей, захватывал поток непонятных и интересных слов: «президиум», «кандидат», «перестройка», «гласность», «кооператив». Его первое воспоминание о себе — как сидел на ковре и строил из кубиков башню. Второе — как ставил кости домино одну на другую, стараясь забраться как можно выше, пока стела не рухнула.

«Исступленное стремление к созиданию изначально есть практически у всех, просто у меня оно осталось по мере взросления и не было вытеснено псевдоценностями общества потребления, — этот пассаж высветился на экране в половину четвертого одного июньского утра. — Возможно, потому что я сохранял голову в чистоте: не смотрел телевизор, не читал газет, не принимал на веру мнение авторитетов».

Мы переписывались восемь часов подряд, отвлекаясь на разговор с редактором (автор) и консультацию разработчиков (герой). Подумав, Дуров добавил: «А может быть, это не причины, а следствия. Все, ухожу, я сегодня еще не ел».

Позднесоветский детский сад мало отличался от современного — раз ты прописан в таком-то районе, значит, твоя тарелка манной каши именно там. Тусклыми утрами мальчик и пожилая женщина выходили из подъезда, пряча глаза от ветра, и ждали троллейбуса. Цепляясь за перила, лезли в него, как альпинисты по веревке, и тратили часы своей жизни, чтобы достичь окраины. Так Дуров возненавидел бюрократию.

Через несколько месяцев мать прилетела и забрала его с собой. В итальянской школе детей учили иначе, никакого принуждения. Тогда-то педагоги и опознали в его брате Николае вундеркинда, а телевизионщики рекрутировали на телешоу.

Павла никуда не звали. Но, во-первых, ему перепадало от эрудиции брата. Родители, уложив их, гасили свет и уходили, после чего старший пересказывал младшему самое интересное из прочитанного за день: созвездия, логарифмы, origin of species и т. д. Они, разумеется, дрались и дулись друг на друга, но старший не жадничал и делился тезаурусом.

А во-вторых, младший брат был одарен по-своему. Когда в семью приходил гость, он брал карандаш и бумагу и под кухонный диспут рисовал прибывшего. Перед тем как портретируемый собирался прощаться, ему демонстрировали картину — и часто сходство сражало; конечно, если учесть, что автор — первоклассник.

Возвращение на родину далось трудно. Павла ждала приличная школа, где он совсем не страдал, пока однажды не понял, что знает английский лучше, чем пришедшая на замену заболевшей англичанке девушка. Он так и сказал ей: «Вы плохо учите». Похожий конфликт тлел между ним и преподавателем русского.

Ученик плевал на субординацию и считал важным лишь то, что англичанка делает ошибки, — и почему в таком случае директор ждет, что он заткнется?! Возраст он не считал чем-то, что обеспечивает авторитетом, — еще с той поры, когда бил банки. Есть факт, и ничто не должно его затмевать. А факт в том, что… и т. д.

«Я боролся со страхом, — вспоминал потом Дуров. — Учитель держит всех в магическом оцепенении — если все не замолчат, произойдет что-то ужасное. Надо расковырять это ужасное. Ну, встану я и заору — что она может сделать? Исключат из школы? Но даже в этом случае есть плюсы. Я и то и другое огреб — и тройку за год, и исключение. А есть люди, которые боятся самого страха».

Родители узнали быстро. Отец подчеркивал, что не надо идти на конфликт, но учителей не защищал. Мать сочла, что сыновья разумны и воспитанны и вряд ли ни с того ни с сего станут хамить учителям; очевидно, учителя проявили недостаточный профессионализм — не смогли справиться с сыном.

Ей самой в старших классах однажды прислали другого физика, и она из чувства протеста подбила класс уйти в кино. На других предметах, если ее что-то не устраивало, выходила к доске нарочито вежливо. «Отвечайте урок». — «Это [допустим, формула] так-то?» — «Да». — «Это [первый ход решения] так-то?» — «Верно. А дальше?» — «Я не знаю…» Класс понимал, что вожак все знает, но протестует и защищается.

Отличница чувствовала за собой право на саботаж. Она росла в Омске, рядом с переселенцами-немцами, и выучила их язык. Блестящие способности. Когда ее мама заболела раком, решила участвовать в изобретении лекарства против опухолей и подала документы в Хабаровск на медицинский. Затем уехала в Ленинград. Выбирая, где учиться, определилась с журфаком и поступила без особых проблем.

Непонятно, какая школа взяла бы ее сына с трудным характером, если бы действие разворачивалось не в Петербурге — колыбели интеллигенции, которая веками строила социальные связи, чтобы выучить детей в приличных заведениях. Друзья отца, филологи Русаковы, после открытия педагогической вольницы возрождали систему классического дореволюционного образования — в собственной школе. Тогда, в 1992 году, им повезло — Академической гимназии при университете достался крупный транш от Министерства образования. Накал энтузиазма в то время был высок, о «пилежке» средств речи не шло — поэтому Русаковы под свои «общеобразовательные классы» получили деньги и арендовали Аничков дворец на Невском.

Педагогическая идея в целом выглядела так. Если ребенка учить с малых лет математике и языкам, он научится думать и воспринимать информацию таким образом, что новые науки и умения освоит без труда. От классического образования оставили латынь, заканчивающуюся в выпускном классе «Записками о Галльской войне», английский, французский и немецкий языки, которые вводились последовательно.

Сперва классы жили в роскоши, учеников возили по Европе, и они едва ли не столовались по талончикам в «Метрополе». Русаковы как люди талантливые, но непрагматичные, считали, что школа должна быть бесплатной — чтобы могли учиться таланты из бедных семей. Затем деньги иссякли, и энтузиасты съехали в плохо отапливаемые помещения университета. Классы предложили родителям сдавать 83 рубля в месяц — в тот момент минимальная оплата труда, — но родители отказались. Гимназия поставила экспериментаторам ультиматум: «Самоокупаемость или роспуск», и Русаковы ушли. Началась эпоха мытарств. Тогда профессор Дуров и привел в классы заносчивого младшего сына.

***

Мальчика пригласили пройти отбор — письменный тест, затем задачи на лингвистическое чутье. Предлагалось ознакомиться с текстом, написанным на несуществующем языке, — и, разобравшись в его структуре, с помощью скудных вводных догадаться, о чем идет речь. Дуров проанализировал имеющуюся информацию и сдал листок с ответом. Все оказалось верно, и последующее собеседование было почти формальностью.

Новый директор Григорий Медников снимал помещение в конструктивистском доме культуры у «Нарвской», где в 60-х на поэтических турнирах являлся публике Бродский. Английский учили в аудитории, которую оккупировал клуб анонимных алкоголиков. Историю — в помещении, где адвентисты разучивали за партами гимны. Рядом «зажигал» клуб «Пляшущий пенсионер». Дорога в эти остросюжетные обстоятельства занимала у Дурова час: автобус до метро, пересадка, эскалатор и немного пешком.

Я помню Петербург того времени. Декабрь, утро. На улицах тусклый свет, аэродинамические трубы подворотен, сугробы, как морены ледника, ползущего по мостовым. Ощущение, что город сплотился, чтобы пережить темень этих месяцев.

Хозяйка, у которой вписывались друзья, жила по адресу Большая Морская, дом 2 — то есть почти в арке, выводящей на Дворцовую площадь. Тревожить ее было неприлично, поэтому мы пробрались переулками к трамвайной линии, чтобы выспаться на протяженном маршруте. Вверху болтались фонари, неслись по касательной люди-футляры, спешащие скорее прятаться от ветра, чем к рабочему месту. Двери в трамвае стреляли, как красные матросы, и вздремнуть не удалось. Надежда скоротать время в Ростральной колонне пропала, когда за дверью, ведущей в ее недра, мы нашли спящих бродяг.

Вывалившись из стреляющих дверей, толкаясь среди замерзших футляров, к метро устремлялся и Дуров: «Я помню очереди на подступах к станции. Метров за сто. Самое опасное место — поручень, туда выносило тех, кто не сопротивлялся».

Он оказался самым младшим в классе. Сначала сидел за партой с девочкой Тасей, которой нравился. Одноклассники вспоминали, что Тася зачем-то носила соседу медяки, копеечки, и он пересыпал их в портфель. Позже Дуров оккупировал первую парту, где пребывал чаще всего в одиночестве, ссутулившись над тетрадями или рассматривая — третья строчка снизу яснее не стала — то, что нацарапано на доске.

До старших классов у него не было друзей. Исключение составил товарищ, с которым они проучились неполных два года. Этот ученик одним своим присутствием спасал общеобразовательные классы от развала.

Каждое утро Слава ехал в школу на лимузине с охранником, разглядывая в окно сонный Кировский район. Он тормозил авто за три квартала, вылезал на тротуар, продевал руки в лямки рюкзака и шагал к Дому культуры, не глядя на проезжую часть. Там, прикидываясь, что хочет припарковаться, полз лимузин. Молодой человек был сыном короля игорных заведений города Михаила Мирилашвили.

В общеобразовательных классах тусовались дети интеллигенции, и не каждая семья с легкостью вносила оплату, которую пришлось ввести. Например, для Дуровых это было существенной тратой. По закону голливудо-болливудских драм столкновение Славы с гордыми детьми, занимающими унизительную вторую, если не третью полку в социальном купе, вело к неизбежному конфликту.

Однако сюжет развивался в колыбели интеллигенции, а не в «Голли-Болли». Слава оказался вежлив, корректен, учился не хуже прочих. На переменах сын миллионера бегал в пышечную и влетал в класс, держа в руках замаслившийся пакет с выпечкой. Дуров оказался едва ли не единственным, с кем подружился Слава.

Жизнь в классе бурлила. Предводители Диевский и Паперно придумали свое государство и написали конституцию. Класс играл в демократию, избирал президента и т. д.

Дурова, может быть, это и волновало, но вида он не показывал, иронически улыбаясь массовым развлечениям. Его одолевали собственные идеи об успехе и власти. Сидя на крыше бункера у аэродрома, он штудировал Кастанеду в компании с Наполеоном Хиллом. «Ты — то, что ты думаешь; думай и богатей».

Однажды класс проходил «Обломова». Илья Ильич как зеркало русской души. Дискуссия. Большинство соглашается, что главный герой добр, безвреден, а Штольц вполне бездушный немчура, механизм и чужеродное тело на славянских просторах.

Руководил обсуждением Николай Гуськов, учитель словесности, известный тем, что любил средневековую литературу. Итальянцу Дурову нравилось, что Гуськов фокусируется на малоизвестных течениях — например, прованских или ломбардских трубадурах. Правда, эта симпатия не отменяла его «идеи фикс» — быть во всем contrarian, противоположным общепринятому взгляду на вещи.

Выслушав про нежную душу Обломова, Дуров (о русские дворянские фамилии!) поднял руку. Гуськов дал слово. «Я считаю, что произведение, поэтизирующее лень, следует исключить из школьной программы», — проговорил Дуров. Класс вздрогнул и вышел из оцепенения. Дискуссия свернула на непредсказуемую дорожку.

«Лень упрятана глубоко у нас в культуре — „работа не волк“ и т. д., но людская лень — это все ж таки плохо с точки зрения развития экономики, науки и искусства, — продолжал менторствовать Дуров. — Ничегонеделанье ведет к регрессу и распаду. Поэтому для всей нашей страны, да и культуры, было бы лучше, если бы люди были по возможности менее ленивыми. А что делает Гончаров? Он поэтизирует лень. Заставляет ей сочувствовать с помощью милого Обломова. Активную жизненную позицию он, напротив, дискредитирует с помощью механистичного Штольца. В итоге роман не мог не отразиться негативно на многих сферах человеческой деятельности в нашей чудной стране».

Гуськов не удивился. Он привык, что резонер не просто гонит против всех, а ищет аргументы и доказывает. Кроме Гончарова под шквал ругани уже попадал Достоевский: «Я считаю, что он ужасный писатель, потому что...» Дальше шло доказательство через психологию, неувязки в сюжете, избыточность языка.

В другой раз класс чуть не передрался из-за «Вишневого сада». Интеллигентные дети порицали купечество в лице Лопахина, влезшее сапогами в кружевную душу Раневской, а Дуров орал, что Лопахин — человек дела; помещики сами сгубили сад по лени и бездарности.

Один из его прадедов был дворянином и помещиком, а другой — зажиточным земледельцем. Обоих лишили собственности красные иждивенцы. Поэтому нелюбовь к грязи, получающей все, содержалась в крови Дурова изначально.

Позже, в университете, он отправится в дискуссионный клуб, где позицию оратора выбирает жребий и считается удачей защитить, к примеру, фашизм. Личные убеждения многие отобьют — а как насчет тех, что признаны преступными?..

Гуськов был доволен — спор заполыхал, девочки набросились на Дурова, доказывая, что Обломов хоть и слабый человек, но порядочный, добрый и т. д.

Директор привлекал таких, как Гуськов, всеми правдами и неправдами. Сам Медников был опытным учителем математики, дети его обожали и называли за глаза и в школьном фольклоре Гризом (от медведя гризли). Он быстро все понял про Дурова и не давил на ученика, подбрасывая задачи посложнее. Когда удавалось заразить идеей, Дуров приносил невиданные объемы решенного. Будучи незаинтригованным, показывал средние результаты.

Медников приглашал ученых, способных рассказывать детям всякие занимательные штуки. Так в классы угодил Евгений Нинбург — известный гидробиолог, который увлекал детей тем, что был не кабинетным теоретиком, а месяцами пропадал на Белом море и возил недорослей в экспедиции. Нинбург преподавал теорию популяции и эволюции.

Как-то раз в ресторане «Терраса» с видом на Казанский собор, разламывая хлеб резкими движениями и скатывая из него шарики, Дуров рассказал, как эти теории взорвали ему мозг. Он отшатнулся от позитивной психологии и Хилла и стал воспринимать людей как продукт среды, естественного отбора. Если дать человеку выбор, он выберет, что хочет, — и результат будет достойным вознаграждением за этот выбор. Да, есть вопрос, стоит ли поручать людям выбор. Люди ведутся на манипулирование, выбирают иррационально. Но и манипуляции, и маркетологическое зомбирование, и политика — это тоже поле интеллектуальной конкуренции, а конкуренция была и осталась главной святыней Дурова.

Еще одно знание, приобретенное через Нинбурга и сыгравшее некоторую роль во всем, что происходило с «ВКонтакте», — о поведении человека. Однажды, спускаясь из штаба по лестнице, устланной ковровыми дорожками, Дуров пересказывал мне известный эксперимент с обезьянами и электричеством.

Обезьян посадили в клетку и регулярно подбрасывали им бананы. Но, как только кто-то брал эти бананы, группа получала удар током. Вскоре тех, кто тянулся за бананом, били свои. Затем старожилов по одному начали менять на новоприбывших особей и в какой-то момент отключили электричество. Но все равно группа саморегулировалась так, что новоприбывшим запрещали касаться бананов. В финале клетка наполнилась приматами, которые ни разу не получали удар током и даже не общались с теми, кто получал, — и эта группа хранила священный ужас перед прикосновением к желанной и безопасной еде.

Когда мы вышли через крутящиеся двери на ночной Невский, я спросил: «И зачем вы это рассказали?» «Да так, размышляя об этом эксперименте, я лучше стал понимать суть человека», — пожал плечами Дуров.

Алексей Руткевич вел у гимназистов спецкурс по психоанализу и рассказывал, как психика может влиять на вербальное и визуальное творчество. Юнг, Фрэзер; развитие мозга человека с внутриутробного периода; как определить психотип. Руткевич учил школьников рассчитывать размер своего мозга, а потом уточнял — у кроманьонцев объем мозга был еще больше, но извилин меньше.

Руткевич навел Дурова на тексты изобретателя IQ-тестов Ганса Айзенка. Айзенка подвергали обструкции, к примеру, за утверждение, что у черной расы пространственная и вербальная логика хуже. Дурова взбесила политкорректность, не позволявшая признать, что люди одной национальности могут быть более или менее успешны в каком-либо роде деятельности, чем люди другой национальности.

Тогда же, в девятом классе, он прочитал Фрейда и позже, когда выбирал цвета и логотип для «ВКонтакте», мысленно слал поклон учителю. Выпуклая женственная буква «В», набранная обычным шрифтом без засечек, Tahoma. Красный огонечек оповещений, загоравшийся в Facebook, Дуров копировать не стал и третий цвет, черный, ввел только вместе с всплывающими окнами оповещений.

Когда он выбирал нейтральные цвета — синий и серый, — вспоминал уроки, на которые приходил художник, друг Медникова, периодически в подпитии, и рассказывал про Рафаэля, Микеланджело, пропорции, свет. Раз в неделю он брал класс с собой в Эрмитаж. Короче, Дуров учился у людей, стосковавшихся по свободе творчества и любящих делиться. Однако их педагогическая синекура цвела на фоне закручивающейся диссидентской истории — школа вечно пребывала в статусе гонимой.

Когда Славу Мирилашвили отдавали в это заведение, педагоги еще как-то выкручивались с арендой. После того как их выгнали из дома культуры с «Пляшущими алкоголиками», Михаил Мирилашвили взялся помогать с арендой нового помещения. Но союз педагогов и хозяина «одноруких бандитов», чей офис квартировал в бронированном особняке, просуществовал недолго.

***

Ночной звонок простучал как пулемет. Медников схватил трубку. Человек, отвечавший за безопасность семьи Мирилашвили, извинился за беспокойство, но дальше говорил настойчиво.

Шефа обвиняют в похищении людей, Славу срочно эвакуируют в Израиль. Надо как можно быстрее передать его личное дело и медкарту; насчет помощи школе решим позже.

Дождавшись утра, Медников приехал в свой кабинет, откопал в сейфе нужные бумаги и выдал их прибывшим посланцам. Слава улетел, после чего они с Дуровым не виделись семь лет.

Классам продолжили «делать биографию». Их хотели приручить, посулив новый дом: выселяйте ПТУ у Смоленского кладбища и забирайте помещение. Полторы сотни учеников и их родители давно осознали, что они диссиденты и подмоги ждать неоткуда. Орда, желавшая учиться по своим законам и у своих учителей, вскрыла замки и вывезла станки.

Когда Медникову дали подписать устав, он с изумлением обнаружил, что в бумаге проставлен другой адрес. Власти оказались хитрее диссидентов, выгнали пэтэушников их руками и хотели передать отбитый дом университету.

Классы подняли бунт, и школу закрыла санэпидемстанция. Ее визиты были чем-то вроде ритуала. Когда мы условились с Медниковым встретиться на Черной Речке, первое, что он сделал при появлении, — протянул мне книжку о классах, с фольклором, славословиями и статьями, зачем обществу нужны люди Ренессанса. Половина песен, которые сочинили ученики, описывала, как среди урока в класс вламываются пожарники, санитары и другие слуги народа.

Октябрьским утром приехавшие со всего города бунтовщики увидели перед носом замки на дверях. Учителей отрезали от личных вещей, оставленных в классах.

Гриз смог войти в здание лишь в январе. В одну из комнат кто-то из учеников принес цветы и аквариум, когда начинали обустраиваться. Отперев комнату, директор увидел сухие стебли и глыбы льда с застывшими кусками рваных оранжевых лент. Присмотревшись, он понял, что это замерзшие рыбы.

Школу приказали размазать по соседним учреждениям. Но диссиденты скандалили громко и умело, созвали митинг у Мариинского дворца. Город обратил внимание, что из-за склок дети пропускают занятия, и решил вернуть классы гимназии — пусть доучиваются, но новых набирать нельзя.

В новом здании впервые возник компьютерный класс и начались приключения, связанные с дуровскими штучками. Павел как раз учился программировать и однажды утром завесил экраны всех компьютеров портретом учителя Михаила Бараза с надписью «Must die». Начались догонялки. Учитель закрывал ученику доступ к сети, а тот раз за разом взламывал пароли.

Дуров так надоел Баразу, что тот дал ему задание написать игру — проект на несколько месяцев. Две недели информатик отдыхал, но отпуск кончился внезапно — к нему явился Дуров с готовой игрой, написанной во Flash.

У хакера был свой раздражитель. Брат Николай попал в систему тех же математических кружков, из которой вырос Григорий Перельман и другие топологи и геометры. Его вычислил на городской олимпиаде известный тренер Александр Голованов и заманил в кружок не менее известного Сергея Рукшина — учителя Перельмана. Вскоре после этого Николая рекрутировали в знаменитую «единичку» — спецкласс 239-й школы, где учились призеры олимпиад. Помимо математики он с головой погрузился в программирование.

Школа славилась тем, что в первые два класса параллели — «единичку» и «двойку» — набирали гениев. Гении росли и начинали понимать следствия из того, что аналоговую эпоху сменила цифровая. Интернет дает возможность им, нёрдам в стоптанных сандалиях, создавать программы, игры, пространства, которые неподвластны тем, кто думает менее изящно и быстро.

Власть капитала пасует перед властью таланта. Если коммунисты прятали нёрдов в институты-ящики, создавая годный для выживания и удовлетворения амбиций климат, — то теперь они вырвались на волю и строили продукты, меняющие мир. Путь им указывали Стив Джобс, Билл Гейтс, Сергей Брин, Линус Торвальдс, Джимми Уэйлс. Все перечисленные слыли ботаниками. Когда программные продукты и интернет-сервисы вплотную приблизились к жизни потребителя и стали ее ежедневным инструментом, как зубная щетка или автомобиль, нёрды ощутили власть и вошли во вкус.

Впрочем, в 239-й школе лишь небольшой процент гениев совпадал с образом аутичного носителя очков с гигантским «минусом». Когда «единичка» приезжала в летний лагерь на озеро Зеркальное, отряда математиков боялись все остальные, потому что парни обыгрывали всех в футбол и были не дураки подраться. На переменах из дверей школы вываливались старшеклассники и расползались по прилегающим дворам под названиями «Дымок-1» и «Дымок-2». В соседней школе сдвинули звонки, чтобы за гаражами не дрались, например, за девочек. Милиция часто наведывалась в «дымки».

Но, конечно, лучшими в классах были хронические нёрды. Именно они — концентрировавшиеся на страсти к математике, реже к физике и биологии — достигали мирового уровня в науке. Остальные превращались в высокообразованных менеджеров, журналистов, маркетологов — в общем, вливались в креативную страту, которая создавала что-то для конечного потребителя. Им, как и в школе, где учился Дуров, внушали, что именно они интеллектуальная элита и что от них зависит будущее страны. Если не мы, то кто?

Николай Дуров относился к хроническому типу. Он выиграл сначала российский чемпионат по программированию, а затем и мировой. Мама, исправно посещавшая родительские собрания, благодарила Медникова за то, что он не давил на Павла так, как в «единичке» тренировали Николая. Медников ругал идейного вдохновителя маткружка Рукшина — мол, когда у ребенка нервный срыв или энурез из-за нерешенной задачи, это ненормально: «Он, наверное, самый великий тренер по математике в мире, но у него на первом месте математическое, а на втором человеческое. Я не отдал бы ему своего внука».

Николая звали судить соревнования. Ученикам раздавали задачи, они их решали, а потом судьи определяли, кто справился элегантнее. Дуров-старший не принимал участия в обсуждениях, рисуя что-то на бумаге, а когда спрашивали его мнение, часто показывал лист с верным решением задачи или просто рассказывал, как правильно было бы с ней разделаться. Коллегия произносила что-то вроде: «Что ж ты молчал!» — и меняла свои вердикты.

Николай был совершенно погруженным в свою страсть человеком, далеким от денежных, карьерных и других суетных стремлений. Когда ему доводилось выступать на публике, он, покачиваясь с ноги на ногу и глядя в потолок, кратко обрисовывал смысл своих изысканий и быстрее отправлялся к доске, где чувствовал себя увереннее, имея перед глазами формулы.

По своему типу Дуров-младший находился где-то между ботаниками и активными умниками, а может, и сбоку. Как-то раз он прочел в эссе Пола Грэма «Почему ботаники непопулярны», что нёрды не хотят быть самыми красивыми или успешными в понимании большинства (хотя глупо думать, что это их не волнует) — они хотят быть самыми умными.

Нельзя утверждать, что Дуров свирепо завидовал старшему брату, но конкуренция с ним подстегивала. Он тоже записался в кружок программирования и летом съездил на Зеркальное. Там его попросили прочесть лекцию о языке паскаль.

Дуров вышел перед несколькими десятками незнакомцев, обвел аудиторию рассеянным взглядом и, запинаясь, начал вещать. Прошло несколько минут, и, почувствовав, что слушают, он заговорил более уверенно и после лекции свободно отвечал на вопросы.

Он превращался из худого мальчика, согнувшегося над партой, в более общительного, но по-прежнему отстраненного товарища. Портрет со слов одноклассников: «Всегда находил способ быть отдельным»; «Некомандный человек»; «Никогда не был ограничен»; «Внутри него шла работа, которая наружу не прорывалась».

Дурова захватывала идея эффективности. Как успевать на отлично сразу по нескольким предметам — это было продолжение вызова кастанедовско-хилловского: «Ты можешь все». Дуров концентрировался на учебе, и даже программирование, которое затягивало его все сильнее, отошло на второй план.

Из всего класса на серебряную медаль тянули двоих — его и Аню Бертову. Впрочем, они, как и большинство учеников, разговаривали без всяких «Ань» — только на «вы» и по отчеству. Это были интеллигентные дети, инфильтрованные диссидентством и порожденным им чувством избранности. «Здравствуйте, Павел Валерьевич». — «Добрый вечер, Анна Дмитриевна». После уроков с ними занимался Гриз.

Закончив тесты, они шли домой и болтали на нравственно-этические темы. Дуров утверждал, что ежели кто беден, то потому, что ленив и неспособен поднять зад для великих свершений. Бертова приводила в пример родителей, астрономов, которые вели себя отнюдь не пассивно, но жили не в роскоши.

Так они спорили до июня, когда получили по серебряной медали — золотая оказалась недостижимой. Бертова как воплощенная педагогическая идея о человеке Ренессанса готовилась на матмех, но потом внезапно передумала и без усилий прошла на японскую филологию.

Дуров перестал сторониться самодеятельности. Если на снимке 8-го класса (был день рождения у Бертовой) он единственный из всех намеренно и гордо смотрит мимо камеры вдаль, то теперь, перед выпуском, как с иронией заметила одна из звезд класса, «с ним уже можно было общаться». Он написал пьесу для утренника по мотивам программы «Кто хочет стать миллионером» и сыграл в ней роль саркастичного ведущего.

Ощущение того, что классы и их обитатели вечно гонимы, не сплачивало его ни с кем, когда речь касалась зависимости его воли от коллективного разума. Перед выпуском параллель хотела сняться для альбома, чтобы каждый получил по экземпляру на память. Староста приступил к Дурову насчет участия в общем котле.

— Какой альбом? — спросил Дуров.

— Ну, вот такой, где мы все.

— А почему именно так будут снимать?

— Ну, вот так договорились.

— Нет, я не буду.

— Ты что, с ума сошел?

— Не буду, и все! — заорал Дуров, взбешенный, что его ставят перед фактом. — Бараны вы этакие, я не хочу, как вы, всем стадом сдавать!

Альбом напечатали без него.

Ночью после выпускного они гуляли по набережным Петроградской стороны. Под утро добрались до квартиры Гриза, пили на кухне чай и по традиции рассказывали, кто кем видит себя в будущем. Дуров молчал.

Диевский задвинул про математику, Паперно — про лингвистику, Русин визионировал насчет кораблестроения, постебались над айкидисткой Бертовой.

Когда Дурова спросили, кем себя видит в будущем, он прервал молчание и сказал, улыбаясь: «Тотемом». Его желания, страсти, умения сложились в одну формулу. Все неинтересное и ненужное отсеялось.

Он повторил то, что окружающие расценили как шутку, не подозревая, что произнесенная фраза определит все, что произойдет дальше: «Я хочу стать интернет-тотемом».

Глава 2
Архитектор

Очередь извивалась от «Капитанского мостика» на лестнице — через коридор «Школы» с ее досками объявлений, завешанными подрагивающими от сквозняков листами («Студенческая карта ISIC», «Семинар по финно-угорским диалектам переносится», «Двоечников, не сдавших хвосты до пятницы, повесят в деканате»), — и тянулась до дверей «Евразии», то есть аудитории № 215. Здесь толкались, делая вид, что с иронией относятся к обстоятельствам, блондинки, брюнетки, рыжие, миниатюрные и дылды — короче, все студентки филфака и востфака, которые сочли себя достойными конкурса. Приклеенная к стене афиша звала на «студенческий конкурс эстетики и дизайна „Олимп“». Внизу ее стояли логотипы спонсоров: Elle, Mary Kay, Motivi.

Время от времени дверь выпускала отстрелявшихся, и к ним подбегали из очереди:

— Что там? Пели-танцевали?

— Да нет, просто говорили.

— Говорили?

— Ну да, говорили, как собеседование.

— А кто они, симпатичные?

— Ну такие, вполне, хи-хи. Дали визитку, смотрите…

Толпа рассматривала черные карточки, напоминавшие те, что имели хождение в гарвардском студенческом клубе. На одной было напечатано «Durov.com Club — Ilya Perekopsky, Vice President». На другой, собственно, — «Pavel Durov, President». Ничего больше.

Те, о ком сплетничала очередь, еле ворочали языком, скулы сводило от болтовни. Они сидели за партой. Первый — коротко стриженный шатен в поблескивающих оправой очках. Второй — бледный брюнет в черном, волосы на прямой пробор, кажется, близорукий. Солировал он.

Зашедшую в аудиторию жертву приглашали к парте. Брюнет демонстрировал рассеянную, чуть неестественную, но в целом убедительную улыбку и спрашивал голосом самоуверенного старшеклассника — про литературу, музыку, философию, вкусы. Какое у вас хобби? Танцы? Ну-ну. Периодически он сбивал ответчиц парадоксальными вопросами, выставлял их убеждения примитивными — короче, вредничал и издевался.

Если конкурсантка о чем-то переспрашивала, он смотрел на нее, пока она говорила, кивая и держа взгляд. Когда вопрос был задан, он продолжал молчать, чуть щурясь и как бы убеждаясь, что соискательница уже закончила. Если требовались размышления (обычно нет), смотрел в сторону, а потом отвечал слегка разухабистым, напористым, но непременно вежливым тоном, из которого нельзя было понять, прошла девушка в следующий тур или нет.

Товарищ вредного чернеца (им был Дуров), Илья Перекопский, поддакивал и шугал мужской пол, заглядывающий в аудиторию с саркастическими, а иногда идиотскими лицами. Кроме этого, он прикидывал, отчего их конкурс выстрелил. Да, на филфаке отсутствовала всякая студенческая активность — и вдруг такое шоу. Да, афиша выглядела не хуже плаката к блокбастеру — черный фон, стальные буквы и логотипы модных спонсоров, которые обещали, что мероприятие статусное. Но аншлаг-то откуда?

Перекопский также размышлял и о том, что, конечно, найдутся обиженные и поднимется народный фронт: «Честные женщины против сомнительного конкурса». Но, во-первых, они покажут декану, на что способны, а во-вторых, как бы то ни было, перезнакомятся с лучшими красавицами факультета. Красота — страшная сила, прелестные кадры объединяют компании, вокруг них вьются активные парни.

Их с Дуровым девушки не принимали участия, считая конкурс чем-то ниже своего достоинства. Но и сцены ревности не закатывали. Дуров учил Перекопского, что отношения надо строить так, чтобы женщины не влияли на творческие эксперименты, к которым имеют гораздо меньше способностей, чем мужчины, и не перехватывали власть. Перекопский был поражен тем, что Дуров как-то в воспитательных целях не разговаривал со своей девушкой две недели.

Впрочем, резоны «приязнь декана» и «знакомство с бьюти-активом» имели для тандема побочное значение. Цель находилась в другом месте — и, чтобы попасть в нее, требовалась спланированная публичная кампания, где конкурс выступал лишь эпизодом закрученного сюжета.

Отсеяв пятьдесят симпатичных и остроязыких филологинь, они выпроводили последнюю конкурсантку, заперли аудиторию и отправились готовиться к следующему туру.

***

Перекопский явился в Петербург из металлургического города Череповца, где окончил лучшее заведение и был натаскан репетиторами. Родители сняли ему квартиру недалеко от Сенной площади и высылали денежное содержание. Перекопский любил деньги, хотел зарабатывать их много и английский язык учил не ради красот, а для деловых связей.

Главная такая связь его жизни установилась в первый же день. Вместе с толпой поступивших Перекопский влился в узкий холл двухэтажной усадьбы, миновал бюсты первых деканов востфака и филфака Александра Казем-Бека и Бодуэна де Куртене и вскоре очутился во внутреннем дворе. Его критический глаз исследовал курс в поисках товарищей.

Товарищи не находились. Один, когда разговаривал с людьми, смотрел в землю. Другой, как в анекдоте про разницу между программистом-интровертом и программистом-экстравертом, смотрел не в землю, но на туфли оппонента. Третий оказался церемонным мажором. Зато наличествовала туча, тьма, стая прекрасных девушек, как и полагается на факультете невест.

И тут толпа извергла из себя Дурова — этакого джокера без легко считываемых свойств, в белой рубашечке. Они как-то стихийно познакомились и разговорились. На первой лекции сели вместе, и их объединило легкое жжение от открывавшихся университетом возможностей и вообще от новой жизни, которая началась и продлится пять лет.

После занятий сутулый мальчик с первой парты шел с новым приятелем через Дворцовый мост до метро «Невский проспект» и, как вспоминал потом Перекопский, трещал про свои общеобразовательные классы и пересказал полжизни. Уроженец города хоккея и едкого дыма из труб умудрялся вставлять какие-то фразы в этот монолог, но редко.

Я повторил их путь от филфака до «Невского проспекта»: 3500 метров, полчаса быстрым шагом с поправкой на ветер. Если Дуров столько проболтал с впервые встреченным человеком и увлек его, это означало лишь одно — сидя на первой парте, он прослыл социопатом потому, что в школе мало с кем хотелось говорить. Ни в классах, ни на озере Зеркальном не встретилось удобного характера, устремленного к проектам, напрямую связанным с людьми и их потребностями.

Перекопский был удобен. Он сразу понял, что Дуров обдумывает далекоидущие идеи и ставит цели точнее, но при этом не любит рутинную работу, необходимую для воплощения этих идей. Роль второго лица в тандеме Перекопского устраивала.

Как-то раз, отвечая на опрос: «Для чего нужно чего-то добиваться?» — он написал: «Чтобы были деньги. Я их коллекционирую. Нужно же что-то коллекционировать?»

Прагматик и визионер осознали, что полезны друг другу, имеют взаимодополняющие сильные стороны, и сдружились.

Сначала их устремления не поражали размахом. Амбиции касались, например, двора факультета — сада со скульптурами и скамейками, где на переменах болтали филологи. Каждый день рядом со скульптурой «Перекур» дискутировал кружок американцев, которые учат русский. Почему-то филологи не снисходили до знакомства с носителями языка, а Дуров с Перекопским увидели в этом шанс перейти на более высокий языковой уровень.

День рождения Дурова они праздновали в англоязычном кругу, зазвав носителей в бар «Идиот» на Мойке. Американцы поразились, что именинник не пьет и утверждает, что даже капля спиртного во рту ему отвратительна.

Первая идея Дурова, связанная с интернетом, выросла из его мании эффективности. Студент английской кафедры считал, что человечество тратит адское количество времени на ерунду, и тот, кто ему поможет, будет если не вознагражден, то по крайней мере удовлетворен как творец.

Готовясь к сессии, его группа использовала вечный метод — каждый взял себе пул билетов и обязался их написать. На трех мальчиков в группе приходилось пятнадцать девочек, и поэтому обязательства выполнялись красивыми разборчивыми почерками. Затем группа встречалась и менялась записями.

Чтобы ускорить этот процесс, Дуров написал сайт и назвал его в соответствии с выпускным обетом — durov.com. Там выкладывались филологические билеты и курсовые. Хостинг стоил дешево, и Дуров легко покрывал расходы из своего заработка — он рисовал сайты, а также писал статьи в журнал «Всемирный следопыт» об исторических персонажах. Редактор заказал первую статью его отцу — о римских гладиаторах, — но профессору было неинтересно заниматься перетолмачиванием науки в популярное чтение, и он сплавил халтуру сыну. Тот с радостью заработал на Эдисоне, Форде и братьях Райт, попутно усвоив один из законов медиа — продавать читателю малоизвестного героя лучше, связав его со знаменитостью или с громким событием. Например, посланника Российской империи в Тибет Агвана Доржиева преподнесли как «друга живого бога».

Durov.com наводнили материалы. Сайт прогремел на факультете, и вскоре все курсы размещали там рефераты с лекциями. Преподаватели разделились на две партии. Те, кто помоложе, советовали заглянуть на durov.com за материалами к следующему коллоквиуму. Профессор классической филологии, в честь которого закуток перед кафедрой называли «уголком Дурова», отнесся к идее сына без восторга, но не критиковал.

Преподаватели-консерваторы сочли сайт злом и дорогой к отупению, списыванию и компиляторству. Сопротивление прогрессу укрепило эйджизм Дурова, верящего в молодость: «Пожилые — люди внутри своих конструктов, давят своим мнимым авторитетом. Меня это бесило».

Популярность не сносила крышу тотему и пока не давала оснований полагать, что mass collaboration может стать его главным занятием в жизни, которое даст не только славу, но и хлеб. Когда он встречался со школьными товарищами, говорил, что метит в переводчики какой-нибудь богатой углеводородной конторы типа «Газпрома».

Старая знакомая Бертова как-то проходила по «Школе» и увидела Дурова, окруженного толпой девиц. По словам Бертовой, Дуров заметил ее и кивнул девицам — подождите, я сейчас. Приблизившись, церемонно склонил голову.

— Здравствуйте, Анна Дмитриевна.

— Здравствуйте, Павел Валерьевич. Как поживаете, чем занимаетесь?

— Да вот думаю, Анна Дмитриевна, поработать летом.

— Неужели? И кем?

— Аспен, Калифорния. Это горнолыжный курорт, для очень богатых людей. Они оставляют чаевые. Думаю, может, официантом поехать.

— Как же, Павел Валерьевич, разве это возможно: вы — и тарелки?

— Возможно, Анна Дмитриевна, все возможно.

***

Осенним вечером Дуров с Перекопским засиделись допоздна в квартире на Сенной. Они часто учили заданные слова или возились с домашним заданием, а потом трепались, пока не клонило в сон. Первый курс закончился, и грянул второй.

Дуров любил проповедовать. Он учил Перекопского правильному отношению к учебе: главное — экзамены и подготовка к ним; если не сдал, не стоит убиваться, следует всегда оставаться хладнокровным. «Преподов», как и всех людей, надо понимать — в смысле потребностей, какие мотивы ими управляют, — а также четко улавливать, что им нужно от тебя, и предоставлять это.

«В девяноста девяти случаях знакомств Дуров хочет понравиться, чтобы отношение к нему изменилось в лучшую сторону», — скажет Перекопский позже. Мы будем сидеть в ресторане на крыше самой дорогой гостиницы Москвы, и за его спиной будут блестеть звезды, а гуляющие на Манежной граждане покажутся кем-то вроде термитов, топчущихся около башен недосягаемого муравейника.

Дуров происходил из семьи менее состоятельной, чем у одногруппников, а Перекопский мог позволить себе больше, но и он был ограничен в средствах. После того как «ВКонтакте» стала стоить миллиарды долларов, оба оторвались и жили в лучших гостиницах, работали в самом дорогом офисе Петербурга. «Мы сделали этот мир...»

Мантра Дурова касалась информации. Интернет стер прежнюю картину мира, люди загружают в сеть все больше данных, их жизнь перетекает в двоичный код. Сообща они создают контент и саморегулирующиеся сообщества — тому примером «Википедия». Деньги не главное в свободном интернете. Главное — власть, которая принадлежит тому, кто контролирует потоки информации.

«Смотри, — проговорил Дуров. — Что такое университет? Это же раздробленная структура с удельными княжествами. Физики в своем Петергофе вообще никого не видят, экономический сидит отдельно, юристы тоже».

Перекопский подбрасывал апельсин. Фрукт долетал до потолка, но вовремя останавливался и падал в руку. «Я слышал, на истфаке процветает жуткое политиканство, студсовет, политические споры, — добавил Перекопский, пряча зевок. — Все кипит».

«Ну да, — кивнул Дуров. — Пассионарная прослойка либо за профком, либо против профкома. Те контролируют бюджет — распределяют деньги на мероприятия. Есть за что бороться. К тому же людям важны титулы, это же круто — стать во главе профкома или студкома». Последние дни он торчал на форумах факультетов и разбирался в законах, по которым разгорались и затухали дискуссии.

Дуров визионировал: «Мы придумаем площадку для всех факультетов и создадим иллюзию, что все уже здесь. Ключевых людей приглашаем на роль модераторов — вместе с ними к нам придет аудитория».

«М-м-м, — бросок апельсином, — а что их заставит уйти со своих площадок на нашу?» «Это будет форум, где можно знакомиться с народом с других факультетов, искать общие темы, создавать альтернативные центры силы, становиться известным, — перечислил Дуров. — Мы будем в двадцать раз сильнее, и каждый из примкнувших к нам сможет найти применение этой силы в бизнесе или личной жизни».

«Смотрю, ты не прочь прославиться», — заметил квартиросъемщик. «Надо заняться этим срочно», — донеслось с дивана. «Надо», — зевнул Перекопский, отложил оранжевый шар и щелкнул выключателем.

***

Дуров зарегистрировал домен spbgu.org и выбрал движок для форума. Они с братом подрихтовали кое-какие опции и протестировали. Все работало: форум как форум, с темами, модерацией, вполне безликим дизайном.

Теперь Дурову предстояло стать местным богом из машины, который бы решал споры, авторитетно выступал на горячие темы и регулировал жизнь сообщества. Он предвкушал, как сыграет на сдержках-противовесах чужих амбиций. Верховному модератору следовало тщательно строить образ.

У них с Перекопским была тайная страсть. Они раз двадцать пересмотрели «Матрицу». Остатки трезвомыслящих людей выкрадывают талантливого программиста и втолковывают ему, что виртуальная реальность реальна, а в «истинном» мире машины навевают людям морок, чтобы высасывать из них, спящих, энергию. Предводитель повстанцев Морфеус объясняет герою, что Пифия предрекла: у него талант не только кодить, но и драться с машинами. «Проснись, Нео. Ты избранный».

Хакер и ментор находятся в некоем белом пространстве, одетые во все черное — рубашки, костюмы, туфли. Вдали падший мир. Киану Ривз немного напоминает чертами Дурова. Оба программисты. Оба с миссией.

Черный цвет приглянулся Дурову. Тотем обожал пафос и, когда кодил, включал речи великих ораторов — Муссолини, Мартина Лютера Кинга, Малькольма Икса. Если лепить себе маску, черный цвет идеален — это цвет пафоса, миссии, строгости, проповеди, начальства. Логотип Durov.com — книга в золотом сиянии на черном фоне — смотрелся символом масонской ложи. Собственно, Дуров интересовался масонами — позже он скажет: «Догма» Альберта Пайка стала для него своеобразным нравственным ориентиром.

А пока он стоял перед зеркалом и прикидывал, как выглядит. Черная бейсболка, костюм, туфли, чемоданчик. Это очень просто — не надо париться с выбором одежды, ты просто носишь черное. Но пока стиль не так важен — людям нужно узнать о форуме, а его творец будет завоевывать доверие уже в онлайне.

Дуров списался с модераторами факультетских форумов, и они начали осваиваться на spbgu.org. Но писали и спорили пока недостаточно, мало скандалов, активность перетекала на новый форум вяловато. Следовало нанести визуальный удар и вручить власть тем, у кого ее нет и кто ее хочет.

Наушники прижаты к голове, реальность растворяется, и, как в «Матрице», создается иной мир: шуршат цифры, зеленый двоичный код. Дуров сидел в кресле и рисовал афиши форума.

«Пора неграм отплатить Америке за 310 лет рабства. Покажем им, как надо бороться! Покажем, как проснуться и начать настоящую революцию! Хватит трепать языком. Вам нужны не разговоры, вам нужны действия»

Светлые тона: зеленый, салатовый. Они нравятся юзерам durov.com больше других. Выделяем адрес сайта. Эта штука перевернет жизнь университета.

«Когда мы выйдем на улицы, мы сразимся за общую цель. Против врага, который у нас один на всех и который не хочет нашей свободы!»

Да, ключевое — свобода. Вот эту плашку вниз — «Без рекламы!». Здесь нет маркетологов. Метастазы общества потребления, порабощающего всех, кто мыслит стереотипами, не дотянутся в наш мир.

Нет, конечно, не будем забывать про инстинкты — ставим анимешную девицу наверх, приоткрываем ей декольте, подчеркиваем талию, бедра, ресницы уже прорисованы. Пафос не должен отрываться от земли, от базовых потребностей, иначе его носителя легко троллить за высокодуховность.

Сам Дуров тоже троллил и стебал. Они с Перекопским выписали диск с «Тупым, еще тупее» — без дубляжа и субтитров; тотем писал курсовую по англоязычному юмору. Если кто не помнит, сюжет заключается в том, что два болвана, ужасно предприимчивых и обладающих каким-то хтоническим чувством прекрасного, выполняют миссию — доставляют брошенный в аэропорту чемоданчик незнакомке.

И вот настает время продать форум людям. Звонит будильник. (Проснись, Нео.)

Дуров сворачивает плакаты в рулон, берет чемоданчик, натягивает бейсболку. (Нео выходит из телефонной будки, чтобы принести людям веру в их неограниченные возможности, под «Wake Up» Rage Against The Machine.)

Спускается на лифте и видит, что какой-то урод опять поставил машину у подъезда — приходится ее огибать. («Посмотрите в окно, это закат человечества, а будущее за нами, — наставляет пленного Морфеуса его враг, агент Смит. — Я хочу поделиться теорией. Все животные приспосабливаются к среде обитания, но человек не таков. Заняв какой-то участок, вы размножаетесь. Чтобы выжить, вам приходится захватывать все новые и новые территории. Есть один организм на земле со сходной повадкой. Знаете какой? Вирус. Человечество — это болезнь, раковая опухоль планеты. А мы — лекарство».)

Дуров мстит достойному сыну автомобилизации — вытаскивает из кармана гвоздь, царапает борт и продолжает свой путь.

Заброшенный аэродром, где он сидел с книгой, начали застраивать — потребительское общество возводит вавилонские моллы. В маршрутке он не платит — считает, что право студента на бесплатный проезд распространяется и на нее. Если громила-водитель орет: «Кто не передал?» — встает и выходит.

Через полчаса он у цели. Холл экономфака, где бродят стада студенток со стаканчиками кофе, конспектами, сигаретами. Кто-то болтает по телефону, кто-то вполголоса материт опаздывающего старосту, кто-то сдает в раздевалку пальто. Трафик. Живой трафик, люди, которым бывает сложно создавать связи в жизни.

(«Я знаю, ты здесь. Я знаю, что ты боишься. Боишься нас. Боишься перемен. Я не знаю будущего. Я не могу рассказать тебе, каким оно будет. Но я могу показать тебе, как начать его менять. Я покажу мир без контроля и границ, мир, где возможно все».)

Доступ к трафику лимитирован вахтером. Студбилет филолога на него не действует. Дуров предельно вежлив, показывает афишу, рассказывает про сайт и улыбается, улыбается, улыбается, мысленно посылая привет американцам из бара «Идиот». Это не всегда срабатывает, но экономический вахтер не слишком подозрителен и впускает человека с чемоданчиком.

Дуров ищет точку, с которой просматривается тусовочный пятачок. Изучает лица, одежду, стиль, жестикуляцию. Мы вербуем сторонников, которые расклеят афиши. Если плакатики сорвут, пришпилим новые — и так, пока администрации не станет ясно, что форум ей не переупрямить.

Кто может быть сторонником? Гламурная девица с клатчем? Нет, в их глазах золото, думает Дуров, одни деньги, такие об улучшении мира не размышляют, все больше о том, как захомутать богатенького. Он вспоминает, как зашел на день рождения к однокурснице и услышал, как она с подругами размазывала по стенке парня, которому нравилась, — а когда тот позвонил в дверь, преобразилась, мило улыбаясь, приняла подарки и т. д.

Нет, не наша клиентура — Дуров анализирует трафик, — если девочка, то должна быть неформалка. Пусть не модель, но с харизмой. Наконец мелькает умный взгляд, приближается интеллигентный вроде тип и не ботан. Запускаем программу знакомства.

Алгоритм прост: подходим с невинным вопросом. Выказываем интерес. Начинаем обсуждать факультет. А я с филфака, заходите, у нас дворик неплохой, декан собирает скульптуры, да. Вы, может быть, слышали, он у нас большой оригинал, на день филолога приехал на карете, ряженный в камзол, в том году на «Харлее», а в позапрошлом вообще на воздушном шаре этаким богом из машины. Система пропусков есть, приходите, закажем.

Знакомство состоялось, и возникает тема форума. Из чемоданчика появляются афиши. Избранник рассказывает про профком, оппозицию — весь расклад сил на факультете и тусовки, где вертятся личности, притягивающие глаза и уши. Если избранник оказывается лидером, прекрасно. Если нет, Дуров добирается через него до агентов влияния.

На филфаке вокруг него теперь тусовались не только одногруппницы, но и активные писатели форума. Между лекциями они собирались во дворе и болтали о высоком — например, про ценности либертарианства. Эти споры продолжались в онлайне. Дуров повесил на свой аккаунт картинку с золотым орлом на красном поле и подписался The Architect (архитектор).

«Какое-то время я старался разжигать огонь, — вспоминал он. — Человек приходил на форум — а ничего нет, пусто и мертвые с косами стоят. И он не оставлял сообщения, уходил. Надо было создать иллюзию наличия критической массы. Я использовал заголовки, которые являются стопроцентным попаданием: возможна ли дружба между мужчиной и женщиной и т. д. Спорщиков приходилось зацеплять. Если с оратором все согласятся, он почувствует, что он красавчик, делать тут больше нечего, и уйдет. Если поспорят с ним, немного унизив, — вернется, чтобы доказать, что он лучший».

Однако шпионские истории с проникновением на факультеты и скандальные темы не привели к необходимому эффекту.

Посещаемость сайта росла, количество высказываний — тоже, но недостаточно быстро. Некоторые факультеты (например, истфак) сидели на своих площадках. А самое главное, среднестатистический студент редко лазал в интернете. Следовательно, нужен катализатор в офлайне — чтобы затянуть людей в онлайн. Что бы это могло быть?

Куранты на башне, с которой не удосужились снять рубиновые звезды, пробили 2004 год. Дуров не знал, что на другом полушарии, в заснеженном Гарварде, раскручивалась история, которая превратила своего демиурга из сетевого задрота в одного из влиятельнейших людей мира. Марк Цукерберг хакнул сервер с фотографиями студенток, выкачал файлы и написал программу, которая позволяла выбирать из двух расположенных рядом снимков тот, где более привлекательная девушка. Общежития прилипли к мониторам, выбирая всенародную мисс Гарвард, и локальная сеть рухнула.

Именно в эти дни Дуров перебирал варианты, как раскрутиться через громкое событие. В конце концов его мысли отправились в том же направлении, что у Цукерберга.

***

Новичок рассматривал кружок вокруг парня в черном. Тусовка едва умещалась на «Седьмом небе», узком коридоре третьего этажа, бывшем чердаке. Забавно, что некоторые участники копировали лидера и тоже носили траур.

Любопытство заставило новичка познакомиться — так же, как когда-то толкнуло заниматься нетипичными для филолога вещами: торговать джинсами, редактировать газету «Метростроевец» и разучивать аргентинское танго. Принадлежность к виду «юноша с филфака» в нем подчеркивали стихи и проза — непременные атрибуты гения, который видит сны о чем-то большем. «Идея с конкурсом красоты забавная, но одно дело — мечтать, другое — воплощать» — так новичок описал первое впечатление от консильери. Совершив ритуал знакомства, он старался говорить мало и в основном наблюдал за компанией. Его звали Михаил Равдоникас, и через месяц он тоже облекся в черное.

Вскоре после тусовки на «Седьмом небе» в приемной декана нарисовались Дуров и Перекопский. Их привел завкафедрой межкультурных коммуникаций, знакомство с которым парни активизировали чуть раньше. Так же, как в Перекопском, Дуров вычислил компаньона в завкафедрой и использовал его как мостик к декану. Тот приходился родственником Перекопскому и не противился идее послужить административной подпоркой.

Декан выслушал идею. «Конкурс красоты и дизайна»: отбор девушек в три тура, никаких бикини, декламация, танец, остроумная пикировка, а вы, конечно, возглавляете жюри. Декан благословил «людей в черном», для порядка прочитав лекцию, что «филологини по роду занятий ориентированы на воплощение идеи любви и красоты», и, пожалуйста, никакой пошлости. Активистам выделили 100 000 рублей.

Дуров с Перекопским вышли, едва сдерживаясь, чтобы не сплясать пого. Равдоникас, пораженный скоростью действий компаньонов, подключился к делу. Срочно разыскивались спонсоры, готовые одеть девушек, научить двигаться на сцене, сфотографировать их и помочь с макияжем. Активисты напечатали визитки и плакаты, а также приобрели факс для рассылки предложений. Волокиту и дозвон принял на себя Перекопский, а Дуров нарисовал афиши и подключался на переговорах. Они условились, что в беседе с контрагентами никогда не спорят друг с другом — даже если один из них бредит.

История с маркетингом развивалась гладко. Спонсоры задавали два-три вопроса по условиям и акцептировали участие. Главный приз, ноутбук, ссудила фирма, торговавшая компьютерами на первом этаже филфака. Motivi поделились платьями, а Mary Kay — макияжем. «Фитнес палас» предоставил зал, где рекрутированный хореограф из Мариинки ставил движение. Elle обещал фоторепортаж — за место в жюри. Ближе к маю Перекопский арендовал свет и звукоусилители, а также заказал статуэтку скульптору.

Но это была лишь офлайн-часть артподготовки. Вскоре Дуров выложил на сайт фотосессии девушек, вышедших во второй этап конкурса, и предложил форуму выбрать № 1. Студенческие голоса давали право называться «Мисс зрительских симпатий». Каждая девушка указывала рост и параметры фигуры.

Это выглядело не столь провокативной бомбой, как у Цукерберга, — но вполне себе гранатой, которая взорвалась прямо перед финалом.

Сначала некоторым участницам кто-то нагнал голосов с одного ip-адреса. Дуров держался роли арбитра и подчеркивал, что он не в жюри, а лишь обеспечивает справедливость выражения воли. После чего блокировал фальш-голоса. На форуме возникло семь тем, в которых студенты негодовали, что фальсификацию придумал сам архитектор, чтобы вызвать к себе ненависть.

Дуров и правда поощрял это чувство — неважно, какие эмоции ты вызываешь; важно, чтобы ты волновал людей. Позже, когда счет угодившим в сети «ВКонтакте» перевалил за 10 млн человек, он строжайше запретил репрессировать группы, разжигающие ненависть к создателю сети. А тогда, перед конкурсом, он отменил студенческую номинацию, хотя проголосовали тысячи человек.

В день финала аудитория громокипела. Первый ряд оккупировали спонсоры, декан и приближенные. Дуров с Перекопским отрепетировали все — от выноса цветов до фонограммы и конферанса кавээнщиков, — а сами сели в зал.

Жюри наградило удобную конкурсантку, которая была хороша во всех упражнениях. Решение взорвало форум во второй раз — в ангажированности обвиняли уже оценщиков. Равдоникас, который наблюдал за тем, как конкурс вырос из идеи, брошенной на «Седьмом небе», все понял про тотема и надел черный костюм. И даже шляпу. «Итальянец» Дуров играл «в мафию» по-серьезному.

Как вспоминал один из однокашников, однажды утром во дворе со скульптурами молодые консильери, придавшие физиономиям выражение убийц, все в заветном черном цвете, — плечом к плечу перегородили путь конкуренту. Конкурента звали Иннокентием. Высокий и нескладный деятель, выпускник, выбил себе комнату под студсовет и пытался играть на поле конкурсов красоты и других тусовок. Сначала «мафия» мочила его на форуме, а потом решила как бы в шутку пугнуть во дворе.

Консильери перегородили ему путь и участливо-холодно заглянули в глаза: «You call it „crime“ — we call it „smart family business“». Рослый Иннокентий оказался к подобному не готов и хоть нависал — даже над шляпой Равдоникаса, — но чувствовал, что сейчас отведет взгляд. И отвел. Консильери по-змеиному улыбнулись и двинули к Неве мимо скульптуры «Нос».

Ко всему прочему, Дуров желал растоптать Иннокентия перед девочками. Архитектор прославился с помощью слабого пола, а теперь хотел использовать авторитет. Он начал стрелять во врага ироничными постами, попутно ругая в комментариях с помощью своего виртуала по имени Kreol. Иннокентий сдулся и не получил сотой доли обожания, доставшегося «мафии».

Дуров убедился, что girl power — великий инструмент. Как-то раз мы разговаривали в комнате с видом на Казанский, за которым фонил революционным колором закат — свидетельство верно выбранного штаба для тех, кто хочет взорвать мир. Вертя в руках бейсбольный мяч, Дуров формулировал осознанное в процессе привлечения людей на spbgu.org.

«Акцент надо делать на красивых девушках. Если они придут — соберутся парни, будут показывать, какие они умные, — сказал он, глядя в сторону. — У всех млекопитающих это самое главное. Есть девушки — есть арена, а зритель найдется. Мне всегда важно их мнение по поводу разных фич: если девушкам нравится, значит, остальные съедят. Они идеальные контент-организаторы, они общаются и объединяют вокруг себя остальных».

Дуров действовал исходя из этого правила. Форум бурлил, и надо было использовать страсти, чтобы поощрять пассионарных девиц писать чаще. Что он, собственно, и делал, задруживаясь с ними в офлайне и подталкивая к более активным действиям — иногда даже отдавал модераторскую власть. Это помогало тащить на свою площадку факультеты, пока не примкнувшие к форуму, и переманивать еще не знакомых с тотемом красавиц. Какими средствами? А какая разница!

***

Осенним вечером студент философского факультета Тимур Качарава вышел из магазина «Буквоед» и направился к метро. Не успел Качарава сделать несколько шагов, как на него с криком «Антантифа!» «прыгнули» скинхеды. В ходе неравной драки его ударили ножом в шею, и он умер в считаные минуты.

Петербург встал на уши — война фашистов и антифашистов достигла апогея. История облетела массмедиа, и исследователи национализма получили возможность сказать с экрана, что больше нельзя закрывать глаза на армию бритоголовых.

Через два дня после убийства Качаравы третьекурсник Макс Петренчук сидел на подоконнике в коридоре истфака. Перед ним лежала тетрадь, в которой то и дело расписывались циркулирующие по этажу студенты. Петренчук собирал автографы под требованием к губернатору начать спецрасследование дела. Некоторые из подписантов сначала глядели с недоверием — эпатируя форум истфака, его модератор прикидывался фашистом, и в конце концов маска приросла. Убийство на Невском заставило Петренчука отскрести ее и прийти на лекции с тетрадью.

Петренчук поразился всеобщему безумию — на филфаке девочки вполне ангельского вида читали ему лекцию, что он продался жидомасонам, собирает голоса за грузина, когда русских убивают сотнями. Затем ему стали звонить и угрожать. Петренчук, человек вполне отмороженный и беззаботный, не остановился. Чтобы его пустили на филфак, он заручился поддержкой декана.

Сорвав очередную гроздь автографов, Петренчук осмотрелся и заметил, что за ним следит тип, в облике которого сквозило нечто опереточное — эспаньолка, черный плащ, кейс. Незнакомец понял, что его раскрыли, и шагнул к собирателю подписей.

— Максим?

— Да. А ты кто?

— Я Паша Дуров. Собираете подписи?

Петренчук опешил от того, как с ним общается звезда, но не растерялся и сунул тетрадь: на, подпишись. Дуров черкнул ручкой и откланялся, но еще пять минут стоял в стороне и наблюдал за Петренчуком, надев вежливую улыбку.

Убедившись, что активист не мошенник, он вернулся домой и написал на форуме, что познакомился с Петренчуком и тот оказался искренним антифашистом. Количество подписантов выросло до 3000 человек. Дело Качаравы взяли под контроль ректорат и опасавшийся шума губернатор.

Дуров нуждался в фигуре, которая перетащила бы историков с их форума «Покемония», где тусовалось 200 человек, на spbgu.org. Петренчук подходил на роль безумца-зажигалки — он гнал против всех, не пробился ни в профком, ни в студсовет и скандалил с обеими ветвями власти. Толкал дикие речи в пьяном виде, нимало не заботясь о высоком штиле. Дуров видел это, но считал, что средства оправданы целью.

Эпатаж и разжигание в исполнении добровольного клоуна загнали раздел истфака выше международников и филологов — по количеству сообщений. Однако чем больше истфаковцев Петренчук перетаскивал с «Покемонии» на форум, тем больше отбивался от рук. Модератор, который ведет себя как фрик и отказывается занимать позицию беспристрастного судьи, стал раздражать главного архитектора.

Нет, конечно, форум истфака бурлил спорами про Путина, гомосексуалистов, еврейскую закулису, результаты Великой Отечественной — и это было прекрасно. Чтобы зажечь танцпол, Дуров сам прикидывался циником и писал: «Жаль, что Гитлер нас не завоевал». Но правила на истфаке нарушались слишком часто. Модератор ввязывался в драки и троллил гостей.

Однажды Петренчук, напившись, опубликовал чрезмерно разнузданный спич и был подслушан конкурентами с «Покемонии», которые не могли ему простить захвата власти и увода глаз с их форума. Самый непримиримый его враг, редактор истфаковской газеты «Студень» (медиапремия Дарвина за название) Даша Бондаренко почуяла запах крови и вцепилась в Петренчука.

Эти два человека давно сошлись в клинче. Петренчук рассказывал, что Даша считала его неприятным идиотом — как-то раз он совершил грубую ошибку, высказав сомнения в ее уме и красоте, чем нажил непримиримого врага. И главное, их интересы пересекались — Даша жаждала власти над истфаком за пределами «Покемонии». Макс, чья популярность держалась на истерике и клоунаде, ее бесил. Она писала резко и эпатирующе: «Я кончаю», — в ответ Равдоникасу, посвятившему ей рассказ. Но поддеть Петренчука так, чтобы дезавуировать раз и навсегда, у пользователя Jennyfer не получалось.

Даша была знакома с Дуровым — брала интервью для «Студня». Ей понравился «горделивый профиль», а также очищенное от стереотипов восприятие мира.

Когда случился скандал с фашистом-модератором, она взяла у декана письмо в стиле «Петренчук подрывает нравственность» и встретилась с Дуровым. Тот внимательно слушал ее — эффектная девушка вместо надоевшего хулигана; очень, очень вовремя она пришла. Очень гладкий, не подкопаться, повод убрать Петренчука. Дуров протянул руку и взял у Даши письмо.

Вскоре Петренчук читал мейл от консильери в духе: «Прости, мне не нравится вмешательство властей, но придется тебя отставить. Тебе не следовало попадать в такую историю. А теперь — сам понимаешь…»

Биться за власть после столь сердечного разъяснения Петренчук не стал.

Спустя четыре года на тусовке выпускников истфака он увидит Дурова, по-прежнему в черном. Согласно рассказу Петренчука, тот придет с Дашей и, обнимая ее, высокомерно кому-то станет растолковывать про уже взлетевший «ВКонтакте». Макс увидит, как странные, вызывавшие сомнения причины и следствия из прошлого сплетаются в прозрачный сюжет, и с горя напьется.

Дуров писал в форум все меньше, разве что в дискуссионных темах и закрытых группах или вмешиваясь в конфликты. Он переводил свой стиль мышления в тексты — предельная очищенность от иллюзий, иногда нарочито «тупой-еще-тупее» юмор, краткость и, главное, поворот против очевидности и стереотипов.

Тогда, в 2004 году, трафик измерялся тысячами посетителей в день. Перекопский вспоминал, как заставал у Дурова дома семейные сцены. Заглянув в счетчик, мать комментировала: «Павлуша, сегодня что-то очень мало». Дуров злился: «Замолчи, пожалуйста, не мешай».

Когда форум поражала бацилла занудства, Дуров подпускал угара репликами выдуманных персонажей. «Очень сочные виртуалы, в их реальность верили: антифеминистка, гомофоб, сталинист. Я отстаивал их точку зрения. На 9 Мая шла моя любимая волна: Сталин преступник; не победа, а поражение; при таких потерях называть случившееся победой — кощунство; лучше бы нас завоевал Гитлер. У меня дед прошел всю войну, защищал Ленинград, и мне непросто было принять эту точку зрения. Но я неплохо вжился в роль, негодовал по поводу оккупации Прибалтики и Польши».

Виртуалам свято верили, объявляли им джихады, жаловались их создателю. А дальше костер горел сам — врукопашную сходились фанаты альтернативных концепций а-ля Анатолий Фоменко, а также тролли с другими перверсиями.

Форум получал предложения о рекламе, но Дуров не ставил ее, держа слово, данное на плакате, — «ad free». На жизнь он зарабатывал, рисуя сайты.

Студенты оживлялись к сессии. Дурова избрали командиром взвода на военной кафедре — его отделение штудировало США. Разбираясь в истории Штатов, он заинтересовался масонами, сыгравшими важную роль в создании ценностей, воодушевляющих американцев как нацию.

Три года подряд он получал «стипендию Потанина», для чего требовалось побеждать в лидерской игре. Со всего университета селектировали тех, кто не только умен, но и способен вести за собой, и сталкивали в одной комнате, дав какое-нибудь задание. Смысл — понять по групповой динамике, кто лидер в среде лидеров. Испытание проходили единицы, и «потанинкой» гордились, как мало чем гордятся на филфаке.

***

В июне 2011 года я заглянул на лекцию потанинского стипендиата Юры Лифшица. Вообразите невысокого, худого и чрезвычайно активного, громкоговорящего Гарри Поттера, разменявшего математику высочайшего уровня на позицию в Yahoo и потом вернувшегося в Россию заниматься образованием и бизнес-инкубаторами. Это Лифшиц.

Лекция была про корпоративную культуру, но оратор взял шире и полтора часа держал аудиторию соображениями, как делать карьеру и строить великие компании. Когда в конце его спросили, почему он бесплатно делится ценными сведениями, Лифшиц хмыкнул: «Из эгоистических соображений. Во-первых, формулируя мысли вслух, я начинаю лучше их понимать. Во-вторых, я верю, что, когда люди делятся друг с другом знаниями, они улучшают качество социальной системы в целом. Экономика дарения выгодна всем — тому, кто дарит, выгода возвращается».

На потанинском отборе состязались ораторы такого уровня и стиля. Дуров отличался от них и выигрывал. Лифшиц вспоминал, что интернет-тотем говорил негромко, но, когда открывал рот, все замолкали. Дело, впрочем, было не в какой-то особенной мудрости, а в трезвости и доходчивости. «Паша был взрослее и взвешеннее нас. Когда он выходил из комнаты, становилось легче говорить, и я снова чувствовал себя лидером». Дуров доминировал, даже когда искали кафе для поствыпускного сбора.

Тролль с первой парты превратился в небожителя, который иногда спускается в народ. Дуров не был оппозиционером власти — он создал параллельную ей структуру, но при этом всегда поддерживал хорошие отношения с ней. Выступал на ученом совете, рекламировал мероприятия. Когда понадобилось выставить кого-то из студактива поболтать для телевидения о «Единой России», не отказался и резонерствовал. На военной кафедре их просили указать в анкете любимого политика, и комвзвода начертал: «Путин» (позже оправдывался, что хотел вписать Рузвельта, но счел такой вариант непатриотичным).

«Я никогда не списывал, — вспоминал брат Николай. — Павел всегда списывал и не терзался. Им на военкафедре сказали, что списывать можно, это как военная хитрость, но если поймают — двойка». Он подумал немного, будто сопоставляя какие-то события, и стал как бы оправдывать брата: «Павел — филолог, там много материала, от которого если не фанатеешь, то запомнить нереально. А мне надо было утверждения учить, теоремы».

«Дуров всегда хотел быть известным, чтобы его все знали, тщеславный, хотел власти над умами, — перечислял Перекопский. — Всегда выпендривался. Его мотивы — смесь тщеславия и благородства».

Сам Перекопский горел идеей открыть свое дело — статуса консильери ему было явно недостаточно. Уже на третьем курсе он убедился, что определяющее значение имеет нетривиальная идея: «Только на халяве и делаются большие деньги. На гениальных идеях, где не требуется много работать, а только немного пошевелить головой». Если Дуров играл во влияние и загадочность, Перекопский казался проще: «Я коллекционирую деньги. Нужно же что-то коллекционировать?»

Для начала Перекопский открыл курсы английского, где преподавали носители языка. Стартовый капитал он взял у отца своей девушки, нефтяника. Что-то типа 2000 долларов, чтобы снять помещение. На мебель потратился сам. Курсы раскрутились, и иногда не хватало учителей. Когда слетел один из знакомцев по бару «Идиот», выручил Дуров: втолковал двум гламурным девицам грамматику, да так, что те требовали «еще того мальчика».

Затем приятельница из финской юридической компании попросила Перекопского найти ей практикантов. Тот нашел и получил заказ еще на несколько позиций. Вскоре у него образовалось бойкое кадровое агентство. Сидевший в жюри конкурса торговец компьютерами подбивал мафию открыть магазин в интернете, но Дуров скривился — торговля не для людей в черном; они про новую нервную систему человечества.

Мама испекла торт на день рождения, и он созвал друзей в буфете. Это походило на собрание масонской ложи. Действо разворачивалось по сложившемуся ритуалу — Дуров доставал из чемоданчика апельсин, чистил его и раздавал дольки приближенным, по значимости. Своей девушке, Перекопскому, Равдоникасу. За апельсином следовал торт, и после славословий трапеза целомудренно завершалась.

Вечером в квартире Перекопского на Сенной снималось другое кино. На диване сидела пятерка победительниц конкурса красоты, и хозяин втирал им, какое блестящее будущее их ждет. Один из участников тусовки вспоминал, как Перекопский невзначай перечислял свои успехи: ищу недвижимость тайскому премьер-министру, подбираю один дом, второй — а ему не нравится! Музыканты «Под водой» хлестали коньяк. Равдоникас заперся в ванной с одной из участниц форума и, видимо, преподавал урок риторики. Дуров сидел на диване и пил апельсиновый сок.

Гоп-компания оставалась ночевать, а тотем и его девушка встали и, накинув пальто, покинули квартиру.

***

Заканчивался последний курс. Spbgu.ru жил своей жизнью. Поколение юзеров, не знавших архитектора лично, считали его едва не привидением. Иногда против власти тотема создавали коалиции, писали воззвания к народу против верховного модератора и т. д. — но Дуров или не обращал внимания, или отщелкивал оппозиционеров краткими репликами.

Что действительно его волновало — как менять ресурс. Идея социальной сети, где люди выступают под настоящими именами, еще не материализовалась, и он сам о ней не думал, хотя интуитивно вводил все больше социальных опций.

У каждого пользователя были: профиль с датой рождения, увлечениями; нечто вроде стены, где можно написать отзыв о ее хозяине;

возможность написать заметку (особенно полюбил ее Равдоникас, печатавший стихи и рассказы), создать фотоальбом и открыть его, выбрав уровень публичности. Сотни юзеров поставили маркеры, отмечающие их дома на виртуальной карте Петербурга, которую тотему помог написать физик Кузнецов, он же Кузя. Дуров отметил на ней свой дом рядом с аэродромом, где теперь царствовали торговцы в нагромождениях стекла и бетона.

Майским утром он и Перекопский зашли в аудиторию, сели за парту и выложили ноутбуки — неуклюжие, похожие одновременно на станцию управления полетами и режиссерский пульт. Группа ходила с толстыми справочниками и бумажными словарями, а у них стояла программа Lingvo. Правила разрешали иметь мини-компьютеры при себе, но пользоваться запрещалось. Начинался третий этап госэкзамена «Английский письменный».

Надзирала за их потоком недавно начавшая преподавать аспирантка. «Не очень симпатичная», — заметил Перекопский. Аспирантка нервничала и принялась терроризировать консильери: «Уберите компьютер». Отличники проигнорировали. Их ноуты были захлопнуты. «Вы слышите? Убирайте компьютеры». «Они же выключены», — отозвался Дуров. И тогда надзирательница допустила ошибку…

Тусовка вокруг группы «Мафия» считала приемлемым — как и в общеобразовательных классах — разговаривать на «вы», а «ты» включать лишь с совсем близкими друзьями. Как говорил Равдоникас, высшая степень близости — когда, перейдя с «вы» на «ты», через какое-то время опять начинаешь употреблять «вы»; как бы высшая форма признательности, когда человеку не нужно подчеркивать, что он твой друг. А вот посторонние, «тыкнув», получали намек, что так обращаться не следует.

— Убери компьютер и не выпендривайся!

Дуров заглянул в глаза надсмотрщице и стальным голосом произнес: «Заткнись, дура, мы пять лет учились, а ты нам мешаешь, коза закомплексованная». Перекопский заспешил добавить что-то более учтивое, но поезд ушел. Аспирантка взбешенно простучала каблуками в деканат. Сдавшим на отлично компаньонам влепили неуды.

Холодея от жажды мести, они сели в буфете и набросали план расследования. Кто такая. Каковы слабые места в позиции деканата. Забросили удочки в форум. Доброжелатели подсказали, куда копать, — через несколько рук они добрались до знания, что в ходе экзамена аспирантка должны была помочь остолопам с платного отделения, незаметно подсунув ответы.

Мафиози явились на кафедру и выдвинули против обвинений свои обвинения. В ситуации, когда слово споткнулось о слово, а одной из сторон был сын уважаемого завкафедрой, факультет сдал назад. Нахалы получили объективные оценки, а их врагу был объявлен строгий выговор. «Я не чувствую стыда за свои поступки, потому что, если и случались какие-то эпизоды, я давно выкинул их из памяти», — отмахнется позже Дуров.

Когда я спросил декана о конфликте, Богданов уклончиво и витиевато, но все же намекнул, что Дуров, безусловно, хам, но и аспирантка не без греха. Декана больше занимала другая тема. Битых полчаса он рассказывал о своем изобретении, которое считал прообразом «ВКонтакте». Это был гигантский складень, «левкас 14 метров, самый большой в мире, 350 лиц». Богданов вклеил туда фотографии всех своих друзей, авторов прочитанных книг и, кажется, даже киноартистов, а также лики святых.

«Идея в том, что каждое индивидуальное существование состоит из множества чужих, — вещал Богданов. — Друзей, врагов, героев, лиц, с которыми я еще встречусь, тех, кого я читал, — и я могу это расширить до человечества. Я даже терял сознание перед складнем — как я мог знать это все?» В глубинах полок его шкафа блестели рамки, в которые были вставлены фотографии студенческих праздников — Богданов в камзоле, на осле, на воздушном шаре. «Паша Дуров сделал гораздо более значимую вещь, — продолжил он, стуча карандашом по столу. — Форум, а потом и „ВКонтакте" — это форма коллективного существования, которая позволяет не просто, стоя рядом с артефактом, чувствовать его, а жить в одном пространстве с людьми, которые что-то для тебя значат. Паша воплотил недоступным мне способом идею всей моей жизни. И он сделал ее доступным инструментом для огромного количества людей».

За университетским дипломом Дуров так и не пришел. Необходимость тратить время на административную волокиту отвратила его. Не то чтобы он боялся контактировать с бюрократией — просто, развязавшись с учебой, Дуров окончательно разделил волнующие и не волнующие его вещи.

Перекопский подначивал: спорим, у тебя через год не будет миллиона долларов, а у меня будет. Дуров уловил вопрос, но оставил где-то на периферии сознания.

Его мысли занимали изменения, происходящие с миром из-за проникновения интернета. Пока они не массовые. Например, в «Википедии» торчат одни гики, но очевидно, что аудитория людей, которые пишут туда статьи, редактируют, спорят, — все они, так или иначе, учатся договариваться и формируют свой авторитет на базе замеченных сообществом поступков, а не лозунгов и деклараций. Ключевое слово в викономике — «делиться». Обогащая среду, ты делаешь себя же сильнее и работаешь на свое будущее.

Дурову нравилось наблюдать, как созданная им среда для общения жила сама по себе, но он понимал, что инструмент коллаборации «форум» устаревает. Какой будет следующая ступень эволюции в том, как люди обмениваются информацией? Он перебирал разные версии, но не слышал щелчка над ухом, который знаменовал бы качественно новый поворот, в который он так хотел вложить все свое желание воздействовать на реальность.

«Миллион так миллион, — очнулся Дуров и с любопытством посмотрел на Перекопского. — Спорим».

Если бы он знал, что через год, когда Перекопский вспомнит о пари, его жизнь навсегда изменится благодаря одной случайной встрече, — свалился бы в обморок, как декан перед тысячеликим складнем.

Глава 3

Мафия открывает глаза

Лежащая на столе газета редко поставляла читателям сенсационные откровения, но для этого круглолицего преппи листать «Деловой Петербург» было чем-то вроде традиции. Поселившись на кампусе, он не бросил это занятие — приходил на сайт dp.ru и читал, что происходит на родине. Когда этот выпускник Tufts University вернулся из Америки с дипломом и начал размышлять, с какого бизнеса взять старт, газета играла роль сводок с фронта.

Шапка про налоги, подвал о пошлинах на вывоз древесины, новости о линии автозавода во Всеволожске и очередном офисе глобальной корпорации в Питере. И закадровым текстом, двадцать пятым кадром: возможности, много возможностей.

За семь лет отсутствия Славы Мирилашвили город изменился — утихли лесные и другие войны за заводы и пароходы, бандиты скрылись в подполье, «крышу» обеспечивал класс силовиков. Еще до того, как Михаила Мирилашвили осудили за похищение похитителей его отца (Славиного деда), мальчика вывезли в Израиль. Он прибыл на Святую землю с выданными Гризом школьными документами и попал в школу для детей дипломатов. Окончив ее, захотел сменить континент и подал документы в Массачусетский университет Лиги плюща.

Оставаться в Штатах выпускник Слава не желал — очевидно, что в России, где стартовал потребительский бум, незанятых рынков было больше. Семейный бизнес выстоял — управляющая компания избавилась от казино и сконцентрировалась на сдаче недвижимости в аренду. Пока отец сидел, дела курировал дед Михаил, с кражи которого началась их семейная эпопея.

Слава листал «Петербург», пропуская большинство заметок. Ему хотелось скорее добраться до полосы о молодых предпринимателях. Нет, про него там вряд ли написали — хотя первый опыт Славы был занимателен. Взяв в долю одноклассника Льва Левиева, отучившегося в канадском университете МакГилл и поработавшего аудитором в Ernst & Young, он расставил платежные терминалы по принадлежащей клану петербуржской недвижимости.

В 2006 году рынок поглощающих деньги автоматов взлетал, но компаньоны быстро убедились, что сыграть вбелую не удастся. Например, если ты не сдаешь кэш фирмам, которые занимаются обналичкой, теряешь прибыль. Или не теряешь (если у тебя низкая ставка аренды), но тогда в проигрыше остается арендодатель. То есть в случае с Мирилашвили — сами Мирилашвили.

Скорее всего, у Славы были и другие резоны бросать терминалы, но в данном случае это неважно. Важно, что он искал, куда вложиться.

Полосу про отроков в бизнесе занимало интервью неизвестного чувака. Слава прочел лид, в котором говорилось, что этот человек создал сайт, где общаются студенты универа. Далее утверждалось, что персонаж зарабатывает на баннерной рекламе приличные деньги. «Прикольно», — подумал Слава, рассматривавший вариант с инвестициями в сеть.

Речь в «Деловом Петербурге» шла о Дурове, а историю с рекламой выдумала Эльнара Петрова, автор интервью. Тотем почти ничего не получал с форума. Просто Эльнара однажды уже допрашивала Дурова насчет рецепта, как выиграть три потанинские стипендии подряд, и, чтобы оправдать второе явление понравившегося героя, продала редактору историю о бизнес-успехах студента. Дуров явился к ней «с этим своим саквояжиком», в черной бейсболке и пиджаке с набитыми поролоном плечами. Открыл рот и не закрывал два часа. Редактор названивал Эльнаре и кричал: «Гони его уже наконец!» Но та не могла прервать Дурова.

Этот факт странен сам по себе, так как я не встречал людей, произносивших в любую единицу времени больше слов, чем Эльнара. Позже она выйдет замуж за главного разработчика «ВКонтакте» Андрея Рогозова, я зайду к ним в гости, и мы будем вспоминать историю ее знакомства с Дуровым.

«Я поняла, что для Павла самое страшное, когда кто-то работает за зарплату, — щебетала Эльнара. — Это осталось до сих пор, он щедрый, но опасается, если люди помешаны на бонусах, этих премиях, перестанут гореть духом. Еще он был нетерпим к людям, которые медленно понимают сказанное и сами плохо говорят, медленно работают, ну, ты понял».

Уходя, я пройду мимо кухни и услышу, как Эльнара моет в одиночестве тарелки и продолжает: «Ну да, Паша все твердил: хочу, хочу создать сообщество, объединять все больше, больше вузов. Конечно. Собрал кучу людей, а что с ними делать, непонятно…»

Так вот, Слава влип в текст. Пассаж, где публике предъявлялся герой, он перечитал несколько раз. Вспомнился Дом культуры с алкоголиками и евангелистами, набеги на пышечную, Тася с ее медяками, деликатно ползущий за спиной лимузин. Его одноклассник и друг Дуров замутил популярный сайт и теперь рассуждает со страниц городской газеты о личной эффективности и сетевых социальных проектах.

Слава понимал, что Дуров интуитивно следует за трендом — в начале нулевых появились и прогремели платформы Livejournal (блоги), Myspace (страницы музыкантов и их композиции), Classmates (связи между старыми друзьями), Friendster (то же, но между всеми подряд). В России успели стартовать «Одноклассники» — клон Classmates. Но больше всего Славе нравилась закрытая соцсеть Facebook, в которую могли попасть только учащиеся североамериканских универов — чтобы получить доступ, он авторизовался через персональную почту на домене Tufts University.

Facebook требовал реальных имени и фамилии, а клонов, троллей и других бестий вычищал. Удостоившиеся чести пользователи обменивались личными сообщениями, публиковали фото, назначали встречи, подмигивали понравившимся персонажам и при этом видели, что нового произошло у друзей.

Дуров произвел схожий ресурс для тех же студентов и владел вниманием пяти тысяч человек в день. Слава взял трубку и набрал Льва Левиева. «Шалом», — отозвался Лев и прослушал композицию «Есть мегакрутой чел, школьный друг, очень умный, с суперпроектом, надо вытащить его поболтать». Возражений не последовало. Слава разыскал мейл Дурова и написал ему.

Получив письмо, тот был не менее удивлен и рад. Старый товарищ, да еще с желанием и возможностями начать бизнес — конечно, встречаемся. Слава и Лев пригласили Дурова в петербургский офис семьи Мирилашвили на Тверскую улицу. Взявший название «мафия» самозванец, озираясь, шагал по коридору штаба, где сидели настоящие консильери. После приветствий и вопросов за жизнь он включил обаяние и быстро снял сомнения, работать с ним или нет. «Разбирается в дизайне, как Джобс, очень хорошо говорит, пишет речи и тексты», — обрисовал первое впечатление Левиев.

После абстрактных дискуссий, что следует строить в интернете, Слава и Лев повернули к оппоненту ноутбук с открытым Facebook. Не изучавший его доселе Дуров всмотрелся и услышал щелчок.

Находка Цукерберга претендовала на гениальность — создать сообщество, где ты действуешь под реальным именем и отвечаешь за свои поступки. Да, жизнь постепенно перетекала в интернет, отражалась в блогах и форумах, но слома парадигмы не происходило. Люди привыкли воспринимать сеть как другую реальность и видеть себя там в льстящем себе фантастическом ракурсе — выдуманные образы, псевдонимы, ники, аватары с героями фильмов и игр.

Должен был найтись кто-то, имеющий наглость взорвать легитимность инкогнито и заманить человека в сеть в его натуральном, библейском виде, без прикрытия срама — под настоящим именем. Не то чтобы Цукерберг совершил этот шаг первым, но в отличие от разных «одноклассников» он воплотил на одном сайте удобный интерфейс и сервисы, обслуживающие базовые человеческие потребности: общение, самопрезентацию, самореализацию. Аудитория Facebook идеально годилась для эксперимента — лучшие университеты мира, люди около двадцати лет.

После просмотра Facebook компаньоны сказали впроброс, без конкретики: думаем, куда нам вложиться; рады делать бизнес с тобой. Дуров возвращался к метро через Таврический сад и слушал себя. Ему еще ничего не предложили, не обещали, но внутри дрожала струна, сообщавшая удивительно спокойные и счастливые колебания. Их частота давала железобетонное ощущение, что теперь все будет хорошо, очень хорошо.

Дуров сошел в метро, вынырнул, распахнул дверь в квартиру, включил монитор, надел наушники. В тишине звучала та же струна.

Когда все изменится необратимо и его личная война за независимость переживет апогей, в три часа ночи, сбившимся, не таким твердым, каким ему хотелось говорить, голосом Дуров скажет: «Вера в это ощущение не покидала меня очень долго. Появились „ВКонтакте“, миллион долларов, на который мы спорили с Ильей, инвестиции — а я уже порадовался, заранее, и пережил, что все эти события произойдут».

Вскоре поступило предложение — продать сайт и написать на его основе русскоязычный клон Facebook. Форум оценили в 10 000 долларов. Дуров взял тайм-аут на размышления и набросился на тех, чье мнение считал полезным. Соглашаться или нет?

Группа «Мафия» выступила скорее за сделку. «Паша, продай форум, купи машину!» — убеждала Дурова Эльнара, сыгравшая медийного

Вергилия. «Не хочу машину, — отмахивался Дуров. — Меня укачивает».

Модератор факультета международных отношений Алексей Кобылянский вспоминал, что вариант с новым сайтом рассматривался как основной и споры велись вокруг названия — в частности, предлагался StudentList. «Я был недостаточно прозорлив, чтобы самому вложиться», — добавил он.

Дуров отказался, хотя, сказав «да», получил бы контроль в создаваемой компании или существенно больше денег. Но Дуров определял, как себя вести, по иным параметрам. Кобылянский сказал об этом так: «Если Павел и предприниматель, то нового толка. Он отодвигал деньги на второй план и концентрировался на социальном эффекте и ценности для потребителей. Это, кстати, послужило поводом для мифа, что „ВКонтакте“ — проект ФСБ, люди не понимали такой благотворительности».

Парадигма социальной сети требовала нового интерфейса, имени, кода. А spbgu.org и так может помочь, решил архитектор и лично анонсировал форумчанам новый сайт, где люди взаимодействуют под реальными именами.

Слава и Лев взяли время на раздумья и предъявили Дурову несколько вариантов участия в предприятии, которому будет принадлежать написанная с нуля соцсеть. От зарплаты за 100 000 рублей и крошечной доли до 25 000 рублей и 20%, включая возможность де-факто блокировать неугодные решения.

Дуров колебался: «Я хотел обеспечить свои финансовые потребности раз и навсегда». Они с братом жили с мамой, которая «как прорывной провинциал любила деньги» и твердила, что пора зарабатывать более трех копеек.

Известный венчурный капиталист Билл Дрейпер однажды сказал: «Не тратьте даже время на размышления в сторону стартап-бизнесов

Silicon Valley Style, если у вас в голове одна идея — как прокормить семью или купить себе ранчо. Это масштаб малого бизнеса — достойного, важного, социального. Но не того, кто запускает проект, — тот не должен думать о том, сколько денег он „поднимет"; только о том, как он изменит мир. И мир, возможно, ему потом заплатит».

Архитектора подмывало разом избавиться от житейских проблем, но ему хватило выдержки, и он предпочел стратегическую выгоду сиюминутной. Дуров верил, что стоимость его сети будет исчисляться в миллионах долларов. Мысль о том, что он, архитектор и творец, станет бесправным менеджером для своего детища, казалась невыносимой.

Друзья обговорили детали. По 20% — Дурову, Мирилашвили и Левиеву. 40% — Славиному деду, компании которого обеспечивали бэкофис и тыл на случай приключений. Дуров — гендиректор с фактическим правом вето.

Последнее пригодилось почти сразу. Управляя проектом, Дуров с самого начала блокировал различные идеи Славы и Льва, которые, например, хотели присоединить к соцсети интернет-магазины — коммерцию, создававшую cash flow. Хотя Перекопский, который был в курсе перемен, предложил привязать к соцсети рекрутинговый сервис ВКадре.ру и получил одобрение. Через год Дуров пожалел об этом решении и уничтожил непопулярный сервис.

Стратегию тройка основателей определила сразу: никакой монетизации и, в частности, рекламы первые несколько лет. За год предстоит набрать миллион пользователей. Все усилия надо приложить к тому, чтобы дать людям удобный инструмент коммуникации, чтобы они тащили в сеть друзей и превратили ее в доминирующее средство общения в интернете.

Слава взял кредит у отцовской фирмы и вложил в дело 30 000 долларов. Еще летом Дуров взял скопленные за три года деньги и купил сервер для будущих проектов. Так стартап обеспечил себя мощностями. Оставалось придумать название, а затем написать код.

Тотем Петербургского университета поступил наоборот.

***

Лабораторию института математики Макса Планка огласило пиликанье телефона. За окном медитативно падали листья и играли оркестры — население Бонна угорало по классической музыке на фестивале памяти Бетховена.

Телефон пропиликал еще несколько раз, пока появившийся аспирант не взял трубку. Мужской голос спросил Николая Дурова. «Его нет, — вздохнул аспирант. — Когда придет, сказать не могу. Он не появляется в какое-то определенное время».

За четыре года, которые Николай занимался высшей алгеброй в Германии и готовил диссертацию на петербургский матмех, родственники привыкли, что дозвониться до него трудно. Мобильная связь была дорога, и мать пользовалась международной телефонной карточкой. Под аккомпанемент струнных коллеги уведомили Николая, что ему звонили, и, когда после очередной нетерпеливой трели он поднял трубку, там оказался брат.

«Я занялся новым проектом», — без преамбулы сообщил Дуров и выдал параметры. Социальная сеть для студентов, профиль, стена, на которой отображается личная активность, сообщения, фотозагрузчик и альбомы. Плюс важнейшее — поиск людей не только по институтам-школам и годам обучения, но и по факультетам. «С чего лучше начинать?»

Николай не особенно удивился. Он помогал брату с первого написанного им куска кода. Программа рисовала Сатурн и посередине Солнце — планета вращалась вокруг него почему-то по прямоугольной орбите. Когда брат придумал форум университета, он улучшал его движок InVision, правил php-код, добавлял новые функции. Форум превратился в проект с приличным трафиком, и Николай оптимизировал распределение нагрузки на сервер. Павел дорабатывал сайт, с большей охотой занимаясь пользовательскими интерфейсами и дизайном.

Но написать социальную сеть с нуля — это звучало как совсем другая история. Это было труднее, чем изменить старый сайт даже на 90%. Николай ответил: «Я бы сначала занялся библиотекой авторизации и входом на сайт, а потом прикрутил остальной функционал».

Времени у братьев на эксперименты не оставалось — «Одноклассники» стремительно росли и, что самое скверное, запустился прямой конкурент — MoiFakultet.ru. Над ним трудились парни из МГУ под руководством каких-то экзотических, по слухам, австралийских инвесторов. Дуров зарегистрировался и стал разбираться, что натворили конкуренты.

Успокоился он быстро. Парни привлекли всего 1700 пользователей. Они не заморачивались со своими фишками и скопировали Facebook — начиная с того, что при регистрации требовали указывать почту на домене вуза. Это была явная глупость. Мало того что не каждый институт имел сайт и выдавал студентам e-mail — еще и редкий студент стремился получить этот почтовый ящик. Позднее MoiFakultet стал просить номер студбилета, но революции это нововведение не произвело.

Дуров начал кодить. Помимо правила реальных имен он ввел схожие с Facebook возможности, которые перечислил в телефонном разговоре брату. По неделе ушло на фото и опцию «назначь встречу». Одним из главных преимуществ он полагал максимально детализированный поиск по вузам и школам. Для последних он ввел поиск по литере класса — «А», «Б», «В» и т. д.

Его девушка скрупулезно коллекционировала данные обо всех факультетах России и Украины, на которые Дуров серьезно рассчитывал. Если не находилось информации в открытых источниках, она звонила в Министерство образования или ректораты самих институтов. База расширяла географию — Москва, Петербург, Новосибирск, Екатеринбург, Челябинск, Нижний Новгород, Самара. Затем Киев, Одесса, Харьков.

Название «ВКонтакте» пришло в голову сразу, без романтического перебора вариантов. Оно звучало легко. Сначала Дуров хотел добавлять названия городов — типа «В Контакте С Хабаровском», но вовремя отказался от этой идеи.

Получившийся сайт в серо-синих тонах стал горючим сырьем, спиртовой таблеткой, валежником для костров амбиций интернет-спорщиков. Лейтмотив все эти годы неизменен: украл «человек в черном» идею Цукерберга или нет. «Тупоконечники» утверждают, что, раз взял основные решения, — вор. «Остроконечники» отвечают, что идеи ничего не стоят и висят в ноосфере, срывай и надкусывай — главное в том, как их докрутить.

Сам Дуров не видел в переработке чужих идей ничего предосудительного: «Стив Джобс учился и декомпилировал „Сони“, разбирая Walkman'ы и ощупывая их полиграфию. Если бы общество послевоенной Японии или Америки 80-х относилось к заимствованиям так, как сегодня относимся мы, там могло бы попросту ничего не вырасти».

Отвечая на прямой вопрос о копировании, Дуров не отрицал, что произвел на свет клон. Когда закрытая версия «ВКонтакте» уже была запущена, на форуме физфака разгорелась дискуссия с парнями из MoiFacultet.ru, сравнимая с самыми кассовыми драками на форуме истфака.

Автор: durov 3.12.2006, 23:33

Ребята, важное объявление.

Данный сайт создан на профессионально низком уровне и имеет десятки дыр, через которые хакеры могут узнать вашу личную информацию. БД со всеми личными данными, внесенными на moifakultet, продается в интернете за 800 долларов. Я бы не поверил этому, если бы мне не предложили купить базу данных, от которой я, разумеется, отказался. Но я отказался, а кто-то согласится.

Почему предложили мне — я один из создателей проекта ВКонтакте.ру. Этот сайт, как и moifakultet, является клоном американского сайта facebook.com, однако мы создаем наш, российский сайт со своей спецификой и рядом функций. Если вас заинтересовал moifakultet, но вам не нравятся баги, слабая функциональность, корявость в альтернативных браузерах и т. д., я советую использовать ВКонтакте.ру.

Друзья, если вы посмотрите сайт и согласитесь, что vkontakte.ru — проект более серьезный и профессиональный, прошу пригласить туда друзей и предупредить их о том, о чем я рассказал. Для всех нас очень важна ваша поддержка — без нее проект и все наши старания бессмысленны. Пожалуйста, напишите, что вы думаете об этом.

Автор: durov 4.12.2006, 7:44

UPDATE!

Только что мне рассказали, что администратор сайта moifakultet.ru теперь обвиняет нас в том, что мы его якобы злостно взломали. Приехали, называется…

Мы сотрудничаем с серьезной командой по информационной безопасности, которая с нами работала некоторое время, — они не занимаются нелегалом. Как оказалось, moifakultet взломали хакеры, которые как-то узнали о работе над параллельными проектами и решили «через них» подзаработать. Продать дыры одного сайта владельцу другого и наоборот. Они связались через нашу команду со мной и предложили купить БД незадачливого конкурента. Не получилось — нам это просто не надо. Не уверен, что та сторона была бы настолько же великодушна, но я хакеров послал. А теперь в благодарность распространяются байки про то, что «они нас взломали».

Автор: Данила 4.12.2006, 12:58

Новый проект Павла и Николая Дуровых стартует с криминальной хакерской атаки и плагиата!

КРИМИНАЛ. Наш сайт (MoiFakultet.ru) 01.12.06 подвергся криминальной хакерской атаке со стороны команды Павла Дурова. Документальное свидетельство (заказ на взлом сайта) смотрите в Яндекс-блогах:

http://blogs.yandex.ru/search.xml?how=tm&rd=2&text=moifakultet.ru [сейчас ничего криминального по этой ссылке найти невозможно. — *Н. К.*].

Вот цитата текста объявления Павла или его подручного: «Большая просьба проверить два сайта на уязвимость: _vkontakte.ru и moifakultet.ru Если найдете во втором сайте серьезные дырки, с меня $. Заранее спасибо».

После этого, 01.12.06, наш сайт был взломан и прекратил работать на 1 сутки...

Возможно, часть мейлов был похищена и будет в дальнейшем использована для увеличения аудитории сайта вконтакте.ру.
ПЛАГИАТ. До хакерской атаки Павел с братом отличились тем, что оперативно скопировали наш сайт. Убедиться в этом также просто: достаточно посмотреть на дату регистрации нашего сайта: (domain: MOIFAKULTET.RU, created: 2006.08.14) и на дату регистрации домена vkontakte.ru (domain: VKONTAKTE.RU, created: 2006.10.01). А после этого сравнить сами сайты.

И то и другое — неправомерные деяния по российскому праву...

Выводы о чистоплотности организаторов сайта и о доверии к ресурсу делайте сами. Для нас очевидно: Павел и Николай не брезгуют никакими методами...

Автор: durov 4.12.2006, 13:02

Не надоело сыпать клевету и ложь?

Ребята, посмотрите сайт facebook.com и оцените, что кто у кого скопировал и когда =]
В СОТЫЙ РАЗ ПОВТОРЯЮ: Я ЭТОГО НЕ РАЗМЕЩАЛ И РАЗМЕЩАТЬ НИКОГО НЕ ПРОСИЛ.
Хватит фантазий.

Умейте отвечать за свои дырки, а не валить все на злые силы.

В суд подадим за клевету!

Автор: Данила 4.12.2006, 13:30

Достаточно прочитать эти две ссылки, чтобы стало все понятно.

Павел просто дружит с криминальными элементами, которые ломают неугодные сайты. При этом в частном разговоре по «аське» Павел признал, что размещал заказ. Да что тут говорить, все и так видно... Заказ размещен, сайт взломан, наши пользователи уже на его сайте... Не надо быть Шерлоком Холмсом...

Автор: durov 4.12.2006, 14:15

Простите, что Вы несете???

Извините, я больше не могу выдержать этого бреда... Надеюсь, Вы успокоитесь и перестанете во всех ваших грехах винить только меня. Бог видит — я Вам не вредил.

Перед остальными могу только извиниться за этот грязный базар. Надеюсь, все эти разборки никому не испортили настроение.

«Facebook подсказал не как надо делать, а как не надо, — объяснял Дуров. — „Одноклассники“ — тоже. Важно было понять, от чего избавиться. Я понял, что главное — стартовая страница пользователя. Человек хочет видеть свой профиль, а не ленту происходящего у друзей и предложение разных возможностей, как у Facebook. Надо выводить личную страницу как стартовую, чтобы человек загружал больше личных данных, чтобы лепил идеального себя».

Догадка Дурова не была оригинальной — с момента возникновения социальных сервисов стало очевидно, что у человека возникают отношения со своей страницей, профилем. Люди не только загружают новые фотографии, но и периодически редактируют данные, любимые цитаты, предпочтения, создают свой образ. Но ставить как стартовую страницу сам профиль и стену — это как раз чисто русская находка.

Разобравшись с функционалом, Дуров ломал голову над дизайном. На мониторе мерцали варианты. Малкольм Икс чеканил в наушниках: «Мы покажем, как проснуться и начать настоящую революцию! Хватит трепать языком. Нам нужны не разговоры, нам нужны действия!»

Логотип? Без наворотов, что-то лаконичное. Наберем «ВКонтакте» Tahoma. Теперь цвет. Мы не должны вызывать ярких негативных эмоций. Какие цвета никого не бесят? Синий, белый, серый. Что ж, мы будем чуть серыми, но узнаваемыми. Выпуклая буква вплыла в его сознание откуда-то из воспоминаний об уроках Руткевича.

«Тема Лебедев может ругаться на наш логотип, — почти кричал Дуров, уворачиваясь от идущих по Невскому прохожих. — Ну и что! Леонардо да Винчи, наверное, тоже ругал строителей древнеримских дорог — типа „почему их будто по прямой прокладывали?“ — а строители создавали инфраструктуру».

Светофор, на противоположном берегу проспекта двери штаба, Казанский за спиной. Дуров помолчал, затем снял кепку, быстрым движением пригладил волосы и водрузил ее обратно. «По крайней мере я никогда не копировал, не применяя мозг».

***

1 ноября 2006 года «ВКонтакте» открылся для узкого круга пользователей. Первые id распространили между владельцами и группой «Мафия». Где-то со второго десятка примкнули старые форумчане.

Конкуренты из MoiFakultet.ru не спали и медленно, но все-таки расширяли аудиторию. Дуров понимал, что ему предстоит не просто внедрить элегантный и понятный человеку инструмент. Надо было затащить во «ВКонтакте» незнакомую с ним, университетским демиургом, аудиторию. Для этого следовало отстроиться от имиджа петербургского локального ресурса.

Специалисты только что образованного IT-сообщества «Хабрахабр» были единодушны: новую социальную сеть создавать бессмысленно, так как тема социальных сетей на 146% исчерпана сетями «Мой круг» и «Одноклассники». «Как это часто бывает, эксперты хорошо предсказали прошлое», — ухмылялся Дуров.

Он списался с форумом «Дубинушка» физфака МГУ. Он даже купил у физиков рекламные баннеры — не столько ради рекламы, сколько ради лояльности москвичей. Раньше гуру social media он сообразил, что прямая реклама среды, где люди коммуницируют без преград, — бессмысленна. Работает только искренний интерес, только сарафанное радио.

Активность на форумах МГУ выстрелила. Конечно, во «ВКонтакте» регистрировалось больше питерцев, но московская диаспора также росла. Через месяц Дуров открыл сайт для всех. Единственным требованием к новоприбывшему он выставил приглашение со стороны уже зарегистрированного пользователя. Эта мера втыкала решетку перед мордами троллей и давала привкус элитарности, что заставляло стремиться во «ВКонтакте» тысячи студентов — хотя бы поглядеть, как там внутри.

Я услышал о «ВКонтакте» весной 2007 года на тусовке бывших одноклассников. Когда школьные товарищи нравственно обнялись, распрощались и одной рукой уже залезли в пальто, кто-то крикнул: «А давайте зафрендимся в социальной сети! „Чтобы не теряться“».

Несколько человек среагировали — клевая идея, давайте в «Одноклассниках», мы там уже есть. Пара умников сказала: нет, ЖЖ интереснее. Внезапно две отличницы (детсадовский воспитатель и бухгалтер) предложили: «Лучше во „ВКонтакте“, там легче искать по школам-классам-факультетам-годам выпуска». — «Можно еще встречи назначать и фотоальбомы составлять». На том и договорились.

Именно такая аудитория — не программисты, а люди, оценившие удобство и интуитивно ясный интерфейс, — повалила тысячами в день.

«ВКонтакте» трудно было бы сделать человеку не из студенческой среды, — писал Дуров. — Я делал для себя». Первые два месяца он лично поддерживал сайт и отвечал на вопросы, а потом передал эту работу id2, Александре Владимировой.

Население «ВКонтакте» за два месяца выросло до сотни тысяч пользователей. Внизу каждой страницы соцсети стояла подпись — «Павел Дуров».

***

Праздный люд, сидящий за чашкой кофе на Невском, не раскусил юношу — темные волосы, небритая щека, модное пальто — и не понял, чем он на самом деле занят. Версии были такие: драгдилер, продавец гербалайфа, мормон, свидетель Иеговы. Он сидел в «Кофехаузе» уже несколько часов, и все это время к нему стояла очередь из студентов.

Студент подходил, назывался, молодой человек искал его в списке, проверял паспорт, вытаскивал из-под полы небольшую коробочку и вручал ее оппоненту. На соседнем стуле лежали пакеты, и, пока они не кончились, мормон выдавал их всем, кто прошел проверку.

Это был Лев Левиев, и раздавал он не гашиш, а айподы. По его версии, идея конкурса родилась у Славы — кто пригласит во «ВКонтакте» больше всего друзей, получит джобсовский плеер. Дуров тогда еще не использовал устройства Apple, но дизайн айподов и идея ему понравились.

По другой версии, эту идею отцы-основатели взяли у MoiFacultet. Правда, у тех количество разыгрываемых плееров ограничивалось десятками. Слава перешиб конкурента числом. Компаньоны купили тысячу айподов.

«ВКонтакте» успел обрести поклонников, и двое из них — откуда-то из области — напечатали фосфоресцирующие футболки с логотипом сети и прислали на Тверскую. Лев прихватил их с собой в кафе. Под конец раздачи голова шла кругом, но страдания дорогого стоили — решающий для любого интернет-проекта набор ранних фанатов, то есть закладка фундамента будущей аудитории, прошел на ура.

Новый год друзья отмечали в победном расположении духа. Цель — миллион пользователей к ноябрю 2007-го — казалась быстродостижимой. Но уже в феврале сайт рухнул.

Месяцем ранее, раскинувшись, как патриций, на глубоких подушках, Олег Бунин затягивался кальяном и пускал дым в потолок. Он, консультант по высоким нагрузкам, больше напоминавший менестреля (кудри, что-то типа кованого амулета на шее, никаких пиджаков-галстуков), слушал чайников, затащивших его в вальяжный азиатский шалман.

Парни не рубили в предмете, но выглядели любопытно. Замкнутый старший брат, обращаясь к собеседнику, редко смотрел в глаза, думал долго, говорил мало, жесты неуклюжие. Младший, наоборот, подвижный, речь поставлена, вопросами попадает в точку — при этом не лезет в лидеры, подчеркивая, что техническими задачами в их соцсети заведует брат, который круче него как программист.

Стороны встретились в кафе «Рубаи». Еще несколько лет у «ВКонтакте» не будет офиса, и Дуров с программистами полюбят обсуждать дела в заведениях Невского. Лишь годом позже тотем посадит соратников в специально приобретенную квартиру.

Окутанный дымом Бунин растолковывал азы — как хранить и отдавать информацию с сервера, какие особенности существуют при расчете необходимых мощностей, масштабировании системы и т. д. По тому, как заказчики схватывали идеи, менестрель чувствовал, что долго консультировать их не придется.

Но он не предполагал, насколько быстро они въедут в тему. Николай хоть и выигрывал олимпиады по программированию, но решать сложные задачи — все равно что учиться колоть штыком манекен. Укрощение трафика, когда он растет в геометрической прогрессии, — иная баталия.

Бунин посоветовал использовать сервер Apache в комбинации с сервером Nginx. Через несколько часов от Николая пришла весточка — я поставил эту конфигурацию, посмотрите. Бунин изумился. Nginx обычно настраивают полнедели. Еще больше поразило, что Дуров-старший все написал правильно.

Консультант «подкрутил параметры», и первая версия запустилась. «Дуровы все быстро поняли и через три месяца перестали советоваться, — резюмировал Бунин. — Мы показали, куда копать, и они перекопали нас».

Мы встретились на конференции HighLoad-2011. «ВКонтакте» прислала разработчика Андрея Илларионова, и набитый битком зал задавал ему недоуменные вопросы по их системе распределения нагрузок. Некоторые решения не то что не приходили никому в голову — даже после выступления не стало яснее, как они работают.

«Когда общаешься с обычным человеком, почти всегда представляешь, что он ответит, — говорил Бунин. — Павел постоянно думал по-другому и масштабно. Знаете, как Цукерберг в фильме „Социальная сеть“ — когда девушка его отвергла, приятель хочет посочувствовать, а он уже думает о своей сети: „Пора расширяться“. Дуров — такой же».

Это наблюдение Бунина повторяли разные деятели рунета. Способность думать иначе стала краеугольным камнем для дуровской команды, спровоцировала изменения личности ее участников и привела к неминуемому конфликту с окружающей реальностью.

Но тогда, первой зимой «ВКонтакте», сентенции Дурова выдавали лишь оригинальный ум. Для интернет-тусовки соцсеть выглядела не более чем любопытным проектом с пассионарным основателем, уверенным, что выведет сайт в топ популярных ресурсов.

Дуровы советовались с консультантами, но вызывали их все реже. «Какие-то вещи я сразу сделал, как считал нужным, — рассказывал Николай. — Например, Бунин советовал хранить фотографии на одном домене и пропускать все через один сервер. А я предложил отдавать фото с того сервера, где они находятся».

Счетчик посещаемости крутился как бешеный, пока однажды февральским вечером Павел Дуров не набил в браузере vkontakte.ru и не обнаружил вместо соцсети «ошибку 502». Вход на сайт для пользователей оказался закрыт.

Дуров набрал телефон хостинг-провайдера. Трубку взял дежурный инженер.

— Алло, привет. Мы висим.

— Привет, сейчас разберемся. (*Пауза.*) Так. Идет огромный поток запросов к сайту, волна полтора гигабита. Канал забился.

— Есть идеи, что делать?

— Если честно, нет.

Звонить в Бонн поздно, брат наверняка ушел из лаборатории. Пальто, штиблеты, ключ, деньги, такси. Дуров ворвался в прохладную комнату со стеклянными стеллажами, нашел свои сервера и перезагрузил их.

Волна шла из Китая, Южной Америки, Украины. Даже если передать провайдерам списки IP-адресов, участвовавших в атаке, чтобы те их заблокировали, — все равно шансы на успех мизерны. Соперник не идиот, атакует с других компьютеров.

Утром Дуров известил брата, и они начали суматошно перебирать способы защиты. Сначала арендовали маршрутизатор, который идентифицирует врага. Зная провайдера, можно его блокировать — но, опять же, провайдеров-то тысячи.

Ночами они с Николаем, который еще не дописал диссер, созванивались и ломали головы, что бы предпринять. Атаки продолжались — их старались заваливать запросами ближе к ночи. Особой популярностью пользовался вечер пятницы, когда в офисе провайдера оставался только дежурный. На форуме СПбГУ жаловались, что «ВКонтакте» лежит, сочувствовали, но ничего посоветовать не могли. Слава и Лев вели свое расследование, и им даже слили переписку с исполнителями атаки, однако установить заказчика не удалось.

Дуров написал письмо юзерам:

«В течение прошедшего дня (18.02.2007) активность доходила до фантастической отметки в 2 млн запросов в минуту. Это позволило предположить, что весомая доля запросов была создана искусственно для того, чтобы часть пользователей не смогла попасть на сайт. 95% из этих искусственно создаваемых запросов шли из-за рубежа.

Также мы получили серию новых коммерческих предложений, часто смешанных с угрозами. Мы по-прежнему отклоняем предложения людей, которые хотели бы превратить студенческое сообщество в обычный бизнес. „ВКонтакте“ никуда и никому не будет продаваться».

Строго говоря, атаки были разновидностью проблемы высоких нагрузок на сайт. Но здесь советы Бунина — да и никого другого — не помогали. Дуров спал по несколько часов в день, метался злой, с мутными глазами, между серверной и компьютером и лихорадочно искал вакцину против эпидемии.

Наконец он наткнулся на статью в журнале «Хакер» о том, как сисадмин на языке Perl написал программу, которая вычленяет IP-адреса нападающих, и сервер блокирует их. Операция происходит каждые три секунды.

Статья подтолкнула их с братом к созданию своего защитного кода. Николай написал нечто похожее. Протестировали, доработали, опять протестировали, опять доработали — и так, пока не удалось частично купировать атаки. Нервотрепка продолжалась, но задача уже начала решаться.

Дуров размышлял, кто мог быть заказчиком. Предположим, конкуренты из MoiFacultet. Простите, но один час такой атаки стоит 500 долларов — а «ВКонтакте» подвергали DDOS-набегам сутками. Откуда столько денег у стартапа? К тому же средства явно эффективнее вложить в продвижение, серверы. Вряд ли это австралийцы и компания. Но кто же?

Пока Дуровы боролись с хакерами, акционеров долбил иной тип атакующих — инвесторы. Стартап, запустившийся без рекламы и аккумулировавший 100 000 юзеров, привлек внимание всех, кто хоть немного разбирался в интернете. Одни хотели сотрудничать, другие — приобрести компанию. Дуров в этих встречах не участвовал; отдувались Слава и Лев.

Установка звучала просто. Не то что контроль, а даже блокирующий пакет не отдадим. И вообще, сделка нужна вам, инвесторам, а не нам — мы органически растем и с каждым днем увеличиваем свою стоимость.

«ВКонтакте» переговаривались с разными деятелями — от Романа Симонова из Delta Private Equity Partners до отца «Одноклассников» Альберта Попкова и его партнеров-латышей из Forticom. Некоторые предложения звучали заманчиво. Но Слава и Лев отвергали предложения, загипнотизированные верой Дурова в то, что надо продаться позже и тому, кто предложит наибольшие деньги и гарантирует минимальное вмешательство во «ВКонтакте».

Впервые что-то искренне заинтересовавшее их партнеры услышали в апреле. Слава позвонил Дурову и сообщил, что ему наверняка интересно поприсутствовать на встрече с Юрием Мильнером. Знаменитый ныне венчурный капиталист, инвестировавший в Facebook, Twitter, Groupon и другх передовиков интернета, в 2007 году был не так известен. Но то, что он собрал под знамена своего Mail.ru «Одноклассников» и игровой холдинг Astrum, — интриговало. Мильнер не напирал. Его оферта звучала как «встретимся и поговорим», а не «продавайтесь, или запустим свою сеть и сотрем „ВКонтакте“ с лица земли», чем грешили некоторые претенденты.

Итак, переговорщики съехались на Тверскую и уселись за стол. Светящийся доброжелательностью Мильнер, не выспавшийся из-за атак Дуров в черной водолазке и черных брюках, очень деловые и вежливые Слава и Лев.

Впоследствии умение Мильнера заключать сделки стало легендарным. Во-первых, он умел разобраться, с кем имеет дело. Стартапу с неочевидной перспективой мирового господства он предлагал рыночную цену. Вот как описывал это на Slon.ru основатель Liveinternet.ru и других проектов Герман Клименко: «Он приходит и говорит: „Вы будете стоить 20 млн долларов, а я вам дам два“. Вы говорите: „Да? Ну и на х… пошел!“ И уходите домой. У вас дома жена и 300 долларов в месяц. Ну или неважно сколько. И вы жене говорите: „Знаешь, дорогая, ко мне сам известный инвестор пришел, 2 млн долларов обещал.

И я ему сказал: „На х… пошел!“ Жена начинает пилить, и через две недели вы сами позвоните и скажете: „Ну ладно, пять!“ А инвестор знаете что ответит? „Один!“ Вы скажете: „Как же так! Вы обещали хотя бы два!“ А он передумал.

Если же Мильнер видел блестящее будущее и пассионарных основателей, то назначал цену выше рыночной. Это было частью прославленного стиля DST Deal — сделки, при которой инвестор гарантирует невмешательство в управление компанией, не настаивает на кресле в совете директоров. А главное — не парит мозг сложносочиненным контрактом, довольствуясь бумагой в три листа. И, опять же, не скряга и не торгуется, как на самаркандском базаре.

Сын академика Мильнера, экономиста, пришел к этому стилю — и вообще к своему пониманию будущего, — наткнувшись в 1999 году на обзор аналитика Morgan Stanley Мэри Микер о перспективах интернета. К тому времени он закончил физфак МГУ и Уортонскую школу бизнеса, затем трудился во Всемирном банке и брокерской компании Ходорковского. Олигарх был его кумиром. (Тролль Дуров не признался Мильнеру, что после посадки кумира повесил в туалет тяжелую раму с портретом Ходорковского, чем эпатировал математиков, заглядывавших к брату.)

Осознав, что интернет — это среда будущего и вести в ней бизнес — великий вызов, Мильнер создал свою компанию. В 2006 году она преобразовалась в холдинг Mail.ru. Стратегия этого спрута заключалась в том, чтобы сожрать все перспективные коммуникационные проекты в рунете и окрестностях. Мильнер догадался, что деньги идут вслед за разными формами взаимодействия людей между собой, и начал скупать соцсети.

Позже, когда он начал инвестировать в мировых гигантов, Кремниевая долина переполошилась — вести дела, как Мильнер, считалось фриковством! Не принято инвестировать в компании на стадии перед IPO. Не принято рассчитывать цену не на основе прибыли, а на основе востребованности идеи в будущем.

Мильнер крутил чужие деньги — с ним сотрудничал металлургический и телекоммуникационный магнат Алишер Усманов. Поговаривали, что тот полез в интернет и медиа по просьбе власти — чтобы контролировать каналы доставки контента, его производителей и саму информационную среду будущего.

Первый вопрос Мильнера касался трафика: «Как справляетесь с нагрузками?» По воспоминаниям Левиева, Дуров был совсем неопытным переговорщиком, почти не имел опыта диспута с бизнесменами. Но тотем почувствовал, что инвестор стоящий, и включил свой навык производить впечатление. Если бы кто-то взялся составить рейтинг боев по интеллектуальному карате, эта дуэль, выглядевшая как умиротворенная беседа, вошла бы туда. Два талантливых пиарщика — Мильнер и Дуров — прощупывали друг друга.

Тотем не стал раскрывать карты и ответил в том духе, что с нагрузками хлебнули дерьма, но сейчас все в порядке. Мильнер сочувственно выслушал и задал второй вопрос: «Как раскручиваетесь?» Дуров бросил: «Органически». Затем добавил, что не считает необходимым тратить деньги на рекламу — айподы и полоса в студенческой газете «Сачок» не в счет. Если проект кому-то нужен, молва о нем разлетится, подобно эпидемии. Несмотря на атаки, аудитория «ВКонтакте» продолжала расти в геометрической прогрессии.

Мильнер приезжал в Петербург еще несколько раз, и в одной из бесед мелькнула тема, что директор Mail.ru Дмитрий Гришин считает «ВКонтакте» конкурентами. Гришин запускал соцсеть на основе почтового сервиса Mail.ru — «Мой Мир». Кроме этого, DST в рамках своей «коммуникативной» стратегии приобретала долю в «Одноклассниках».

Дуров не придал сведениям о ревности Гришина большого значения, так как считал конкуренцию благотворной. Но однажды он сопоставил даты визитов Мильнера и атак на сайт. Выяснилось, что они практически совпадают.

Впрочем, железных доказательств версии, что инвестор таким образом санкционировал проверку «ВКонтакте» через своего менеджера, Дурову заполучить не удалось.

Первая встреча закончилась безоблачно. Дуров понравился Мильнеру. Человек в черном сознавал, как интернет меняет человеческую жизнь, какие потребности он может удовлетворить, и не стремился быстрее накосить денег. Последнее выглядело важным, так как Мильнер сознавал: проекты, выжимающие копейку, рано или поздно начинают бесить пользователя.

Летом речь зашла уже о конкретных условиях. Мильнер оценил «ВКонтакте» в 40 млн долларов. Стороны начали торговлю — здесь на первый план вышел Слава. Он заявил, что соцсеть стоит 60 млн. Свои позиции он оборонял настолько яростно, что Мильнер согласился отдать 15 млн за 24,99%. При этом капиталист выбил себе право на увеличение доли до 49%.

Сделку оформили быстро — изящный договор в стиле DST Deal был подписан в июле. Если бы теперь Перекопский спросил Дурова, где заработанный миллион, тот предъявил бы ему счета. Но Перекопский вспомнил о споре нескоро — перспективы, нарисовавшиеся после альянса с Мильнером, ослепляли своим блеском сильнее золота.

Глава 4
Сок черешни

Это была странная квартира. Едва не в полтораста квадратных метров, с четырьмя комнатами, глядящими узкими вытянутыми окнами во двор-колодец. Со стороны фасада шумел и клокотал человеческий трафик Невского. Население квартиры менялось от одного до десяти постояльцев. Средоточием жизни служила тесная комнатушка. За сдвинутыми столами стучали клавишами люди, останавливаясь лишь в шесть утра, когда по провайдерскому обыкновению падала сеть. Тогда люди обсуждали богословские вопросы типа: «Какой должна быть платформа для разработчиков?» или «Что хотят люди от соцсети?» Затем, утомленные кодом и схоластикой, валились на кровати и спали до часа дня.

Чтобы попасть во двор, Лев свернул с проспекта в подворотню с дверями неясного назначения и крадущимися по стенам проводами. Раньше дом занимали контора и квартиры банкира Блокка, который реконструировал здание и воздвиг на фасаде аллегории Правосудия и Адвокатуры. Дуров питал слабость к символике, и наличие аллегорий сыграло роль в выборе квартиры, к которой, гулко топая по лестнице, поднимался акционер его компании, нагруженный коробками.

Часто ночами одна из теней отвлекалась от ноутбука и бросала клич: «Кто за суши?» Коллеги неохотно отрывались от экранов и выдвигались в сторону двери и вниз по лестнице — к бару на углу Фонтанки и Невского. Но в эту ночь они были заняты настолько, что Дуров набрал номер Льва и попросил привезти еды.

Лев добрался до двери, перевел дыхание. Позвонил. Шаги. «Пи-иццу заказывали?» — крикнул он. Дверь отворил Дуров и, улыбаясь, отошел в сторону. Лев, хоть и не впервые заглядывал сюда, с удивлением осмотрел пустующую квартиру. Его приход будто не заметили.

Программисты сгрудились в каком-то чулане. Николай восседал в кресле и стучал по клавиатуре, время от времени прикладываясь к шоколадному батончику. За самым большим из сдвинутых столов согнулся кто-то худой и растрепанный. Некоторые из аутистов все-таки поздоровались, но, взяв еду, вернулись к коду.

Лев поговорил с предводителем, по которому было видно, что он тоже не прочь уткнуться в десктоп. Впрочем, Дуров, как всегда, был вежлив и прохладно приветлив. Висело ощущение шабаша, на который заглянула человеческая душа. Лев чувствовал себя не совсем уютно.

После сделки с Мильнером осенью 2007 года Дуров получил на счет деньги и с помощью матери, устроившейся риелтором, вложил их в квартиры — одну купил недалеко от дома, другую как офис, в сердце города. Николай вернулся в Петербург, и вот они с братом осматривали анфиладу комнат — две спальни, гостиная, подобие чулана для прислуги, кухня. Дуров как истинный петербуржец привык жить в декорациях к историческим спектаклям, хотя, впрочем, признавал, что в последнее время репертуар измельчал и театр пробавляется одноактными оперетками про весенние сосули.

Команда расширялась, и вскоре в девятиметровом пенале за сдвинутыми столами толкались четыре человека. Изредка кто-то уходил на кухню и кодил за столом для готовки. Прочие метры оставались невостребованными.

Четырьмя годами позже я сел в лифт, напоминавший золоченую клетку, устланную коврами в духе советского министерства тяжелой промышленности, и поднялся на один из двух этажей «ВКонтакте» в доме Зингера. Перед дуровской бандой здесь обитали юристы, которые хоть и скрепляли транснациональные сделки, но существовали без изысков — дешевые панели, подвесные потолки, ковролин.

Дуров въехал на этаж и изменил ровно четыре вещи. На стойке появился логотип сети, рядом с кабинетами возник механизм, выжимающий из апельсинов сок, и длинный диван с валиком в виде коров, высовывающих языки. На двери повесили доски с магнитным шрифтом (конечно, Tahoma) — «Сквот ИЕ. Кости в танке», «Наркомпросвет», «Злые пользователи», «Музей Павла Дурова».

Все прочее осталось неизменным — включая торчащие провода, отваливающиеся панели и другие предметы быта от прошлых хозяев. Дуров бросил в бой программистов и почти не отвлекался на офисные заморочки.

Проходя по штабу, я вспомнил, во-первых, тропинки, от которых муравьи не отклоняются, а во-вторых, свою квартиру летом, когда семья уехала на дачу и жизнедеятельность происходит только по тем маршрутам, где я, пользуясь свободным временем, живу и пишу с перерывами на сон. Так я понял, что приехал к близким по духу товарищам.

А тогда, в блокковском доме, кодеры сидели друг у друга на голове. Толкотня в пенале — братья перед десктопами, остальные за ноутбуками — никак не отражалась на результате. За год после ночного визита Льва с пиццей «ВКонтакте» открыла сервисы, которые обеспечили ей рост трафика в геометрической прогрессии. В первую очередь — видеохостинг и аудиохостинг с собственными плеерами. Во вторую — системы рейтингования юзеров через платные sms и подарки, мобильная версия.

Прежде чем врубаться в разработку сервисов, впоследствии принесших ему скандалы и судебные иски, Дуров охотился за головами. Позиции его были привлекательны: сайт входит в пятерку самых посещаемых в России, молва сделала его культовым в Петербурге, быстрее него летает только Google.ru. Его умение обаять и желание нравиться должны были притягивать гениев.

Одного из его самых ценных кадров пробовал сманить Google, но кадр, не моргнув глазом, ответил хедхантеру:

«Hey Nina,

It is the best company in Russia and possibly in the world.

I'm very happy to be able to create magnificent software and design at VK.

Regards, N.

P. S. Here's an address for CVs in case some of your programmers would like to apply».

Знакомые еще по группе «Мафия» Кузнецов и Столбовский занялись аудиохостингом и мобильной версией. Эти сервисы выглядели естественным выражением идеи Дурова об открытости информации. «Давайте сделаем русский YouTube», — предложил он банде.

Люди должны обмениваться контентом без преград. Закон позволял соцсети не нести ответственность перед правообладателями — «ВКонтакте» лишь предоставляла платформу для выкладывания песен. Загружать музыку, слушать ее, составлять плейлисты — короче, использовать соцсеть одновременно как полку для пластинок и проигрыватель — что может быть притягательнее?

Пиратские сайты были неудобны и не имели преимуществ соцсети, где действуют люди под настоящими именами. Myspace содержал мало русской музыки, а другие сервисы и вовсе были неизвестны. Очевидную лакуну взялся заполнить программист Александр Кузнецов, он же Кузя.

В отличие от музыки, спешка с версией для телефонов казалась странной. Люди редко использовали трубку как точку входа в интернет. Мобильный трафик рунета в 2007 году рос не такими мощными, как сейчас, темпами, и можно было потерпеть год-другой. Однако Дуров свято верил, что если писать версию сразу, то к мобильному буму подойдешь во всеоружии — и пользователь привыкнет.

«Одноклассники» и «Мой Мир» от Mail.ru решали другие проблемы. Первые выжимали из пользователей копеечку через платные опции, включая регистрацию, вторые находились под впечатлением экспертного шума на тему: «Все умрут, а блоги останутся». Столбовский был отряжен писать мобильную версию, и через год она увидела свет.

На этих двух разработчиках университетский ресурс Дурова иссяк. Требовалась новая кровь. И в этот момент ему подвернулись два друга-программиста, которым предстояло превратить «ВКонтакте» в то, как он выглядит сейчас.

***

Олег Андреев и Андрей Рогозов познакомились на том же нёрдском озере Зеркальном, где тотем, краснея и запинаясь, читал лекцию о паскале, а его брат блистал в математическом отряде. Оба торчали на программировании и переписывались после того лета. Рогозов попал в олимпиадную «единичку» 239-й, а Андреев окончил Аничков лицей, где искусство кода преподавалось как предмет. Поступив в Политех, они создали что-то типа артели, которая писала сайты и сервисы для коллег. Они прославились в узких кругах и получали заказы со всего мира — в том числе соцсети; хорваты оплатили создание локальных «Одноклассников», staryiprijatel.hr.

Архитектор сразу опознал в Андрееве единомышленника. Дуров фанател от книг Пола Грэма, программиста и создателя инкубатора стартапов Y Combinator. Грэм доступно и емко излагал философию программирования и независимости от IT-монстров. Ты творец, меняющий кодом реальность. Программист — художник новой эпохи, который, экспериментируя, создает миры по своему вкусу. Он свободен от уродливых корпоративных этик, практик и дурного шлака.

«Для нас программирование — это инструмент, — рассказывал Рогозов об Андрееве. — А для него это как оперный спектакль. Важен не столько результат, сколько красивый код, язык, архитектура». Андреев вечно что-нибудь придумывал и пользовался языком ActionScript3, которым Дуров не владел. Случай проверить его в бою выпал быстро.

Дуров придумал приложение, где пользователь мог виртуальным баллончиком рисовать граффити. Ему не терпелось показать эту штуку публике, но требовалось переписать ее на ActionScript3. Андреев согласился помочь. Вечером они начали менять «Граффити» — Андреев в своей квартире, Дуров в своей. Переписывались по ICQ, где у предводителя остался ник Mr.President.

Они стучали по клавишам всю ночь. Как вспоминал Андреев, он едва не валился спать, но Дуров подгонял его. Все, кто работает во «ВКонтакте», поражались умению архитектора в моменты истощения генерировать дополнительную энергию. Перекопский вспоминал, как тот мог не спать несколько ночей; при этом не был как-то особенно бледен, разве что зол.

Слушая подобные разговоры, я воображал дух Кастанеды, приземляющийся на брошенный аэродром. Если не знать о ненависти Дурова к веществам, можно заподозрить в нем кокаиниста или амфетаминщика.

Андреев стряхнул с себя сон и продолжил фиксить ошибки. Он дорожил мнением тотема и рвался посмотреть, как отреагируют юзеры на граффити. «Павел в отличие от большинства программистов понимал, чего хочет от жизни школьник и студент и как это выглядит в дизайне, — рассказывал он по скайпу из Франции. — Он умел смотреть глазами человека, у которого старая версия браузера и медленный интернет».

Сквозь шторы просачивалось утро. Наконец все было готово, и Дуров запостил приложение во «ВКонтакте». Несколько минут хакеры ждали пользовательских рисунков, а когда те появились, проверили на предмет глюков и рухнули спать.

Дуров предложил Андрееву создать платформу для видео, связанную с «ВКонтакте»: «ВКадре». Тот согласился и первым делом получил от Николая советы, как хранить видео. Впрочем, воспользовался только теми, с которыми был заранее согласен. Видеохостинг он написал достаточно резво, но с управлением проектом возникли проблемы. Хакер-художник не ладил с маркетингом, к тому же сказывалась усталость от темы. Николай Дуров вспоминал, что с сайтом, написанным на языке Ruby on Rails, возникли проблемы масштабирования — когда пошел мощный трафик. Аналогичная история случилась с Twitter, который пришлось переписывать на Scala. Серверы не справлялись с нагрузками. Все эти факторы наложились друг на друга, и Андреев ушел.

Его жизнь обрела другие цели. Слушая докладчиков на пражской конференции по Ruby on Rails, Андреев внезапно увидел среди толпы свою школьную подругу — Ольга уехала учиться во Францию, и теперь код свел их. Последовал роман и отъезд в галльские палестины.

Другая версия гласила, что Андреев был мощным лидером, и они с Дуровым трудно уживались. «Некомандный игрок, такой „скорпион", который хочет захватывать мир, — щебетала Эльнара, нарезая торт, с которым я явился в сквот петербургских предпринимателей на Рубинштейна. — Мне казалось, что под каждой страницей сайта он хочет написать „Олег Андреев", а не "Павел Дуров"».

Так или иначе, Андреев собрал вещи и улетел во Францию. Удаленно трудиться над «ВКонтакте» не представлялось возможным. Дуров сетовал: «Надо было по-другому мотивировать, я потерял сильного человека». После ухода Андреева тотем неустанно возносил ему хвалу и подчеркивал заслуги в части видеохостинга.

Раздел «Видео» стартовал и подвергся нашествию миллионов. Клипы, блокбастеры, мультфильмы, порно — все подряд лилось широкой рекой. Популярность принесла изменение аудитории. Раньше во «ВКонтакте» сидели, как и декларировалось на старте, «студенты элитных вузов». Теперь в сеть хлынули широкие народные массы. Чтобы справиться с потоком, Николай бился с нагрузками с удвоенными силами, а штат администраторов, поддерживающих порядок, теперь исчислялся десятками.

«ВКонтакте» рос, но пока оставался стартапом энтузиастов, купавшихся в эйфории оттого, что махом сдвинули с пьедестала гигантов рунета. Дуров декларировал, что тратить ресурсы на удаление порнографии и блокбастеров будет только в том случае, когда нарушен закон, — по запросу прокуратуры. Иначе понадобились бы не десятки, а тысячи админов, а несокрушимое преимущество его соцсети — вал пользовательского контента — обернулось бы против него.

Как почти всякий житель социального интернета со стажем более пяти лет, Дуров укрепился в цинизме и превратился в гурмана трэша, угара и содомии.

Однажды в штабе он отловил дизайнера Добромыслова и спросил, что тот думает про идею виртуального кладбища для умерших юзеров. Добромыслов подумал и ответил: «Трудно понять, кто на самом деле умер, кто нет, — куча фейков появится. А также любителей создать виртуала своего врага и отправить в могилу. Нам и так постоянно пишут, чтобы закрыли аккаунты умерших».

«Ха! Если бы врага! — воскликнул Дуров. — Недавно один товарищ выложил эротические фото своей девушки, а потом так получилось, что она умерла, и его попросили убрать их. Он не убрал и пририсовал фотошопом льющуюся кровь и пятна!»

Добромыслов широко улыбнулся — нельзя было понять, из вежливости или он уважает трэш так же, как начальник. «Нет, ну какая у человека душа! — не унимался Дуров. — Подрисовал кровь. Какая душа!»

Программиста, который стал ключевым разработчиком «ВКонтакте», он нанял, как Джобс директора «Пепси-колы». Известный эпизод из истории Apple: отец яблок агитировал Джона Скалли уйти из рядов «красно-синих» и невзначай бросил: «Ты планируешь всю жизнь торговать подслащенной водой или хочешь изменить мир?» Скалли подал заявление об увольнении из PepsiCo, правда, вскоре уволил самого Джобса.

Рогозов попался на ту же удочку. Сидя за столиком кафе, он мучительно ждал, когда от человека в черном отклеятся телевизионщики. Человек говорил и говорил, а корреспондент зачарованно кивал. Наконец фонарь на камере погас, и Дуров переместился за столик. «Ну что, — спросил он. — Вы готовы заняться проектом, который меняет жизнь миллионов людей?»

Рогозова не надо было агитировать. Он пришел удостовериться, что намерения тотема серьезны. Узрев мерцание миссии вокруг фигуры, сидящей напротив, он, не колеблясь, ответил: «Готов».

Последнее время Рогозов работал в контракторе Motorola, изготавливал им софт, то есть вполне торговал подслащенной программной водой. Для «ВКонтакте» он когда-то писал виджет с всплывающим окном, когда кто-то присылал пользователю сообщение или комментарий. Причем медлил и изготовил версии не для всех браузеров.

Тут опять вступила в дело ангел-связной «ВКонтакте» Эльнара. Она схватила Рогозова за воротник и тряхнула: дуровские разработчики сейчас допилят свой виджет, и ты будешь никому не нужен! Рогозов очнулся и за ночь написал версию для Opera. Дуров приобрел его виджет за тысячу долларов.

Затем Рогозов прислал код на конкурс комментариев для блога и получил приглашение на встречу с архитектором. Завербовав талант, Дуров подключил его к прорывному проекту — платформе для сторонних разработчиков. Идея заключалась в том, что, взяв за основу открытый код «ВКонтакте», любой человек может создать свой сайт или использовать возможности соцсети для своих проектов — сообщества, магазина, краудсорсингового проекта, да чего угодно. Такие платформы запустили лишь Myspace и Facebook.

Дуров декларировал, что рассматривает открытие API как базу для интернет-герильи. «Мы считаем, что будущее интернета находится в руках отдельных пассионарных личностей, многие из которых сейчас читают это сообщение, — писал он, обращаясь к пользователям. — Поэтому мы запускаем во „ВКонтакте“ проект User API, который позволяет любому желающему без затрат создавать отдельные социальные сети в различных странах мира».

Однако его мотивы касались не только создания идеального инструмента коммуникации. Гендиректор Дуров разрывался между своими целями и требованием приносить прибыль. Время беззаботного стартапа как бы длилось, но «ВКонтакте» неумолимо превращалась в бизнес, и это превращение было неотменимо — росло количество серверов, штат, издержки.

«Компании-посредники, которые стремятся дешево купить талантливые команды, старательно поддерживают миф, что продвижение игры в социальных сетях требует больших расходов, — писал он на сайте „Частный корреспондент“. — На самом деле никогда порог входа для желающих создать что-то существенное не был таким низким. По мере того как растет платежеспособная аудитория социальных сетей и падают цены на хостинг, порог входа для новых игроков опускается еще ниже. Фактически единственное, что нужно инвестировать начинающим разработчикам или дизайнерам в создание игры, — это свой труд».

После сделки с Мильнером прошел всего год, а Дурову пришлось пойти на компромисс со своими ценностями. Будучи циником и любителем трэша, он сохранял романтический пуризм в части обороны его сети от метастазов общества потребления. Пользователя ничто не должно раздражать — и точка. И вот теперь деньги инвестора кончались, денежный поток был слаб. Эти обстоятельства принудили Дурова заключить первый рекламный контракт.

Продолжать в том же духе не хотелось. Как еще зарабатывать? Весной 2008 года «ВКонтакте» ввели платное повышение рейтинга. Ранее рейтинг применялся для сортировки людей в поисковой выдаче, а теперь служил монетизации тщеславия. Дуров гордился его пирамидальной схемой — за приглашение в сеть новых друзей юзеры повышали свой рейтинг: «Как заработать на бессмысленной опции? Я придумал как и сумел».

Однако рейтинг не нес существенных денег, и Дуров придумал сервис «Подарки». Ты можешь оказать знак внимания другому человеку, подарив ему, допустим, виртуальную розу. Или плюшевого единорога. Или еще какую-нибудь слюнявую ерунду. «ВКонтакте» ввели валюту — «голоса», которые можно было оплачивать через мобильный счет.

Этот сервис принес несколько миллионов долларов, но было ясно, что подарки служат временной подпоркой.

Размышляя о том, за что еще люди готовы платить, Дуров пришел к выводу, что в соцсеть логично затащить игры. Facebook уже сотрудничал с Zynga. Юзеры режутся в них под виртуальными именами — зачем, если можно под настоящими? Разработчики игр — творческие конторы, это один из самых драйвовых бизнесов цифровой эпохи. Сидят суровые дяди и спорят, какой уровень защиты нужен кирасам джедая восьмого уровня.

«ВКонтакте» создал платформу для этих рыцарей и окончательно превратился в государство с валютой, которое позволяет зарабатывать на своей территории, развлекая граждан и уплачивая с дохода налоги. «Мне показалось, что все должно быть доступно сторонним разработчикам, и тогда сотни пассионариев на основе API нас раскрутят», — объяснял Дуров.

Идея архитектора выглядела логично. Мильнер не уставал им восхищаться и рекомендовал в разговорах не иначе как гения: «Если бы Дуров жил в Америке, он был бы Цукербергом». Однако платформа не взлетела. Могло показаться, что дело в инертности кодеров, не готовых к революции, но на самом деле ошибся сам зодчий.

Рогозов предлагал детально проработать API, а Дуров, наоборот, хотел запустить ее как можно быстрее, упростив до минимума. Рогозов быстро согласился. Как когда-то Перекопский; в отличие от «самого-себе-и-неба-и-луны» Андреева он не упирался насмерть и не претендовал на роль лидера.

Платформа оказалась неудобной для разработчиков, и взрыв пассионарности не прогремел. Дурову не хватило рук. Как он сам признался, можно было бы отвлечь Кузю и Рогозова от их задач, но тогда компания прекратила бы бои на других направлениях. Он не стал отвлекать их, и мечта о вирусном распространении «ВКонтакте» по миру не сбылась.

Это был драматический момент, потому что в 2008 году Facebook еще не захватил мир и пока штурмовал высоту «150 млн пользователей». Если бы у Дурова с его 20 млн получился идеальный API с кроссплатформенной авторизацией и другими возможностями, соответствующими тренду сближения разных устройств, платформ, сервисов, — неизвестно, как бы выглядел расклад соцсетей. По крайней мере, гегемония Facebook выглядела бы не столь однозначно.

С другой стороны, пассионарии и без платформы осознали «ВКонтакте» как инструмент распространения информации и организации событий. Сервис, назначающий встречи, был страшно популярен, а количество групп неуклонно росло.

Сначала юзеры подражали Facebook, регистрируя группы узконаправленного веселья типа «Группа для тех, кто любит пылесосить и петь знаменным распевом». Затем в соцсеть перетекли все группы интересов — от революционеров и озабоченных родителей до фанатов аниме и азартных игр. География ширилась: все регионы России плюс Украина, которую Дуров захватил и до сих пор никому не отдал.

Среди новоприбывших юзеров мало кто понимал, что из себя представляет «ВКонтакте». Немногие осознавшие пытались достучаться до Дурова, чтобы поделиться идеями. Тот часто писал в блоге о нововведениях и достижениях, иногда отвечал на комментарии. Но по мере роста аудитории между ним и активными пользователями росла стена.

От: Д. [студентка, Златоуст]

Кому: Б., администратору «ВКонтакте»

Вы самое мощное средство массовой информации, которое сейчас у нас (русских, тех, кто любит свою страну) есть. Телевидение, газеты, журналы, радио — все это куплено, фальшиво, не развивается, поэтому морально устаревает с большой скоростью. А миллионы пользователей — не шутка. Как вы думаете, почему этот ресурс так быстро развивается? Только лишь потому, что люди могут теперь сократить расстояние? Можно найти и еще кучу причин, главная из которых — люди понимают (неважно, сознательно или бессознательно), что существует потребность в социальном развитии, что у нас все морально устарело.

Этот ресурс не для манипуляции, люди намного умнее, чем вы можете подумать, и вообще, обманывать неэффективно, особенно с нашей скоростью передачи информации — все же будет известно очень быстро, репутация может быть испорчена.

Общество (я, вы, наши друзья, родители, преподаватели и т. п.) как-никак развивается, но у нас это происходит медленно, а с помощью этого ресурса можно ускорить процесс развития. Везде проблемы одинаковые. Везде, и в Москве, и в Златоусте, и в Челябинске, где я училась (я про большое количество гопников, отсутствие места времяпрепровождения и т. п.). Но дело в том, что люди не понимают, что это с ними что-то не так, что они не умеют общаться. А их можно научить.

Про государственный аппарат, который должен этим заниматься, можно забыть. Они там думают о перераспределении прибылей, о том, как построить завод, как перепродать нефть повыгоднее. Короче, о себе любимых они думают.

Поэтому я предлагаю описать на видном месте (чтобы люди не искали), как именно пользоваться vkontakte.ru. Ведь это очень важно, это как предисловие у книги, инструкция по применению у телефона или фотоаппарата.

От: Б.

Кому: Д.

Много буков, Павел не осилит. Я с ним в icq общаюсь и знаю, что говорю.

Павлу надо писать кратко, ясно и по делу. Иначе игнорировать будет. Такова жизнь. Я ему не близкий человек, так что и меня игнорировать начнет, если пару подобных воззваний передам. Объясните, что же Вы хотели бы сделать, стоит в 3–5 предложениях, а то он не увидит сути и заигнорит. <…> Рекомендую все-таки с группы начать. Мы, техподдержцы и админы, на нее посмотрим, порадуемся и вот тогда уже Павлу расскажем — когда что-то будет осязаемое. Да, я так понимаю, о коммерции речи не идет. Я всю свою деятельность веду совершенно бесплатно.

***

В узкий двор валил снег, и жители странной квартиры наблюдали, как колодец наполняется им, а гипсовая аллегория правосудия поправляет белый берет. Квартиру по-прежнему наводняли тени, но этим вечером они не сбились в чулан, а, бросив десктопы и ноуты, сошлись за столом в гостиной. Чтобы не сидеть в темноте, включили свет, покинули сумрак и образовали круг.

Подступал 2009 год, и Дуров хотел обсудить, как развиваться дальше. Дилемма простая. Остаться небольшой группой, где каждый кодер выполняет титанические работы, или строить компанию с офисом, нанимать программистов и учиться делегировать задачи. Ясно, что с улетающим в небо ростом аудитории придется расширяться — но когда? Прямо сейчас или позже?

Голоса разделились. Рогозов выступал за офис и рост численности кодеров. Дуров-старший допускал оба варианта. Его младший брат склонялся к подпольной деятельности. Кузя и Столбовский сохраняли нейтралитет.

Разгорелся спор в классическом стиле «ВКонтакте». Дуров вбросил провокационное предложение — забить на офис, — и сразу образовались партии консерваторов и умеренных обновленцев (отчаянных радикалов, как архитектор, до сих пор не завелось). Партии часами обсуждали свои концепции с самых разных сторон — а потом было принято быстрое решение, противоположное тому, что вроде бы выкристаллизовалось в дискуссии.

Как-то я поинтересовался у Николая Дурова, продуктивна ли эта шокотерапия. Николай откусил половину шоколадного батончика, вдумчиво прожевал и ответил: «Павел специально устраивает провокативные формы, чтобы стимулировать дискуссию и устранить сомнения, правильно ли мы все делаем. Например, говорит: „Это ненужный сервис“. Или: „Откроем все личные сообщения без учета приватности“. Или: „Давай дадим разработчику, который устроился, доступ к исходникам“. Я сразу говорю, что так нельзя делать — с точки зрения приватности, безопасности».

«А часто удается его переубедить?» — спросил я, вспомнив разговор с разработчиком Илларионовым, который утверждал, что в компании свобода мнений, но не смог вспомнить случая, когда кто-то уломал Дурова отменить желанное нововведение.

Николай погрузился в размышления. «Была идея приглашать в беседу человека через e-mail — это в том числе моими усилиями было отменено, — наконец ответил он. — Если бы мы начали рассылать спам, все почтовые службы могли нас забанить. Нет, Павел вряд ли предложит что-то безумное — например, сделать доступными публике все фотки пользователей. Он очень хорошо понимает, как использовать провокации и что можно и нужно делать».

«В его голове есть переключатель углов обзора, фокусировки, он видит ракурс проблемы, с которого видна заноза, — сформулировал

Равдоникас. — Дурова в такие моменты ненавидишь — когда надо, он перевернет все с ног на голову. Как в „Матрице“, его голова на 360° поворачивается. Ты бьешься целый день — ушел в какую-то сторону и углубляешься, а он приходит и с этого важного ракурса разрушает все твои построения, надо переделывать».

Разработчик Андрей Мима писал, что провокации Дурова — способ менять продукт быстро, без ненавидимых им бюрократических проволочек. Если основатель в чем-то уверен, то не сдает позиций, пока не оттестирует свои идеи в бою. (Набрасывая этот пост, Мима уходил из «ВКонтакте» запускать свой стартап и, хотя рассчитывал на дальнейшее сотрудничество с Дуровым, был вполне искренен в своих восторгах.)

«Лучшее будущее создается каждый день, порой в коридоре, и без оглядки на возможную панику, — писал он. — Нереально круто, что изменения придумываются; еще круче — что внедряются, несмотря на вой пользователей; а что совершенно нереально круто — что все потом оказываются очень довольны. Часто от придумывания радикальных изменений до внедрения проходит меньше недели! Нет другого выхода, кроме как заранее четко понимать, что будет лучше».

Превращаясь в главу государства с многомиллионным населением, Дуров заражал соратников своей религией. Имя ей — максимальная, до полной отстраненности чистота восприятия и мышления. Это касалось как никотина-алкоголя-мяса, которых Дуров не потреблял, — так и риторики, культуры рассуждения и принятия решения.

У нас нет иллюзий, предрассудков, мы стараемся видеть вещи такими, какие они есть. Мы боремся с манекенами, оперирующими стереотипами. Чтобы заставить человека думать, надо встряхнуть его. Как главный герой своего любимого фильма «Пролетая над гнездом кукушки», Дуров хотел пробудить в соратниках свободу ума и воли.

«Мир вокруг нас развивается так быстро, что общепринятые убеждения на наших глазах становятся издевательством над здравым смыслом, — писал он позже. — Сопротивление шума вокруг — устойчивый ориентир для всех желающих внести весомый вклад в развитие человечества. Слушать внутренний голос не означает оставаться глухим к мнению окружающих. Однако забудьте про демократию среди тех, кто вас окружает, — голос деятельного мыслителя, меняющего мир, должен быть для вас стократ более значим, чем голос праздного обывателя с его правом на мнение».

Проповедуя, Дуров не забывал заземлять религию. Он рос как лидер, но оставался изрядным троллем, не любителем платить в маршрутках и фанатом «Тупого, еще тупее».

Журналист Злата Николаева, первой из московских репортеров добившаяся у Дурова интервью, пересказала мне разговор между пиарщиком «ВКонтакте» Цыплухиным и мафиози Равдоникасом, которого пригласили заняться «словесным оформлением» сети. Влад злился, что в ресторанах недалеко от офиса жалуются на Дурова. Типа он приходит и заказывает стакан свежевыжатого черешневого сока. И пока фрустрированные официанты ищут черешню и выжимают сок, Дуров ест, расплачивается с чаевыми и уходит. Официант стоит со стаканом черешневого сока и думает: ну что, самому выпить?

«Что ж, — заметил Равдоникас. — Каждый официант, выжавший раз в жизни сок черешни, имеет право выпить стакан получившегося сока».

Даже если это апокриф, умение Дурова сшибать с привычного хода мысли оказывало на оппонентов магнетическое воздействие. «Когда с ним общаешься, всегда уходишь вдохновленным, — восхищался Бунин. — Он рассказывает то, чего не ждешь. Как Цукерберг в фильме — того грузят ерундой, а он смотрит в окно и вдруг: «идет дождь». «За год я научился у него многому, пропитал свое сознание простотой мышления», — вторил Рогозов.

Предновогоднее собрание закончилось победой Дурова. После дебатов насчет офиса победила точка зрения, что он не нужен. Год решили прожить в квартире и с незначительным расширением команды. Программисты не протестовали.

Такой стиль принятия решений имеет известные изъяны. В системе, которая держится на восхищении, штраф за фейлы зачисляется на счет вдохновителя. Двигаясь на ощупь в части продукта, Дуров совершал стратегические ошибки роста.

Отложив наем кодеров на год, он затормозил развитие компании. «Через год поняли, что нельзя дальше действовать маленькой командой, — признался Дуров. — Мы делали втроем работу, которую могут делать двести человек, а у конкурентов — тысяча. Нет психологического удовлетворения — конкуренты успевают больше. А офис лучше предназначен для дисциплинирования молодых сотрудников. В квартире они теряют ощущение, что здесь надо работать».

Кроме того, для десятков миллионов юзеров «ВКонтакте» отсутствовала служба техподдержки. Публика, не читавшая посты Дурова, не знала историю сети и не понимала ценностей ее создателей. С журналистами и сетевыми авторитетами никто не коммуницировал.

Впрочем, рефлексия настигла архитектора через три года, а тогда, после рождественских праздников, «ВКонтакте» меняли сайт семимильными шагами, не вылезая с Невского, 65, по выходным, с утра до ночи. Начали разрабатывать систему таргетинга рекламы, переделывали систему поиска по людям, вузам, фильмам, песням. Новый движок Николай пригласил писать Андрея Лопатина, тренера сборной России по программированию. Предстояло ускорить сайт — базы данных хранения не справлялись с росшим объемом информации.

Рогозов перекроил платформу. Коллеги одобрили новую версию, и оставалось лишь написать документацию — как кодерам пользоваться API. Дело было перед выходными, на которые он собирался ехать в Таллин. Рогозов пришел отпрашиваться к Дурову.

Тот выслушал его и сказал: «Нет, это нужно сейчас». — «Но у меня автобус в семь утра!» — «У тебя достаточно времени до семи».

Проклиная все на свете, Рогозов сел за текст, поручив взбешенной Эльнаре упаковать чемоданы. Они успели на автобус.

***

Солнце красило муравейник в охру и бликовало в его стеклянных панелях. Муравьи жили свою жизнь и к вечеру затихали — накидывали на плечо рюкзаки и исчезали. Они одевались похоже — либеральный casual: тенниски, шлепанцы, джинсы. Их исход напоминал вечерний отлив на шумящем неподалеку океане.

Компьютеры с погасшими мониторами напоминали коконы с людьми из «Матрицы». К каждому из-под потолка шла пуповина кабеля, через которую машины высасывали энергию. Там же, под потолком, покачивались флаги Индии, Китая, Чехии и других стран, чьи граждане до шести вечера трудились в коконе.

Консильери бежали сквозь муравейник, чтобы успеть на встречу с его правительницей, и успели, но разговор получился малопродуктивный. «О, гости из России, сейчас я принесу вам сувениров», — сказала правительница, известная тем, что умела отстаивать интересы муравейника в самых высоких кабинетах. Вернувшись, она вручила каждому синий значок с надписью Facebook. Это напоминало обмен вымпелами перед футбольным матчем, когда через минуту после свистка начинаются тычки и грязные подкаты.

Содержательный разговор между Дуровым и коммерческим директором Facebook Шерил Сэндберг так и не состоялся, хотя «ВКонтакте» проторчали в штаб-квартире конкурентов несколько дней. Впрочем, Дуров не расстроился. Главная встреча была впереди — Марк Цукерберг позвал их с Рогозовым на ужин. До этого дня два тотема даже не переписывались.

Диспозиция выглядела так. Известный любовью к тусовкам своих подопечных Мильнер старался, чтобы гении взаимодействовали друг с другом, и пригласил Дурова и компанию в тур по США. Мильнер крутил деньги мощного партнера — Алишера Усманова — и договорился инвестировать около 800 млн долларов из кошелька этого участника списка Forbes в интернет. Объектом он выбрал новые медиа — социальные платформы, на которых люди общаются и сами создают контент. «Могильщик веба», — писал о Мильнере журнал Wired. Очарованию DST поддались Facebook, Groupon и Zynga.

Спустя полгода работы на износ, летом 2009 года, Дуров и команда прилетели в Нью-Йорк, встретились с Равдоникасом, который на несколько лет уехал к отцу в Канаду. Парни отрывались. Садились в такси и, пока «желтый король» пробивался через пробки в аэропорт, дебатировали идеи, куда лететь. Их ждали в Сан-Франциско, но они направили стопы в Майами.

Перемещаясь зигзагами с севера на юг, шайка достигла Калифорнии. Нёрды поселились в отеле с видом на Сан-Франциско и залив. Мир лежал под ногами Дурова, который экономил на маршрутке.

Их ждали инвесторы Twitter, венчурные фонды и Марк Пинкус из Zynga. Последний забил стрелку в пиццерии. Zynga еще не была лидером среди производителей социальных игр с капитализацией под десяток миллиардов долларов. Но ее игры уже завоевали топ приложений Facebook. Дуров слышал, как невысокий, худой, похожий на подростка Пинкус мотивирует команду: «Почему я тут прыгаю перед вами в драной майке? Потому что наши приложения скачали всего пять миллионов человек!»

Дуров предложил ему запустить игры во «ВКонтакте». «Мы готовы русифицировать за свой счет», — прибавил он и назвал два хита: FarmVille и CityBuilder. Пинкус не задирал нос, расспрашивал про платформу и комиссию, но чувствовалось, что он делает одолжение. Zynga отказалась.

«В 2009 году Россия не была для Пинкуса приоритетом, половину доходов они не хотели отдавать — чтобы не создавать прецедент, который мог бы использовать Facebook, — пожал плечами Дуров и добавил: — Спустя два года Zynga решила выйти в Россию, пытались с нами встретиться. Я заранее знал, что они хотят — поддержка, команду найти, — и мне были неинтересны эти переговоры. Сейчас они нам не нужны, у нас разработчики лучше. Zynga первой захватила лидерство — а когда у тебя есть игры с сотнями тысяч юзеров, раскручивать новые игры не так сложно».

Когда они с Рогозовым тусовались в муравейнике Facebook, вице-президенты и маркетологи глядели на них свысока — клонировали нас, ну и ладно. Разработчики встречали по-другому — как вы добились, чтобы «ВКонтакте» из долины загружался быстрее, чем Facebook?!

Дуров спросил Цукерберга: «Что вы ответите Twitter?» Создатель микроблогов Джек Дорси привлек миллионы людей простотой использования — на высказывание 140 знаков, легко делиться ссылками. Информация крутилась в интернете все быстрее, люди привыкали плавать в ее потоках, а не потреблять дискретные образы и идеи, как в гутенберговскую эпоху. Дорси шагнул на следующую ступень эволюции — от сети друзей и знакомств к Twitter, где люди быстро и активно делятся мыслями, чувствами, ссылками. Он взял из модели Livejournal идею односторонних связей, гениальность которой стала очевидна только сейчас. Ты можешь подписаться на интересующего тебя вещателя в одностороннем порядке, без его благословения.

Цукерберг не раскололся про Twitter и пустился в рассуждения о соцсетях. Либертарианец Дуров почувствовал в нем брата-революционера. «У нас оказалось больше общего, чем с бизнес-персонажами, — заявил он после. — Марк — анархист, но не в смысле отрицания власти и порядка, а в плане понимания устаревшей природы государства». Архитекторы сошлись на том, что соцсети выступают надстройкой над человечеством, позволяющей информации распространяться мимо централизующих рупоров государства.

Безумное чаепитие происходило вечером. Цукерберг пригласил гостей в свой дом, надел галстук, позвал переманенного из Google повара приготовить несколько блюд, как в гурманском ресторане.

Дуров ерзал на стуле и морщился не от официоза, а от кухни. «Для желудка много ингредиентов — деструктивно, — жаловался он. — Желудочный сок зависит от того, что вы перевариваете, чем однороднее еда, тем лучше. Поэтому я ем как животное — отдельно фрукты, потом, допустим, пюре». К вину он не притронулся — уверял, что не пил с тех пор, как в школе химик Шпаков рассказывал об убийстве клеток спиртом.

Разговор напоминал танец боксеров на ринге:

— Какую комиссию берет «ВКонтакте» с разработчиков приложений?

— Ну, вообще 50%, но так происходит не со всеми. С каждым поразному. А когда вы начинаете экспансию в Россию?

— Россия нам интересна, как и другие развивающиеся рынки. А ваши пользователи сразу восприняли валюту?

— Не совсем.

Пока архитектор трепался, Рогозов наблюдал за Цукербергом. «Очень странный тип, — делился он ощущениями. — Как робот зомбированный — глаза бешеные, когда разговаривает, мышцы лица не двигаются». Оппоненты танцевали друг вокруг друга несколько часов и раскланялись глухой ночью.

Дуров догадался по вопросам, что Facebook скоро введет свою валюту, а также начнет международную экспансию — причем и в Россию тоже. Вернувшись, он начал вавилонскую кампанию по переводу «ВКонтакте» на тридцать языков — с помощью университетских друзей и добровольцев.

Но если сам Цукерберг понравился Дурову, то от Facebook он плевался. То есть, конечно, признавал мощь аналитиков, гибкость в выборе стратегии роста в зависимости от страны, ценил умение учиться на ошибках и амбицию согнать Google с пьедестала. Но гораздо важнее для него было ощущение, что Цукерберг прогнулся под ценности коммерсантов. «ДНК компании определяет Шэрил Сэндберг, бывшая вашингтонская лоббистка, — объяснял он. — Если Цукерберг скажет: „У нас будет пятьдесят разработчиков, а не двести“, — у нее найдется туча аргументов, чтобы заблокировать эту идею».

Сидя в самолете домой, Дуров размышлял о том, что «ВКонтакте» и Facebook расходятся все заметнее. Цукерберг монетизировал сеть все интенсивнее. Свободные места на страницах забиты баннерами. Раскручены инструменты для продвижения брендов — от промоутирования страниц до вылезающих подсказок с их названиями.

«ВКонтакте» отводил рекламе меньше места, а с маркетологами вовсе не работал. Дуров согласился продавать рекламу через компанию Media+ — за фиксированную сумму в год плюс бонусы, если план перевыполнен. Заниматься рекламой он поставил Перекопского, финансами — его брата, а сам только одобрял или заворачивал баннеры. Их размер напоминал Facebook: небольшие картинки снизу слева.

Позже Дуров признавал, что ошибся со схемой продажи рекламы. Следовало создать свою службу.

Это было характерным симптомом. Дуров нехотя втягивался в коммерческую историю. Гораздо охотнее он проводил время, выспрашивая звезд своей сети, где секрет успеха и чем сеть может им помочь.

Инопланетянка просочилась сквозь дверь и протянула тотему прозрачную руку. Перед встречей Дуров напялил коричневую кожанку, которая была ему велика, и узкие очки а-ля Нео. Пожимая руку, он разглядел существо в серебристом скафандре и ее компаньонку, обтянутую медицинским халатом, заимствованным из немецкого порно.

Пришелица по кличке Нахема перекочевала во «ВКонтакте» из Livejournal и затащила в свою группу про эзотерику сотни тысяч пользователей. Часть их обожала отфотошопленные снимки Нахемы в бикини, часть стебалась над ней. Жестом призвав гостей к монитору, Дуров похвалил группу. «У меня тоже мистическое мышление, — улыбнувшись, добавил он. — Часто я знаю, что надо поступить так-то, но не могу объяснить почему».

Инопланетянка раскрепостилась и сделала несколько замечаний. Потом выдвинула предложения, как улучшить функционал. Дуров улыбался из-за очков. Когда гостьи раскланялись и покинули штаб, позвал дизайнера и сказал что-то вроде: «Фотографии стоит выводить крупнее, а вот эти пиксели лишние».

Правда, разбираясь в продукте и потребностях инопланетян, он допускал ляпы в управлении структурами, бóльшими, чем партизанский отряд нёрдов.

Архитектор видел, что горячая любовь пользователей, как на первом году запуска, понемногу тает. Реклама убивала ощущение площадки сотрудничества а-ля «Википедия» — но выхода у Дурова не оставалось.

Сделки со своими убеждениями стоили все дороже. Казалось бы, раз «ВКонтакте» превратилась в государство, глупо игнорировать желание людей торговать. Лев и Слава настаивали на идее пустить в сеть интернет-магазины, и Дуров согласился.

Сначала требовалось определить, как сотрудничать с торговцами. Наиболее крупный и опытный игрок был очевиден. Его возглавлял экспат, что как бы намекало — можно договориться об удобной модели взаимодействия и гибких условиях.

Однако, сидя в переговорной комнате с видом на Казанский и слушая про разный процент на разный товар, Дуров почувствовал, что вот она, точка, когда он не хочет больше тратить ни секунды на уговоры людей, чуждых ему по духу, убеждениям и ценностям. Он ощутил, что стервенеет, и закричал: «Вы не понимаете разницы между торговлей и творчеством! Вы считаете, что мы набиваем себе цену. Вы просто тратите наше время».

Пока он выговаривал свою ненависть к мелкотемью, за 700 километров от дома Зингера зрела война против «ВКонтакте», поражение в которой означало утерю нёрдами их острова бизнеса в стиле панк.

***

Враг пришел изнутри. Русские компании Юрия Мильнера объединились в холдинг Mail.ru Group. Доля во «ВКонтакте», доведенная по соглашению с Мильнером до 32%, принадлежала именно этой структуре. С Дуровым конкурировала соцсеть «Мой Мир», которая автоматически записала в своих юзеров всех обладателей почты на Mail.ru, а также «Одноклассники».

Дуров не уделял конкурентам много внимания. «Мой Мир» был не так удобен, лишен возможности делиться контентом и плелся за «ВКонтакте» и более боевыми «Одноклассниками». А главное, разработчики Mail.ru не демонстрировали способности изобретать что-то крышесносящее.

Тем сильнее штаб в доме Зингера поразился, когда конкуренты выкатили свою платформу для разработчиков приложений. Изучив ее, Рогозов убедился, что Mail.ru передрал у них некоторые решения. Дело напрямую касалось денег, поэтому компаньоны обсуждали ответные действия в расширенном составе. К Дурову, Левиеву и Мирилашвили-младшему примкнул Мирилашвили-старший, недавно вышедший на свободу. Ему удалось сохранить свои компании. Позже власти запретили игорный бизнес, и Мирилашвили сделал акцент на недвижимости. Назначив на ключевые посты надежных менеджеров, он улетел в Израиль и в Петербург старался не заглядывать. Слава отправился вслед за ним.

***

Дуров ломал голову, как убедить игровые компании не пользоваться платформой конкурентов. Конечно, он понимал, что задавить эту инициативу Mail.ru не удастся и «ВКонтакте» перестанет быть монополистом, но москвичам требовалось дать ответ. Мирилашвили-старший предложил выдвинуть игровикам ультиматум: или вы с нами, или против нас. Кто пользуется «Моим.Миром», ни копейки у нас не заработает.

Если бы речь шла о заметном рынке, антимонопольная служба вкатила бы Дурову предупреждение. Он и сам не радовался мере, казавшейся архаичной, — в интернете глупо опускать шлагбаумы. Это свободная среда, где барьеров нет, а если кто-то что-то запрещает — следует взломать, обойти, скопировать. Но партнеры настаивали, и Дуров согласился на шоковую терапию.

Идея была симпатична тем, что к Mail.ru, который уже намекал, что стремится контролировать «ВКонтакте», хотелось прийти с плеткой. То есть отреагировать максимально свирепо. Дуров улавливал настроения, витавшие в Mail.ru, по разговорам с Мильнером. Два года назад тот вскользь упомянул, что москвичи следят с интересом за его сетью, а теперь по разговорам с представителями инвесторов Дуров почувствовал, что независимость его детища ставится под вопрос.

Тотем разделил песни на личной странице на две вкладки — «s [e] x» и «w [a]r». Эти две мании вели его, но страсть к сражению, похоже, была сильнее. Конфликты неминуемо должны была возникнуть после того, как «ВКонтакте» превратился в мощный инструмент влияния.

Создав этот инструмент, Дуров должен был однажды обернуть его против захватчиков. Теперь момент настал. Он увидел первого врага у ворот и напал первым.

Набросав письмо о выборе между «ВКонтакте» и Mail.ru, Дуров поставил в копию игровиков, которые зарабатывали на его аудитории, пробежал глазами текст и кликнул «Отправить».

Глава 5
Стена

И казалось бы, куда ему деться, но он несся дальше и дальше. Мелькала трасса, холмы, пригорки, пилот уклонялся от опор мостов и, не сбрасывая скорости, входил в повороты, где обычный водитель сломал бы себе шею. За стеклом летела монохромная картина, пейзаж без свойств. Пилот управлял «Альфа-ромео» легким касанием пальцев и, когда пересек финишную черту, откинулся на стуле и нажал Escape.

«Ну что, — повернулся он к посетителю, который топтался за спиной. — Покупаю. Приноси еще чего-нибудь». Посетитель вздохнул с облегчением.

Наблюдая за гонкой, он изрядно нервничал, потому что учился в девятом классе и демонстрировал эксперту свою первую игру. Он написал ее на первобытной машине БК-2101, закинул на кассету, положил в карман и направил стопы свои в магазин «Руслан и Людмила». Саратовский посперестроечный ГУМ, кроме одежды и бижутерии, держал закуток, где сидел специальный человек и записывал игры.

Девятикласснику не хватало денег на дисковод, и он решил их заработать на интересе к автомобилям. Школу охватила мания коллекционирования вкладышей от жвачек — девочки фанатели от Love is, а мальчики дрались за Turbo с автомобилями «Формулы-1». Классы облепляли подоконники, бросали по вкладышу с игрока и стучали, пока не засинеют ладони.

Операция прошла удачно: автор избрал модную тему, кассета пропела свое «шшшш, трынь-трынь-трынь», торговец одобрил игру, и полученные рубли тут же возвратились в его карман как вознаграждение за дисковод.

«Так я понял, где в игровом бизнесе кусок пирога издателя, где разработчика и где дистрибьютора», — усмехнется автор через двадцать лет, сидя в кабинете, закрытом от внешнего мира жалюзи. Чтобы попасть в этот кабинет, я прошел по длинному коридору бывшего института кинематографической техники. Справа и слева мелькали кьюбиклы, набитые людьми, которые большей частью сидели в наушниках и задумчиво стучали по клавишам. Это напоминало даже не улей, а муравейник Facebook.

Перед дверью, за которой расположился бывший девятиклассник, задвинувший «Альфу-ромео» в саратовском универмаге, возникла секретарша в сером костюме. Она сделала примиряющий жест «секундочку» и подняла трубку: «Приемная генерального директора, слушаю».

Дмитрий Гришин теперь управлял крупнейшим в России интернет-холдингом Mail.ru. Собственно, он и не собирался становиться предпринимателем, предпочитая заниматься интересующими его продуктами, а не бизнесом. Начал работать в двадцать два года, доучиваясь в Бауманке, и угодил в List.ru. Занимался интернет-аукционом, продвинулся до технического директора.

Port.ru входил в состав компании NetBridge, основанной будущим инвестором «ВКонтакте» Мильнером. Посмотрев на западные коммуникационные сервисы, Мильнер решил клонировать лучшее из того, что есть, в России.

Однако в 2001 году интернет-рынок подкосил кризис «доткомов». Западные инвесторы были фрустрированы падением акций крупнейших компаний, и, чтобы развиваться, Мильнеру пришлось искать партнера в России. NetBridge объединился с Port.ru, владевшей множеством сайтов.

Обе компании сидели в минусе. Мильнер сменил на посту директора основателя Port.ru и сократил 80% персонала. Способного Гришина он двигал по карьерной лестнице. Разрозненные сайты плохо продавали рекламные площади, и коммерсанты решили вытянуть из колоды брендов самый быстрорастущий и консолидировать остальные под его маркой. Этим якорем стал Mail.ru.

Из почтового сервиса он превратился в портал с разделами «Работа», «Новости» и т. д. Мильнер с Гришиным создавали его во многом по подобию Yahoo. Правда, в дальнейшем они пошли по пути, позволившему выжить — в отличие от теряющей юзеров компании Джерри Янга.

В 2003 году Гришина повысили до генерального директора. Он продолжал кодить и разрабатывать продукты. Новых идей, как делать деньги в интернете, помимо рекламы, у него не было. Неизвестно, чем закончилось бы дело, если бы Mail.ru не поддержали высокотехнологичные рекламодатели. Разбирающиеся в интернете и верующие в его будущее менеджеры Intel, Microsoft, МТС, «Билайн» и «Мегафон» фактически спасли портал, массово покупая рекламу.

Гришин был постоянно озабочен финансовым результатом и при этом не имел радикальных идей, как еще зарабатывать, кроме размещения баннеров. Куда двигаться, они с Мильнером поняли: строить линейку коммуникационных продуктов. Чем пользуются люди? Почтой, мгновенными сообщениями типа ICQ. Значит, надо развивать, а позже интегрировать эти направления. А вот с источниками дохода несколько лет Mail.ru ничего не изобретал.

Впрочем, в мировом интернете над монетизацией ломали мозги более изобретательные парни, и в конце концов модели нарисовались сами. В состав акционеров Mail.ru вошел китайский Tencent, и, общаясь с новыми партнерами, Гришин заметил два тренда.

Во-первых, коммуникации в сети — своего рода развлечение. Почта, соцсети, мессенджеры и игры постепенно сливаются в одно пространство.

Во-вторых, монетизировать сервисы, тупо взимая деньги с юзеров, нельзя. Будущее за моделью «фримиум» — базовой версией пользуешься бесплатно, а платишь за дополнительные возможности, причем такие, которых нет у конкурентов. Например, Гришин рассказывал, что китайский аналог ICQ даром раздавал аватарки, но подсветить или «раскрасить их можно было за денежку». (Выражение «за денежку» в ходе интервью Гришин употребил шесть раз.)

История Mail.ru — зеркало того, что произошло с Гришиным. В отличие от «Яндекса» и, в меньшей степени, «ВКонтакте», компания не имела уникального продукта — лишь копировала или скупала сервисы, комплементарные ее стратегии.

Гришин так и не научился генерировать прорывные идеи. Дух компании возник в эпоху выживания, а потом, когда пришли большие деньги и холдинг разросся, гендиректор столкнулся с внутренними интригами. Не будучи диктатором или визионером, воле которого беспрекословно подчиняются окружающие, он защищался от желающих сесть в его кресло.

Кроме этого, болезнь роста превратила Mail.ru в структуру с тысячами сотрудников, где вышли на первое место корпоративные фишки: бонусы, тренинги, митинги с разрисовыванием флипчартов, молебны на бизнес-показатели.

***

Гришин и Дуров родились с разницей в пять дней — 15 октября против 10 октября. Оба юзали MacBook Air. Оба одевались неброско. Оба ботаники и злостные нёрды. Оба начинали путь программиста с написания игры. Оба любили кодить. Но трудно было найти столь непохожих друг на друга военачальников.

Один формировал команду, собирая единомышленников-партизан на герилью с корпорациями, и обращался к миллионам пользователей через личный блог. Другой строил корпорацию, лично утверждая макеты визиток для сотрудников, и обожал такой жанр разговора с миром, как пресс-релиз.

Один — про свободу и раздачу людям новых возможностей. Другой — про контроль над сотрудниками и удовлетворение акционеров.

Один — про маниакальное следование своему вкусу и пользовательским надеждам, еще не воплощенным. Другой — про работу с уже испытанными на юзерах моделями.

Когда Mail.ru решил скупить все многообещающие соцсети рунета, Дуров не подозревал, что когда-то эта стратегия выльется в открытый конфликт. Да, в «Одноклассниках» холдинг приобрел контрольный пакет и последующие два года свирепо конфликтовал с другими акционерами. Правда, те были сами хороши. Желая быстрее снять сливки, они прикрутили соцсети платную регистрацию и за каждый шаг юзера драли монету.

Вход в капитал «ВКонтакте» прошел более гладко. Мильнеру нравилось, как Дуров развивает продукт, а петербуржцев устраивала независимость, и они не просили помощи. У инвестора и основателя случилась любовь, которая до поры до времени хранила стартап от конфликтов.

Однако Мильнер помимо переговорщических качеств обладал изощренным политическим чутьем. Он знакомил подопечных друг с другом, возил в Кремниевую долину, гладил по головке и называл светочами, но, когда менеджеры сцеплялись между собой, поднимался над схваткой. Скрестив руки на груди, он наблюдал, кто кого съест, и не склонялся ни на чью сторону.

Услышав, что Дуров грозит извергнуть из сети всех, кто перебежал на платформу «Мейла», Мильнер не стал звонить и давить на второго Цукерберга, а занял выжидательную позицию.

Гришин жестом пригласил просителя за длинный стол и откинулся в кресле, приготовившись слушать. В окне маячили крыши хрущевок и краны, поднимающие блоки на возводящийся небоскреб. Проситель был крупным игровиком — насколько крупным можно быть на рынке, чей объем исчисляется миллионами долларов. Он не собирался утомлять хозяина спичем и просто спросил: «Что за хрень с вашей платформой?»

«В смысле — хрень?» — изумился Гришин. «Ну как, Дуров прислал ультиматум, что или мы остаемся у него, или выбираем вас, но ни копейки больше во „ВКонтакте" не заработаем». Гришин переспросил: «Уверены, что это не шутка?» «Какие шутки, — сдерживаясь, проговорил игровик. — Мы зарабатываем у них кучу денег. Хотели бы зарабатывать и у вас, конечно. Но боимся потерять „ВКонтакте"».

Гришин задумался. Казалось бы, Mail.ru владел акциями «ВКонтакте» и мог разбомбить выскочку Дурова, предъявив претензии насчет неэтичного поведения.

Но, во-первых, холдингу скандал не нужен, а во-вторых, давить на питерских ботаников никто не пробовал, а Дуров непредсказуемый, кто его знает, чем ответит. Пока надо вести себя тихо. К тому же ультиматум — ошибка, в интернете такие методы не работают.

Гришину промыли мозг еще несколько игровиков, и он понял, что сам собой конфликт не рассосется. Требуется контррешение. Схватка так схватка, и раз соперники ведут себя как дети, следует этим воспользоваться. Гришин вызвал пиарщика и сел составлять пресс-релиз.

Они придумали красивый ход: отменить комиссию для приложений. 100% дохода с игр падали в карман разработчикам. Конечно, не навсегда, на первые месяцы, но тем не менее. Игровики больше не колебались и отправились в «Мой Мир» стройными рядами, и за последующие месяцы платформа Mail.ru взлетела, как ракета. Дуров смирился и дезавуировал ультиматум.

***

Прошло полгода. «ВКонтакте» въехала в дом с валькириями и земным шаром. Акционеры уже не сомневались, что офис нужен. «У меня слабость к красивым видам», — объяснял Дуров. Он выбрал три варианта: на Михайловской и Маяковской улицах, а также дом Зингера. Первые два, впрочем, выступали как фиктивные участники тендера.

Дуров нечеловечески хотел окопаться в штабе, которому раскрыл объятья Казанский собор и где под окнами не иссякал человеческий трафик. Глобус, опять же. И Заболоцкий, конечно:

Там Невский в блеске и тоске,
В ночи переменивший краски,
От сказки был на волоске,
Ветрами вея без опаски.
И как бы яростью объятый,
Через туман, тоску, бензин,
Над башней рвался шар крылатый
И имя «Зингер» возносил.

Они с Перекопским, путешествуя, выбирали самые умопомрачительные гостиницы как знак покорения мира денег. Теперь Дуров настаивал на Зингере из-за его привлекательности для гениев, которых намеревался поймать в свою сеть. Разрабатывать продукт, который от сказки на волоске, в легендарном доме, на первой линии Невского — это была уловка хитрого охотника за головами.

Совершив променад по двум этажам, Дуров восхитился пыточной переговорной, выходом по витой лестнице наверх в стеклянный глобус, где умещалось одно рабочее место. Конечно, два этажа «ВКонтакте» были не нужны, но Дуров выбил из Льва и Славы дорогущую аренду — под предлогом инвестиций в таланты, рост компании, создание службы поддержки и т. д.

Въехав, нёрды не изменили в быту ничего. Скелет, испанский сапог, дешевый ремонт на этаже, где сидели сам архитектор и топменеджеры, — все осталось. Добавились магнитные доски со шрифтом

Tahoma, диван с коровьими головами и автомат с апельсиновым соком.

В университетской столовой Дуров раздавал дольки приспешникам, а теперь выжимал апельсины в промышленных масштабах.

Гришину тоже предстояли перемены. До осени 2009 года Mail.ru выпускал свои игры, но сейчас холдингу предстояло купить Astrum, владеющий множеством студий-разработчиков. Компанию основал Игорь Мацанюк, начинавший карьеру с торговли джипами в Мурманске, впоследствии бросивший стремный бизнес и занявшийся играми.

Мильнер оплатил сделку с Мацанюком деньгами и акциями Mail.ru. Но на этом интерес игровика не кончался — он желал возглавить холдинг и поставить директора по маркетингу Astrum Алису Чумаченко на позицию вице-президента. Мильнер не стал принимать ничью сторону, оставив Гришину и Мацанюку выяснить, кто прав, в корпоративном бою.

Произошедший после этого конфликт имеет две версии. Согласно первой, Гришин заблокировал назначение Чумаченко и Мацанюка, а те создали компанию Game Insight. Взяв куски кода игр, разработанных Astrum, они нарушили пакт о ненападении (non-compete agreement) и стали выпускать игры, конкурирующие с Mail.ru.

Вторая версия гласит, что Чумаченко не очень-то хотелось трудиться с Гришиным, а вот создать свой бизнес — другое дело. Найдя инвестора (Мацанюк не подтверждает, что Game Insight создан на его деньги), она начала писать свои собственные игры. Ни у кого ничего не копировала, а Гришин, мол, выдумал копирайтные войны, чтобы выжить Мацанюка до IPO, на котором тот бы заработал больше, чем при выкупе акций до выхода на биржу.

Конфликт перестал быть тайной и взорвался в публичной сфере, когда на сайте разработчиков Mail.ru был опубликован сворованный, по мнению холдинга, кусок кода. За несколько дней до этого Гришин пошел на манипуляцию, схожую с дуровской. «ВКонтакте» поставили в известность, что код краденый, и затребовали исключение игр Game Insight из сети. Когда Дурову сообщили об этом, он спросил, правда ли код тупо скопирован, и, получив ответ «нет», велел отказать Mail.ru.

Вскоре на его айфоне высветился звонок — беспокоил Гришин. Дуров привык брать трубку далеко не всегда и воспитывал этим Льва со Славой и других менеджеров. Теперь он применил это к сопернику. Гришин перезвонил еще пару раз и прекратил попытки.

Еще через некоторое время Дурову набрал Мильнер. В подобных случаях тотем брал трубку. Поговорив о том о сем, инвестор намекнул вундеркинду, что неплохо бы снять спорные игры. Дуров хоть и ненавидел переливание из пустого в порожнее, когда ответ уже дан, но в важных разговорах умел маскировать нежелание идти на компромисс выжидающей позицией. Да-да, разработчики посмотрят код, разберемся объективно.

Разумеется, итоги разбора были предсказуемы. Дуров понял, что военные действия начались и следует не держаться за позиции, а нападать первым. Если пойти на уступки Гришину — все, съедят. Надо подчеркнуто твердо отказаться убирать игры.

Дуров открыл ноутбук, зашел в систему рекламы и на свои деньги создал кампанию играм Game Insight. Затем он вызвал недавно нанятого пресс-секретаря Влада Цыплухина и велел предупредить Чумаченко, что со дня на день Mail.ru опубликует скандальный пост о краже кода и под этим предлогом отключит монетизацию их игр. О кампании за счет начальника Влад не знал.

Он предупредил Game Insight, и игровики встретили скандал во всеоружии. Для них решение Mail.ru лишить их средств к проживанию — более половины выручки капало с платформы Гришина — выглядело едва ли не смертельным. Конфликт закончился недружелюбными переговорами и поиском посредника для замирения сторон.

Впрочем, потом Чумаченко утверждала, что эта история заставила ее взглянуть на новые рынки — социальные игры на платформе Google Android и в джобсовском AppStore. Именно там Game Insight издала свои лучшие приложения и стала одной из крупнейших игровых компаний в России. От «ВКонтакте» Чумаченко получала все меньше дохода, потому что сконцентрировалась на мировом рынке.

Если с Game Insight Гришин наладил какие-никакие отношения, то с Дуровым мира не предвиделось. Отложив боевые действия на потом, Гришин с помощью Мильнера нанял сильного продакт-менеджера Илью Широкова перезапускать «Одноклассников» — соцсеть, которая могла бы покончить с гегемонией «ВКонтакте» в стране. Mail.ru приготовился к затяжной осаде дома Зингера.

***

— Все здесь?

— Вроде все.

— Ты считал?

— Да, конечно. Если хочешь, пересчитай сам.

Лев кивнул сисадмину и направился по проходу между сиденьями. В автобус набились безмолвные пассажиры. Еще недавно вкалывавшие, работавшие, так сказать, с огоньком, они умолкли и заснули, откинувшись на спинки кресел.

Лев встал у дверей и, отдышавшись, еще раз посчитал перетащенный им и коллегами груз. Все были на месте: в креслах ехали серверы, которые предстояло развезти нескольким хостинг-провайдерам.

Он вернулся к водителю, убежденный, что ничего не забыли. Как ни странно, Лев был рад, будто недавно подрался и хотел бы продолжить.

«Давить, — сказал ему Дуров перед началом операции. — Давить этот чертов картель. Пусть засунут себе свой трафик куда-нибудь». Водитель повернул ключ, и автобус с серверами отчалил.

Безумное путешествие было продолжением противостояния. Не столько с Mail.ru, сколько с тем, что Дуров считал злом.

«ВКонтакте» вырос настолько, что вторгался в сферу интересов и власти, и конкурентов, и просто отраслей, с которыми соприкасался и на которые влиял не так, как хотелось бы оппонентам. Казалось, реальность ополчилась против них. Впрочем, Дуров не искал в том, что на него посыпалось, политики или происков каких-то автохтонных сил.

«Что есть зло? — писал он в блоге. — Зло — это наш враг. Добро — это мы. Если увеличить масштаб, можно понять простую истину: то, что в итоге побеждает, становится добром. Побеждать и вытеснять врага — его основная характеристика. Поэтому язычество и рабство — зло, а монотеизм и общество потребления — добро. Почему они победили? Потому что оказались более эффективными в изменяющихся условиях».

История с автобусом началась, когда растущей «ВКонтакте» понадобился хостинг-провайдер для обслуживания серверов. Мильнер указал партнерам на «Голден Телеком». Дуров согласился, не до конца понимая рисков. «Голден» входил в неформальный клуб трех крупнейших провайдеров страны и фиксировал цены на выгодном себе уровне.

Когда версия «ВКонтакте» для телефонов раскрутилась, трафик пошел мимо «Голдена» к сотовым операторам. Провайдер начал давить на клиента. Смысл — сделать так, чтобы соцсеть работала только через него. Несколько раз серверы падали на два-три часа — провайдер отвечал, что не имеет возможности расширить канал вовремя. Затем присылал письма, что поднимет стоимость обслуживания в десять раз. Не нравится? Уходите.

Компаньоны взяли билеты в Москву. Лев вспоминал, что дорогой они настраивались на победу: «Паша стоял твердо, что или мы их ломаем, или мы должны оказаться достаточно сильными, чтобы послать на фиг».

Офис. Круг стульев. Напротив бледного юноши, наряженного в черное, расположились импозантные мужчины — менеджеры подразделения, курировавшего интернет-трафик.

— Предлагаю подписать эксклюзивный договор на пять лет, — начал директор.

«Уверены, что у нас нет вариантов», — подумал Дуров.

— Вы не расширяете каналы вовремя. Есть гарантии, что это не повторится?

— Поймите, мало ли что может случиться, у нас много подрядчиков.

(«Монополисты, создали систему, когда все, кто от них не зависит, гонят трафик через Европу и переплачивают».)

— В таком случае нам выгоднее сотрудничать с несколькими независимыми провайдерами.

— Сомневаюсь, Павел.

(«Понимают, что у независимых нет столько мощностей, сколько нам надо».)

— Привязываться на пять лет к одному оператору — это слишком!

— ОК, подпишем эксклюзив на три года.

(«Менеджерье плевало на наши идеи, жируют при хозяине. Уверены, что, если я откажусь сейчас, приползу позже…»)

— Это все, что вы можете предложить?

— Да.

Дуров удержался от того, чтобы выдернуть чеку из воображаемой гранаты и взорвать офис к чертовой матери. Недавно он смотрел фильм

«Святые из трущоб», где братья-ирландцы после убийства девочки на глазах у струсивших обывателей берутся за оружие и вершат правосудие.

Братья врываются в суд, который намерен оправдать мафиози, приставляют к его затылку дуло и произносят: «Теперь вы примете нас. Нам не нужны бедные и голодные. Нам не нужны уставшие и больные. Мы взыщем с продажных. Мы взыщем со злодеев. Пусть ваши мелкие гнусности не выходят за рамки и не переходят границ настоящей скверны, которой занимаемся мы. Ибо если это случится, то однажды вы обернетесь и увидите нас троих, и в этот день вы пожнете плоды».

Дуров встал и отодвинул стул. Перед ним, конечно, не злодеи, а корпоративная шушера, но их манипуляции мешают «ВКонтакте» расти. Пришел черед произнести свою речь. Побелев от гнева, он сказал: «Мы уходим. Вы нарушаете законы России. Я пожалуюсь на вас в антимонопольную службу. Вы выкручиваете руки стартапам. Вы действуете не в русле высказываний президента, который говорил о помощи высокотехнологичному бизнесу».

Переговорщики открыли рты. Вместе с ними застыл Лев, почувствовав, что Дуров зажег спичку и вот-вот бросит ее на мост.

«Более того, — холодно продолжил Дуров. — Я считаю, что вы ведете себя как уголовники. Следует подумать о том, чтобы отдать вас под суд, потому что, похоже, вы ставите свои интересы выше интересов акционеров „Голден Телекома“».

Мост вспыхнул, и змейка огня побежала к противоположному берегу. Оппоненты выходили из ступора.

Первым очнулся линейный менеджер и возмутился: этот наглец рассказывает, как нам вести бизнес! Видимо, в голове директора всплыли словосочетания «худой мир» и «добрая ссора», и он затоптал огонь: «Давайте не торопиться».

Но было поздно, Дуров вылетел из кабинета. Вслед за ним, попрощавшись, исчез Лев. Шагая по коридору, архитектор проговорил: «Ищем других провайдеров и перевозим серверы». Лев не стал возражать.

Спустя несколько дней они встретились с человеком из «Ростелекома». Тот обещал найти канал на 60 Мбит. Нашлось в итоге на 25, но «ВКонтакте» договорилась с другими провайдерами, в сумме набрав необходимые мощности. Лев вызвонил автобус, и демонтаж серверов закончил их роман с «Голденом».

Менеджеры, правда, выкатили претензии, что «ВКонтакте» им недоплатила, и попытались взыскать около 15 млн рублей. Но Дуров платить отказался; тяжба продолжается до сих пор.

Тогда же акционеры «ВКонтакте» убедились, что нужно строить свои каналы — «дороги будущего», — чтобы не зависеть ни от кого. Слава и Лев создали компанию «Селектел» и занялись развитием независимого хостинг-провайдера.

Дуров написал и передал письмо президенту Дмитрию Медведеву. Телекоммуникационный картель искусственно завышает цены. Надо строить дороги XXI века, а не гнобить интернет-компании. У русских продуктов недостаточный авторитет в глазах журналистов, которые восхищаются всем западным. Мы рассуждаем о модернизации, а истинная модернизация — снизу; ей нужно помогать и т. д.

Политических претензий к власти Дуров не имел. Власть управляет страной, где осталось крепостное сознание и право, — и крутится как может. Не то чтобы Дуров не видел свинцовых мерзостей нулевых, когда бюрократам и силовикам позволили облагать оброком и сажать предпринимателей. Он все прекрасно понимал, но воевал с носителями зла и устранял помехи на пути компании, а не бодался с системой. «Демократия и тирания различаются скорее формой, чем содержанием, — писал он. — Попытки установить всеобщее равенство оканчиваются печально, потому что равенство не предусмотрено биологически.

Но хочется верить, что открытая конкуренция делает свое дело. И если остается хоть небольшая лазейка, самые способные и энергичные постепенно проникают наверх».

Проблема вымахавшего до полсотни миллионов юзеров «ВКонтакте» заключалась в том, что количество желающих перекрыть лазейки или вставить палки в колеса росло на глазах. Дуров неуклонно стервенел с каждым иском.

«Это 30 млн уголовников, и соучастники известны! — кричал на пресс-конференции директор кинокомпании „Амедиа" Александр Акопов. — Всех посадить в тюрьму нельзя, но 10 000 — можно!» Пресса радостно строчила в блокноты, предвкушая скандал.

Акопов инициировал холивар против «ВКонтакте» за то, что соцсеть фактически держала крупнейшее хранилище пиратского контента. Это было объяснимое негодование — не только русские, но и западные пираты бесплатно хостились у Дурова. К 2010 году примерно половина показов видео в рунете приходилась на «ВКонтакте» — и это было конкурентным преимуществом сети.

Дуров считал свободу распространения информации органической чертой интернета. Но правообладателей следовало успокоить, и ему вновь пришлось идти на сделку со своими убеждениями. «ВКонтакте» дала мейджорам возможность удалять видео и предложила продвигать их страницы. Первой под «отличника с двойкой за поведение» прогнулась 20th Century Fox. За ней последовала «Централ Партнершип».

Но за ними поспешили далеко не все. Английская Virgin Media закрыла клиентам доступ к «ВКонтакте». Акопов (как и телекомпания ВГТРК) все-таки подал в суд. Несмотря на проигрыш исков (контент выкладывала не сеть, а пользователи), правообладатели не успокоились и при удобном случае пинали «ВКонтакте». После этого на лбу манекена для избиения в тренажерном зале дома Зингера кто-то начертал: «Акопов».

Однажды я слушал откровения монстра копирайта: «Вот мы пришли с сериалом ABC, на который у нас есть эксклюзивные права на российскую территорию. Заглядываем во „ВКонтакте“, а там 65 000 видеозаписей — и мы вручную должны все это удалить. ОК, попыхтели, удалили, а еще через четыре дня там еще 30 000 видео — ну это издевательство, слушайте!»

Пересказав этот вопль Дурову, я услышал следующее:

«Мы занимаемся технологиями и средствами коммуникации. Проблемы индустрии развлечений, которую интернет вынуждает пересматривать бизнес-модели, волнуют нас только в плане соблюдения законов. Мы обязаны удалять видеоролики, если получаем письменное уведомление о ролике с документами, доказывающими авторские права на данный контент.

Но мы пошли дальше — дали правообладателям возможность бесконтрольно удалять видеоролики, которые, по их мнению, нарушают их права. Мы даже почти не проверяем списки удаленных видеороликов, полностью полагаясь на честность.

Тогда они стали говорить о том, что пользователи загружают те же видеоролики заново. Мы снова пошли навстречу — создали систему, которая запрещает повторно загружать видеоролики.

Но и этого оказалось мало. Жаловались именно те издатели, которым мы помогали все удалять. А западные издатели тем временем молча собирали рекордные прибыли в российских кинотеатрах при существующих копиях своих фильмов „ВКонтакте“ и на других российских UGC-ресурсах. При этом американские мейджоры покупали рекламу фильмов, а большинство отечественных кинопродюсеров — бойкотировали. Например, из США на нас жалуются скорее издатели музыки.

У некоторых российских издателей или у всей нашей киноиндустрии есть какие-то внутренние проблемы, которые они не осознают или которые им не хотелось бы признавать. С ними невозможно договориться, они живут в прошлом веке и хотят заставить людей платить немалые деньги за то, что лежит в торрентах в более качественном формате бесплатно».

Позже я общался с главой «Одноклассников» Ильей Широковым — после того, как они запустили аудиохостинг. Широков подчеркивал, что, в отличие от «ВКонтакте», он горой за правообладателей.

«А, так у вас на выложенные песни подписаны контракты?» — поинтересовался я. Широков сделал жест, символизирующий сложность вопроса. Оказалось, они с Гришиным бились с правообладателями два года, а потом махнули рукой и запустили хостинг, куда любой может закачать песню. Мейджорам они продали эту новацию как «тестовый вариант».

Дуров считал хозяев контента, отказавшихся конструктивно сотрудничать, кем-то вроде избалованных работорговцев. По его мнению, вместо того чтобы менять стратегию и каналы дистрибуции, правообладатели хотели руками «ВКонтакте» душить юзеров, а после отказа призывали государство к репрессиям.

С другой стороны, Дуров задумывался о том, чтобы вывести компанию на биржу — так можно было поднять денег на дальнейший рост и удовлетворить желание Славы и Льва зафиксировать прибыль. И здесь начинались проблемы.

Продавать дальше акции значило потерять контроль. Акционеры не приветствовали идею опционов для лучших сотрудников — Дурову с трудом удавалось выбивать инвестирование части дивидендов в развитие. Партнеры хотели денег и не принимали идею вложить в развитие всю прибыль.

Между тотемом и основателями расширялась трещина. Они попрежнему дружили и часами спорили о Торе, которую изучал Слава, — но разница в отношении к деньгам бесила обе стороны.

Еще один риск при выходе на биржу крылся в контенте. О размещении акций на западных биржах с дуровским подходом к интеллектуальной собственности можно было не мечтать. Например, банкир, участвовавший в IPO «Яндекса», утверждал, что без урегулирования всех вопросов о пиратском контенте «ВКонтакте» вряд ли что-либо светит.

Учитывая эти факторы, Дуров пятился, отдавая правообладателям все больше прав.

Схожая история происходила с порнографией, наличие которой пришлось бы объяснить инвесторам перед IPO. Соцсеть жестко блокировала детскую порнографию, но к остальной относилась прохладно. Если в поиск по видео вбить запросы на тему секса — независимо от дней недели и времени суток, — примерно половина выдачи окажется порнороликами, выложенными в обход спам-робота.

Неудивительно, что в сети появилось письмо «к администрации и акционерам социальной сети „Вконтакте"»:

«Ничто не мешает тому, чтобы в поиске внутри сайта пользователи без труда находили порно и пересылали его друг другу. Такое попустительство равно поощрению. Фактически вы потворствуете развращению целого поколения юных интернет-пользователей. <… > В то время как уже сегодня настройка эффективной фильтрации порно и незаконного контента технологически и организационно осуществима, и это сделано на всех крупных интернет-площадках цивилизованных стран».

Письмо подписали больше десятка интернет-деятелей — в том числе партнеры правообладателей. Дуров не расстроился. Ему нравилось быть объектом ненависти для внезапно сколоченной армии спасения. Тестировать, как работает тэгирование фото, они с Цыплухиным отправились в стрип-клуб Golden Dolls.

Раскинувшись на диване в блуждающих лучах световых пушек, зажигающих блестки на телах танцовщиц, Дуров сфотографировал сцену с шестами и подписал что-то типа: «Следует запретить курение в общественных местах». Затем поставил тэг и отправил миллионам подписчиков.

Первые минуты сеть молчала, а затем подписчики сообразили, в чем прикол. Офлайновая реальность тоже не дремала, и посетители начали подгребать к столику с вопросами: «Не вы ли Дуров?» Влад спросил шефа: ну что, исчезаем из этих благословенных широт? «Пожалуй», — отозвался Дуров, и парочка исчезла так же стремительно, как появилась.

Пробовать, что вышло с геотэггингом — помещением на карту точки, где находится юзер, — они явились в ночной клуб «Максимус». Повторилась схожая сцена, и Дуров с удовольствием сменил подпись в личном твиттере с «CEO ВКонтакте» на «Porn King». Позже он выложил фотографию, снятую на пляже: морда хаски с капающей слюной на фоне женских поп.

На письмо о морали он ответил публично:

«Модераторы „ВКонтакте“ расчистили результаты стандартного поиска по видеозаписям от обилия порнографических материалов. Сотни поисковых запросов занесены в черный список, десятки тысяч видеороликов изъяты из перечней результатов поиска. Найти порнографические материалы во „ВКонтакте“ сложнее, чем сделать то же самое при помощи более очевидных инструментов — поиска „Яндекса“ или Google.

Безусловно, при большом желании вы все равно можете найти порнографию во „ВКонтакте“. Однако в результате слаженной работы модераторов и разработчиков порнография теперь никак не затрагивает пользователей, которые в ней не заинтересованы… Оградить ребенка от порнографии можно только на уровне домашней сети».

Постепенно шум затих, правообладатели успокоились. Борцы с порнографией если не сняли претензии, то сконцентрировались на иных объектах ненависти. Mail.ru тоже не шумел.

Но штилем не пахло — ко «ВКонтакте» подкралась новая проблема, причем с той стороны, откуда давно не ждали удара.

***

Вагон мотало из стороны в сторону, как шлюпку на волнах. Пассажиры уткнулись кто в газету, кто в ридер, кто в телефон — поворот от бумажных книг к цифровым уже произошел. На Дурова и Илларионова, вцепившихся в поручень, никто не обращал внимания, но подручный порнокороля все равно озирался, ожидая, что их окликнут.

«Слушай, может, снимешь бейсболку? — наконец спросил он у CEO как бы в шутку. — Сейчас узнают и вломят». Тот поправил кепку с литерой «В» и засмеялся: «Кому мы нужны».

Московское метро фонило безразличием, но Илларионову мерещились враги, которые последние дни слали письма с угрозами оторвать руки. Они исписали полсоцсети граффити в духе «Дуров чмо», «Дуров, верни стену» и «Дуров, убери свой микроблог».

За неделю до визита в столицу «ВКонтакте» окончательно открыла все записи на личных страницах пользователей и позволила любому юзеру писать на их стенах что угодно. Это можно было ограничить в настройках, но гневные телеги катились тысячами. Илларионов трясся не зря.

«Сначала нас ненавидят, потом начнут любить», — перекрикивая лязг вагонов, ответил Дуров. Железный голос объявил «Кропоткинскую», и товарищи продрались к дверям. Выйдя невредимыми из подземки, они пересекли площадь и зашагали по переулкам, сбегающим к Москве-реке, к залу, где проходило мероприятие HighLoad.

Старый знакомый Бунин позвал «ВКонтакте» рассказать, как они оптимизируют высокие нагрузки на серверы. Соцсеть в сутки навещало около 20 млн человек. Увидев ожидающих его спича программистов, сидящих друг у друга на шее, Илларионов забыл про хейтеров, мысленно пробежал план выступления и взял микрофон.

Самая скандальная реформа «ВКонтакте» началась с того, что Дуров, вышагивая руки-в-черные-брюки мимо апельсинового автомата и коровьего дивана, придумал очередную провокацию. Он бережно донес ее до двери, за которой сидел Илларионов, и вкрадчиво сказал ему: «А что если открыть все стены?»

Немедленно был созван консилиум во главе с братом Николаем, который оценил идею как безумную. «Единственное, чего ты добьешься, — это массовые волнения и уход в другие соцсети!»

Однако Дуров стоял на своем твердо — он не изобретал велосипед, похожую манипуляцию осуществил Facebook, и ничего, все съели. Мир становится более открытым; людей следует приучать к прозрачности намерений и поступков. Все, что ты пишешь, а также что друзья написали тебе на стену, надо показывать другим. Ограничивать — можно. Но по умолчанию — открывать.

За нововведением стояла не только религиозная вера, но и желание сильнее вовлечь людей в интеракции с другими юзерами. Тем самым «ВКонтакте» увеличивала и без того лучшее в Европе вовлечение — пользователи ежесуточно сидели у Дурова часами.

Несмотря на яростное сопротивление Николая, Кузи и других, Дуров настоял на своем. Кодеры разработали новую стену и 2 августа показали ее сети.

Тотем недооценил пользователей. Как он предсказал несколько лет назад, страница «ВКонтакте» стала второй личностью человека. Вмешательство было расценено как покушение на личную жизнь.

«Дуров ублюдок», «Ты нарушил тайну личной жизни», «Верни все как было», — писали люди. Участок народного мозга, отвечающий за фольклор, родил мем: «Проснулся утром, гляжу — а Дуров всю мебель в комнате переставил!»

Читая это, Дуров ощущал жар костров амбиций. Он Доктор Зло. Он персонализирован. Он тотем.

Волна негодования не спадала — ее гнали миллионы пользователей. Пришлось впервые устроить опрос: хотите микроблог или нет? Большинство проголосовавших восстали против микроблога.

«ВКонтакте» пришлось идти на попятную. Нёрды сделали новую стену опциональной — то есть дали возможность выбирать старую. Но это был не более чем обходной маневр. Дуров только укрепился во мнении, что демократия вредна. Разработчики перепиливали новый микроблог, чтобы ввести его принудительно.

В дом Зингера наняли новых бойцов — партизанская ячейка разрасталась. Прибывшие напоминали кого угодно, но не нёрдов. Вася Бабич, сын академиков, отличник, бегал на работу по набережным в зеленых физкультурных штанах. Эти штаны, а также недовольную физиономию Васи увековечила вирусная реклама, призывающая студентов наниматься «под сень валькирий». Рядом трудились Илларионов и проходящий по качеству футбола в дубль «Зенита» Игорь Жуков.

Эти превосходно социализированные юноши оттеняли не бросающуюся в глаза гостю комнату со странными людьми. Территория оптимизации высоких нагрузок и антиспама выглядела местом с искаженными временны́ми и пространственными характеристиками. Люди разговаривали обрывками кода и птичьим языком.

Задав вопрос, здесь стоило рассчитывать на ответ не ранее чем через десять минут. Просто обитатели привыкли очень хорошо думать. Дуров с Равдоникасом на их фоне выглядели образцами нормы.

Например, среди «сишников» работал человек, который не отзывался ни на какие внешние раздражители, кроме голоса Николая. Он исправно писал на C++, но, например, Дурова-младшего не воспринимал. Также он ходил днями в бессменной одежде, размышляя, видимо, о горнем.

К этому диковатому племени примкнул тренер сборной России по программированию и друг Николая Дурова Андрей Лопатин. Помимо high load он вел холивар против сетей ботов, а также помогал приятелю не терять остатки человечности в окружении нёрдов. Сам Николай не сменил поля деятельности — мать, по-прежнему вникающая в происходящее с проектом сыновей, убедила его, что надо полноценно помогать брату, получать приличные деньги, а на науку выкраивать время от основной работы.

Готовясь возвести новую стену, Дуров переехал из кабинета под стеклянным глобусом в тесную комнату напротив соковыжималки и взял в товарищи Равдоникаса. Тот днями корпел над «словесным оформлением сайта», а ночами выкладывал в сеть стихи. Позже, смирившись с тем, что во «ВКонтакте» люди не воспринимают буквы без пиктограммы, начал пририсовывать что-нибудь к своим хореям — авторучкой на клетчатой бумаге.

После истории со стеной Равдоникас запостил полотно с избиением младенцев и подписал: «Саша (слева), Игорь (по центру) и Вася (справа) отнимают у пользователей стену, новости и поклонников соответственно. 1625/26; Paris, Musée du Petit Palais».

Час икс пробил 20 октября. Зингер превратился в блестящую капсулу, готовую к взлету. Шар зловеще поблескивал, валькирии заметно нервничали. Команда пристегнулась, проверила ремни безопасности, убедилась, что все системы функционируют нормально, готовность три, два, один… Дуров совершил вояж по кабинетам, отметил, что люди горят духом, и запалил шнур.

Старые стены рухнули, и на их месте проступили водяные знаки микроблога. Дуров настучал в макбуке: «С сегодняшнего дня мы включаем этот режим для всех страниц. Для большей части активных

пользователей „ВКонтакте“ переход пройдет незамеченным, так как порядка 70% уже включили режим микроблога в настройках». (Цифру кое-как натянули — на самом деле абсолютный процент пользователей, перешедших на микроблог, был ниже.)
Сеть отреагировала мгновенно. Юзеры создали сотни групп с призывом вернуть старую стену. Многие администраторы использовали возможности микроблога и рекрутировали друзей в движение против микроблога. Команда с чувством глубокого удовлетворения вводила в строку разработанного Николаем поиска запрос «Дуров» и знакомилась с трехэтажными ругательствами.

Равдоникас, следивший за пользовательской реакцией чуть более пристально, чем кодеры, не смог остановить льющуюся из него литературу:

«22.02. Возле Казанского собора начинает собираться толпа. В отсветах факелов там и тут поблескивают вилы. Люди преимущественно спокойны и сосредоточенны, песен и лозунгов не слышно. Висит недобрая тишина, нарушаемая глухим кашлем и шумом дождя.

22.13. Толпа приходит в движение. В окна летят первые камни. В лазарет, спешно организованный в кабинете Алексея Богатова, доставлен Добромыслов с травмой левой брови и множественными порезами от осколков.

22.29. Для тяжелого пулемета на ресепшене оказалось всего три ленты. Похоже на саботаж. Переходим на легкое автоматическое оружие. Запасов пресной воды хватает.

22.53. Важное наблюдение: большинство наступающих — в лаптях. Добромыслов вырвался из лазарета и бубнит: „Великий день, великий день!“ Настроение праздничное. К стрекотанию и звону привыкли. С начала осады отжали 170 апельсинов».

Сводки с полей не сильно отличались. По «ВКонтакте» рассылали сообщения с призывом не заходить на сайт 22 октября. Цель — дать понять, что юзеры готовы уйти из «ВКонтакте», если к ним не прислушаются.

Штаб нанес ответный удар: ночью в блоге, где фиксировалась история «ВКонтакте», опубликовали запись — в прошедшие сутки рекорд посещаемости побит. Чуть позже Дуров обратился к хейтерам: «Пару дней вы будете нас ненавидеть, затем — любить еще сильнее. Но ради вас мы готовы смириться даже с вашей ненавистью».

Написав эти строки, Дуров начал восхождение к образу просвещенного диктатора. Он запретил банить любые группы, разжигающие вражду к его персоне. «В репутации Доктора Зло есть что-то для добротного маркетинга», — признается он позже.

Впрочем, то, что сработало с юзерами, не говоря о служителях копирайта, не проходило с источником главной угрозы. Спустя несколько месяцев конфликт с Mail.ru разросся из маленькой разборки в большом Токио в громкий скандал.

***

Бомбу заложил Мильнер. Три года назад, когда Дуров, Мирилашвили и Левиев оформляли с ним сделку, в документах не регулировалась возможность инвестора переводить свою долю в другие юридические лица. Поэтому, когда у Мильнера прошел интерес к рунету и он обрел миллиард долларов для глобальных инвестиций (олигарх Алишер Усманов интересовался крупнейшими мировыми сервисами), все доли в «Одноклассниках», «ВКонтакте» и других компаниях он слил в холдинг Mail.ru Group. Группа основывалась на активах Mail.ru, и рулить ею назначили Гришина.

Дуров слышал о планах сколотить суперкомпанию, которая могла бы противостоять натиску Google и других корпораций добра, но не придавал им серьезного значения. К тому же и речи не шло о передаче «ВКонтакте» под командование московских менеджеров. В итоге случилось так, что Дуров внезапно обнаружил у себя в совладельцах агрессивно настроенного автора игры «Альфа-ромео».

Первое время Гришин не давал о себе знать — он определялся, как решать проблемы слияния, и разбирался с управляющими поглощенных продуктов. Некоторые из них — например, Илья Широков из «Одноклассников» — сопротивлялись тотальному контролю человека, подписывавшего макеты визиток своим менеджерам.

Однако через пару месяцев раздался первый звонок. Перекопский узнал, что сейлзы Mail.ru Group обещают клиентам, что скоро начнут продавать рекламу во «ВКонтакте».

Второй звонок прогремел как гонг на ринге. Корреспондент Forbes Андрей Бабицкий брал интервью у Гришина и поинтересовался, что тот думает о будущем «ВКонтакте». Гришин, не моргнув глазом, ответил: «Стратегически для нас правильно приобрести контроль в социальной сети, а лучше даже выкупить все 100%».

Тратить время на диверсии не входило в планы тотема. Он по-прежнему желал изобретать новые штуки в кругу единомышленников, но после взорвавшейся информационной бомбы у него не осталось иного выхода. Маска воина прирастала к его лицу.

Дуров созвал шабаш под стеклянным шаром. Перекопский, Равдоникас и Цыплухин заслушали доклад на тему «менеджерьё окружает». После недолгих прений Дуров опубликовал ответ акционеру:

«Контрольный пакет „ВКонтакте“ принадлежит основателям. Планов менять текущее положение дел не существует. Слухи о том, что Mail.ru Group находится в процессе переговоров о покупке компании „ВКонтакте“, не соответствуют действительности. Ситуацию, при которой „ВКонтакте“ полностью входит в холдинг, мы исключаем и считаем утопичной».

Среди песен во вкладке «война» у него появилась Sweet Dreams из блокбастера «Запрещенный прием», ремикс хита Eurythmics:

Some of them want to use you,
some of them to get used by you.
Some of them want to abuse you,
some of them want to be abused.

Сюжет выглядит так: отчим сдает девочку-подростка в психушку, чтобы завладеть имуществом ее умершей матери. Падчерица знакомится с такими же несчастными, упрятанными в клинику. Ее приговаривают к лоботомии, но внезапно реальности наслаиваются друг на друга, и они с сокамерницами оказываются труппой стрип-шоу, а главврач — сутенером. Еще смена реальностей, и они в средневековой Японии. Еще — и в эпоху Первой мировой. У каждой прозвище-амплуа: Куколка, Милашка, Ракета, Блонди.

Обитатели Зингера напоминали такую же банду — циник и любитель денег Перекопский, танцор и поэт Равдоникас, пиарщик Цыплухин, превратившийся из сутулого очкарика в героя радиошоу «Школа соблазнения». Нёрды перезарядили оружие и приготовились обороняться.

Если насчет прошлых войн были какие-то сомнения, кем они начаты и кому выгодны, то противостояние с Mail.ru показало: Дуров ценил врагов и обожал конфликты как средство поддержания духа.

Впрочем, он вряд ли рассчитывал, что боевые сценарии однажды станут плотью от плоти реальности.

Глава 6
Запрещенный прием

Звук трубы навевал тоску и ярость. Трубач выдувал один и тот же набор — «кукарачу», «хаву нагилу» и далее без остановок. Денно и нощно он торчал на парапете, на углу канала и Невского в ушанке с залихватски задранным ухом. Прохожие швыряли ему мелочь — в сумку на колесиках — скорее из жалости, чем из любви к искусству. Стояли приличные морозы, и выше –15 ртуть не заползала.

Шестой этаж Зингера готовил бунт против музыки. Труба достала всех, чьи окна выходили на канал. «Заберите его кто-нибудь», — молил читателей Равдоникас. Они с дизайнером Добромысловым работали допоздна и как-то раз в приступе вдохновения примотали бутафорскую трубу ко лбу манекена для избиения (того, который «Акопов»).

Обряд подействовал. Назавтра человек с парапета играл недолго и к вечеру укатил свою сумку. Город праздновал 23 февраля 2011 года. Ночной Невский был чуть более оживлен, чем обычно. Дуров, Равдоникас и Добромыслов сидели за полночь и, проголодавшись, отправились в ближайший «Сабвэй».

Агрессия насыщала воздух. В начале месяца Равдоникас запостил очередное эссе:

«Когда мы шли втроем по набережной канала, все со своими ломиками, я почуял власть диспозиции. Метель, слякотная в центре города, — идеальная погода для любого преступления, все слишком заняты собственными ногами. Ты замечаешь лом в руке у человека слишком поздно, чтобы не стать частью его истории, какой бы она ни была.

Мы шутили, я говорил, что минимальные жесты наиболее угрожающи: похлопывание куском железа по ладони мультипликационно, но стоит просто изменить слегка положение предмета в руке — или же снять его с плеча. Без фейерверков приведение объекта в боевую готовность страшно, потому что общение со зрителем происходит на досознательном уровне; деятель обращается не к мозгу, а к животному и говорит ему следующее: „Сейчас тебя будут бить“.

Животное понимает при этом, что никакой рационализации не будет; но рационализация ему и не нужна, оно уважает свое чутье. И все же его страх приводит к оцепенению. Не потому ли, что разум пытается отогнать страх? В одиннадцать утра, и в нескольких минутах от проспекта, и без какого-либо повода. Отпусти, мозг, у тебя не хватит времени выстроить цепочки, если мы не скроемся сейчас.

Сегодня, конечно, уже поздно, момент был упущен еще в самом начале, из-за снега. Мы как раз начинаем проходить мимо; и именно здесь я чувствую власть контекста. Она в том, что не бывает действительно никакого повода, есть только условия. И при необходимых условиях, которые сложились сейчас, мы изметелим человека ломами на берегу канала. Я не уверен, что мы этого не сделали».

Спустя три недели, ночью, по дороге к «Сайгону» их окликнули банальным: «Есть закурить?» Равдоникас ощутил то самое, животное чувство. Он не успел сообразить, какую выбрать интонацию, как Дуров одарил просителей взглядом — каким отвечал назойливым официантам или не узнающим его на входе в штаб охранникам: с брезгливым поворотом головы.

Из тройки ростом выделялся Добромыслов, и инстинкт подсказал гопникам, кому врезать первому. Выдуманная и реальная жизнь скрестились, и предсказанные Равдоникасом булыжники с монтировками самовоспроизводились. Денди из пригорода прижимали их к какой-то витрине.

Дуров получил мощный удар в затылок и отступал. У Добромыслова заплыл глаз, и тот едва мог обороняться. Их наверняка прижали бы и изметелили, если бы Равдоникас не начал вязать нападавшим руки, крича что-то примиряющее.

Тотем вырвался и побежал к Дворцовой площади. Добромыслов бросился в штаб и вызвал скорую: если повреждена сетчатка, пора осваивать новую профессию.

Справа неслись сверкающие огнями заведения, слева машины, а милиции все никак не находилось. Дуров остановился перевести дух и увидел автомобиль с синей полосой и мигалкой. Он постучался в закрытое окно. «Это не наша территория», — ответили изнутри.

Дуров вспомнил, как шел с Равдоникасом по галерее Гостиного двора, через которую можно попасть на проспект, избежав торговых рядов. Обсуждали, как меняется понятие личности в соцсетях. Высокоумную беседу прервали барышни в серой форме и пилотках: «Сюда нельзя». За их спинами кипел пятачок между метро и проспектом, куда на 31-е числа сходились оппозиционеры — недобитая демшиза и иные антипутинцы. Их было мало, не тысячи, как в Москве на Триумфальной, и они требовали исполнения статьи Конституции о свободе собраний. Кого-то винтили и волокли в автозак.

Дуров посмотрел на барышень с ласковой ненавистью: «Представьтесь, пожалуйста, и скажите номер удостоверения». Милиция замешкалась. «Вы не понимаете, что делаете! — крикнул Дуров, посмотрел в сторону и продолжил: — Вы не можете ограничить свободу передвижения. Ограничивая свободу, вообще любую, можно лишь разогреть протестные настроения». И так далее, в том же регистре.

Их с Равдоникасом пропустили. Пока они шагали к штабу, тотем возмущался, насколько слаба репрессивная машина, если два чувака смогли продавить милицейский кордон с помощью слов.

Теперь, стоя на Невском в бессилии, у равнодушного авто с синей полосой, обхватив болевшую от удара голову, владелец компании ценой в миллиарды думал о том, что все оказалось хуже. Все сгнило.

Люди чувствуют это и не верят, что государство способно их защитить. Лишь подсознательно они цепляются за эфемерное обещание безопасности.

Скоро, очень скоро государства рухнут и на их место придут конкурентоспособные компании, в том числе охраняющие граждан. Граждане будут выбирать место жительства, исходя из своих компетенций. Государства станут бороться за привлечение тех или иных специалистов. Это произойдет не так быстро, как хотелось бы. Наше дело — приближать этот момент, погружая все большее количество социальных транзакций в сеть, где все процессы текут прозрачнее, чем по бумажным процедурам. Наши идеи как кислота — растворят консервативные установки и станут мейнстримом. Лет через двадцать.

В штабе Дурова ждал Добромыслов, избежавший отслоения сетчатки и чувствовавший себя счастливым — что, впрочем, было не очень заметно на фоне адреналина, фрустрации и размышлений, куда свернула бы его судьба, если бы.

Добромыслов не собирался становиться оформителем соцсети. Он учился торговать акциями, и если увлекался дизайном, то скорее автомобильным. Зарегистрировавшись во «ВКонтакте», он начал администрировать группу «Студенты.ру» и был замечен штабом. Затем он выиграл конкурс дизайна, получил приглашение, был очарован Дуровым и вступил в секту.

Они часами сидели над редизайном — архитектор с черной коленкоровой тетрадью, Добромыслов с айпадом — и обсуждали, как ложится свет на каждую кнопку страницы. Добромыслова, как и других, поражала способность Дурова вбросить неожиданную идею — и отследить, чтобы она была воплощена за короткий срок (если производство растянулось, значит, идея негодная). Однажды они таким образом придумали выводить в профиле пользователя его фотоальбом, а личную информацию ужимать.

После вечера с мордобоем Добромыслов перестал оставаться в общежитии. Сквот располагался в восьмикомнатной квартире, которую Дуров купил в близлежащем переулке, — там ночевали закодившиеся программисты. Это было огромное пространство с пустынными комнатами и прихожей с люстрой, напоминавшей краба. Ключи от апартаментов на Невском, 65, СЕО отдал Васе Бабичу, который женился и нуждался в жилье.

Дуров утверждал, что не хотел ни к чему привязываться, и жил на разных квартирах; чаще всего в сквоте. Он редко приезжал в штаб раньше полудня, а задерживался до трех-четырех утра.

После сцены с дракой история «ВКонтакте» окончательно приняла вид самосбывающегося пророчества. Дуров раззадоривал себя, и теперь боевой дух не надо было поддерживать, он горел сам. Архитектор носил черное и сеял революции и провокации во всем. Он все больше убеждался, что преград не существует и растущее число пользователей — это и база для исследований, и журналисты его коллективного медиа, и потенциальные последователи.

***

Дуров продолжал дружить с Мильнером, летал на различные семейные празднества, а также ежегодные тусовки подопечных инвестора в Калифорнии. Однако венчурный капиталист, выполнивший свой долг перед Усмановым и получивший свободу, мирить «ВКонтакте» с Mail.ru не намеревался.

Тотем продолжал выбирать врагов для поднятия духа. Тем более, «Одноклассники» и правда догоняли по численности аудитории, правообладатели не успокаивались, а вслед за ними были забанены производители алкоголя и сигарет, желавшие разместить рекламу.

И вот после непродолжительного затишья проявился Mail.ru. После публикации интервью Гришина в Forbes интернет зашумел: сказка кончилась, холдинг сожрет нёрдов и не подавится. Резкий ответ Дурова не успокоил скептиков.

Тогда они с Перекопским решили обратить сильные стороны врага в слабые. Перекопский заявил: холдинг, предъявлявший претензии к соцсети, что та недомонетизирована (мало рекламных мест на страницах), продает баннеры на коррупционной основе. Отсюда и супермонетизация.

Обвинения имели под собой почву. Рынок медийной рекламы устроен так, что между площадкой и рекламодателем существует цепочка из двух-трех посредников. Каждый из них, борясь за бюджеты, предлагал контрагентам так называемые суперкомиссии — вознаграждение за приведенные деньги, которые проходили в контрактах как «белые», но по факту оседали в карманах посредников. Перекопский жаловался, что Mail.ru портил рынок, загоняя эти суперкомиссии до уровня 70% от суммы размещения.

Наиболее взвешенно оценил этот конфликт на Roem.ru Игорь Ашманов:

«Не знаю, как на Mail.ru с этим, но обычно при покупке медийки каким-то крупным брендом имеется цепочка из трех-пяти посредников (рекламный отдел бренда → прикормленное рекламное агентство → медиабайер → медиаселлер → рекламное агентство площадки → площадка), и там не только откаты по цепочке, но и просто распил на комиссии — купив на 100 рублей рекламы, крупный бренд может получить открутку на 25, а остальное осядет в цепочке или/и будет употреблено его же рекламным отделом. Но факт этой усохшей открутки (или выросшей цены за показ) будет запрятан в отчетах, и будет заплачен откат, чтоб заказчик „не заметил“. Так в среднем устроен этот рынок, и именно поэтому так взлетела контекстная реклама, где нет посредников и распилооткатов».

Вслед за своим заявлением Дуров заблокировал ссылки с «ВКонтакте» на файлообменный сайт Mail.ru. Когда интернет осведомился, в чем изъян, он написал на том же Roem.ru: «Все очень просто, files.mail.ru является безвкусным складом вирусов и вареза, как и любые другие обменники».

Mail.ru подвис от такой наглости. Через какое-то время «ВКонтакте» обвинили, что принадлежащий Льву и Славе провайдер «Селектел» закупал серверы у своих же компаний, то есть нарушал условия честной конкуренции и выводил таким образом деньги в карманы акционерам. Дуров вновь посетил комментарии и назвал выпад Гришина «словами типичного менеджера». Что касается вывода денег, он ограничился репликой, мол, смешно комментировать подозрения в махинациях с сотнями тысяч рублей со стороны долларовых миллионеров.

Когда я спросил у Гришина, почему он не стал нажимать на «ВКонтакте» и доказывать обвинения насчет серверов, тот ушел от ответа. Мол, мы в одной лодке и, несмотря на натянутые отношения, стараемся вести себя интеллигентно — в отличие от Дурова, заигравшегося в шоу-бизнес и пиар.

Выгода от операции с серверами и правда не шла ни в какое сравнение с масштабами бизнеса «ВКонтакте» — 114 млн долларов выручки за 2011 год. Тотем по-прежнему с трудом отвоевывал прибыль, чтобы пустить ее на строительство дата-центра и каналов связи, которые считал дорогами будущего.

Гришин все же выступил с ответными обвинениями. Правда, сделал он это неконкретно и обтекаемо — без имен-фамилий. Дуров радостно загасил поднятую над кортом «свечу», повторив тезис, что это речь типичного скользкого менеджера.

Разделив мир с точки зрения ценностей на чужих и своих, Дуров сколотил преданную команду. Рассуждая о своем кумире-военачальнике, он говорил: «Джобс — шестидесятник; его ценностями были свобода, человек — хозяин своей судьбы, художник с мини-компьютером. Та же реклама „1984“. Apple — пираты, дающие бой протухшему

„айбиэму". Захват продуктом широких слоев населения. Айфон против уродства и безвкусия мобильных устройств. Мы тоже восстали против тухлого дизайна, застоя, коррупции и повальной монетизации».

Внутренних диссидентов — тех членов команды, кто восставал против ее ценностей, — Дуров выжигал огнем. Например, одному из старожилов, Кузнецову-Кузе, надоело работать в ритме стартапа, и он ослабил хватку. Тотем терпел, но когда однажды Кузнецов забрел к нему, чем-то занятому, в кабинет, жуя колбасу, и что-то расслабленно начал спрашивать, рассвирепел.

— Выйди, пожалуйста.

— Почему я должен выходить?

— Выйди, ты меня раздражаешь.

— Не буду.

Дуров вскочил со своего архитекторского кресла, схватил Кузнецова за грудки и вытолкал из кабинета. Тот подал заявление об уходе. На юбилей соцсети, совпадающий с его днем рождения, Дуров снял ресторан. Как всегда, стол утопал во фруктах, парни созвали своих девушек, алкоголь и сигареты отсутствовали. Кто-то из программистов решил сфотографировать Дурова, жующего кусок дыни, и тот показал в камеру fuck.

Из персонажей внешнего мира он мог взаимодействовать с кем угодно, даже с представителями государства — лишь бы это приносило пользу и не касалось инструмента коммуникации, над которым друзья валькирий корпели день и ночь.

Когда Мирилашвили уехали из России в Израиль, перед «ВКонтакте» встал вопрос об отношениях с властью. Попасть в зависимость от Mail.ru казалось Дурову синонимом краха, и тогда Цыплухин взялся наладить связи с Кремлем. Точнее, с человеком, курировавшим информационную повестку страны, — Владиславом Сурковым. Дуров согласился. Ему, в общем, было все равно, кто им поможет.

Сурков, руливший политическими событиями в стране, казался ему умным человеком. Вполне искренне Дуров считал, что власть имеет дело с полукрепостной страной, изуродованной рабством и тоталитаризмом, и поэтому на политическом поле нет партий, которые предлагали что-то толковое.

Первую встречу с Сурковым назначил Мильнер. Политтехнолог помог сделать так, чтобы государство и близкие ему деятели не мешали развиваться «ВКонтакте» по дуровскому плану. Второй разговор организовал Цыплухин, подгадав приезд кремлевского деятеля в Петербург и зазвав в штаб.

Сурков поднялся в золоченой клетке на шестой этаж, не без удовольствия осмотрел переговорную с механизмом для скрепления сделок кровью. Затем Влад пригласил его заглянуть к кодерам, предусмотрительно обогнув резервацию «сишников». Увидев диван с валиками-коровами, Сурков поинтересовался у Дурова: «Это, конечно, вы выдумали?»

Откинувшись в кресле, он посмотрел на тотема и произнес: «Мне говорили, что вы гений». Дуров постарался, чтобы мышцы лица не отреагировали на лесть, и ответил: «Ну, про нас многое говорят».

Гостя волновали две вещи. Первая неслась на гребне информационной волны — создание аналога GPS «Глонасс», смартфона от «Ситроникс» и т. д., а также ажиотаж вокруг государственных высокотехнологических проектов. Дуров пожал плечами — он концентрировался на своей цифровой стране и только теоретически мог о чем-то рассуждать.

Второй вопрос, который волновал Суркова, — как развивать проект «Сколково». Дуров сослался на своего любимого писателя Пола Грэма — точнее, на текст о том, как создавать инкубаторы для инноваций. Кроме этого, добавил Дуров, произнося «Скол-ко-во», иностранец сломает язык. Другое дело — «Со-чи». Если строить русскую долину, то в теплом климате, у моря. Шаттлы от Ростова и Краснодара снимут транспортную проблему.

Собеседники расстались, удовлетворенные друг другом. Оба умели нравиться и понравились. Политтехнолог помог сделать так, чтобы «ВКонтакте» государство и близкие ему деятели не мешали развивать по дуровскому плану. Когда я попросил Суркова об интервью насчет его роли в судьбе «ВКонтакте», он уклонился от разговора.

***

Продукт под названием «социальная сеть» эволюционировал. Однажды Дуров заметил странное изменение ленты новостей. Раньше друзья постили больше личного, а теперь выросла доля статей и ссылок на медиа.

Это объяснялось тем, что журналисты и их работодатели осваивали новые каналы распространения своих творений. Но тренд заключался далеко не только в этом — значительная часть пользователей привыкла не только потреблять, но и распространять информацию в Facebook и особенно Twitter. Создатель последней, Джек Дорси, устроил свою сеть микроблогов так, чтобы люди могли делиться новостями, ссылками, картинками за считаные секунды, а лента с новыми событиями ползла вниз сама, без лишних кликов.

Казалось бы, в эпоху социальных медиа новости перестали существовать, став общим достоянием, но Дорси придумал инструмент для их генерации. Следуя за ним, Цукерберг внедрил виджеты для сайтов традиционных медиа, а также опцию подсасывания красивой картинки к ссылке и некоторые другие шаги — в общем, все, чтобы превратить Facebook в персонализированную газету, оставив Twitter поле информагентства.

Вслед за Дорси Цукерберг внедрил находку создателя Livejournal Брэда Фитцпатрика — односторонние связи. Чтобы читать публичные посты интересного тебе автора, ты не обязательно должен получить его одобрение насчет дружбы.

Дуров колебался. Его бесили новости. Он спрятал из ленты всех друзей, кто увлекался обсуждением злободневных тем.

Внедрять то, что необходимо тебе самому; делать соцсеть для себя — он исповедовал эту стратегию, и это приносило успех. Односторонние связи ему понравились, и, следуя за желанием еще сильнее облучать аудиторию своими идеями, он убедил кодеров, что необходимо перевести желающих стать друзьями юзера в его подписчиков. Настройка приватности, над которой по-прежнему тряслось большинство пользователей, осуществлялась выбором режима записи — если хочешь писать для друзей, пиши.

Но с news feed Дурову было трудно переубедить себя. На выходные он поехал в Милан и бродил по улицам, размышляя, стоит ли превращать стартовую страницу из личной в поток ссылок на контент, расшаренный друзьями. Он помнил, как Слава вбрасывал идею обыгрывать событийную картинку дня чем-то вроде «Яндекс.Новости».

Дурову не нравилось, когда ему навязывали идеи. Тем более когда это проходит в Славином стиле — внедрять предложения постепенно, возвращаясь к одним и тем же темам. Архитектор терпел повторы, пока не взрывался и не отвечал на мягкое давление категоричным письмом. На звонки он по-прежнему отвечал не всегда, воспитывая акционеров.

Часть проблемы заключалась в том, что новости не просто толкали пользователей на создание добавочной стоимости к ним — в виде картинок, смешных подписей и т. д. Они влекли «премиальную» аудиторию. Facebook агрессивно захватывал мозг отечественных медиаменеджеров, предлагая им красивые виджеты, которые можно было вставлять на их сайты, чтобы одной кнопкой рекламировать статьи и фото.

«Образованная и хорошо зарабатывающая публика использует Facebook для коммуникации с иноязычными друзьями», сладкие рекламные возможности, многократная мантра «во „ВКонтакте“ сидит школота, а администрация ненавидит журналистов» — все это перетягивало сетевых авторитетов к Цукербергу.

Российские медиа охотились за полумифической «премиальной» аудиторией Facebook, исчислявшейся парой миллионов юзеров, и сами начали загонять своих читателей к Цукербергу — создавая брендированные страницы СМИ. Во «ВКонтакте» царили Виктория Боня и сонм поп-звезд.

Дуров отправил на переговоры Цыплухина. Редакторы не сразу поняли, что им втирает хипстер в очках и клетчатой рубашке. «ВКонтакте» — это школьники и студенты, а нам какое дело?

Цыплухин раскинул офлайновую сеть связей и добился, чтобы к статьям и роликам выдавались кнопки «ВКонтакте», а СМИ завели группы в его соцсети. Но проблема заключался в тренде потребления информации, а он был неумолим — Facebook сменил модель уютной сети для друзей на модель глобальной газеты.

Дуров решил, что сопротивляться бессмысленно. Он заменил стартовую страницу с личного профиля на поток новостей от друзей. Затем велел переписать фото — чтобы снимки расхлопывались почти на весь экран и группировались в альбомах более симпатичным образом.

Спустя год журналист Wired заглянул во «ВКонтакте» и был поражен сходством с Facebook образца 2005 года. Но потом, вглядевшись, написал, что «это как если бы Facebook оставил черты сети „для своих“, но при этом выполнял роль информационного хаба с удобным просмотром картинок и библиотекой пиратского видео».

Когда Дэниэл Эк из музыкального сервиса Spotify, легально проигрывавшего песни и бравшего с пользователя абонентскую плату, приехал к Дурову договариваться о сотрудничестве, то получил от ворот поворот. «У нас в разы больше песен, чем у вас, нам невыгодно», — отрезал Дуров. Эк понял, что крыть нечем, распрощался и шагнул в позолоченный лифт.

***

Два человека уселись в кресла друг напротив друга. Вид на строящиеся небоскребы скрывали жалюзи. Спустя месяцы контрударов обоим было тяжело казаться приветливыми, но они старались. Хозяин встретил гостя у кабинета, к которому тот прошел через галерею кьюбиклов, недобро поглядывая на программистов в сотах-отсеках.

Собеседники походили друг на друга. Расположившись за длинным столом, они открыли свои MacBook Air. Оба одевались неярко. Оба — ботаники и злостные нёрды. Оба начинали путь программиста с игр. Оба любили кодить. Но было трудно найти более полярных друг другу деятелей.

— Закажете что-нибудь поесть, Павел? У нас внизу есть ресторан.

— Давайте, если там готовят рыбу, я бы ее съел.

Секретарь получил указания и отправил гонца в заведение. Деятели перекинулись парой фраз о том о сем и наконец перешли к делу.

«Ну что, — сказал Гришин, считая это самое дело решенным. — Когда мы все подпишем, выпустим совместный пресс-релиз, где „ВКонтакте“ будет указана не как компания, а как проект».

Дуров, слушая, излучал нордическое спокойствие, хотя внимательный человек сказал бы, что это дается тотему с трудом. Много раз тактика «я обхожу острые углы, если меня не оскорбляют» играла ему на руку, но теперь он чувствовал себя несколько в тупике. Гришин напирал на переход контрольного пакета к Mail.ru.

«„ВКонтакте“ уникальна как независимая организация со специфической атмосферой и стилем, — ответил Дуров. — „Синергия“ — это, конечно, приятное для инвесторов слово, но в данном случае преимущества слияния неочевидны».

За несколько недель до визита в кинофотоинститут Дуров шагал к Фонтанке, изредка поднимая взгляд, чтобы не столкнуться с прохожими. Мимо него, завывая, неслись черные автомобили с мигалками.

Сквозь тонированные стекла можно было разглядеть страдающих одышкой седоков. Автомобили дышали так же тяжко — их радиаторы шумели, как вытяжные трубы, утомившись от солнца и пробок.

Дуров направлялся туда, куда ехала знать. Алишер Усманов собирал гостей петербургского форума на прием в снятый для этого Шереметьевский дворец. Полтора километра через мосты, и он, не сразу признанный охраной, поднялся во дворец.

Усманов желал познакомиться и нащупать ключевые мотивы в позиции Дурова. Конфликт с Mail.ru его не очень раздражал — у олигарха, который до сих пор собирал активы «Газпрому», были дела поважнее, чем распря двух программистов. Но, с другой стороны, капитализация холдинга на Лондонской бирже могла бы вырасти, если бы он поглотил русскоязычную соцсеть № 1.

Самый простой вариант поглощения — выкуп акций у Льва и Славы — обламывался. Им предлагали исходить из оценки компании, превышающей сумму последней сделки (1,5 млрд долларов) едва ли не вдвое, но аргумент об IPO, где можно выручить еще больше денег, сдерживал основателей. Кроме этого, Слава, даже раздражаясь на партнера, умел держать слово и не сдавал архитектора.

Помимо Дурова Усманов пригласил во дворец Гришина, финдиректора Mail.ru Верди Исраэляна, «смотрящего» за телекоммуникационными активами Ивана Стрешинского и представителя в «Мегафоне» Ивана Таврина.

О чем беседовали Усманов и Дуров, обе стороны рассказывать отказались. Однако, сопоставляя данные из источников, близких к ним, канву удалось восстановить. Беседа развивалась примерно так — с учетом лексики Усманова, которая поразила коллег из Forbes в ходе интервью:

— Будете расти?

— Будем.

— На биржу когда можно пойти?

— Ну, года через три.

— Ладно, твои пассажиры [Левиев и Мирилашвили] торгуются — но ты-то чего хочешь?

— Есть вариант: мне контроль над принятием решений, вам контроль над собственностью. В таком раскладе все выигрывают — у меня остается мой пакет, а у вас, если парни продадут, больше 50%. «ВКонтакте» будет расти.

— Хорошо, подумаю, а ты тряхни своих друзей.

Когда Гришин спросил Усманова о результате разговора, тот, вероятно, ответил что-то такое, из чего глава холдинга заключил, что «ВКонтакте» готовы продаться Mail.ru. Дурова позвали продолжить разговор. Перед встречей в кабинете напротив башен-близнецов он заехал к юристам прояснить свои права и возможности, если доли в компании будут меняться.

В дверь постучали. Переговорщики прервались, и секретарь внес тарелки.

Дуров прикидывал сценарии переговоров. Его раздражала уверенность Гришина, что холдинг съест его детище, как эту ловкую, но угодившую на сковороду рыбину.

Впрочем, Гришин лишь менеджер. За ним стоит Усманов, с которым прекрасно сотрудничал Мильнер и почему бы не посотрудничать ему самому. Если повести себя с менеджером чрезмерно агрессивно, можно лишиться возможности наладить отношения с собственным акционером.

Подчеркивая, что ничего личного, только бизнес, Дуров повторил, что слияние с Mail.ru нежелательно, и повернул разговор в сторону глобальных трендов и т. д. — подальше от темы слияния. Ему показалось, что Гришин понял.

Однако это был тупик и спор на разных языках. В нем, как и во всем конфликте, не было злых и добрых. Столкнулись настолько разные типы, менталитеты, что понимания между ними возникнуть не могло. Менеджер убеждал предпринимателя, что тому стоит перейти из «состояния независимости» в «состояние подчинения». Гришин искренне думал, что Дуров выторговывает шоколадные условия продажи «ВКонтакте» — ведь все имеет цену.

Неудивительно, что, вернувшись к валькириям и глобусу, Дуров получил письмо. Mail.ru предлагал вариант: он становится акционером холдинга, продав долю во «ВКонтакте».

Архитектора взбесило, что ему опять пихают деньги. Прямым текстом он дал понять: зеленые бумажки — совсем не то, чего он хочет. И в данный момент, и в жизни. В конце концов, он уже миллионер. Мало того, соглашение подразумевало, что, если Дуров продолжит плохо себя вести — негативно высказываться о компании, — ему устроят ата-та и поставят в угол. Отнимут долю, например.

Дуров вдохнул поглубже, распахнул дверь в общежитие с люстрой-крабом, устроился в своей комнате и открыл почту на айфоне.

Главное — спокойно объяснить, на английском языке, выбирая точные слова, почему эта сделка невозможна. То есть невозможна никогда. Указываем, что вся история спровоцирована Mail.ru, и ставим в копию Мильнера, чтобы он видел: мои мотивы прозрачны, агрессии нет. Переговоры завершены.

Нажав «Отправить», Дуров задумался. Чего-то не хватало. Красивого широкого жеста, коды.

Отбросив пару вариантов, он покрутил пришедшую в голову мысль. Мысль вызывала защитную реакцию — с Усмановым не хотелось портить отношения. Но, извините, пакостит не он, а менеджеры, выдумывающие схемы поглощения и унизительные условия, о которых мы не договаривались. «ОК», — подумал Дуров и запросил у службы тыла фугас.

Фото с праздника в ресторане упало в ящик, и он открыл Twitter. Подпись сформулировалась сразу: «Официальный ответ трэш-холдингу Mail.ru на его попытки поглотить „ВКонтакте“».

Картинка нерезкая, зато демонстрируемый fuck не вызовет двояких толкований. Все разделилось вокруг на чужое и наше. Жмем «Tweet».

Фотографию мгновенно заметили информагентства. Когда я разговаривал с Гришиным, Широковым и другими людьми из Mail.ru, их реакция была ошеломленно-прибитой. Как публичная компания, холдинг не мог перевести конфликт в медийную сферу. Поведение Дурова нарушало все возможные этики и эстетики. Консолидированное мнение менеджеров: парень зарвался и ведет себя как гопник с высоким IQ.

Не уверен, что тогда Дуров сознавал это, но на самом деле ситуацией управлял он. Журналист Forbes Валерий Игуменов брал интервью у Ивана Стрешинского, который отвечал у Усманова за интернет, и тот, совершив реверансы перед талантами Дурова, сказал: «Он считает программистов творцами, а всех остальных — людьми второго сорта. Интернет-бизнес так устроен, что огромное значение имеют компетенции, которыми мы не владеем. Условно говоря, если начнутся недружелюбные действия по отношению к „ВКонтакте“, Дуров может выключить рубильник и уйти».

Фобии Стрешинского выглядели знаковыми. Сильные мира сего не придали значения трещине, которая рассекала мир и пробиралась из стран с развитой демократией в государства с вертикалью власти, — высокие технологии по природе своей отдавали власть интеллекту и способствовали распространению демократии. Нёрды захватили ноосферу.

То, как понимал «ВКонтакте» менеджер Усманов, говорит о средневековье в уме даже очень хитрых людей. Проклятые маги сидят, варят свое зелье, и как президент держит в чемоданчике ядерную кнопку, так эти очкарики где-то спрятали рубильник, который в случае опасности выключает все. Бизнес стоимостью в миллиарды долларов рушится, в стране полыхают восстания. Пользователи бегут во враждебный

Facebook — хорошо, что небольшой кусочек этой сети Усманов купил заранее.

Интернет дал власть интеллекту, но, чтобы воплощать свои идеи в России, требовались твердость и умение контролировать страх, схожее с тем, каким владеют альпинисты, привыкшие лезть вверх по стене, имея под ногами километровую пропасть. Дуров обладал тем и другим.

Подувшись на строптивого ботаника, менеджеры Усманова продолжили переговоры. Убедившись, что Слава со Львом готовы обсуждать оценку стоимости компании, но не готовы продаться Mail.ru, они нацелились на вход в акционеры самого олигарха.

***

Россию штормило. Подходил к концу первый срок президента в синем костюме с айпадом под мышкой. Страна имела в анамнезе волнения в городах-миллионниках. Средний класс разбогател и хотел повысить качество государственных услуг, а также лишить чиновников коррупционной ренты.

Пресс-секретаря «ВКонтакте» Цыплухина больше волновали собственные проблемы с властью. Ему стоило больших усилий свести на нет гнев Кремля, когда Дуров отказался ехать на встречу президента со столпами рунета.

Узнав, что разговор пройдет под телекамерами, Дуров манкировал тусовкой. Это в университете он лавировал в отношениях с деканатом, произнося в камеру слова о «Единой России», а теперь у него были сотня миллионов зарегистрированных пользователей и буддистская готовность потерять все и сразу.

Услышав, что шефу неохота заниматься популизмом, Цыплухин известил об этом Левиева. «ВКонтакте» опаздывала на встречу. Лев разгневался и попробовал надавить на Дурова, но тот был непреклонен.

Последние месяцы Левиев с Цыплухиным общались теснее. Чтобы сплотить штаб и бэк-офис, сидевший на Тверской, они придумали воскресный футбол.

Закончив интервью, Лев пригласил меня попинать мяч, и мы отправились на стадион. Лев опаздывал и потому гнал на ревущем «Гелендвагене» по трамвайным рельсам, со свистом тормозя у светофоров. Перед спортивным магазином, куда мы заглянули за бутсами, он припарковался во втором ряду с мигающей «аварийкой». Вспомнился гвоздь в кармане Дурова.

Наступившая зима усугубила проблемы власти. Президент анонсировал последователя, который по совместительству был его предшественником. Парламентские выборы принесли такую волну фальсификаций, что на следующий день оппозиция вышла на Чистые пруды, прорвала кордон полиции и добралась до Лубянки. Сквозь стекла здания ФСБ на протестующих смотрели силовики, а площадь разглядывала их. «Вы нас даже не представляете».

Бунт огорошил Кремль. На Новый год оппозиционные группы на Facebook и «ВКонтакте» координировали действия перед митингами на столичной Болотной площади и у Исаакиевского собора в Петербурге. Власть оказалась не готова, и «интеллектуала» Суркова сменили его замом Володиным, жестким администратором.

Когда новый владелец кабинета с портретом Че Гевары еще не вступил в должность, а прошлый уже съезжал, в дом Зингера принесли бумагу из прокуратуры. Бумага настойчиво рекомендовала Дурову закрыть группы против «Единой России» и несколько подобных. Мотивировка: экстремизм.

Несмотря на анархистские взгляды, Дуров старался блюсти закон. Обычно группы закрывались по запросу прокуратуры, подкрепленному законными основаниями. Но в данном случае внутри тотема что-то воспротивилось. Дело пахло ограничением свободы и предательством пользователей. Дуров решил не прогибаться и отказался закрывать группы.

Цыплухину позвонили из администрации президента и попросили убрать группы по-хорошему. Лев с Владом осадили Дурова, умоляли, просили и грозили. Тот вежливо улыбался и максимум, на что согласился, — написать письмо Суркову. Мол, удалить протест — что заливать костер бензином: вспыхнет ярче и перекинется на соседние дома.

Вскоре Влад постучался к нему с взволнованным лицом. Прокуратура прислала Дурову повестку на допрос. Ровно в тот день они с Мильнером запускали проект StartFellows, выдающий стартапам 25 000 долларов без требования доли в них. Дуров селекционировал заявки, а Мильнер переводил деньги.

Я позвонил Дурову по скайпу. Тот сидел в бейсболке, на которую накинул капюшон худи, и жевал что-то типа вегетарианского гамбургера, запивая минеральной водой. На лице его застыло выражение растерянного безумца, которое поразило меня на первом интервью.

За год до разговора на благотворительном аукционе Дурова попросили нарисовать картинку для детдома. Он разделил лист на четыре части — красную, желтую, зеленую и синюю, а поверх нарисовал собаку с черными зрачками. Один глаз собаки был крупнее другого и сверкал, как дуло или тоннель. Ухо украшал зашитый шрам. Это наиболее точный портрет Дурова из всех, что я знаю.

«Что вы намерены делать?» «Ничего, — пробормотал Дуров. — Опять звонили, просят закрыть группы. Влад и Лев, наверное, будут уговаривать. Я уже привык. Они знают, что я не боюсь». Мы обсудили стартапы и распрощались.

Через час в твиттере Дурова появилась фотография хаски в наброшенном капюшоне и с высунутым языком. Внизу красовалась подпись, что это ответ прокуратуре. Твиту предшествовал скан повестки, к которому Дуров приписал, что на допрос не успел, бумага пришла слишком поздно.

Как я теперь понимаю, в тот день Дуров боролся со страхом потерять все. Одно дело — переговоры, где ты, чувствуя за спиной многомиллионную аудиторию, стоишь на своем. Другое дело — состязание с государством, чья компетенция — давить. Ценивший тотема Сурков уходил из Кремля на пост главного по технологиям в правительстве. С Володиным Дуров не был знаком.

Вернувшегося в квартиру на Крестовском острове Дурова потревожил звонок в дверь. На лестничной площадке суетились омоновцы в камуфляже и, видимо, следователь. Дуров отшатнулся. Страх полз по телу, и надо было решить — пускать его, кормить надеждами, что само рассосется, или выбрасывать из тела. Вспомнилась школьная борьба с ужасом перед скандалом и эксперимент с обезьянами. Прими как факт, что ты ничем на самом деле не владеешь, — и тебе будет не страшно терять.

Дуров не открыл. Осторожно выглянув в окно, он увидел пятна камуфляжа во дворе. Позже служба безопасности рассказала, что чуть не устроила перестрелку, не желая пускать маски-шоу внутрь. Дуров выслушал, зашел во «ВКонтакте» и процитировал 2,7 млн подписчиков Карлейля: «Насколько человек побеждает страх, настолько он человек».

Ни на следующий день, ни позже санкций не последовало. То ли система отвлеклась на многотысячные акции протеста — вязала оппозиционеров у Исаакиевского и катала их по городу в автозаках; то ли Сурков шепнул что-то коллегам.

Дуров гнал страх дальше от блестящего глобуса. Группа поддержки Алексея Навального, адвоката-антикоррупционера, известного проектами «Роспил» и «Добрая машина пропаганды», исчерпала лимит пользователей — Дуров велел программистам убрать этот лимит.

Позже он написал в «Ленту.ру» колонку о том, что оставил группы не из-за любви к оппозиции, а из-за того, что, закрой их, юзеры перетекут на Facebook. Это не был жест лояльности ни власти, ни Mail.ru, ни пользователям или кому-либо еще. Это была попытка объяснить поступок самому себе.

«Люди оправдывают свои действия в прошлом, — рассуждал Дуров позже, когда все кончилось и началась совсем другая история. — Я в этом смысле не совсем материалист, у меня мистическое отношение к таким вещам. Я, конечно, красиво объяснил все на „Ленте“, но не знаю, почему тогда отказался закрывать группы. Что-то внутри меня воспротивилось. Не знаю».

***

Кривые пересекались лишь один раз, в самом низу графика, когда синяя догнала оранжевую и больше уже не пропускала ее вперед. Впрочем, ближе к концу горизонтальной оси, которая обозначала время, оранжевая подбиралась к сопернице вплотную. Казалось, соприкоснувшись, они заискрят.

Когда я зашел в гости к Mail.ru, война с «ВКонтакте» приутихла, и стороны изредка обменивались колкостями. Присутствовало ощущение, что это временное затишье и холдинг обдумывает ход, который повергнет дом Зингера в руины.

Раскинувшись на оранжевом пуфе в застекленном отсеке зала «Одноклассников», где за партами сидели программисты и дизайнеры, Илья Широков объяснял, как перегонит Дурова. «Одноклассники» запустили свою платформу для игр, причем хиты рекламировали за свой счет. Аудио- и видеохостинги привлекали юзеров удобством и дизайном — например, песни одной группы можно собрать в альбом и загрузить его оригинальную обложку.

Широков открыл свою страницу и показал, как треки Pink Floyd скомпонованы в диск The Wall. Соцсеть сменила логотип на аббревиатуру ОК, изображенную в виде человечка, перевернутого набок.

Превратив «Одноклассников» в продукт, интуитивно понятный даже новичку, Широков отбил у «ВКонтакте» малые города и поселки городского типа.

Дуров реагировал как сноб: «Как только утихнет волна новоподключившихся к интернету, провинциалы сами постепенно перейдут на более качественный ресурс. Готовы ли мы разменять наше доминирование в столицах и мегаполисах (9 млн человек ежедневно заходят во „ВКонтакте“ только из Москвы и Петербурга) на пенсионерок из провинциальных поселков и деревень ради того, чтобы остаться „самой массовой сетью“? Нет, не готовы. Потому что опыт показывает — если вас вышибли из столиц, в регионах вы можете иметь лишь временный успех. Рано или поздно провинциалы подтягиваются за жителями столиц. Если „Одноклассники“ и догонят „ВК“, то лишь до тех пор, пока более прогрессивные пользователи не покажут им то, что несоизмеримо удобнее и современнее. Каждый из нас знает множество людей, перешедших из „ОК“ в „ВК“, но обратных случаев практически нет».

До поры до времени он смотрел сквозь пальцы на сокращающийся аудиторный разрыв. В январе 2012 года разница оказалась мизерной — 30 млн против 31 млн пользователей в сутки. Выступая на мартовской конференции, «Одноклассники» заявили, что почти догнали. Но именно в этот момент «ВКонтакте» уходил в новый отрыв, и к лету разница в аудитории колебалась вокруг 5 млн пользователей.

Через месяц Усманов встретился с Гришиным и Широковым. В Москву приехал и Дуров — олигарх собирал подопечных на серьезную беседу. В Mail.ru, похоже, не знали истинной цели Усманова.

Так же как и переговоры в Шереметьевском дворце, детали этой встречи участники не комментировали, но сопоставив впечатления разных сторон (в том числе с помощью коллег из Forbes), удалось восстановить примерный ход разговора. Сначала Усманов огорошил

Гришина и Широкова известием, что слиться Mail.ru и «ВКонтакте» не суждено. Произносимые им слова — вроде «две разные культуры», «конкуренция», «стимулировать друг друга» — вызвали лютый баттхерт менеджеров.

Еще сильнее они загрустили, когда Усманов намекнул, что Дурову следует самостоятельно управлять компанией. Фактически это означало, что ему отдадут в управление пакет Mail.ru. Тотем получит право одобрять свои же решения, и парни из кинофотоинститута ему не указ.

Затем Усманов анонсировал то, что они с Дуровым обсуждали во дворце, — он думает о выкупе долей Мирилашвили и Левиева. Это были лишь планы, но любом случае Гришин был шокирован, а его амбиции слегка поутихли.

Понимая, что стратегические позиции надо удерживать с любым акционером, Дуров предложил пофантазировать — может быть, ему выкупить, скажем, 60%? А что: он основатель, заслужил контрольный пакет. Лица у Широкова с Гришиным вытянулись, а Усманов произнес спич на тему скромности. Позже, в интервью коллеге Игуменову он скажет: «Вот Дима Гришин, нормальный русский программист, управляет компанией, и у него все будет хорошо. А Дуров не такой: он непростой, ему большего надо».

Когда встреча закончилась и Дуров отдельно говорил с Широковым в президентском номере Ritz, снятом по случаю со скидкой, в дверь постучали. Дуров отпер, и мимо него, не говоря ни слова, прошествовали агенты Смиты с проводками в ушах. Дуров открыл рот, чтобы поинтересоваться: «В чем дело?» — но агенты уже обстукивали шкафы, проверяли карнизы под окнами, щупали ковры.

Это не сбывалась «Матрица». Это президент Казахстана снял апартаменты с видом на Кремль, а в суете со встречами Дуров забыл продлить бронирование. Им с Широковым пришлось переместиться в соседний номер. Широков спросил, зачем Дуров рвется к контролю.

Дуров ответил что-то общее, а сам задумался — почему им не нужно большее, чем кресло менеджера или опцион 1% компании? Почему они боятся и не хотят пойти на шаг дальше? Широков вроде запустил свой стартап «Мой круг», «сеть профессиональных контактов», отучился в Стэнфорде — и… И что? Не хватает дерзости идти до конца, наглости, за которую они меня не любят?

Позже Усманов, выступая по телевидению, рассказал, что да, управлять должны основатели, то есть Дуров. Рунет возликовал по поводу развязки мыльной оперы «„ВКонтакте" против Mail.ru». Но ее пузыри продолжали летать.

Слава и Лев общались с Усмановым по поводу стоимости их доли, и Дуров случайно оказался в курсе кое-каких новых сведений о компании. Тотем не сомневался в порядочности школьного друга, так как знал, что Мирилашвили не продался Mail.ru и не нарушал их договоренностей. Если бы Слава клял и ругал самого Дурова, тот бы отнесся с пониманием, но партнер пересек его границы добра и зла. Похоже, Дуров услышал что-то вроде того, что вес команды разработчиков в стоимости компании переоценён; «ВКонтакте» ценна скорее другими активами, не программистами. Не следует превозносить нёрдов.

Рассвирепевший Дуров вернулся в номер с коврами, вазой с орешками и запахом парфюма. Сел за круглый стол из дуба с вертящейся крышкой, будто для вызова духов. Выпил энергетического напитка с фруктовым вкусом. Решение оформилось так же быстро, как fuck в твиттере. Пусть парни торгуются, но знают свое место.

Жернова игры «Мафия» вертелись все стремительнее. Консильери закрывают глаза. Утро. Жители города проснулись. Акционеры открывают глаза и видят, что аккаунты двоих из них удалены.
Позиции id3 и id4, которые пять лет назад получили Слава и Лев, оказались пустыми. Мало того, архитектор написал во все социальные сети, что запускает аукцион на вакантные места.

Юридически виртуальное убийство было оформлено чисто — пользовательская оферта «ВКонтакте» гласила, что администрация может удалить любой аккаунт без объяснения причин.

Лишившись своих профилей, фотографий и записей, Слава и Лев остолбенели. Дружба, походы за пончиками, бегство от неуместного лимузина, встреча через семь лет, раздача айподов в «Кофехаузе», вывоз серверов — жест Дурова разом обрушил все это.

Партия катилась к эндшпилю.

Но Дурова эта игра уже не занимала. «Пассажиры» не знали, что человеку в черном надоела торговля вокруг «ВКонтакте» и он обдумывает новый увлекательный квест.

Глава 7
Пятно Роршаха

Чайка совершила круг, примериваясь, куда опуститься, и выбрала жестяной знак, торчавший на парапете набережной. Стоило ей повернуться в профиль, как фотограф, чью личность теперь установить вряд ли возможно, нажал кнопку. Кадр расшарили в интернете — птица сидит на знаке, изображающем ее же силуэт, перечеркнутый красным: «Кормить чаек запрещено!»

Дуров покрутил-повертел снимок. Выбрал черный фон, как у модных картинок-демотиваторов, и приписал снизу лозунг, висевший у его профиля во «ВКонтакте»: Subvert The Paradigm. Разрушь парадигму.

При всей любви к своему детищу архитектор утомился и искал новые идеи. Сначала он, конечно, пробовал запустить глобальную экспансию «ВКонтакте». Купил домен vk.com и почти договорился о приобретении загибающейся студенческой соцсети Studi VZ, первой в Германии. Но выяснилось, что выдающихся программистов из этой компании схантили конкуренты, в том числе Facebook, захвативший местный рынок.

Дурову стало очевидно, что тягаться с Цукербергом бессмысленно — в том числе потому, что русский проект по умолчанию вызывал за рубежом не самые светлые эмоции (все опрошенные мной интернет-предприниматели говорили то же самое). Плюс к тому шлейф пиратского и порнографического имиджа тянулся за «ВКонтакте» несмотря на то, что «Централ Партнершип» и другие правообладатели подружились с домом Зингера.

Он задумался, как зайти на рынок персональных коммуникаций с тыла. Люди все больше общаются, пользуясь соцсетями, через мобильный интернет. После переговоров в Шереметьевском дворце

Дуров, давая интервью, вскользь упомянул, что можно сначала запустить «остроумное мобильное приложение», позволяющее людям общаться, суперюзабильное и красивое — и распространить его по миру. Вскоре он уточнил идею: сделать такое приложение для телефона, которое будет удобнее sms- и mms-сервисов и при этом построит социальный граф на основе записной книжки.

Разумеется, не одни «ВКонтакте» были такими умными. Apple улучшил на айфонах свои iMessages — картинки красиво отправляются, быстро делишься контактами, телефонная книжка связана с Facebook, можешь прикрутить фото абонента, связать телефонную книжку с Facebook. Украинец Ян Кум, эмигрировавший в долину, написал сервис WhatsApp, с которого можно бесплатно посылать тексты, фото и видео другим пользователям приложения.

Однако эти два конкурента имели бреши. Насладиться всеми фишками сервиса Apple можно, только если оба абонента используют iPhone или iPad. WhatsApp не желал вкладываться в борьбу с высокими нагрузками и не хранил на своих серверах историю переписки. Оба сервиса не произвели над телефоном то, что в последние годы обозначалось глаголом «твикнуть».

Это слово — от английского tweak (улучшить) — актуализировал писатель Малькольм Гладуэлл в эпитафии Стиву Джобсу, напечатанной The New Yorker. По его мнению, Джобс не получал по голове яблоком гениальности — он совершенствовал чужие изобретения. Доказывая, что такие люди двигают прогресс сильнее изобретателей, Гладуэлл приводит в пример английскую индустриальную революцию конца XVIII века. Нация инженеров улучшала недостаточно продуманные ноу-хау — внедряя докрученные разработки, империя укрепляла позиции правительницы морей.

Эпоха приложений для мобильных платформ подтолкнула массовый твикинг всего. Фотосервис Instagram — типичный пример.

Учиться фотографировать — долго, техника дорога, освоить Photoshop дано не каждому; при этом камера встроена в большинство телефонов. Следовательно, надо дать возможность преобразить натюрморт с завтраком из подгорелых тостов или нерезкий автопортрет в искусство — с помощью фильтров.

Размышляя об этом, Дуров трезво оценивал себя и понимал, что он не великий творец, а твикер. Пять лет назад он твикнул для России идею Facebook, а теперь задавал себе вопрос — как бы я хотел, чтобы выглядел телефон? Что он должен уметь? Какие есть в мобильнике упущения и анахронизмы? Как продолжить идеи социальных сетей в телефоне?

Еще не оставив планов экспансии «ВКонтакте», он попробовал получить глобальное признание. Написал в Wikimedia Foundation письмо, что хочет пожертвовать Wikipedia 1 млн долларов. Основатель сетевой энциклопедии Уэйлс как раз собирался выступать в Мюнхене на конференции DLD. Дурова вписали в программу рядом с ним.

Тотем старался. Возникнув на сцене в черном — штиблеты, жилет с капюшоном — он с улыбкой пережил конферанс «приветствуем клон Facebook из страны медведей и водки» и рассказал о «ВКонтакте», не без сарказма поясняя слайды о ее аудиторном величии. Vk.com номер один среди соцсетей по времени, которое пользователь проводит внутри. «Если хотите профукивать еще больше времени, будьте любезны, присоединяйтесь к нам».

Затем он перескочил на величие Wikipedia, сказал, что 70% его личного поиска информации в интернете заканчиваются в творении Уэйлса. Показал график, на котором полезные, образовательные сервисы оказали человечеству бóльшую услугу, чем развлекательные. Под конец речи он анонсировал пожертвование фонду Wikimedia, и конференция зааплодировала.

Дав зрителям похлопать, Дуров сбил аплодисменты и уступил место Уэйлсу. Тому надлежало выказать осмотрительность и не бросаться в объятия черного человека. Вы такой молодой, сказал он, двадцать семь лет, и спускаете миллион долларов.

Уэйлс намекнул, что в курсе сложных отношений «ВКонтакте» с правообладателями и полицией морали. Дуров отреагировал как всегда: мы действуем строго по закону.

После выступления его интервьюировал Businessweek. Вопросы те же — контент, контент, контент; легкое недоверие. Дуров включил доброжелательность на максимум, бурно жестикулировал, вертел в руках невидимый кубик Рубика, и вспомнил историю со Spotify. Мол, приезжали, а мы им р-раз — и от ворот поворот, потому что у нас музыки больше, чем у них. Законы не нарушаем, нет-нет.

Уэйлс принял миллион, но отношение к «ВКонтакте» не изменилось. Facebook засобирался на IPO, и журнал Wired нарисовал карту конкурентов Цукерберга. В России, констатировал автор, соцсеть безнадежно проигрывает команде из Зингера. «ВКонтакте» он описывал как копию раннего Facebook. Автор ностальгировал, но его всхлипы отдавали сарказмом.

«Я хотел бы совершить небольшую революцию в том, как люди общаются, — рассказывал Дуров, сидя в баре на последнем этаже Ritz, который оккупировали пожилые американцы. — „ВКонтакте" вряд ли будет перерождаться. Из зайца нельзя сделать слона. Мне жаль Цукерберга и Брина — они построили империи и теперь стареют на глазах. Они не могут отключиться и сфокусироваться на том, что важно сейчас. Дорси ушел из Twitter и тогда изобрел Square». Кто-то из американцев поперхнулся чаем, и остальные с громкими криками застучали его по спине.

«У Цукерберга — дом, семья, кампус, — пробормотал Дуров, оборачиваясь, чтобы разглядеть соседей. — А я живу в съемной квартире, чтобы не быть ни к чему привязанным». Вскоре он наткнулся в твиттере на запись «Цукерберг вступил в брак, теперь пора Дурова женить» и ответил: «Проще убить».

Вернувшись из Лондона, он зачудил. Разбрасывал пятитысячные банкноты из окна штаба на День города (внезапный эксперимент над самоорганизацией граждан — они объединялись в кланы и определяли вожаков), троллил сталинистов. Затем сорвался и полетел в Неаполь к основателю сервиса знакомств Badoo Андрею Андрееву.

Андреев предложил ему авто, но Дуров сел в поезд, открыл ноутбук и покатил, переписываясь со штабом. От станции до места встречи он брел пыльными пустырями, где шатались стаи ободранных псов. Поговорив с Андреевым о телефонной идее, составил тому компанию на фестивале Le Web. Парни вырядились — один в тройку, другой во что-то ужасающе спортивное — и позировали папарацци.

Вернувшись, Дуров поручил Цыплухину нанять моделей для эротической фотосессии в Зингере. После сессии они раздавали футболки с монохромной собакой народу на Дворцовой площади.

Казалось, все это — полеты банкнот, игры в Нео, мокрые майки и забеги по Дворцовой, глубокомысленные цитаты — выдает катастрофическое отсутствие вкуса.

Дуров продолжал цитировать философов в личном блоге, а в медиа опубликовал программы переустройства Петербурга и системы образования. Слог напоминал одновременно Хилла и Грэма. Казалось, из его текстов можно надергать таких же манифестационных кусков, разрезать и написать код, который составляет из этих ошметков новые тексты.

«Мы зовем в новый мир, свободный от оков невозможности. Возможно все, если ты готов умереть за свой путь. Знания и возбужденная ими свобода, которая несется по каналам, построенным нами, рано или поздно заставят ветхие мехи прохудиться. Вино само выльется из них. Новые виноградари должны ждать и верить. Верить, что будущее невозможно без них».

Почему человек, который с малолетства изучал искусство, так любил этот стиль?

Когда Дуров прилетел в Москву и позвал встретиться в том же Ritz, я сел в машину с намерением допросить тотема, зачем, решая принять ли «телефонный» вызов — потенциальную новую жизнь, ответ на вопрос, глобальных ли масштабов его талант, — он вытряхнул из закоулков сознания эту патетику.

***

Полночная Тверская генерировала человеческий трафик не слабее Невского. Поток бурлил, завивался и крутил водовороты из встреченных знакомых, прохожих, зевак, глазеющих на рубиновые звезды, которые мерцали с той стороны площади. Все были заняты.

Вход в отель Ritz оккупировали фанаты с картонными плакатами, беснующиеся у ограждения. Пара голливудских звезд заглянула в столицу раскрутить новый фильм, и охранники едва сдерживали поклонников.

Потягивая чай, Дуров рассказал, как выбрал из банды не очень занятых во «ВКонтакте» и угорающих по мобильным приложениям парней. Основного разработчика — первокурсника Григория Клюшникова — он вытащил из толпы конкурсантов, писавших приложение vk.com под операционную систему Android. Григорий получил зарплату, сопоставимую с компенсацией кодеров «ВКонтакте», и продолжил учиться на программиста.

Лобби отеля оккупировали зализанные мафиози, телохранители звезд и менеджеры с аккуратными портфельчиками. Вокруг вертелись фрачные и декольтированные тени. Разговор свернул на будущее соцсети и продолжался беспрерывно около часа.

«Мне правда не так важны деньги: что 20 млн, что 200, — говорил Дуров. — Если бы я телефоны хотел делать — тогда да, нужны. А приложение недорогое — хоть сто вариантов пиши. Поэтому я не хочу продавать свою долю „ВКонтакте“. Продажа — это не свобода.

Продажа с демпингом — рабство, бегство с поля боя. Это как-то не по-русски».

«Слушайте, — сказал я, — люди, с которыми вы в одной лодке, — они довольно жесткие. Их стиль из девяностых, они хитры и опытны, участвовали в грандиозных переделах собственности, вхожи в кремлевские приемные. Как вам удается не просто переговариваться с ними, но защищать свои идеи?»

«Ничего особенного, главное — верить в то, что будете говорить, — пожал плечами Дуров. — Запрограммировать себя не на вранье. Врать вредно для духовной целостности. Нужно добиваться отрешенности — какая разница, продаем, не продаем. Обязательно в переговорах всплывает история, мол, „если вы не сделаете так, будет то-то". Или запугивание присказками типа: „Вы же помните, в какой стране живете". Я выбираю позицию: компанию отбирать — отбирайте; крест на моей репутации ставить — ставьте; но я не прогнусь. Таким образом, манипулятивные переговоры вести невозможно».

«То же с прокурорскими запросами?»

«Абсолютно. Если ты безыдейный, это видно, и на тебя возможно влиять. Со мной это не пройдет. Идеология — это в конечном счете главное, что движет людьми. Нужно создавать более глубинные убеждения для возникновения у людей веры в свои силы и свое мнение. Глубинные убеждения, сходные с религиозными. У современных политиков нет мечты, цели, куда мы все должны стремиться. У Гитлера, кстати, была мечта».

Догадка, внезапно пришедшая в голову, поразила меня. Я сидел, придавленный не Гитлером, а пониманием того, что проглядел сквозной сюжет, шедший через историю героя.

Что Дуров — необычный предприниматель, оригинальный полководец, умник, фанат нетривиальных эвристических ходов, эпатажник и нёрд, воспитавший в себе воина, — это, в общем, и так можно понять по записям в твиттере, фейсбуке, редких статьях и постах в блоге. В конце концов, его сеть уловила 100 млн человек, и это не нуждается в комментариях.

Но теперь мне казалось, что его история о другом.

Если посмотреть на путь Дурова — это, по сути, путь политика, который работает напрямую с людьми, вокруг партийной системы и других сред коммуникации. Он создавал свои такие среды — еще с университета. Его форум выступал государством, объединяющим разбросанные по Петербургу и пригородам княжества-факультеты. Глава этого государства контролировал правила игры, был открыт разговору и лишь регулировал сообщество.

Сеть как среда была обязана сформировать запрос на такого лидера, и вот в русскоязычном интернете появился Дуров, чья «ВКонтакте» служила замахом на приобретение паствы совершенно других масштабов. Все, что он делал, — это была чистейшей воды сетевая политика и рекрутинг единомышленников.

Он произвел негромкую революцию — если понимать революцию в духе Ханны Арендт: не как освобождение («свобода от...»), а как создание среды, территории свободы. Итогом такой революции выступает res publica, дающая гражданам новое политическое измерение — в данном случае это «ВКонтакте».

Политики старого типа понимают веб как инструмент, и даже Алексей Навальный, троллививший госслужащих-коррупционеров, применяет старые приемы в новой среде. Декларируя, что нет смысла лезть в партийную систему, он придумал «Добрую машину пропаганды» — сеть единомышленников, информирующих население о гадостях режима. Но идея Навального упирается в недостаточное доверие населения интернету, а также в контроль власти над обеспечением нужного результата выборов.

Дуров строил свою res publica. Восхождение он преодолевал постепенно. Разрешив регистрироваться несовершеннолетним и оставляя свое имя внизу каждой страницы, он притягивал будущих последователей. «Идеи, которые исповедуем мы [в Зингере], будут популярны лет через двадцать».

Так говорил сетевой авторитет и не навязывал свои взгляды, ничего не лоббировал, кроме здорового образа жизни и культа ума. Эта ненавязчивость и прямые коммуникации, уравнивающие всех, способствуют меритократии — то есть самореализации талантливого человека.

Похожую роль старался играть другой политик, которого с Дуровым объединила готовность быть для каждого человека таким, каким этот человек хочет видеть лидера, защищающего его интересы. Дэвид Ремник в книге «Мост» окрестил этого политика «пятном Роршаха».

Готовясь ко вторым президентским выборам, человек по имени Барак Обама сознавал, что за четыре года мир изменился — люди обменивались идеями, убеждали, агитировали друг друга совсем не так, как раньше. Доля смартфонов в карманах американцев серьезно выросла, и Обаме предстояло использовать эту новую среду и для фондирования кампании, и для достижения результата на выборах.

Обама честно признавал, что не рубит в «мобайле», и нанял политтехнолога Джима Мессину. Тот все прекрасно понял о цифровом веке и отправился консультироваться, как выстраивать новую кампанию, к основателю Google Ларри Пейджу и другим интернет-гуру. Команда Мессины написала приложение для избирателей, где публиковались новости и обсуждались программы. Параллельно создавалась офлайновая соцсеть, похожая на MLM: приведи десять продавцов идей, которые продадут их еще десяти гражданам. Этот офлайн координировался с помощью того же приложения.

Мессина объяснил Обаме, что тому не следует как-то специально ломать себя — с помощью его сильных качеств можно выгодно проповедовать в интернете. Открытость, прозрачность позиции, искреннее желание нравиться — соцмедиа абсолютно про эти вещи. Будучи политиком нового типа, Обама тем не менее сделал усилие над собой, чтобы начать постить фоточки с семейных пикников, сжимать мысли до 140 знаков твиттера и отвечать на выборочные комментарии.

Дуров чувствовал себя в этой среде как рыба в воде — просто потому, что сам конструировал инструменты новой политики: сервисы «встречи», «диалог» на несколько пользователей, «работа над документом» и т. д. Свойства «пятна Роршаха» были присущи ему органически.

Прежде обучения программированию Дуров вырастил в себе умение нравиться и ловить души, угадывая ожидания оппонента. В его убеждениях многие найдут созвучные себе мотивы. Сочетание «роршахности» с умом, настойчивостью и опытом в сетевых коммуникациях дало тотему шанс, и он им воспользовался.

Забавно, что сочетанием своих сильных сторон и устремлениями он походил на политика, под которого кодил, — Мартина Лютера Кинга. Журналист Гэри Уиллз писал в очерке «Дело М. Л. К. живет и побеждает»: «Кинг стремился к обретению достоинства как к конечной цели всех возмущений негров. Его талант, сообразительность, обучаемость, годы, посвященные теологии (к которой он не питал особой склонности), были направлены на получение власти. Все его ученые степени и книги — лишь инструменты, оружие, чтобы каждый негр Юга получил приставку „мистер“ перед своей фамилией. И они это понимали. Они ощущали его достоинство как свое».

Не правда ли, чем-то напоминает отношения с юзерами?

Размышляя о «роршахности» как черте политика нового времени, я вспоминал Послание апостола Павла к коринфянам: «Ибо, будучи свободен от всех, я всем поработил себя, дабы больше приобрести: для Иудеев я был как Иудей, чтобы приобрести Иудеев; для подзаконных был как подзаконный, чтобы приобрести подзаконных; для чуждых закона как чуждый закона, не будучи чужд закона пред Богом, но подзаконен Христу, чтобы приобрести чуждых закона; для немощных был как немощный, чтобы приобрести немощных. Для всех я сделался всем, чтобы спасти по крайней мере некоторых».

Политика бессмысленно осуждать, что он вышел за грань вкуса, — всякий политик должен убить в себе эстета, чтобы стать внятным, доходчивым и максимально понятным разным возрастам и социальным стратам.

«Слушайте, — прервал Дуров размышления, — давайте пройдемся, все равно спать уже глупо, а здесь сидеть надоело».

В три часа ночи людские потоки ослабли, и течение выносило навстречу только загулявшие парочки и пьяниц. Замигала огнями Манежная площадь, и мы прошли в сад с выкопанной из преисподней рекой Неглинной.

«Эмоция как сто лет назад была движущей силой агитации и пропаганды, так и осталась, — рассуждал Дуров. — Чтобы увеличивать свою власть, не надо ничего делать. Надо ждать неизбежного результата процесса, когда люди проводят больше и больше времени в интернете. Бюрократы однажды проснутся и поймут, что оставили от своей системы пустую скорлупку».

«Вы типичный либертарианец, ждущий краха государств», — сказал я, рассматривая панков у Вечного огня.

Дуров, будто не слыша, продолжал мысль: «Люди держатся за государство как за спасжилет и за часто эфемерную, некачественную защиту интереса готовы терять независимость. Возьмем каналы информации — как власть общается с населением. Государство сейчас учится интернету, производит вирусные ролики, но у него нет монополии.

Получается, страна существует только потому, что все верят, что она существует. Когда вы получаете каналы, демонтируете систему власти де-факто. Люди теряют веру в то, что она легитимна».

Ворота сада, ведущие к Красной площади, кто-то запер. Мы потоптались немного напротив башен. «Вам это нравится?» — спросил Дуров и указал на Исторический музей. Я закачал головой, потому что никогда не любил пряничные домики.

«Москва — красивый город, — невпопад заметил Дуров. — Да. Но это какое-то нагромождение кирпича».

Я сказал что-то насчет неудачи жить в межвременье, когда старая нервная система человечества еще бьется в конвульсиях, не желая меняться, а новая еще не проникла повсюду.

«История с бюрократией устроена так, что стать наверху можно, только когда старое государство сгниет», — бросил Дуров.

«И вы, конечно, готовы?»

«Пока это все слишком умозрительно, меня не интересует политика. Разве что в плане эксперимента, — усмехнулся он. — Как отцы-основатели Америки создали либертарианское государство».

Что-то трогательное было в этой сцене: рассуждения о сломе ветхого мира в зассанном переходе, где грелись у труб драгдилеры, а безразличный охранник лущил семечки, — на пути от груды бурого кирпича к псевдоклассицистическому отелю. Адски хотелось спать, и две сомнамбулы заканчивали свой глубокомысленный моцион.

«Однажды я начал видеть, как некоторые люди терпят поражение не из-за того, что не умеют считать, — а из-за неумения понять, почему так произошло. Отговорки они умели находить, но понять — нет», — сказал вдруг Дуров.

«Любопытно. А что вы имели в виду, когда утверждали, что у вас „мистическое мышление“?»

«Ну как. Все, в общем-то, просто, — ответил Дуров. — Нелогично, что я не хочу продавать „ВКонтакте“. И я не знаю, почему не закрыл группы перед митингами, — хотя потом все красиво обосновал «Ленте.ру». Смотрите: события происходят или не происходят не из-за умения или неумения все просчитывать. Я гляжу на сотрудников и себя. Если есть энтузиазм и вера — все ОК. Чуть-чуть страха — все рушится».

«Страх ускоряет негативный сценарий?» — продолжил я.

«Да, и я могу объяснить это биологически, но это будет лишь теория. Важно не это. Важно знать, что ты на самом деле ничем не владеешь, и быть готовым потерять то, что у тебя якобы есть, — сказал Дуров, протянув на прощание руку. — Что из этого следует?» — спросил он.

Из этого следовало со всей возможной в четыре утра ясностью, что отсутствие страха приближает момент, когда ветхие мехи прохудятся и вино выльется само. Политика не производит интересных лидеров. Часть новых фигур придет из бизнеса, часть — из медиа. Необходимое условие для входа — ты должен создать что-то для большого количества граждан. Имя этому движению activist capitalism, и Дуров предвосхитил его, описывая в квартире на Сенной изменения в мире, которые принесет смена информационной парадигмы, и дал людям то, чего они хотели.

Назначение предпринимательства меняется. Зарабатывая на свое развитие, бизнесмены генерируют интеллектуальный потенциал, притягивая таланты, и конкурируют с политиками, государством, академией. Новые виноградари должны верить, что будущее невозможно без них. Мы не можем рассказать, каким оно будет. Но мы можем показать, как начать его менять.

Человеческие потоки пересохли — не более чем на два часа. Скособочившись и поправив очки на переносице, чайка по имени Павел Дуров во френче с поролоновыми плечами двинула к колоннаде отеля. Там, прикрывшись от дождя картонным плакатом, спали фанаты, уставшие ждать старых кумиров.

Об авторе

Николай Кононов — журналист, главный редактор ежедневного издания о предпринимательстве Hopes&Fears (hopesandfears.com). Окончил МГУ, работал репортером в газетах «Известия» и «Столичная вечерняя». Писал о бизнесменах разного масштаба — от деревенских подвижников до миллиардеров — сначала в журнале «Эксперт», а затем на протяжении семи лет в российском издании Forbes. Автор книги «Бог без машины: Истории 20 сумасшедших, сделавших в России бизнес с нуля».

Максимально полезные книги от издательства «Манн, Иванов и Фербер»

Об издательстве

Как все начиналось

Мы стартовали в июне 2005 года с двумя книгами. Первой стала «Клиенты на всю жизнь» Карла Сьюэлла, второй — «Маркетинг на 100%: ремикс». «Доброжелатели» сразу же завертели пальцами у виска: зачем вы выходите на этот рынок? Вам же придется бороться с большими и сильными конкурентами!

Отвечаем. Мы создали издательство, чтобы перестать переживать по поводу того, что отличные книги по бизнесу не попадают к российским читателям (или попадают, но не ко всем и зачастую в недостойном виде). Весь наш опыт общения с другими издательствами привел нас к мысли о том, что эти книги будет проще выпустить самим.

И с самого начала мы решили, что это будет самое необычное издательство деловой литературы — начиная с названия (мы дали ему наши три фамилии и готовы отвечать за все, что мы делаем) и заканчивая самими книгами.

Как мы работаем

— Мы издаем только те книги, которые считаем самыми полезными и самыми лучшими в своей области.

— Мы тщательно отбираем книги, тщательно их переводим, редактируем, публикуем и активно продвигаем (подробнее о том, как это делается, вы можете прочитать на сайте нашего издательства mann-ivanov-ferber.ru в разделе «Как мы издаем книги»).

— Дизайн для наших первых книг мы заказывали у Артемия Лебедева. Это дорого, но красиво и очень профессионально. Сейчас мы делаем обложки с другими дизайнерами, но планка, поднятая Лебедевым, как нам кажется, не опускается.

Мы знаем: наши книги помогают делать вашу карьеру быстрее, а бизнес — лучше.

Для этого мы и работаем.

С уважением,
Игорь Манн,
Михаил Иванов,
Михаил Фербер

Предложите нам книгу!

Когда я не умел читать на английском бегло, я часто думал: «Как много я пропускаю! Какое количество книг выходит на английском языке и как ничтожно мало издается на русском!»

Потом я научился читать на английском, но проблемы мои не закончились. Я не умел читать на немецком, японском, китайском, итальянском, французском языках... И мимо меня проходило (и проходит) огромное количество хороших деловых книг, изданных на этих и других языках. И точно так же они проходят мимо вас — я не думаю, что среди нас много полиглотов.

Потом вышла моя книга «Маркетинг на 100%», где в одном из приложений были опубликованы рецензии на более чем 60 лучших, на мой взгляд, книг из тех 300, которые я прочитал на английском. Издательства деловой литературы начали издавать их одну за другой — и ни слова благодарности, ни устно, ни письменно.

Теперь я сам немного издатель. Поэтому хочу обратиться к таким же активным читателям, как я. Предложите нам хорошую книгу для издания или переиздания!

Мы вам твердо обещаем три вещи

— Во-первых, если книга стоящая — деловая и максимально полезная, то мы обязательно издадим или переиздадим ее (если права на нее свободны).

— Во-вторых, мы обязательно укажем в самой книге и на ее странице на нашем сайте, кем она была рекомендована. Читатели должны знать, кому они обязаны тем, что у них в руках отличная книга.

— В-третьих, мы подарим вам три экземпляра этой книги, и один будет с нашими словами благодарности.

Мы внимательно читаем все письма. Если предложенная вами книга заинтересует нас, мы обязательно свяжемся с вами.

И если вы хотите проверить твердость наших обещаний, то заполните, пожалуйста, специальную форму на нашем сайте mann-ivanov-ferber.ru

Мы ждем!

Игорь Манн

Где купить наши книги

Специальное предложение для компаний

Если вы хотите купить сразу более 20 книг, например для своих сотрудников или в подарок партнерам, мы готовы обсудить с вами специальные условия работы. Для этого обращайтесь к нашему менеджеру по корпоративным продажам: +7 (495) 792-43-72, b2b@mann-ivanov-ferber.ru

Книготорговым организациям

Если вы оптовый покупатель, обратитесь, пожалуйста, к нашему партнеру — Торговому дому «Эксмо», который осуществляет поставки во все книготорговые организации.

142701, Московская обл., Ленинский р-н, г. Видное,
Белокаменное ш., д. 1; +7 (495) 411-50-74, reception@eksmo-sale.ru

Санкт-Петербург
ООО «СЗКО», 193029, г. Санкт-Петербург, пр-т Обуховской
Обороны, д. 84, лит. «Е»; +7 (812) 365-46-03 / 04, server@szko.ru

Нижний Новгород
Филиал ТД «Эксмо» в Нижнем Новгороде,
603074, г. Нижний Новгород, ул. Маршала Воронова, д. 3;
+7 (831) 272-36-70, 243-00-20, 275-30-02, reception@eksmonn.ru

Ростов-на-Дону
ООО «РДЦ Ростов-на-Дону», 344091, г. Ростов-на-Дону,
пр-т Стачки, д. 243а; +7 (863) 220-19-34, 218-48-21, 218-48-22,
info@rnd.eksmo.ru

Самара
ООО «РДЦ Самара», 443052, г. Самара, пр-т Кирова, д. 75/1, лит. «Е»;
+7 (846) 269-66-70 (71…79), RDC@samara.eksmo.ru

Екатеринбург
ООО «РДЦ Екатеринбург», 620007, г. Екатеринбург,
ул. Прибалтийская, д. 24а; +7 (343) 378-49-45 (46…49)

Новосибирск
ООО «РДЦ Новосибирск», 630105, г. Новосибирск, ул. Линейная,
114; +7 (383) 289-91-42; eksmo-nsk@yandex.ru

Хабаровск
Филиал «РДЦ Новосибирск» в Хабаровске,
680000, г. Хабаровск, пер. Дзержинского, д. 24, лит. «Б», оф. 1;
+7 (4212) 21-83-81, eksmo-khv@mail.ru

Казахстан
«РДЦ Алматы», 050039, г. Алматы, ул. Домбровского, 3а;
+7 (727) 251-58-12, 251-59-90 (91, 92, 99), RDC-Almaty@mail.ru

Мы в Facebook!

Присоединяйтесь к нам в Facebook! Все самое интересное из первых рук: http://www.facebook.com/mifbooks

Мечтай, создавай, изменяй!

Как молодые предприниматели меняют мир и зарабатывают состояния

Сара Лейси

Brilliant, Crazy, Cocky
How the Top 1% of Entrepreneurs Profit from Global Chaos
Sarah Lacy

О чем эта книга

Увлекательное путешествие Сары Лейси по разным странам с динамично развивающейся экономикой показало: яркие и харизматичные предприниматели могут появиться где угодно.

Книга «Мечтай, создавай, изменяй!» — это ее приглашение зарядиться жизненной энергией и энтузиазмом от молодых и успешных предпринимателей со всего мира. Одновременно с этим книга позволяет заглянуть в будущее глобальной экономики, где самые сумасшедшие и влиятельные бизнесмены устанавливают свои правила.

Почему мы решили издать эту книгу

Эта книга способна изменить ваши взгляды на мир, познакомив с удивительными людьми, создающими новые ценности в мире стартапов и венчурного предпринимательства.

Фишка книги

Эта книга написана на основе собственных впечатлений автора от поездок в далеко не самые безопасные и благоустроенные уголки планеты. Но за «невидимой» инфраструктурой, политическими и социальными проблемами Сара Лейси сумела разглядеть формирующийся слой предпринимателей, обладающих теми же универсальными качествами, что и стартаперы Кремниевой долины, ставшие символом «нового информационного мира».

От автора

Работа на рынках развивающихся стран — не для слабонервных. Жить и инвестировать там трудно. Культурные, деловые и этические проблемы подстерегают на каждом шагу. Многие западные инвесторы и бизнесмены уже поняли, что потенциал этих рынков слишком велик, чтобы его игнорировать, особенно с учетом замедления экономического роста в западных странах.

Суть «американской мечты» в том и состоит, что, если не боишься рискнуть, можешь выиграть многое. Мозг великих предпринимателей работает не так, как у остальных людей. Они ясно видят решение проблемы. И хотя оно кажется очевидным после того как его вам объяснят, найти его самостоятельно способны немногие. Великие предприниматели отличаются не типом основанной ими компании, возрастом, национальностью или образованием, а уникальным способом мышления.

Переворот

Проверенная методика захвата рынка

Люк Уильямс

Disrupt
Think the Unthinkable to Spark Transformation in Your Business
Luke Williams

Тематика

Инновации, креативность в бизнесе

О чем эта книга

Люк Уильямс убежден в том, что в постоянно меняющемся мире бизнеса выиграть можно только одним способом: перевернуть все с ног на голову. Он подробно рассказывает о том, как рождаются прорывные стратегии и откуда берутся неожиданные решения. Вы узнаете, как соединить творческую гибкость и аналитическую жесткость и за пять простых шагов сделать прорыв на любом рынке. Это не очередное пособие по «мозговому штурму». Предлагаемая модель мышления научит вас не просто выявлять прорывные изменения на рынке и реагировать на них — она научит их внедрять. Вы научитесь держать в голове то, что обычно выпускаете из виду, обращать внимание на неочевидные вещи. А главное — находить прорывные решения за несколько дней и недель, не растягивая это на месяцы и даже годы.

Для кого эта книга

Эта книга для тех, кто не боится перемен, кто готов не только отличаться от других, но и быть совершенно непохожим на других, единственным в своем деле.

Об авторе

Люк Уильямс — известный консультант, специализирующийся на прорывном мышлении и инновационных стратегиях. Более десяти лет он работает на международном рынке с такими отраслевыми лидерами, как American Express, GE, Sony, Crocs, Virgin, Disney, Hewlett-Packard, разрабатывая для них новые продукты, услуги и бренды. Уильямс — партнер и креативный директор в компании frog design, одной из самых влиятельных в мире инновационных компаний. Преподает в Школе бизнеса Штерна при Нью-Йоркском университете.

Уходим в отрыв

Построение эффективной компании

Кэмерон Герольд

Double Double
Cameron Herold

О чем эта книга

Эта книга о росте — о том, как его добиться и как управлять растущей компанией. Здесь нет общих теорий и тактик. Будучи опытным бизнес-консультантом, Кэмерон Герольд дает только практические советы — простые и максимально действенные.

Как спланировать успешное будущее и «заразить» идеей роста сотрудников? Как организовать работу в компании? Какие показатели контролировать? Автор рассматривает все аспекты бизнеса — от привлечения в команду настоящих профессионалов и выстраивания коммуникаций до организации бесплатного маркетинга и PR и повышения личной эффективности.

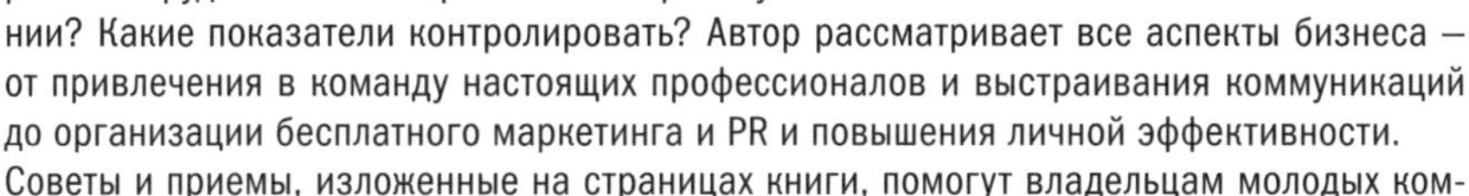

Советы и приемы, изложенные на страницах книги, помогут владельцам молодых компаний избежать ненужных ошибок, сконцентрироваться на достижении цели и «уйти в отрыв».

Автор раскрывает приемы, которые помогли десяткам его клиентов более чем в 17 странах мира в несколько раз увеличить размеры бизнеса. Как написал один из его американских читателей, «Не знаю, почему Герольд делится своей “золотой стратегией” даром, — но от таких подарков не отказываются!»

Для кого эта книга

Для успешного предпринимателя со стабильным доходом, которому нужен драйв и рост прибыли не на проценты, а на порядки. Для всех, кто хочет заразиться «вирусом» высокой доходности и не выздоравливать!

Об авторе

Кэмерон Герольд — наставник, бизнес-тренер и консультант по вопросам управления. Имеет 20-летний опыт создания, развития и консультирования стартапов и растущих компаний США и Канады.

Дважды занимал первую строчку рейтинга самых популярных лекторов в рамках совместной программы MIT и Организации предпринимателей — Entrepreneurial Master Program.

В настоящее время — генеральный директор созданной им компании BackPocket, помогающей предпринимателям развивать бизнес.

Ранее на протяжении 7 лет возглавлял компанию 1-800-GOT-JUNK?, где ему удалось увеличить размеры бизнеса с 2 до 105 млн долларов без долгов и сторонних акционеров.

И ботаники делают бизнес

Максим Котин

Тематика

Предпринимательство, бизнес, менеджмент, маркетинг, продажи, ритейл

О книге

Это не банальная и приукрашенная «история успеха» американского предпринимателя — это абсолютно правдивая и супероткровенная история создания бизнеса в жестких российских условиях, с неоднозначным финалом. Это не сухое повествование об инвестициях и рентабельности, а яркий рассказ, который читается как художественное произведение и при этом содержит массу практической информации как для начинающих, так и для состоявшихся предпринимателей.

Герой книги вел блог, в котором пытался честно описывать, что с ним происходит. На полях книги публикуются комментарии читателей этого блога, которые дополняют повествование автора, порой неожиданно. Ведь у многих читателей от происходящего с героем чуть ли волосы на голове не шевелились, и они писали герою так: «Вы не бизнесмен. Вы экстремал. Вам следует ловить руками акул на мелководье». Или так: «Это капец». Герой неизменно отвечал: «Все, что не убьет, сделает сильнее».

Для кого эта книга

Для каждого человека, который уже начал или еще только мечтает в наши дни начать свое дело, а также для всех, кто хочет знать, как устроен бизнес по-русски. Для владельца бизнеса, директора компании, директора по продажам, директора по маркетингу.

Об авторе

Максим Котин — журналист, специальный корреспондент журнала «Сноб» и редактор серии «Реальные истории» издательства «Манн, Иванов и Фербер». Автор бестселлера «Чичваркин Е..гений».

Для новых идей

Для новых идей

Для новых идей

Для новых идей

Для новых идей

Для новых идей

Для новых идей

Николай В. **Кононов**

Код Дурова

Реальная история «ВКонтакте» и ее создателя

Некоторые эпизоды могут быть реконструкцией происходивших событий

Ответственный редактор *Анна Высочкина*
Литературный редактор *Елена Казаринова*
Дизайн переплета *Иван Шустов*
Верстка *Эрик Брегис*
Корректоры *Наталья Витько, Ярослава Терещенкова, Надежда Болотина*

Подписано в печать 17.10.2012.
Формат 70×100 $^{1}/_{16}$. Гарнитура Чартер.
Бумага офсетная. Печать офсетная.
Усл. печ. л. 16,7.
Тираж 10 000 экз. (1-й з-д 1-5000). Заказ 6473/12.

ООО «Манн, Иванов и Фербер»
mann-ivanov-ferber.ru
ivanov@mann-ivanov-ferber.ru
facebook.com/mifbooks

Отпечатано в соответствии с предоставленными материалами
в ООО «ИПК Парето-Принт», г. Тверь, www.pareto-print.ru